Building a Black Criminology

In light of the Black Lives Matter movement and protests in many cities, race plays an ever more salient role in crime and justice. Within theoretical criminology, however, race has oddly remained on the periphery. It is often introduced as a control variable in tests of theories and is rarely incorporated as a central construct in mainstream paradigms (e.g., control, social learning, and strain theories). When race is discussed, the standard approach is to embrace the racial invariance thesis, which argues that any racial differences in crime are due to African Americans being exposed to the same criminogenic risk factors as are Whites, just more of them. An alternative perspective has emerged that seeks to identify the unique, racially specific conditions that only Blacks experience. Within the United States, these conditions are rooted in the historical racial oppression experienced by African Americans, whose contemporary legacy includes concentrated disadvantage in segregated communities, racial socialization by parents, experiences with and perceptions of racial discrimination, and disproportionate involvement in and unjust treatment by the criminal justice system.

Importantly, race specificity and racial exceptionalism are not mutually exclusive perspectives. Evidence exists that Blacks and Whites commit crimes both for the same reasons (invariance) and for different reasons (race-specific). A full understanding of race and crime thus must involve demarcating both the general and specific causes of crime, the latter embedded in what it means to be "Black" in the United States. This volume seeks to explore these theoretical issues in a depth and breadth that is not common under one cover. Again, given the salience of race and crime, this volume should be of interest to a wide range of criminologists and have the potential to be used in graduate seminars and upper-level undergraduate courses.

James D. Unnever is a Professor of Criminology at the University of South Florida Sarasota-Manatee.

Shaun L. Gabbidon is a Distinguished Professor of Criminal Justice at Penn State Harrisburg.

Cecilia Chouhy is an Assistant Professor in the College of Criminology and Criminal Justice at the Florida State University.

Building a Black Criminology: Race, Theory, and Crime

ADVANCES IN CRIMINOLOGICAL THEORY

Volume 24

Editors

James D. Unnever
University of South Florida, Sarasota Manatee

Shaun L. Gabbidon
Penn State Harrisburg

Cecilia Chouhy
Florida State University

Building a Black Criminology

Race, Theory, and Crime

Advances in Criminological Theory
Volume 24

Edited by
James D. Unnever,
Shaun L. Gabbidon,
and Cecilia Chouhy

Routledge
Taylor & Francis Group

LONDON AND NEW YORK

First published 2019 by Routledge

2 Park Square, Milton Park, Abingdon, Oxfordshire OX14 4RN
52 Vanderbilt Avenue, New York, NY 10017

Routledge is an imprint of the Taylor & Francis Group, an informa business

First issued in paperback 2020

Library of Congress Cataloging-in-Publication Data
A catalog record for this book has been requested

ISBN: 978-1-138-35372-5 (hbk)
ISBN: 978-0-367-50491-5 (pbk)

Typeset in Times New Roman
by Apex CoVantage, LLC

We dedicate our book to the three people who, through their unique contribution, made this book possible:

William Edward Burghardt (W.E.B.) Du Bois
Katheryn Russell-Brown
Francis T. Cullen

Contents

Contributors

Michael L. Benson is a Professor in the School of Criminal Justice at the University of Cincinnati.

Callie H. Burt is an Associate Professor of Sociology at the University of Washington.

Leah Butler is a Ph.D. student in the School of Criminal Justice at the University of Cincinnati.

Christina Campbell is an Assistant Professor in the School of Criminal Justice at the University of Cincinnati.

Cecilia Chouhy is an Assistant Professor in the College of Criminology and Criminal Justice at the Florida State University.

Joshua C. Cochran is an Assistant Professor in the School of Criminal Justice at the University of Cincinnati.

Francis T. Cullen is a Distinguished Research Professor Emeritus and Senior Research Associate in the School of Criminal Justice at the University of Cincinnati.

John E. Eck is a Professor of Criminal Justice at the University of Cincinnati.

Ben Feldmeyer is an Associate Professor in the School of Criminal Justice at the University of Cincinnati.

Shaun L. Gabbidon is a Distinguished Professor of Criminal Justice at Penn State Harrisburg.

Amanda K. Graham is a Doctoral Candidate in the School of Criminal Justice at the University of Cincinnati

Jay P. Kennedy is an Assistant Professor in the School of Criminal Justice at Michigan State University.

Heejin Lee is a Ph.D. student in the School of Criminal Justice at the University of Cincinnati.

Hannah D. McManus is a Doctoral Candidate in the School of Criminal Justice at the University of Cincinnati.

Steven F. Messner is a Distinguished Teaching Professor of Sociology at the University at Albany, State University of New York.

Ojmarrh Mitchell is an Associate Professor in the Department of Criminology at the University of South Florida.

Akwasi Owusu-Bempah is an Assistant Professor in the Department of Sociology at the University of Toronto.

Katheryn Russell-Brown is the Chesterfield Smith Professor of Law and Director of the Center for the Study of Race and Race Relations at the University of Florida, Levin College of Law.

Jillian G. Shafer is a Doctoral Candidate in the School of Criminal Justice at the University of Cincinnati.

Paula Smith is an Associate Professor in the School of Criminal Justice at the University of Cincinnati.

Brian J. Stults is an Associate Professor in the College of Criminology and Criminal Justice at Florida State University.

Kristin Swartz is an Associate Professor in the Department of Criminal Justice at the University of Louisville.

James D. Unnever is a Professor of Criminology at the University of South Florida Sarasota-Manatee.

Pamela Wilcox is a Professor in the School of Criminal Justice at the University of Cincinnati.

Preface

We put together this book of outstanding scholarship out of frustration with the White essentialism of the prevailing general theories of crime (e.g., strain, social disorganization, low self-control, learning theory, and social bonds). We are frustrated with the general theories of crime because they ignore the simple and obvious fact that Black people have encountered and continue to encounter the toxic consequences of systemic racism (see chapters by Unnever). Indeed, ignoring this simple fact is rather incredulous given that Du Bois (1899) laid the theoretical foundation for a Black Criminology over a century ago by showing how the "color line" increases offending among Black people (see chapter 2 by Gabbidon). Moreover, it has been decades since Russell-Brown (1992) published her seminal article that called upon criminology to develop a Black Criminology (see chapter 5 by Russell-Brown). In fact, to this day, few theorists fully incorporate into their analyses the reality that systemic racial subjugation has deleterious everyday consequences for Black people living in the United States, experiences that are not reproducible among Whites or even among other ethnicities (e.g., Latinos, Native Americans). In short, the general theories cannot generate a holistic understanding of offending among Black people because they are a White criminology (see chapter 3 by Cullen, Chouhy, Butler, and Lee).

In fact, it is only over the last decade or so that scholars have begun to unravel more systematically the profound and nuanced ways in which systemic racism increases offending among Black people. For example, Unnever and Gabbidon's (2011) *A Theory of African American Offending: Race, Racism, and Crime* presents a systematic treatment of how experiencing the toxic consequences of systemic racism enhances the likelihood that some Black people will engage in problematic behaviors. Because of these efforts, scholars are now more intently exploring the multitude of ways that systemic racism causes a *minority* of Black people to offend.

The purpose of this book is to move beyond the often-misguided approaches devoted to understanding African American offending and the value of a Black Criminology (Onwudiwe & Lynch, 2000; Penn, 2003; Russell, 1992). Our purpose is to lay the foundation for the creation of a Black Criminology. The starting point for a Black Criminology is that the United States is a racially stratified society and that systemic racism (e.g., racial segregation, stereotype threats, and racial discrimination) increases offending among Black people (see chapter 1 by Unnever and Owusu-Bempah). A Black Criminology assumes that similarly situated Blacks and Whites would have the same levels of offending if Black people never experienced the deleterious consequences of systemic racism. We argue that a Black Criminology will provide a coherence—a broad tent—that will illuminate the innumerable ways in which systemic racism produces offending among some Black people. A Black Criminology will also cause scholars to revisit whether they have fully incorporated race and racism into their analyses of crime.

This will be a tall order because most criminologists, regardless of their theoretical orientation, have failed to integrate into their analyses how systemic racism increases offending among some Blacks. Toward this end, the authors in this book have outlined a multitude of ways that scholars should expand their analyses in order to illustrate the causal pathways between racial subjugation and offending among some Black people. These efforts should include developing macro measures of systemic racism (see chapter 6 by Messner and Stults), showing how interpersonal racial discrimination increases crime (see chapter 9 by Burt), and discussing how systemic racism uniquely produces a code of the street (see chapter 7 by Swartz and Wilcox). In addition, the authors discuss how centuries of racial segregation have produced racialized areas in which place managers neglect their minority tenants (see chapter 8 by Eck), whether the causes of white-collar crime are equal for Blacks and Whites (see chapter 10 by Benson and Kennedy), and how racial threats lead to greater social control (see chapter 11 by Feldmeyer and Cochran). Furthermore, the authors examine whether Blacks and Whites equally perceive and receive procedural justice (see chapter 12 by McManus, Shafer, and Graham), outline how mass incarceration and prosecutor discretion have disproportionately affected Black communities (see chapter 13 by Mitchell), and whether race-specific rehabilitative policies are more efficacious (see chapter 14 by Smith and Campbell). In short, the authors of each of the chapters in this book have provided novel ways to bring race and racism back into the analyses of crime within the United States.

We recognize that there will be a serious pushback to our collective efforts. The White essentialism of the general theories of crime has dictated that scholars can either ignore or marginalize how systemic racism increases offending among a minority of Black people. In addition, scholars have built prestigious careers upon the edifice of the assumption that there is "no need to study the Negro boy" separate from White boys (Hirschi, 1969, p. 80). Therefore, change will be difficult. Nevertheless, the reality that systemic racism is a chronic experience that is deleterious to the well-being of Black people is undeniable. Scholars across the scientific spectrum have reproduced this fact. We are absolute in our belief that the time for criminology to embrace and promote a Black Criminology is now.

References

Du Bois, W. E. B. (1899). *The Philadelphia Negro: A social study*. New York, NY: Schocken Books.

Hirschi, T. (1969). *Causes of delinquency*. Berkeley, CA: University of California.

Onwudiwe, I. D., & Lynch, M. J. (2000). Reopening the debate: A reexamination of the need for a black criminology. *Social Pathology: A Journal of Reviews, 6*, 182–198.

Penn, E. B. (2003). On black criminology: Past, present, and future. *Criminal Justice Studies, 16*, 317–327.

Russell, K. K. (1992). Development of a black criminology and the role of the black criminologist. *Justice Quarterly, 9*, 667–683.

Unnever, J. D., & Gabbidon, S. L. (2011). *A theory of African American offending: Race, racism, and crime*. New York, NY: Taylor & Francis.

Part I

Foundations

1

A Black Criminology Matters*

James D. Unnever and Akwasi Owusu-Bempah

One key issue dominates the theoretical discussion of the relationship between race and crime. This issue is whether African Americans offend for the same reasons as Whites—the racial invariance thesis. This thesis is the foundational assumption of the existing general theories of crime. Thus, the existing general theories recognize that race needs to be included in their models that explain criminality because of the elevated levels of offending among African Americans. However, general theorists relegate race to the status of a control variable along with other variables such as age and gender because they assume that African Americans and Whites offend for the same reasons. Once controlled, general theorists then posit that the only reason why some but not other African Americans offend is that they, for example, are more likely to live in disorganized neighborhoods, have weaker social bonds, affiliate more often with delinquent peers, are labeled more often, have greater episodic strains, or exhibit less self-control. Thus, Hirschi's (1969) long ago declaration that there is no need to study the "Negro boy"—that is, the hegemony of White essentialism—remains a vibrant component of the general theories of crime (Cullen, 2011). Notably this assumption requires that had Hirschi (1969) and the other general theorists only studied African Americans, their theories of crime would have delineated the exact same causes and explanations of crime as they do now.

We recognize that race and racism have affected the development of the general theories of crime. For example, scholars note that the etiology of social disorganization theory was in part a progressive refutation of racist beliefs that suggested that biological or cultural inferiority caused African Americans to commit crimes (Gabbidon & Greene, 2012; Shaw & McKay, 1949). Social disorganization theorists refuted these racist beliefs by arguing that place causes crime. However, we contend that criminologists have "thrown the baby out with the bathwater" in their attempts to refute racist theories of crime. In essence, scholars have focused more on what White and African Americans have in common rather than their dissimilarities, including the fact that African Americans have a long history of racial oppression. As a result, the general theories of crime have ignored how the interactions that African Americans have with racist formations increase their likelihood of committing (Omi & Winant, 2004).[1]

The Formal Development of a Black Criminology

Scholars have challenged relegating the "Negro boy" to the periphery in understanding why some African Americans offend. In fact, nearly a quarter of a century ago, Russell (1992, p. 681) published an article in *Justice Quarterly* that called for criminology to develop a Black Criminology; "a call for criminologists to expand their theorizing and testing of the causes of crime committed by blacks."

Scholars have responded to her clarion call for the development of theories that detail the causes of crime exclusively among African Americans. Tatum (2000) developed a neocolonial theoretical model of offending among African Americans, and Unnever and Gabbidon (2011) have put forth a comprehensive theory that explains why some African Americans but not others commit crime. In addition, ethnographers have generated groundbreaking analyses that solely examine offending among some African Americans. For example, Potter (2008) presents a Black Feminist criminological understanding of intimate partner violence among African Americans, and Jones (2010) investigates the causes of violence among teenaged African American girls in an inner city. In addition, Goffman (2014) analyzes how unprecedented levels of policing, imprisonment, and supervision have affected the lives of young African American men and women living in a poor segregated community. However, despite these pioneering efforts, Russell's (1992) clarion call for the formal development of a Black Criminology has not been accepted by the discipline of criminology (Unnever, Cullen, Mathers, McClure, & Allison, 2009).

In this chapter, we renew Russell's (1992) clarion call for criminology to develop a Black Criminology. We argue that criminology has escaped from its "theoretical time warp" and now can explore, without reservations, the relationship between systemic racism and crime (Russell, 1992, p. 675).[2] However, we concur with Russell (1992, p. 675) that criminology's continuing failure to acknowledge and accept a Black Criminology calls "into question the integrity of the discipline's policy recommendations related to race and crime." And that its "failure to develop and cultivate a Black Criminology will not cause the problems associated with race and crime to go away. Rather, it will limit the discipline's ability to help explain this relationship and to guide policy accordingly" (Russell, 1992, p. 675).

We also agree with Russell (1992) that a Black Criminology is as warranted as a feminist criminology, especially given that women disproportionately underoffend, whereas according to the official statistics, African Americans disproportionately overoffend (Gabbidon & Greene, 2012; Like-Haislip, 2014). Therefore, we consider the unique lived racialized experiences of being an African American in a racist society as worthy of study as the inimitable lived experiences of being a woman in a sexist society.[3] As there are gendered pathways to crime, we argue there are racialized pathways to offending (Jones, 2010; Kruttschnitt, 2016; Miller & Mullins, 2006; Nuytiens & Christiaens, 2016; Potter, 2008; Yun, Kim, & Morris, 2013; Unnever, Barnes, & Cullen, 2016a; Unnever, Cullen, & Barnes, 2016).

Note that our conceptualization of a Black Criminology encourages the development of multiple perspectives using diverse methodologies within its larger theoretical framework (Simpson, 1989). These perspectives can incorporate the intersectionality of offending among African Americans (racialized class, race, and gender effects) with the intent of delineating the causes for the different rates of offending between African Americans and Whites (and others)—group differences—and why some African Americans but not others offend (Goffman, 2014; Jones, 2010; Potter, 2008; Tatum, 2000; Unnever & Gabbidon, 2011). Together, these efforts should reveal the multitude of ways that systemic racial oppression produces offending among some African Americans. In what follows, we propose some guiding assumptions for the development of a Black Criminology.

Guiding Assumptions of a Black Criminology

It is beyond the scope of this essay to outline the tortuous history of Black America. However, it must be recognized that African Americans are the only group who were forcefully brought to the U.S., enslaved, suffered the atrocities of Jim Crow laws, were forced to live in segregated areas (e.g., urban ghettos), and currently are massively policed, incarcerated, and supervised (Alexander, 2010; Bolton & Feagin, 2004; Goffman, 2014). Consequently, the legal and social constraints that limit African Americans are pervasive and run deep—they are systemic (Smångs, 2016). Indeed, the resiliency of Black America is found in their enduring struggle to dismantle the legal, social, and cultural apparatus of their racial oppression (Feagin, 2013; Gines, 2014).

Therefore, we suggest that scholars can build a Black Criminology upon three assumptions.

1. A Black Criminology assumes that Whites purposefully constructed a racially stratified society that oppresses African Americans.
2. A Black Criminology assumes that because the United States has been and is a racialized society, the history of African Americans is incomparable to the histories shared by Whites (and other minorities).
3. A Black Criminology assumes that a minority of African Americans commit crimes because of their inimitable past and current racial subordination.

In sum, we suggest that the overarching assumption or starting point of a Black Criminology is that the creation and maintenance of the United States' system of racial stratification has caused African Americans to have historical and contemporary racialized experiences that are incomparable to those of others (Bonilla-Silva, 2015; Feagin & Elias, 2013; Gines, 2014). The all-embracing hypothesis of a Black Criminology is that their past and current racial subjugation causes a minority of African Americans to commit crimes.

The Racial Invariance Thesis

Obviously, the assumptions of a Black Criminology are incompatible with the prevailing general theories' postulation that Black and White people commit crime for identical reasons. A Black Criminology assumes that most African Americans have unique racialized experiences that are born out of their past and current racial subjugation and that these experiences uniquely produce their offending. This does not rule out the reality that Black and White people experience similar risk factors such as poverty. However, a Black Criminology argues that African Americans and Whites may not perceive, interpret, and react to these risk factors in exactly the same way. Thus, it is the purpose of a Black Criminology to discover when, why, and how there are differences in offending between African Americans and Whites. In short, the formal development of a Black Criminology (as does a feminist criminology) rests upon the rejection of the racial invariance thesis.

The racial invariance thesis is the foundational assumption of the general theories of crime. It assumes that (1) there are no risk factors related to crime that only African Americans experience and (2) the size of the effects of crime-causing variables are the same for African Americans and Whites; that is, the effects of crime-causing factors do not significantly vary across Black and White people. We suggest that there are risk factors related to crime that only African Americans experience and that the effects of crime-causing variables are not always equal across Black and White people. We concur with Peterson (2012, p. 319) that "When a society is organized along race/ethnic lines, we cannot assume that the sources and responses to crime, or the application of criminal justice, are race neutral in their effects and consequences." In short, we contend that the evidence indicates that "race" may be a scope condition that "is a core organizing construct that operates to generate the patterns, sources, and consequences of crime" (Peterson, 2012, p. 309).

There are three reasons why the assumptions of a Black Criminology are incompatible with the racial invariance thesis. First, a Black Criminology argues that African Americans have unparalleled racialized experiences (and experiences similar to Whites) that can only be understood in the context of their past and existing systemic racial oppression (Bonilla-Silva, 2015; Feagin, 2013). By definition, Whites—the superordinate group—do not systematically oppress other Whites because of their skin color. Of course, some Whites may episodically perceive that they are being oppressed—discriminated against—because of their skin color. Nevertheless, a Black Criminology argues that a White person who episodically experiences oppression because s/he is White is incomparable to African Americans as a group experiencing chronic systematic oppression (Feagin, 2013). For example, only African American men continually confront the racist microaggression stereotype threat that they are "super-predators" or the "criminalblackman" (Dilulio, 1995; Russell-Brown, 2009; Steele, 1997).[4]

Gates and Steele (2009) add that African Americans cannot escape from the noxious consequences of stereotype threats such as the *criminalblackman* because they are as omnipresent as if they were "in the air." In addition, because of their history and current experiences, most

African Americans racially socialize their children in order to prepare them for their racial oppression, which includes giving their children—especially their boys—"the talk" ("the talk" prepares them for their possible racist encounters with the police) (Coates, 2015; Owusu-Bempah, 2014). Thus, African Americans have racialized experiences not shared by Whites that may both propel them toward crime—the pejorative stereotype of the "criminalblackman"—and prevent them from offending—positive racial socialization experiences (Burt & Simons, 2015; Unnever, 2014).

Shaw and McKay (1949) illuminate another crime-related experience that only African Americans encounter—their unique exposure to racialized areas of compounded deprivation (Hagan, 2010; Perkins & Sampson, 2015). Shaw and McKay (1949, p. 617) report that the rates of delinquencies for African American boys were higher than for White boys in comparable areas, but "it is impossible to reproduce in white communities the circumstances under which Negro children live. Even if it were possible to parallel the low economic status and the inadequacy of institutions in the white community, it would not be possible to reproduce the effects of segregation and the barriers to upward mobility."

More contemporarily, Peterson (2012, p. 310) highlights the incomparable living circumstances of African Americans as she states that "one direct product of the racial organization of society is noncomparability in local social circumstances across areas of different colors" (see also Griffiths, 2013). Sharkey's (2008, p. 962) analyses also reaffirm the rejection of the racial invariance thesis, as he found that "the most common experience for black families since the 1970s has been to be surrounded by poverty over consecutive generations. This type of persistent contextual disadvantage is nonexistent for whites." Thus, areas of compounded deprivation that racist Whites purposefully constructed to subjugate African Americans encapsulate, define, and concentrate the systemic racial oppression of only African Americans (Massey, 1990; Perkins & Sampson, 2015). In short, a Black Criminology considers areas of compounded deprivation as *racialized* areas of compounded deprivation—that is, they are racial formations (Omi & Winant, 2004).[5]

A Black Criminology further recognizes that the efficacy of prevention and treatment programs may not be invariant across races—that is, there is a need for culturally and ethnically sensitive approaches to prevention and treatment (Halgunseth, Jensen, Sakuma, & McHale, 2016; Liddle, Jackson-Gilfort, & Marvel, 2006; Moore, 2001; Stams, 2015; Stepteau-Watson, Watson, & Lawrence, 2014; Watson, Washington, &

Stepteau-Watson, 2015). Anderson, McKenny, Mitchell, Koku, and Stevenson (2017) examined a race-based prevention and treatment program—Engaging, Managing, and Bonding through Race (EMBRace)—which was specifically designed to help African Americans families address racial stress and trauma in their lives while promoting familial bonds and positive coping strategies after racial encounters. The program promoted strategies that are more effective for African American caregivers and children to discuss racial encounters in their lives and to reduce racial stress and trauma as a family unit. These strategies included increasing cultural socialization messaging and behaviors (e.g., exploring their family histories, discussing pride within the race and culture), understanding the basis for techniques that prepare African American youth for a racially biased environment, exploring past and current trauma that may promote a sense of distrust in others, and promoting hope for equality in the future while coupling this hopefulness with current realities of inequality facing African American youths. Anderson et al. (2017) preliminary found—based on a small sample—that the EMBRace program improved the coping skills of African American parents and children.

Chu and Sung (2009) analyzed the Drug Abuse Treatment Outcome Study (DATOS), which is a prospective study designed to determine the outcomes of drug abuse treatments across eleven U.S. cities. They tested whether African Americans and Whites reported different levels of religious involvement and whether its effect on recovery from substance abuse was invariant across race. Chu and Sung (2009) found that African Americans reported significantly higher levels of religious involvement than did Whites. Most notably, they found that higher levels of religious involvement significantly predicted desistance from drug use for African Americans but had no effect on Whites' desistance. Chu and Sung (2009) conclude that treatment programs will be more efficacious if they acknowledge and incorporate the peerless experiences of African Americans. In addition, Potter (2008, p. 203) reports that programs to combat intimate partner violence among African American women need to be a collaborative effort between African Americans "who have specialized training in counseling and performing therapy with Blacks" and are educated about the issues of African Americans and intimate partner abuse.

Second, a Black Criminology posits that African Americans have a racialized narrative that gives meaning to how they experience racial oppression (Goodman, 2014). This interpretive framework is a personal narrative that can translate racial oppression into a challenge to over-come or a motivation to offend. For example, it is widely recognized that there is a relationship between crime—especially violent crime—and poverty. Moreover, there is no doubt that African Americans are disproportionately poor. However, the correlation between poverty and crime ignores the reality that some African Americans may interpret their reasons for being poor through a unique racial lens. Thus, some African Americans may interpret their poverty as an inevitable result of their racial oppression (Hunt, 1996).

Indeed, a 2016 Pew poll found that when respondents were asked about the underlying reasons why African Americans may be having a harder time getting ahead than Whites, large majorities of African American adults pointed to societal factors (Pew Research Center, 2016). The overwhelming majority of African Americans responded that structural factors such as failing schools (75%), racial discrimination (70%), and a lack of jobs (66%) are major reasons why they are having a harder time getting ahead. Note that the attitudes of African Americans differed significantly from those of Whites on each of these items (Pew Research Center, 2016). But, by far, the biggest gap was on the issue of racial discrimination, where only 36% of Whites responded that it is a major reason why African Americans are struggling to get ahead, which was 34 percentage points lower than the response by African Americans. In addition, the poll found that 71% of African Americans stated that they have experienced racial discrimination or unfair treatment due to their race or ethnicity at some point in their lives in comparison to 30% of Whites (Pew Research Center, 2016). Thus, we suggest that the inter-pretive framework for understanding the relationship between poverty and crime may vary across African Americans and Whites.

Third, a Black Criminology argues that the effects of some crime-related experiences will significantly vary across African Americans and Whites. A case in point is the effect of perceived racial discrimi-nation by the police on offending. A Black Criminology suggests that African Americans have a racialized narrative regarding police brutal-ity that is not shared by Whites.[6] This racialized narrative about police brutality originated with the role that the criminal justice system had in institutionalizing slavery, continued because the criminal justice sys-tem was the primary enforcers of the Jim Crow laws, and is found in the contemporary Black Lives Matter movement (Edwards & Harris, 2016; Oshinsky, 1997). This historically and contemporarily grounded racialized narrative indicates that African Americans will significantly differ from Whites in how they interpret and react to perceived police discrimination. Unnever, Barnes, and Cullen (2016b) found that African Americans who perceived racial discrimination by the police were significantly more likely to offend than Whites and Hispanics when other covariates were controlled. This research suggests that these racialized events define the history of African Americans. Consequently, criminal justice injustices have particularly devastating consequences if they are personally or vicariously experienced. In brief, perceived criminal justice injustices may "strike a raw nerve" among African Americans, ushering them down racialized pathways to offending.

Research has revealed other racialized pathways to offending. Unnever, Cullen, and Barnes (2016) analyzing the 9- and 12-year-old cohorts of African American youths included in the Project on Human Development in Chicago Neighborhoods, Longitudinal Cohort Study (PHDCN-LCS), tested a core hypothesis of Unnever and Gabbidon's (2011) theory of offending. Unnever et al. (2016) tested whether racial oppression, as measured by self-reports of racial discrimination, undermined the ability of African American youths to build bonds with conventional institutions, such as their schools, which in turn increased their probability of offending. They reported that that the more African American youths reported being discriminated against, the less they were attached to their teachers and were less committed to their education while controlling for the degree to which the youths were bonded to their mother and father and other covariates. In addition, their analyses revealed that the influence of racial discrimination on changes in externalizing behavior from wave 1 to wave 3 was both direct and indirect via the measures of school bonds while controlling for parental bonds and the other covariates. Unnever et al. (2016) concluded that racial discrimination can increase externalizing behaviors directly among African American youths, and it can escalate their level of externalizing behaviors by weakening their attachment to teachers and their commitment to their education.

In a subsequent study, analyzing the same two cohorts in the PHDCN-LCS, Unnever et al. (2016a) examined another school-based racialized pathway to offending. Unnever and Gabbidon (2011) posited that racial discrimination should cause African American youths to disidentify with their education, leading to two racialized pathways to offending: (1) dropping out of school and (2) associating with other youths— delinquent peers—who also are in the process of disengaging from their school. Unnever and Gabbidon (2011) argue that disidentified youths are likely to turn to criminal behavior as a way to feel "successful," as crime can be readily and easily accomplished (Gottfredson & Hirschi, 1990).

Unnever et al. (2016a) revealed that racial discrimination amplified a change in offending from wave 1 to wave 3 by increasing (1) the likelihood that African American youths will drop out of school and (2) increasing their association with delinquent peers from wave 1 to wave 3. Unnever et al. (2016a) found evidence in support of this racialized pathway between racial discrimination, associating with delinquent peers, and offending after introducing controls for demographic, social, and individual trait factors. Together, these studies support Unnever and Gabbidon's (2011) core assertion that racial oppression is a debilitating force in the lives of African American youths, compelling some down racialized pathways that lead to offending behaviors.

Similarly, evidence shows that racialized mass incarceration or the rise of the carceral state has uniquely affected African Americans (Alexander, 2010; Bobo & Thompson, 2010; Morris, 2016; Schlesinger, 2011). Indeed, the "deadly symbiosis" that exists among prisons, gangs, and ghettos has solidified into an institutionalized racial formation (Johnson, 2000; Wacquant, 2001). Scholars also have found that the inmate code of conduct has become codified along a race axis that has strict rules of conduct governing interracial and intraracial exchanges (Goodman, 2014). Walker (2016, p. 1064) reports in his ground-level study that in some cellblocks, "inmates must follow a set of racialized norms known as the 'politics.' The politics tell inmates where they can go, with whom they can interact, which resources they can use, when they have access to those resources, and why they must behave in particular ways. As a microinteractional racial project, the politics reify and institutionalize race and mobilize resources in support of racial constructs." Furthermore, research reveals that the mass incarceration of African Americans has negatively affected their communities' by increasing the rates of crime especially among African American men (Alexander, 2010; Clear, 2007).[7] This is particularly troubling, as audit research shows that employers are more likely to hire a White male with a criminal record than African American men who have never been arrested (Pager, 2003).[8]

Resiliency

The resiliency of African Americans to the debilitating forces of systemic racial oppression is found throughout their history (Agnew, 2015;

Jones, 2010; Potter, 2008). This resiliency explains why the vast majority of African Americans do not offend. This means that there is substantial individual variation in how African Americans perceive, interpret, and respond to racial oppression. In other words, racialized narratives vary among African Americans. An intersectional understanding of crime would recognize that the experiences of racial oppression are embedded within other contexts such as place, gender, and class. For example, Gabbidon, Higgins, and Potter (2011) found that African American women that resided in the South were less likely to report experiencing unfair treatment by the police and that older, higher-income men were less likely to report being treated unfairly.

Scholars have identified other characteristics that predict how African Americans construct their racialized narratives and how these narratives are related to resiliency/offending. For example, Potter (2008, p. 190) highlights the resiliency of African American women as they continuously refer to themselves and other African American women as "Strong Black Women." Other research recognizes that there are salient differences in how foreign-born and third-generation and greater U.S. born African Americans respond to perceptions of racial oppression and how they form their racial identity (Waters, Kasinitz, & Asad, 2014). Research shows that foreign-born African Americans make up nearly 15% of the Black population in the U.S. (Unnever, 2016). A Black Criminology must also recognize that there may be ethnic differences (e.g., Haitian, Jamaican, Canadian, and African-born) in how African Americans perceive, interpret, and respond to racial oppression (Waters et al., 2014).[9] In addition, research reveals that "colorism" may be a salient predictor of individual responses to racial oppression among African Americans (Hunter, 2016). Jones (2010, p. 161) reports that colorism is particularly divisive among African American teenage girls: "Colorism, notably the privileging of light skin and other related characteristics, has lingered since the end of slavery and continues to permeate girls' sense of self-worth in a way that divides them from one another. Colorism is one of the most dehumanizing and divisive elements of contemporary Black life and it limits the quality of relationships among adolescent, Black girls" (Jones, 2010, p. 161). Other factors that predict individual differences include education, racial socialization experiences, affiliation with the Black Church, exposure to racial discrimination, coping strategies, and having a positive racial identity (Unnever & Gabbidon, 2011).

In sum, there is no one Black experience. One shoe does not fit all. Race and racism are social constructs and formations (Omi & Winant,

2004). Therefore, a key challenge for a Black Criminology is to illuminate the consequences while revealing the diversity of individual responses to racial oppression (Ferdinand, 2015; Hayward & Krause, 2015; Isom, 2016; Gabbidon et al., 2011; Gabbidon, Higgins, & Wilder-Bonner, 2013; Hunter, Case, Joseph, Mekawi, & Bokhari, 2016; Unnever & Gabbidon, 2015). Thus, a Black Criminology must explain the variation in the degree to which African Americans are cognitively aware of their racial oppression and explain variations in how they respond to their racial subjugation.

Place and Gender

Place

According to Uniform Crime Reports (UCR) reports, the police arrested 8,248,709 people in the United States in 2015. African Americans constituted 26.6% of these arrests (2,197,140). The UCR data also show that the police made the vast majority of those arrests (5,580,654; 68%) in cities. African Americans constituted 29% of all the arrests made in cities (1,716,106). Together, these data show that the police arrested approximately 78% (1,716,106/2,197,140) of African Americans in 2015 in cities. Based on these data, a reasonable conclusion can be made that place is significantly related to offending among African Americans. Therefore, a Black Criminology must incorporate an analysis of how and why place is related to crime.

Research clearly reveals that crime disproportionately occurs in areas of compounded deprivation (Perkins & Sampson, 2015). Social disorganization theorists argue that the higher rates of crime in urban areas are not race related but rather result from residing in locations of compounded deprivation that have little collective efficacy (i.e., neighbors scold if a child is disrespectful, neighbors break up fights in front of their home). However, there are no areas of *compounded deprivation* where nearly all the residents are White (see also Farrington, Loeber, & Loeber, 2003; Hagan, 2010; Peterson, 2012; Sampson, 2013; Sharkey, 2008; Shaw & McKay, 1949). The lack of comparable White neighborhoods to those occupied by some African Americans renders testing the racial invariance problematic while illuminating the inimitability of the experiences of African Americans.

A Black Criminology begins its analysis of the relationship between race, place, and crime by recognizing that racist Whites purposefully constructed areas of racialized compounded deprivation to specifically isolate and circumscribe the life chances of African Americans (Hirsch, 2009; Kusmer, 1978; Massey, 1990; Sugrue, 2014). A Black Criminology could then explore whether place affects the formation of a positive racial identity; whether it restricts the ability of African Americans to interact positively with Whites; whether place enhances the mistrust of Whites and diminishes bonds to historically White-dominated institutions; whether it enhances perceptions of race-based schooling inequality; whether place intensifies perceptions and encounters with racialized criminal justice injustices; and whether it negatively affects racial socialization. In short, a Black Criminology could investigate the racialized narrative that African Americans construct as they come to terms with the knowledge that that they live in areas that were deliberately constructed by racist Whites to subjugate them.

A Black Criminology also notes that racist Whites purposefully constructed "Black ghettos"—areas of compounded deprivation—in order to contain crime and who would be victimized (Hirsch, 2009; Robinson, 1981). Research shows that elite White decision makers knew that the segregation of African Americans into poor, isolated areas would result in higher rates of crime and victimization but were willing to turn a blind eye as long as the levels were not threatening and the consequences remained within the Black community (Kusmer, 1978; Robinson, 1981). Indeed, the data show that the vast majority of crime is intraracial principally because most victims of crime live near the offender in racially segregated neighborhoods (Kim, Willis, Latterner, & LaGrange, 2016).

A Black Criminology encourages research that explores the consequences of intraracial crime within Black communities (Oliver, 1994). We suggest three possible avenues of research. First, researchers could explore whether intraracial crimes disrupt the community's ability to mobilize against the forces that now maintain "Black ghettos" (e.g., White hostility, racial steering, discrimination by landlords, job displacement, racial profiling, racial discrimination in mortgage lending and insurance, and violence) (Hagan, 2010; Hirsch, 2009; Massey, 1990; Peterson, 2012; Sharkey, 2008; Sugrue, 2014). In other words, scholars may wish to investigate whether the intraracial crimes tear "at the fabric of everyday life, sowing fear and suspicion into the networks of family and friends that have long sustained poor Black communities" (Goffman, 2014, p. 197). Second, scholars might explore how intraracial crimes affect the racial socialization process and how African Americans construct their racial identity. Do African Americans racially socialize their children differently, and is it more difficult to construct a positive racial identity if they are victimized by other African Americans? Third, scholars could investigate whether the high rates of crime and victimization within Black communities reinforce the racist stereotype of the *criminalblackman* and its consequential deleterious consequences (Unnever, 2014).

Gender

A Black Criminology must incorporate into its analysis the role of gender in offending (Jones, 2010). Scholars could establish two tracts of research. The first tract could investigate how and why African American and White females differ in their offending (Potter, 2008; Jones, 2010). Simpson (1989, p. 618) argues that "the unique structural and cultural positioning of African American women produces complex cultural typescripts that exert push-pull pressures for crime, pressures that may not exist for white women."

The second tract could examine why there are gender differences in offending. This line of research could begin by outlining the differences in the degree to which racist Whites constructed gender-specific forms of racial oppression. The key would be in cataloging these gender-specific forms of racial oppression and then determining whether they produce gender differences in offending. For example, scholars argue one reason why African American men offend more than African American women is that they are uniquely affected by stereotype threats that negatively depict them as criminals.[10] Only African American men are confronted with the deleterious depiction that they are super-predators or are the "criminalblackman" (Russell-Brown, 2009; Unnever, 2014).[11] These omnipresent stereotype threats could differentially impact African American boys/men as they attend school, seek employment, decide where to live, and interact with the police. Indeed, research suggests that African American boys/men report higher levels of perceived racial discrimination, particularly by the police, than African American females (Unnever, 2014).

Research also highlights other factors that may explain gender differences in offending. For example, studies suggest that the formation of a racial identity may be different for African American females than African American males and that African American caregivers may racially socialize their daughters differently than their sons (McNeil, Reynolds, Fincham, & Beach, 2016). Jones (2010, p. 155) found that

African American teenaged girls that embrace the identity of a "ghetto chick" are most likely to engage in violence. However, she also reports that African American teenage girls have a fluidity in their "racialized, classed, and gendered" form of racial identity that allows some "to use physical aggression when appropriate without sacrificing any and all claims to a respectable feminine identity" (Jones, 2010, p. 155). Research also indicates that African American women more often attend the Black Church; they are less likely to perceive racial discrimination; and they employ different coping skills than African American men when encountering racial oppression (Burt & Simons, 2015; Gabbidon et al., 2011; Unnever & Gabbidon, 2011).

Why a Black Criminology?

Critics will argue that there is no need for a Black Criminology (and a feminist criminology) because the existing general theories of crime (e.g., labeling theory, learning theory, strain theory, social control theory, learning theory, social disorganization, and low self-control) can incorporate its key concepts into an understanding of African American offending. For example, general strain theorists argue that racial and ethnic discrimination are just another form of strain that should predict offending among all minorities (e.g., African Americans, Asians, Jews, and Latinos) (Hartshorn, Whitbeck, & Hoyt, 2012; Salas-Wright, Clark, Vaughn, & Córdova, 2015; Unger, Schwartz, Huh, Soto, & Baezconde-Garbanati, 2014). Likewise, social control scholars could argue that any findings that African Americans with weak social bonds are more likely to offend supports the theory of social control. In short, critics will argue that a Black Criminology will not shine any new light on the causes of crime or allow criminologists to explain any more variance in their models of offending. It simply is not needed.

We suggest that there are three reasons why the general theories of crime cannot subsume a Black Criminology. First, the starting point for a Black Criminology is that the United States has been and is a racialized society (Bonilla-Silva, 2015). It also assumes that African Americans have unique racialized experiences that do not generalize to other Whites and other minorities (e.g., Latinos, Jews, Asians, and Native Americans).[12] This means that the racial oppression of African Americans cannot generalize to Whites and is not identical to ethnic oppression (Feagin, 2013). In addition, general theories of crime are ahistorical explanations of offending.[13] A Black Criminology assumes that the reasons why a minority of African Americans offend today is inextricable related to and embedded within their collective history of racial oppression. In sum, the general theories of crime are incompatible with the Black Criminology assumption that African Americans have unique racialized experiences that they interpret within an inimitable racialized framework born out of centuries of racial oppression (Feagin & Elias, 2013). In short, a Black Criminology is race-specific.

Second, a Black Criminology is larger than the sum of its parts. This means that the tenets of a Black Criminology would lose their theoretical coherence if scholars disassembled and stripped them of their historical meaning in order to have them "fit" into existing general theories. A neutered concept of *episodic* discrimination (e.g., strain) is not the equivalent of arguing that a significant component of African American offending stems from their *past* and present *systemic* racial oppression with specific instances of *racial* discrimination just being a minute component of their overall racialized subordination (Feagin, 2013). In addition, a Black Criminology understands that the reactions that African Americans have to individualistic episodic instances of racial discrimination flow from a "sea of hostility" or from a "reservoir of bad will" that has accumulated over centuries (Noble, 2006, p. 91; Tyler, 1990, p. 235).[14] Similarly, to argue that racial socialization is just another form of coping with strains (e.g., like meditation) sterilizes the fact that African Americans must continuously provide their children with a critical race consciousness that may allow them to overcome their systemic racial oppression in all of its variegated forms (Agnew, 2013; Sullivan & Esmail, 2012).

Third, a Black Criminology pinpoints alternative causes for why African Americans offend than those posited by the general theories of crime. For example, a Black Criminology assumes that African Americans deplete their reservoir of self-control as they are confronted with the profound and daily microaggressions of their racial oppression (Gibbons, O'Hara, Stock, Gerrard, Weng, & Wills, 2012; Haslanger, 2014; Unnever, 2014). Gottfredson and Hirschi (1990) argue that *the* cause of low self-control is bad parenting (Unnever, Cullen, & Agnew, 2006). Social control theorists contend that the likelihood of developing weak social bonds generally arises when parents fail to instill within their children a sense of commitment to conventional institutions and a strong belief in the law. A Black Criminology argues that some African Americans fail to strongly bond with "conventional" institutions because they perceive them as White-dominated racist institutions that have been and are integral to their racial subordination. It is also likely that African Americans encounter racial discrimination when interacting with conventional institutions. Likewise, a Black Criminology assumes that the reason why African American youths failed to respect the Richmond police (the question Hirschi [1969] used to measure belief) was that they likely either personally or vicariously experienced racial injustices by them. We argue that the synergy between a Black Criminology and the general theories will ultimately cause criminology to develop a more holistic historically grounded empirical understanding of why a minority of African Americans offend.

The Balkanization of Criminology

Critics also may be hesitant to endorse a Black Criminology over concerns that it will balkanize or factionalize the discipline of criminology. We offer two responses. First, we suggest that a feminist criminology has enriched rather than divided the discipline. A synergy exists between feminist criminology and the prevailing theories that has deepened the understanding of the gendered pathways to crime (Kruttschnitt, 2016; Miller & Mullins, 2006). We contend that the same synergy will occur between a Black Criminology and the discipline enriching the understanding of why offending is disproportionately high among African Americans and why some but not other African Americans offend.

Second, a Black Criminology will be no different from any of the existing theories of crime. Each is balkanized by having a unique starting point or set of foundational assumptions that are not shared. Labeling theory focuses on secondary deviance, low self-control concentrates on self-control, control theory scrutinizes weak social bonds, learning theory details the learning of crime, strain theory concentrates on stressors, and social disorganization studies an area's level of collective efficacy. Thus, a Black Criminology will be an additional paradigm within the discipline of criminology. The only difference will be that a Black Criminology focuses on how systemic racism produces crime. Unfortunately, none of the existing theories of crime has the same focus.

Conclusion

A leading intent of the discipline of criminology is to produce a deeper understanding of the multifaceted reasons why people engage in criminal activity. The formal development of a Black Criminology will add to this complex task by generating a fuller understanding of the causes of crime among African Americans. A Black Criminology can bring to the forefront causes of crime that scholars have largely neglected or omitted from most of the prevailing theories of crime such as the multilayered consequences of racial oppression and the multi-dimensional methods of resiliency that most African Americans use to negate their racial subjugation. In short, the empirical findings of a Black Criminology coupled with the cumulating evidence generated by the existing theories of crime will produce a fuller understanding of why a minority of African Americans commit crime.

A Black Criminology is essential for accomplishing this task. It will direct researchers to collect data that other datasets omit or poorly measure. For example, Unnever and Gabbidon (2011) highlight that racial discrimination is a salient cause of African American offending. They also state that to assess its true impact on African American offending, researchers must measure it along some of the same axes as child abuse. This would include measures such as age of onset, who racially discriminated against the individual (e.g., was it a person of trust such as a teacher or police officer?), how frequently was the person discriminated against (e.g., daily, weekly, monthly), was the person chronically exposed to racial discrimination (e.g., was it across the lifespan?), what was the severity of the person's experiences with racial discrimination (were the experiences profound or were they mostly racial microaggressions?), and what was the extent of the injuries that resulted from the racial discrimination (e.g., was the person physically attacked?). Unfortunately, we do not know of any existing datasets that fully measure racial discrimination along these axes. However, the development of a formal Black Criminology will cause researchers to be more expansive and inclusive in their data collection and analyses of crime among African Americans.

In addition, we agree with Russell (1992) that failing to acknowledge the need for a Black Criminology undermines the integrity of the discipline of criminology. Certainly, the development of a feminist criminology enhanced its legitimacy as an inclusive science, and we argue that the development of a Black Criminology would further heightened its legitimacy (Kruttschnitt, 2016; Miller & Mullins, 2006). A Black Criminology would give voice to the racialized experiences of African Americans. It may also help diversify the undergraduate and graduate curriculums and, perhaps, even attract more African Americans to the field (Russell, 1992).[15] Moreover, we agree with Russell (1992, p. 675) when she argues that the failure to develop a Black Criminology "will call into question the integrity of the discipline's policy recommendations related to race and crime."

In sum, the intersections of race, crime, and the criminal justice system have always been at the heart of race relations in the United States (Oshinsky, 1997; Spohn, 2014, 2015). In addition, the evidence is clear that racial oppression—in all of its ramifications including racial discrimination—increases the likelihood that some African Americans will offend. Therefore, we suggest that criminology as a discipline would be further enriched by formally developing a Black Criminology, a Black Criminology that recognizes the racialized nature of African American offending, details the racialized pathways to crime, illuminates how race is related to the criminal justice system and the carceral state, and advocates for race-centered approaches to prevention and rehabilitation. However, the formal development of a Black Criminology does not preclude the likelihood that African Americans may share similar reasons for committing crimes as Whites and other stigmatized groups. In short, we argue that the formal development of a Black Criminology creates the theoretical impetus for scholars to discern when, how, and why race matters (Kruttschnitt, 2016; Miller & Mullins, 2006).

Notes

* The authors thank Robert Agnew, J.C. Barnes, Eric Baumer, Callie Burt, Francis Cullen, Richard Felson, Shaun Gabbidon, Candace Kruttschnitt, John Laub, Michael Leiber, Dan Mears, Ruth Peterson, Alex Piquero, Katheryn Russell-Brown, Robert Sampson, Benjamin Steiner, and Eric Stewart for their insightful comments.

1. Thus, we find it ironic that racism significantly affected the development of the general theories, yet these theories posit that racial oppression, in all of its variegated forms, is not a unique cause of why some African Americans commit crime.

2. Other evidence includes the historical precedent that the president and vice president of the American Society of Criminology (ASC) are both African American, the ASC has a Division on People of Color and Crime, which sponsors a journal, *Race and Justice*, and the ASC provides the Ruth Peterson Fellowship for Racial and Ethnic Diversity.

3. Simpson (1989, p. 610) argues that "feminist criminologists must seriously consider the nature of gender relations and the peculiar brand of oppression that patriarchal relations bring."

4. The stereotyping of African Americans as criminal was integral to the scientific racism that legitimated the legal segregation system of Jim Crow. This belief of white supremacy "portrayed African Americans as imminently endangering whites and their communities," and the notion of racial degeneration was "most powerfully captured in the image of the "black beast rapist"" (Smångs, 2016, p. 1341).

5. However, even though Shaw and McKay (1949, p. 617) noted that Jim Crow racism negatively affected only African Americans, they concluded that the higher rates of crime for African American youths in comparison to whites youths resulted both from "low-income and from the fact that the institutions of migrating Negroes have been singularly unsuited to the problems of urban life."

6. Perceptions of police brutality could be considered as "events" that Smångs (2016, p. 1334) argues are critical for creating "collective identity narratives" that produce and reproduce "group boundaries, identities, and, as it may apply, inequalities." Smångs (2016, pp. 1328) defines narratives as the person's "conceptions of racial or ethnic differences and similarities as well as the consequences of such conceptions for relations and behaviors among and between racially and ethnically defined groups." Smångs (2016, pps.1334,1369) states that "The perhaps most powerful and consequential events are in that regard dramatic ones involving conflict in general and violence in particular . . ." and that "violent practices of past racial domination impart directionality to the beliefs and practices through which contemporary racial conflicts are understood and played out on the local as well as national level."

7. Lee, McCormick, Hicken, and Wildeman (2015) report that 44% of African American women and 32% of African American men but only 12% of white women and 6% of white men have a family member imprisoned.

8. Notably, Galgano (2009) replicated Pager's (2003) audit study for African American women versus white women in Chicago for entry-level positions and did not find significant racial disparities. These findings suggest that the effects of the "criminalblackman" stereotype may not generalize to African American women.

9. A Black Criminology would argue that the history of Black America is unique from the histories of other stigmatized groups (e.g., Native Americans, Jews, and Latinos) and differs from the history of African Americans in other countries such as those residing in the Caribbean. In brief, every oppressed group has its own ethnic/racialized narrative.

10. Of note, research shows that in an experimental setting, lenders perceived white men and African American women to be equally fundable, white females as less fundable, and African American males as the least fundable. Harkness (2016) concludes that there is an intersectionality of race and gender because when lenders assess borrowers, they implicitly are guided by cultural stereotypes about the borrowers' status.

11. Jones (2010, p. 160) notes that a gendered stereotype specific to African American girls is the "video hos."

12. For example, research indicates that the children of immigrant groups (including African Americans born in the Caribbean) who maintain a biculturalism have fewer adjustment problems and that each immigrant group has distinct attributes associated with their racial/ethnic socialization (Bailey, 2016; Bentley-Edwards & Stevenson, 2016; Choi, Tan, Yasui, & Hahm, 2016; Dennis, Fonseca, Gutierrez, Shen, & Salazar, 2016; Juang, Shen, Kim, & Wang, 2016; Sanchez, Whittaker, Hamilton, & Zayas, 2016; Waters et al., 2014). Obviously, these findings are inapplicable to African Americans born in the United States because they have lived in racialized areas of compounded deprivation across multiple generations (Sharkey, 2008).

13. For example, Hirschi (1969) failed to connect the reasons why African Americans may have weak bonds with conventional institutions, such as the criminal

justice system and schools, to the fact that many of these institutions were integral to their historical and current racial subjugation. In addition, social disorganization theories do not include in their analyses the reality that areas of compounded deprivation are racist formations specifically created by whites to subjugate and constrain only African Americans. In short, social disorganization theorists fail to reveal how the history of racialized areas of compounded deprivation has created current racialized pathways to African American offending.

14. This contention parallels Kruttschnitt's (2016) argument that when scholars measure strain by the presence of adverse events, its effect on offending is invariant across gender. However, "when we look at a more complex model that allows the responses to strain to vary by emotions and behaviors, we find significant differences by gender" (Kruttschnitt, 2016, p. 8).

15. When Russell (1992) first called for the development of a Black Criminology in 1992, fewer than 50 African Americans in the United States had been granted a doctorate in criminology or criminal justice. In fact, just 27 of the 399 doctoral degrees in criminology between 1980 and 1990 were awarded to African Americans (8%) (Russell, 1992, pp. 675–676). Of concern, data that are more recent reveal that the percentage of African American doctoral students in criminology and criminal justice has decreased since 1990. According to a 2013 survey of the Association of Doctoral Programs in Criminology and Criminal Justice (ADPCCJ, 2013), only 7.25% of doctoral students were Non-Latino African Americans. In addition, the most recent data that are available from the ASC show that in 2014, only 175 of its 3,505 members (5%) self-identified as African American.

References

ADPCCJ Executive Board. (2013). *Association of Doctoral Programs in Criminology and Criminal Justice (ADPCCJ) 2013 survey report*. Retrieved from www. adpccj.com/surveys.html

Agnew, R. (2013). When criminal coping is likely: An extension of general strain theory. *Deviant Behavior*, *34*, 653–670.

Agnew, R. (2015). Race and youth crime: Why isn't the relationship stronger? *Race and Justice*, *6*, 195–221, published online.

Alexander, M. (2010). *The new Jim Crow: Mass incarceration in the age of colorblindness*. New York, NY: The New Press.

Anderson, R. E., McKenny, M., Mitchell, A., Koku, L., & Stevenson, H. C. (2017). Embracing racial stress and trauma: Preliminary feasibility and coping responses of a racial socialization intervention. *Journal of Black Psychology*, *44*, 25–46, published online.

Bailey, E. K. (2016). "I am studying in the US but": Observations and insights from Caribbean college students. *Social Identities*, 1–17, published online.

Bentley-Edwards, K. L., & Stevenson, H. C. (2016). The multidimensionality of racial/ethnic socialization: Scale construction for the cultural and racial experiences of socialization (cares). *Journal of Child and Family Studies*, *25*, 96–108.

Bobo, L. D., & Thompson, V. L. (2010). Racialized mass incarceration: Poverty, prejudice, and punishment. In H. R. Markus & P. M. Moya (Eds.), *Doing race: 21 Essays for the 21st century* (pp. 322–355). New York, NY: W. W. Norton.

Bolton, K., & Feagin, K. (2004). *Black in blue: African-American police officers and racism*. New York, NY: Routledge.

Bonilla-Silva, E. (2015). The structure of racism in color-blind, "post-racial" America. *American Behavioral Scientist, 59*, 1358–1376, published online.

Burt, C. H., & Simons, R. L. (2015). Interpersonal racial discrimination, ethnic-racial socialization, and offending: Risk and resilience among African American females. *Justice Quarterly, 32*, 532–570.

Choi, Y., Tan, K. P. H., Yasui, M., & Hahm, H. C. (2016). Advancing understanding of acculturation for adolescents of Asian immigrants: Person-oriented analysis of acculturation strategy among Korean American youth. *Journal of Youth and Adolescence, 45*, 1380–1395.

Chu, D. C., & Sung, H-E. (2009). Racial differences in desistance from substance abuse: The impact of religious involvement on recovery. *International Journal of Offender Therapy and Comparative Criminology, 53*, 696–716.

Clear, T. R. (2007). *Imprisoning communities: How mass incarceration makes disadvantaged neighborhoods worse.* New York, NY: Oxford University Press.

Coates, T-N. (2015). *Between the world and me.* Melbourne, AU: Text Publishing.

Cullen, F. T. (2011). Beyond adolescence-limited criminology: Choosing our future—the American Society of Criminology 2010 Sutherland address. *Criminology, 49*, 287–330.

Dennis, J. M., Fonseca, A. L., Gutierrez, G., Shen, J., & Salazar, S. (2016). Bicultural competence and the Latino 2.5 generation: The acculturative advantages and challenges of having one foreign-born and one U.S.-born parent. *Hispanic Journal of Behavioral Sciences, 38*, 341–359, published online.

Dilulio, J. (1995). The coming of the super predators. *The Weekly Standard, 1*, 23–30.

Edwards, S. B., & Harris, D. (2016). *Black lives matter.* Minneapolis, MN: ABDO.

Farrington, D. P., Loeber, R., & Stouthamer-Loeber, M. (2003). How can the relationship between race and violence be explained. In D. F. Hawkins (Ed.), *Violent crimes: Assessing race and ethnic differences* (pp. 213–237). New York, NY: Cambridge University Press.

Feagin, J. (2013). *Systemic racism: A theory of oppression.* New York, NY: Routledge.

Feagin, J., & Elias, S. (2013). Rethinking racial formation theory: A systemic racism critique. *Ethnic and Racial Studies, 36*, 931–960.

Ferdinand, R. (2015). Skin tone and popular culture: My story as a dark skinned black woman. *The Popular Culture Studies Journal, 3*, 324–349.

Gabbidon, S. L., & Greene, H. T. (2012). *Race and crime.* Thousand Oaks, CA: Sage.

Gabbidon, S. L., Higgins, G. E., & Potter, H. (2011). Race, gender, and the perception of recently experiencing unfair treatment by the police: Exploratory results from an all-black sample. *Criminal Justice Review, 36*, 5–21.

Gabbidon, S. L., Higgins, G. E., & Wilder-Bonner, K. M. (2013). Black supporters of racial profiling: A demographic profile. *Criminal Justice Policy Review, 24*, 422–440.

Galgano, S. W. (2009). Barriers to reintegration: An audit study of the impact of race and offender status on employment opportunities for women. *Social Thought and Research, 30*, 21–37.

Gates, H. L., & Steele, C. M. (2009). A conversation with Claude M. Steele. *Du Bois Review: Social Science Research on Race, 6*, 251–271.

Gibbons, F. X., O'Hara, R. E., Stock, M. L., Gerrard, M., Weng, C-Y., & Wills, T. A. (2012). The erosive effects of racism: Reduced self-control mediates the relation between perceived racial discrimination and substance use in African American adolescents. *Journal of Personality and Social Psychology, 102*, 1089–1104.

Gines, K. T. (2014). A critique of postracialism. *Du Bois Review: Social Science Research on Race, 11*, 75–86.

Goffman, A. (2014). *On the run: Fugitive life in an American city*. Chicago, IL: University of Chicago Press.

Goodman, P. (2014). Race in California's prison fire camps for men: Prison politics, space, and the racialization of everyday life. *American Journal of Sociology, 120*, 352–394.

Gottfredson, M. R., & Hirschi, T. (1990). *A general theory of crime*. Stanford, CA: Stanford University Press.

Griffiths, E. (2013). Race, space, and the spread of violence across the city. *Social Problems, 60*, 491–512.

Hagan, J. (2010). Foreword: America's deadly and duplicitous divide. In R. D. Peterson & L. J. Krivo (Eds.), *Divergent social worlds: Neighborhood crime and the racial-spatial divide* (pp. xvii–xxi). New York, NY: Russell Sage Foundation.

Halgunseth, L. C., Jensen, A. C., Sakuma, K-L., & McHale, S. M. (2016). The role of mothers' and fathers' religiosity in African American adolescents' religious beliefs and practices. *Cultural Diversity and Ethnic Minority Psychology, 22*, 386–394.

Harkness, S. K. (2016). Discrimination in lending markets: Status and the intersections of gender and race. *Social Psychology Quarterly, 79*, 81–93.

Hartshorn, K. J., Whitbeck, L. B., & Hoyt, D. R. (2012). Exploring the relationships of perceived discrimination, anger, and aggression among North American indigenous adolescents. *Society and Mental Health, 2*, 53–67.

Haslanger, S. (2014). Studying while black. *Du Bois Review: Social Science Research on Race, 11*, 109–136.

Hayward, D. R., & Krause, N. (2015). Religion and strategies for coping with racial discrimination among African Americans and Caribbean African Americans. *International Journal of Stress Management, 22*, 70–91.

Hirsch, A. R. (2009). *Making the second ghetto: Race and housing in Chicago 1940–1960*. Chicago, IL: University of Chicago Press.

Hirschi, T. (1969). *Causes of delinquency*. Berkeley, CA: University of California.

Hunt, M. O. (1996). The individual, society, or both? A comparison of black, Latino, and white beliefs about the causes of poverty. *Social Forces, 75*, 293–322.

Hunter, C. D., Case, A. D., Joseph, N., Mekawi, Y., & Bokhari, E. (2016). The roles of shared racial fate and a sense of belonging with African Americans in black immigrants' race-related stress and depression. *Journal of Black Psychology, 43*, 135–158, published online.

Hunter, M. (2016). Colorism in the classroom: How skin tone stratifies African American and Latina/o students. *Theory into Practice, 55*, 54–61.

Isom, D. (2016). Microaggressions, injustices, and racial identity: An empirical assessment of the theory of African American offending. *Journal of Contemporary Criminal Justice, 32*, 27–59.

Johnson, R. (2000). American prisons and the African-American experience: A history of social control and racial oppression. *Corrections Compendium, 25*, 6–30.

Jones, N. (2010). *Between good and ghetto African American girls and inner-city violence*. New Brunswick, NJ: Rutgers University Press.

Juang, L. P., Shen, Y., Kim, S. Y., & Wang, Y. (2016). Development of an Asian American parental racial—ethnic socialization scale. *Cultural Diversity and Ethnic Minority Psychology, 22*, 417–431.

Kim, S., Willis, C. L., Latterner, K., & LaGrange, R. (2016). When birds of a feather don't flock together: A macrostructural approach to interracial crime. *Sociological Inquiry, 86*, 166–188, published online.

Kruttschnitt, C. (2016). The politics, and place, of gender in research on crime. *Criminology, 54*, 8–29.

Kusmer, K. L. (1978). *A ghetto takes shape: Black Cleveland, 1870–1930*. Chicago, IL: University of Illinois Press.

Lee, H., McCormick, T., Hicken, M. T., & Wildeman, C. (2015). Racial inequalities in connectedness to imprisoned individuals in the United States. *Du Bois Review: Social Science Research on Race, 12*, 269–282.

Liddle, H. A., Jackson-Gilfort, A., & Marvel, F. A. (2006). An empirically supported and culturally specific engagement and intervention strategy for African American adolescent males. *American Journal of Orthopsychiatry, 76*, 215–225.

Like-Haislip, T. (2014). Racial and ethnic patterns in criminality and victimization. In S. M. Bucerius & M. Tonry (Eds.), *The oxford handbook of ethnicity, crime, and immigration* (pp. 107–134). New York, NY: Oxford University Press.

Massey, D. S. (1990). American apartheid: Segregation and the making of the underclass. *American Journal of Sociology, 96*, 329–357.

McNeil, S., Reynolds, J. E., Fincham, F. D., & Beach, S. R. H. (2016). Parental experiences of racial discrimination and youth racial socialization in two-parent African American families. *Cultural Diversity and Ethnic Minority Psychology, 22*, 268–276.

Miller, J., & Mullins, C. W. (2006). The status of feminist theories in criminology. In F. T. Cullen, J. P. Wright, & K. Blevins (Eds.), *Taking stock: The status of criminological theory* (Vol. 15, pp. 217–249). New Brunswick, NJ: Transaction.

Moore, S. E. (2001). Substance abuse treatment with adolescent African American males. *Journal of Social Work Practice in the Addictions, 1*, 21–32.

Morris, M. W. (2016). *Pushout: The criminalization of Black girls in schools*. New York, NY: The New Press.

Noble, R. (2006). *Black rage in the American prison system*. New York, NY: LFB Scholarly Publishing.

Nuytiens, A., & Christiaens, J. (2016). Female pathways to crime and prison: Challenging the (us) gendered pathways perspective. *European Journal of Criminology, 13*, 195–213.

Oliver, W. (1994). *The violent social world of African American men*. New York, NY: Lexington Books.

Omi, M., & Winant, H. (2004). *Racial formation in the United States*. New York, NY: Routledge.

Oshinsky, D. M. (1997). *Worse than slavery*. New York, NY: Simon and Schuster.

Owusu-Bempah, A. (2014). *Black males' perceptions of and experiences with the police in Toronto* (Unpublished doctoral dissertation). Toronto: University of Toronto.

Pager, D. (2003). The mark of a criminal record. *American Journal of Sociology, 108*, 937–975.

Perkins, K. L., & Sampson, R. J. (2015). Compounded deprivation in the transition to adulthood: The intersection of racial and economic inequality among Chicagoans, 1995–2013. *RSF: The Russell Sage Foundation Journal of the Social Sciences, 1*, 35–54.

Peterson, R. D. (2012). The central place of race in crime and justice—the American Society of Criminology's 2011 Sutherland address. *Criminology, 50*, 303–328.

Pew Research Center. (2016). *On views of race and inequality, African Americans and Whites are worlds apart about four-in-ten African Americans are doubtful that the U.S. will ever achieve racial equality*. Retrieved from www. pewsocialtrends.org/2016/06/27/on-views-of-race-and-inequality-African Americans-and-whites-are-worlds-apart

Potter, H. (2008). *Battle cries: Black women and intimate partner abuse*. New York, NY: New York University Press.

Robinson, C. D. (1981). The production of black violence in Chicago. In D. F. Greenberg (Ed.), *Crime and capitalism: Readings in Marxist criminology* (pp. 366–404). Philadelphia, PA: Temple University Press.

Russell, K. K. (1992). Development of a black criminology and the role of the black criminologist. *Justice Quarterly, 9*, 667–683.

Russell-Brown, K. (2009). *The color of crime*. New York, NY: New York University Press.

Salas-Wright, C. P., Clark, T. T., Vaughn, M. G., & Córdova, D. (2015). Profiles of acculturation among Hispanics in the United States: Links with discrimination and substance use. *Social Psychiatry and Psychiatric Epidemiology, 50*, 39–49.

Sampson, R. J. (2013). The place of context: A theory and strategy for criminology's hard problems. *Criminology, 51*, 1–31.

Sanchez, D., Whittaker, T. A., Hamilton, E., & Zayas, L. H. (2016). Perceived discrimination and sexual precursor behaviors in Mexican American preadolescent girls: The role of psychological distress, sexual attitudes, and marianismo beliefs. *Cultural Diversity and Ethnic Minority Psychology, 22*, 395–407.

Schlesinger, T. (2011). The failure of race neutral policies: How mandatory terms and sentencing enhancements contribute to mass racialized incarceration. *Crime & Delinquency, 57*, 56–81.

Sharkey, P. (2008). The intergenerational transmission of context. *American Journal of Sociology, 113*, 931–969.

Shaw, C. R., & McKay, H. D. (1949). Rejoinder. *American Sociological Review, 14*, 614–617.

Simpson, S. S. (1989). Feminist theory, crime, and justice. *Criminology, 27*, 605–632.

Smångs, M. (2016). Doing violence, making race: Southern lynching and white racial group formation. *American Journal of Sociology, 121*, 1329–1374.

Spohn, C. (2014). Racial disparities in prosecution, sentencing, and punishment. In S. M. Bucerius & M. Tonry (Eds.), *The Oxford handbook of ethnicity, crime, and immigration* (pp. 166–193). New York, NY: Oxford University Press.

Spohn, C. (2015). Race, crime, and punishment in the twentieth and twenty-first centuries. *Crime and Justice, 44*, 49–97.

Stams, G. J. J. M. (2015). From criminogenic risk to rehabilitation: Is there a need for a culturally sensitive approach? *International Journal of Offender Therapy and Comparative Criminology, 59*, 1263–1266.

Steele, C. M. (1997). A threat in the air: How stereotypes shape intellectual identity and performance. *American Psychologist, 52*, 613–629.

Stepteau-Watson, D., Watson, J., & Lawrence, S. K. (2014). Young African American males in reentry: An Afrocentric cultural approach. *Journal of Human Behavior in the Social Environment, 24*, 658–665.

Sugrue, T. J. (2014). *The origins of the urban crisis: Race and inequality in postwar Detroit*. Princeton, NJ: Princeton University Press.

Sullivan, J. M., & Esmail, A. M. (2012). *African American identity: Racial and cultural dimensions of the black experience*. Lanham, MD: Lexington Books.

Tatum, B. L. (2000). Toward a neocolonial model of adolescent crime and violence. *Journal of Contemporary Criminal Justice, 16*, 157–170.

Tyler, T. R. (1990). *Why people obey the law: Procedural justice, legitimacy, and compliance.* New Haven, CT: Yale University Press.

Unger, J. B., Schwartz, S. J., Huh, J., Soto, D. W., & Baezconde-Garbanati, L. (2014). Acculturation and perceived discrimination: Predictors of substance use trajectories from adolescence to emerging adulthood among Hispanics. *Addictive Behaviors, 39*, 1293–1296.

Unnever, J. D. (2014). A theory of African American offending: A test of core propositions. *Race and Justice, 4*, 98–123.

Unnever, J. D. (2016). The impact of immigration on indicators of the well-being of the black population in the United States. *Western Journal of Black Studies, 40*, 42–60.

Unnever, J. D., Barnes, J. C., & Cullen, F. T. (2016a). Racial discrimination and pathways to delinquency: Testing a theory of African American offending. *Race and Justice, 7*, 350–373, published online.

Unnever, J. D., Barnes, J. C., & Cullen, F. T. (2016b). The racial invariance thesis revisited: Testing an African American theory of offending. *Journal of Contemporary Criminal Justice, 32*, 7–26.

Unnever, J. D., Cullen, F. T., & Agnew, R. (2006). Why is "bad" parenting criminogenic? Implications from rival theories. *Youth Violence and Juvenile Justice, 4*, 3–33.

Unnever, J. D., Cullen, F. T., & Barnes, J. C. (2016). Racial discrimination, weakened school bonds, and problematic behaviors: Testing a theory of African American offending. *Journal of Research in Crime and Delinquency, 53*, 139–164.

Unnever, J. D., Cullen, F. T., Mathers, S. A., McClure, T. E., & Allison, M. C. (2009). Racial discrimination and Hirschi's criminological classic: A chapter in the sociology of knowledge. *Justice Quarterly, 26*, 377–409.

Unnever, J. D., & Gabbidon, S. L. (2011). *A theory of African American offending: Race, racism, and crime.* New York, NY: Taylor & Francis.

Unnever, J. D., & Gabbidon, S. L. (2015). Do African Americans speak with one voice? Immigrants, public opinions, and perceptions of criminal injustices. *Justice Quarterly, 32*, 680–704.

Wacquant, L. (2001). Deadly symbiosis: When ghetto and prison meet and mesh. *Punishment and Society, 3*, 95–133.

Walker, M. L. (2016). Race making in a penal institution. *American Journal of Sociology, 121*, 1051–1078.

Waters, M. C., Kasinitz, P., & Asad, A. L. (2014). Immigrants and African Americans. *Annual Review of Sociology, 40*, 369–390.

Watson, J., Washington, G., & Stepteau-Watson, D. (2015). Umoja: A culturally specific approach to mentoring young African American males. *Child and Adolescent Social Work Journal, 32*, 81–90.

Yun, M., Kim, E., & Morris, R. (2013). Gendered pathways to delinquency: An examination of general strain theory among South Korean youth. *Youth Violence and Juvenile Justice, 12*, 268–292.

2

Pioneering Black Criminology: W.E.B. Du Bois and *The Philadelphia Negro*

Shaun L. Gabbidon

It has been nearly 30 years since I first discovered the work of W.E.B. Du Bois. During my education as an undergraduate and graduate student no one discussed him or his work. By chance, when I resided in the Washington, DC metro area I frequented a bookstore that was owned by Mr. Payne, a West Indian immigrant who often recommended, "must reads." Mr. Payne introduced me to many Black classics that had somehow been absent from my college courses. One of the first books I read was *The Souls of Black Folk* (1903). After reading it, I was hooked. Du Bois's insights on race relations would not only be relevant on the eve of the 20th century but also at the dawn of the same century. I had to read more. Once I was firmly planted in graduate school, each night after completing the assignments for the required courses, I spent the wee hours of the morning combing through Du Bois's massive collection.

Publication after publication, Du Bois grappled with the same issue I had gone to graduate school to understand—racial disparities in the justice system. Thus, more than a century ago, Du Bois recognized the need to create a race-centered specialized research program to address the significant racial disparities in all areas of American society. Crime was but one of these issues—but he recognized that it was being used as a means to denigrate the entire Black race. Rather than leaving the task of researching the Black experience to the abundance of racist social scientists at his time, he decided to pioneer his own research program at the historically Black institution Atlanta University (Gabbidon, 1999a; Wright, 2002a, 2002b, 2002c, 2016).

The best representation of Du Bois's scholarship that likely serves as the founding Black Criminology treatise is *The Philadelphia Negro* (1899a). The publication was the culmination of Du Bois's 15-month study on the condition of the Black residents living in Philadelphia's Seventh Ward in the late 1800s. This brief essay reviews Du Bois's background and the contribution of *The Philadelphia Negro* (1899a), discusses how Du Bois might have viewed the emerging Black Criminology movement (Russell, 1992; Russell-Brown, 2018), and reviews why the discipline remains tone deaf to the contributions of one of the earliest contributors to American criminology.

Brief Background on Du Bois

Born in Great Barrington, Massachusetts, a few years after the end of slavery, William Edward Burghardt Du Bois was the product of a single-family home. His dad left the home when he was young and never returned (Lewis, 1993). The community helped raised Du Bois, and by all accounts, they did an excellent job. He was an outstanding student who received a partial scholarship to Fisk University in Nashville. Du Bois talked about his experience in the South as being eye-opening, giving the contrasting social norms from his New England home. After graduating from Fisk, he returned north and took a second bachelor's degree at Harvard University, where he also earned an M.A. in history. Unsatisfied with the limited opportunities to study the social sciences at Harvard, he secured funding to study for a doctorate in economics at the University of Berlin under Gustav Von Schmoller. At the time, Schmoller, along with Max Weber and Adolph Wagner, were the leading figures at the important Historical School of Economics at the University of Belin. It is the same place where Robert Park and others went to study what, at the time, was the closest thing to sociology (Boston, 1991).

With his funding cut short just prior to the completion of his doctorate, Du Bois returned to Harvard and received his doctorate in history, studying under the renowned historian Albert Bushnell Hart. Ironically, his M.A. thesis and doctoral dissertation were devoted to the criminal actions of White slave traders who devised all kinds of illicit schemes to continue the transatlantic slave trade despite international laws outlawing it (Du Bois, 1891, 1896). This emphasis on crime by and against Blacks would continue throughout his life.

Elite training in hand, Du Bois was remarkably unable to secure a faculty position at any major university. Instead, he was forced to take a position at Wilberforce University in Ohio, a small historically Black college. After a short period, he was offered the opportunity to conduct a study in Philadelphia, with no faculty appointment attached. Social welfare agencies in Philadelphia were concerned about the social disadvantage and crime in Philadelphia and wanted someone to study it. Du Bois was ideally suited for the task and was hired. He and his new bride, Nina, packed up and headed to the City of Brotherly Love. It was during his tenure in Philadelphia that Du Bois masterfully produced the first true work of a Black Criminology.

The Philadelphia Negro: A Social Study

Elsewhere, I and others have discussed Du Bois and his pioneering criminological research in Philadelphia (Gabbidon, 1996, 2001, 2007; Hanson, 2010; Henderson, 2013). Much like today, Du Bois readily understood the "double consciousness" of being Black and being a social scientist studying the Black community. On the one hand, he was intent on producing a serious scholarly work. On the other hand, he knew that he could not be a completely detached observer of the dire plight facing his people. Hence, to ensure the integrity of the research, he produced one of the most thorough, and likely first, urban ethnographies ever conducted in a major American city (Jerabek, 2016). The resulting tome also constituted the first comprehensive study of a Black community (Du Bois, 1899a). Covering nearly every aspect of Black life in Philadelphia's Seventh Ward and beyond, Du Bois intertwined insights on crime throughout the publication.

Methodological Details. Du Bois recognized that the mere tabulation of statistics could not tell the whole story of the social condition of Blacks in Philadelphia. Thus, he believed that the Verstehen approach he learned from Max Weber at the University of Berlin was the most appropriate method. In some ways, this approach rejected positivism and called for Du Bois to seek a firsthand understanding of the plight of Blacks in Philadelphia. He could only achieve this by living among the residents. With his new wife accompanying him, Du Bois move to the Seventh Ward, where he resided for 15 months. During this time,

Du Bois conducted a comprehensive door-to-door canvass of the Seventh Ward (p. 1). Seeking to capture the full breadth of the near 9,000 residents, he used eight survey schedules that captured family information, individual data, home information, data on the streets and alleys, information on institutions and organizations, and data on servants living in the homes of their employers (p. 2).

Du Bois triangulated his data collection by relying on his multitude of surveys, personal observations, and a review of official statistics. Du Bois informed readers of the value of triangulation by asserting that: "the use of . . . these methods which has been attempted in this study may perhaps have corrected to some extent the errors of each" (p. 3). After constructing this comprehensive methodology, Du Bois began his quest to uncover the reasons for some of the social problems observed among Seventh Ward residents and the larger Black community in Philadelphia.

He divided the final product of his research into two historical chapters, with the remaining chapters devoted to the general condition of the Black community, group life including social maladjustment, and observations devoted to poverty, crime, and alcoholism. He also discussed race relations and social reforms.

Crime in Philadelphia's Seventh Ward

General Statement on Negro Crime

In his pioneering chapter "The Negro Criminal," Du Bois discussed crime among Blacks. He did not make any substantive comparisons to Whites. Moreover, in contrast to the prevailing racist dogma of the period pointing to biological inferiority, Du Bois pointed to two key reasons for the high involvement of Blacks in the Philadelphia justice system. First, he wrote that

Crime is a phenomenon of organized social life, and is the open rebellion of an individual against his social environment. Naturally then, if men are suddenly transported from one environment to another; the result is lack of harmony with the new conditions; lack of harmony with the new physical surroundings leading to disease and death or modification of physique; lack of harmony with social surroundings leading to crime. (p. 235)

Du Bois's early insights dig deep into the specific experiences of Black Americans. In particular, he attributed crime in the Black community to the sudden movements from one environment to another. What were these two movements? The first included the transatlantic slave trade that fed the American slave system in the colonies including Philadelphia. The second was Black migration to the North following Emancipation. And relatedly, the transition of northern slave-holding states, such as Philadelphia, into "free" states. These dramatic transitions resulted in disease, death, and crime. During Colonial times, the crime involved Black rebellions against the institution of slavery; and later, crime resulted from their movement out of the South and their arrival in the north, where racial discrimination restricted their options in the workforce and often landed them under the control of the justice system.

Du Bois recognized the presence of Black slaves in Philadelphia during the late 1600s and their treatment by the local authorities. Records show that, among others, Whites passed one ordinance that restricted the movement of Black slaves who were gathering for entertainment purposes without the approval of their masters. The penalty was one night in jail without food or drink and 39 lashes on their backs, for which their masters would need to pay the whipper $15. These actions speak to the early criminalization of the simple leisure activities of Blacks. The historical records showed additional measures meant to further racially subordinate Black slaves—including the introduction, by William Penn, of distinctive trial procedures and punishments for Blacks, a race-based criminal justice system.

In 1780, Pennsylvania passed legislation that would gradually emancipate the slaves in Philadelphia. By 1790, there were approximately 2,500 Black residents in Philadelphia. A century later, there were nearly 40,000 residents (approximately 6% of the total population). This increase represented another massive transition that transformed the Black community in Philadelphia. In a city where the relationship between the races began as a master–slave one, it progressed into competition for employment and other opportunities within a framework of racial apartheid. Du Bois concluded that these movements would naturally lead to high rates of disease, death, and crime in the Black community. Next, Du Bois turned his attention to arrest and prison statistics. His early insights sound eerily familiar in 2018.

Explaining the Prison Population

Relying on prison data from Eastern Penitentiary, Du Bois analyzed the total number of commitments, the number of Black commitments, and the percentage of Blacks in the population. While commitments were from eastern counties in the state, many of the prisoners were from Philadelphia. Reviewing the numbers, Du Bois quickly pointed out the disproportionate number of Blacks that were populating the prison. Using data from 1830 to 1850, he identified part of the problem being a criminal class in the Black community that resulted in "less than one-fourteenth of the population [being] responsible for nearly a third of the serious crime committed" (p. 238). Moreover, when examining the reduction in disproportionality from the mid-1800s to the late 1800s, Du Bois acknowledged that

> It must be remembered that the discrimination against the Negro was much greater then than now; he was arrested for less cause and given longer sentences than whites. Great numbers of those arrested and committed for trial were never brought to trial so that their guilt could be proven or disproven. (p. 239)

To explore the topic further, Du Bois generated a special study on crime, relying on a decade of prison commitment data from 1885 to 1895. This more focused analysis examined the commitments from residents of Philadelphia. Specifically, he focused on 541 Blacks who had committed serious crimes. After again acknowledging the disproportionate share of Black involvement in serious crimes, Du Bois transitioned into a discussion challenging the reliability of the figures. To begin, he writes about class and race differences that influence who is sentenced to prison:

> This of course assumes that the convicts in the penitentiary represent to a fair degree of accuracy crime committed. The assumption is not wholly true; in convictions by human courts the rich always are favored somewhat at the expense of the poor, the upper classes at the expense of the unfortunate classes, and whites at the expense of the Negroes. (p. 249)

Du Bois then commented on how the nature of offenses affected who is in prison. He notes:

> We know for instance that certain crimes are not punished in Philadelphia because the public opinion is lenient, as for instance embezzlement, forgery, and certain sorts of stealing; on the other hand a commercial

community is apt to punish with severity petty thieving, breaches of the peace, and personal assault or burglary. (p. 249)

Finally, Du Bois addressed the potential role of racial discrimination in the number of Blacks in prison. He opined that

It has been charged by some Negroes that color prejudice plays some part, but there is no tangible proof of this, save perhaps that there is apt to be a certain presumption of guilt when a Negro is accused, on the part of police, public and judge. (p. 249)

Du Bois also pointed to the role of White privilege in the administration of justice. He did so by acknowledging "the influences of social position and connections in procuring white pardons and lighter sentences."

The Criminals

Later in the chapter, Du Bois provided a profile of Black criminals. Notably, his observations related to age and sex are the same as today: "The mass of criminals are, it is easy to see, young single men under thirty" (p. 252). Du Bois's analysis was not isolated to male criminals. He also found that the Black women in Eastern Penitentiary mostly engaged in stealing, fighting, and prostitution. Du Bois further found that many of the more serious criminals were from outside the city. In contrast to the prevailing sentiment at the time, Du Bois found that the level of intelligence (in the form of educational achievement) among the criminals in Philadelphia had increased from 50% literacy in 1885 to 79% in 1895. In comparison, 90% of the Seventh Ward residents were literate in 1896. Given these numbers, Du Bois dismissed the connection between intelligence and crime, writing that

This shows how little increased intelligence alone avails to stop crime in the face of other powerful forces. It would of course be illogical to connect these phenomena directly as cause and effect and make Negro crime the result of Negro education—in that case we should find it difficult to defend the public schools in most modern lands. Crime comes either in spite of intelligence or as a result of misdirected intelligence under severe economic and moral strain. (p. 254)

One final discussion in the chapter was devoted to recidivism. With little official data on the topic, Du Bois relied on the self-reports of inmates to determine that nearly 42% of the criminals had been previously convicted. This self-reported data revealed that nearly 40% of the recidivists had three to four previous convictions. Du Bois concluded the chapter reminding people that, the problem of crime in Philadelphia is largely one tied to a criminal class of Blacks, "not the great mass of Negroes" (p. 259).

Du Bois on Black Criminology

Du Bois's research provides foundational support for the creation of a Black Criminology that focuses on studying crime and its policing in the Black community. Throughout his life, he recognized the seriousness of the crime problem in the Black community and was committed to studying it as a prelude to developing practical policy solutions. With his publication of *The Philadelphia Negro*, Du Bois initiated several key ideas that point to the need for a Black Criminology.

First, he was intent on studying the problem firsthand—not through the detached lens of official statistics. He obviously grasped the importance of understanding the character of the Black population through government statistics but felt the Verstehen (inductive) approach would provide a more complete picture of crime in the Black community. Make no mistake, Du Bois embraced a holistic methodological approach that, as Russell (this volume) mentioned, is a hallmark of Black Criminology. *The Philadelphia Negro* includes a deluge of statistics and detailed maps that, based on his daily observations in the community, illuminate the character of the Seventh Ward neighborhoods (Varner, 2018). Thus, rather than rely on official statistics generated by government agencies, he produced his own quantitative and qualitative portrait of the community through the use of "on road" methods that accord with Black Criminology (Glynn, 2014; Russell-Brown, 2018).

Largely devoid of comparisons to Whites, Du Bois recognized that Whites were not former slaves and were not suffering from the pungent racism that existed in Philadelphia and throughout the United States. In short, Whites could never be in the same situation as Blacks. Thus, adhering to a core aspect of Black Criminology, he restricted most of his crime-related analyses to Black offenders. Even in the late 1800s, Du Bois clearly did not support the notion of racial invariance or the belief that "all things being equal," Black and White offending would be the same. He knew better.

Reflective of Du Bois's commitment to generating race-specific analyses, he developed a research program devoted to the study of Black Americans at the Atlanta University School of Social Scientific Research. Du Bois was committed to studying every aspect of Black life in a 10-year cycle (Du Bois, 1898, 1903a). Before he left Atlanta University in 1914, he had devoted two major studies and conferences to "Negro crime" that were widely praised in the U.S. and abroad (Du Bois, 1904; Du Bois & Dill, 1913).

Second, Du Bois was not an apologist for crime in the Black community. At times, his writings include a moralist tone toward Black criminals. Despite this moralistic tenor, in nearly every crime-related publication, he acknowledged that racial discrimination is a cause of Black offending and that it causes racial disparities in the justice system. In multiple publications following *The Philadelphia Negro* (1899a), racial discrimination is a central theme (Du Bois, 1899b, 1901, 1904). In 1913, for example, Du Bois and his colleague, Augustus Dill, identified racial discrimination as one of the key factors for the large numbers of serious offenses committed by Blacks in the South. They write:

> [the] criminologist passes no judgement on the right or wrong of this discrimination. He simply recognizes it as a fact, but he knows: (a) That many economic forces of the South depend largely on the courts for a supply of labor. (b) That public opinion in the South exaggerates the guilt of Negroes in certain crimes and enforces itself thru police, jury, magistrate and judge. (c) That Southern public opinion over-looks and unduly minimizes certain other Negro misdemeanors, which lead to immorality and crime. (Du Bois & Dill, 1913, p. 41)

Thus, nearly two decades after the publication of *The Philadelphia Negro*, Du Bois was still espousing the significant role of racial discrimination in Black offending and racial disparities in the justice system.

Black Criminology, while recognizing the key role of racial discrimination in past and present Black offending, does not explain all criminality using this lens. It fully recognizes that, as in all communities, there is a small group of criminals that commit a large share of the crime in the Black community. Even though Du Bois would have supported a Black Criminology, he would have been cautious concerning the labeling of all Blacks as criminals because he recognized, much like Wolfgang,

Figlio, and Sellin in their ground-breaking work, *Delinquency in a Birth Cohort* (1972), that a small number of offenders were responsible for a large share of the overall crime and an even larger share of the more serious crime. Wolfgang et al. (1972) referred to these individuals as habitual offenders, the same term Du Bois used to describe active offenders. In addition, Du Bois also referred to habitual offenders in the Seventh Ward as the "Negro criminal class."

Third, Du Bois would have been supportive of researchers of any race working within Black Criminology. During his life, he was influenced by and collaborated with a multitude of scholars with diverse backgrounds. Further, as he transitioned into a scholar-activist, he became a founding member of the Niagara Movement (1905–1909) and the National Association for the Advancement of Colored People (NAACP). The former organization was for most of its existence solely populated by Black activists, while the NAACP, which was largely an outgrowth of the Niagara Movement, was and remains an integrated effort devoted to racial equality.

Finally, as alluded to earlier, Du Bois's double consciousness is relevant for Black criminologists today. In 1903, Du Bois published his literary masterpiece, *The Souls of Black Folk*. In the following passage, Du Bois (1903b) discusses the concept of the double consciousness:

> It is a peculiar sensation, this double-consciousness, this sense of always looking at one's self through the eyes of others, of measuring one's soul by the tape of a world that looks on in amused contempt and pity. One ever feels his two-ness—an American, a Negro; two souls, two thoughts, two unreconciled strivings; two warring ideals in one dark body, whose dogged strength alone keeps it from being torn asunder. (p. 3)

This passage relates to the challenge Black criminologists face that Du Bois also encountered on multiple levels. Du Bois recognized that, as a Black American, one often had to reconcile the often daily racism one encountered with one's additional identity as an American citizen. Living and striving to make a mark in a racist society pushes many Blacks to the edge—even today. Often, Black criminologists go through a similar struggle. Given the nature of how the justice system has treated Blacks in the past and present, Black criminologists face intense conflicts about whether the scales of justice are, or can ever be, balanced.

In fact, this leads some to understandably question everything the system does. Thus, like Du Bois, today, many Black criminologists question the notion that being a "detached observer" is possible while racial injustices permeate the system. Du Bois faced this same question and chose to conduct rigorous social science research—but he also became a model scholar-activist. In the final section, I consider why Du Bois is neglected within modern criminology.

Du Bois's Exclusion From Criminology

Pondering why Du Bois is not considered a pioneer in the field of criminology is a bit mind-boggling. He did all the so-called right things. He attended and/or graduated from elite institutions in America and abroad. He pioneered the use of social science methods in early research studies. He established a race-centered university-based research program at Atlanta University that was unparalleled at the time. In regard to his criminological contributions, he pioneered urban ethnography, produced one of the most thorough studies on community and crime that pioneered the concept of disproportionality, habitual criminals, white-collar offenses, and social disorganization, and the list goes on. Despite these many contributions, Du Bois is simply not a standard name that resonates in the halls of criminology.

African American criminologists have long been aware of Du Bois's contributions and relied on them for insights into early analyses of crime in the Black community (Gabbidon, 2007; Greene & Gabbidon, 2000; Gabbidon, Greene, & Young, 2002). Only recently has the larger discipline even considered Du Bois's criminological scholarship (Belknap, 2015; Bursik, 2009; Hanson, 2010; Hayward, Maruna, & Mooney, 2010; Peterson, 2012, 2017; Rafter, 2010). Notably, in the early 2000s, the National Institute of Justice created the Du Bois Research Fellowship for scholars interested in studying race-related topics. This minimal incorporation of Du Bois into the pantheon of the discipline can be potentially explained by several factors. Some of these are considered in what follows.

First, Du Bois was a Black man studying Blacks in the late 19th and 20th centuries, a period of virulent racism evidenced by the segregationist polices embedded within the apartheid of Jim Crow. Thus, racist White gatekeepers who controlled the flow of information within the social sciences segregated his seminal insights. In addition, Du Bois became a socialist later in life, and more politically White conservative scientists may have neglected his sophisticated analyses because of his political ideology. He was even indicted (the charges were later dropped) by the Department of Justice in the 1950s based on his political activism. Ironically, the same Department of Justice now sponsors the Du Bois Fellowship.

Second, contemporary criminologists exclude Du Bois because they realize his inclusion would cause a revision of the history of the development of criminology. This rewrite would include the acknowledgement that Du Bois was a methodological pioneer that enabled the development of a quantitative criminology. A recent article shows that from 1895 to 1917, only 22% of the articles published in the *American Journal of Sociology* (AJS) provided information on methods. During the same period, every study published by Du Bois at the Atlanta School of Social Scientific Research included methodological details (Gabbidon, 1999a; Green & Wortham, 2018; Daniels & Wright, 2018). In actuality, this placed him at the vanguard of American social science, a full two decades before the rise of the Chicago School of Sociology.

Second, the leading figures in contemporary criminology are largely White, male sociologists (see ASC Fellows listing). They were primarily trained in programs where there was likely minimal interest in race and very little discussion of Du Bois. It is also apparent from the literature that he certainly wasn't considered a pioneering sociologist (Coser, 1977; Morris, 2015). Thus, it was natural for them to consider early White scholars such as Durkheim, Marx, Mead, Park, and Sellin and more contemporary ones such as Solomon Kobrin, Edwin Lemert, Becker, and others the pioneers of sociology and the emerging discipline of criminology (see Jacoby, Severance, & Bruce, 2011; Laub, 1984; Mutchnick, Martin, & Austin, 2008).

Nearly a decade ago, Gabbidon and Martin (2010) surveyed more than 1,000 scholars in the field on their perceptions of the classic books in the field. The results, based on open-ended responses, were separated by eras. In the pre-1900 era, the book with the most nominations was Becarria's *On Crimes and Punishment*, which received 147 nominations. Other books that received multiple nominations included ones authored by well-known European scholars Cesare Lombroso (46 nominations for *Criminal Man*) and Emile Durkheim (*Suicide*, 36 nominations; *Division of Labor in Society*, 12 nominations). Ironically, the only American publication on the list during this era was *The Philadelphia Negro*, which received only two nominations. These results were not surprising. They confirm that scholars in the discipline (the survey participants were nearly 82% White and 58% male) simply do not view *The Philadelphia Negro* as a serious contribution. Given that most of the faculty in the field are White males, there are simply not enough people in the field that have taken interest in Du Bois's work. Even with the minimal increase of minority faculty—who are often familiar with Du Bois's work—in doctorate-granting criminology/criminal justice programs (Greene, Gabbidon, & Wilson, 2018), it is likely that the results of the study would be similar today.

Finally, Jerabak (2016) argues that disciplines such as criminology anoint their pioneers based on theoretical contributions. As such, there might be a sense that Du Bois's work did not provide a longstanding theoretical contribution such as the social disorganization/ecological approach that is linked to the "Chicago school" at the University of Chicago. This suggestion is obviously not supported in the case of Du Bois because the theoretical ideas he developed during his early and later years mirrored social disorganization and conflict theory (see Gabbidon, 1998, 1999b), while his community study of Philadelphia produced extensive mapping that clearly served as a precursor to the ecological approach that flourished during the 1920s to 1940s at the University of Chicago (Rabaka, 2010; Wright, 2016).

Conclusion

I have promised myself this is the last time that I will write about Du Bois. It is unimaginable that two decades after my first article highlighting his work and publishing an entire book on the subject, he remains hardly a footnote in the discipline. In reality, I know this chapter will only be read by people who are open-minded to the question of race, so it is likely that, decades from now, Du Bois's exclusion from the criminological canon will remain. Despite this dismal forecast for the integration of Du Bois into the discipline, there remains much to be learned from a review of his work. One can only wonder how more advanced the discipline would be in its understanding of Black offending had the field taken the time to consider Du Bois's seminal contributions. In a similar vein, had the discipline adopted a race-centered approach like Du Bois, the criminalization of Black Americans based on comparisons to White offenders would have been limited or even prevented. This could have changed how the social sciences approach the question of race by focusing more on the unique historical experience of each racial/ ethnic group.

One of Du Bois's greatest contributions to the discipline is the recognition that racial oppression is an important contributor to offending among Blacks. In addition, Du Bois recognized that researchers must perform race-specific analyses because the lived experiences of Blacks are unparalleled. Truly, Du Bois was the first criminologist/sociologist to develop a theoretical and methodological foundation to generate a holistic understanding of Black offending. It is for these reasons that I argue that criminologists/sociologists must recognize Du Bois as the founder of Black Criminology, a Black Criminology that embraces Du Bois's theoretical and methodological contributions in order to generate race-specific holistic understandings of how racial oppression in all of its variegated forms produces Black offending.

In closing, I can only hope that the next wave of Du Bois "discoverers" will penetrate the doctoral programs in the discipline so future criminologists will be introduced to W.E.B. Du Bois: the first American sociological criminologist, director of the Atlanta School of Social Scientific Research, and the founder of Black Criminology.

References

Belknap, J. (2015). Activist criminology: Criminologists' responsibility to advocate for social and legal justice. *Criminology*, *53*, 1–22.

Boston, T. D. (1991, May). W.E.B. Du Bois and the historical school of economics. *American Economics Association Papers and Proceedings*, 303–307.

Bursik, R. (2009). The Dead Sea Scrolls and criminological knowledge: 2008 Presidential address to the American Society of Criminology. *Criminology*, *47*, 5–16.

Coser, L. A. (1977). *Masters of sociological thought: Ideas in historical and social context* (2nd ed.). New York, NY: Harcourt Brace Jovanovich.

Daniels, K. S., & Wright, E. (2018). "An earnest desire for the truth despite its possible unpleasantness": A comparative analysis of the Atlanta University publications and *American Journal of Sociology*, 1895 to 1917. *Sociology of Race and Ethnicity*, *4*, 35–48.

Du Bois, W. E. B. (1891). The enforcement of the slave trade laws. *American Historical Association, annual report, 1891*.

Du Bois, W. E. B. (1896). *The suppression of the African slave-trade to the United States of America, 1638–1870*. Cambridge, MA: Harvard University Press.

Du Bois, W. E. B. (1898). The study of the Negro problems. *Annals of the American Academy of Political and Social Science*, *11*, 1–23.

Du Bois, W. E. B. (1899a/1996). *The Philadelphia Negro: A social study*. Philadelphia, PA: University of Pennsylvania Press.

Du Bois, W. E. B. (1899b). The Negro and crime. *The Independent*, *51*, 1355–1357.

Du Bois, W. E. B. (1901). The spawn of slavery: The convict-lease system in the South. *The Missionary Review of the World*, *14*, 737–745.

Du Bois, W. E. B. (1903a). The laboratory in sociology at Atlanta University. *Annals of the American Academy of Political and Social Sciences*, *21*, 160–163.

Du Bois, W. E. B. (1903b/1969). *The souls of Black Folk*. New York, NY: Signet Books.

Du Bois, W. E. B. (Ed.). (1904). *Some notes on Negro crime, particularly in Georgia*. Atlanta: Atlanta University Press.

Du Bois, W. E. B., & Dill, A. G. (1913). *Morals and manners among Negro Americans: Report of a social study made by Atlanta University under the Patronage of the trustees of the John F. Slater Fund; with the proceedings of the 18th annual conference for the study of the Negro problems*. Atlanta: Atlanta University Press.

Gabbidon, S. L. (1996). An argument for the inclusion of W.E.B. Du Bois in the criminology and criminal Justice literature. *Journal of Criminal Justice Education, 7*, 99–111.

Gabbidon, S. L. (1998, November/December). W. E. B. Du Bois on crime: Rethinking the beginnings of American criminology. *The Criminologist, 23*(6), 1, 3, 21.

Gabbidon, S. L. (1999a). W. E. B. Du Bois and the "Atlanta school" of social scientific research: 1897–1913. *Journal of Criminal Justice Education, 10*, 21–38.

Gabbidon, S. L. (1999b, January/February). W. E. B. Du Bois on crime: American conflict theorist. *The Criminologist, 24*(1), 1, 3, 20.

Gabbidon, S. L. (2001). W. E. B. Du Bois: Pioneering American criminologist. *Journal of Black Studies, 31*, 581–599.

Gabbidon, S. L. (2007). *W. E. B. Du Bois on crime and justice. Laying the foundations of sociological criminology*. New York, NY: Routledge.

Gabbidon, S. L., Greene Taylor, H., & Young, V. D. (Eds.). (2002). *African American classics in criminology and criminal justice*. Thousand Oaks, CA: Sage.

Gabbidon, S. L., & Martin, F. (2010). An era-based exploration of the most significant books in criminology/criminal justice: A research note. *Journal of Criminal Justice Education, 21*, 348–369.

Glynn, M. (2014). *Black men, invisibility and crime*. London, UK: Routledge.

Green, D. S., & Wortham, R. A. (2018). The sociological insight of W.E.B. Du Bois. *Sociological Inquiry, 88*, 56–78.

Greene, H. T., Gabbidon, S. L., & Wilson, S. (2018). Included? The status of African American Scholars in the discipline of criminology and criminal justice since 2004. *Journal of Criminal Justice Education, 29*, 96–115.

Greene, H. T., & Gabbidon, S. L. (2000). *African American criminological thought*. Albany, NY: State University of New York Press.

Hanson, L. J. (2010). W.E.B. Du Bois. In K. Hayward, S. Maruna, & J. Mooney (Eds.), *Fifty key thinkers in criminology* (pp. 53–57). London, UK: Routledge.

Hayward, K., Maruna, S., & Mooney, J. (Eds.). (2010). *Fifty key thinkers in criminology*. London, UK: Routledge.

Henderson, H. (2013). Historical book review: W.E.B. Du Bois, *The Philadelphia Negro: A social study*. *Journal of Qualitative Criminal Justice and Criminology, 1*, 194–196.

Jacoby, J. E., Severance, T. A., & Bruce, A. S. (Eds.). (2011). *Classics of criminology* (4th ed.). Prospect Heights, IL: Waveland Press.

Jerabek, H. (2016). W.E.B. Du Bois on the history of empirical social research. *Ethnic and Racial Studies, 39*, 1391–1397.

Laub, J. L. (1984). *Criminology in the making: An oral history*. Boston, MA: Northeastern University Press.

Lewis, D. L. (1993). *W.E.B. Du Bois: Biography of a race*. New York, NY: Henry, Holt, and Company, Inc.

Morris, A. D. (2015). *The scholar denied: W.E.B. Du Bois and the birth of modern sociology*. Oakland, CA: University of California Press.

Mutchnick, R., Martin, R., & Austin, W. T. (2008). *Criminological thought: Pioneers past and present*. New York, NY: Pearson.

Peterson, R. D. (2012). The central place of race in crime and justice—The American Society of criminology's 2011 Sutherland address. *Criminology, 50*, 303–328.

Peterson, R. D. (2017). Interrogating race, crime, and justice in a time of unease and racial tension. *Criminology, 55*, 245–272.

Rabaka, R. (2010). *Against epistemic apartheid: W.E.B. Du Bois and the decadence of sociology*. Lanham, MD: Lexington Books.

Rafter, N. (2010). Silence and memory in criminology—The American Society of Criminology 2009 Sutherland address. *Criminology, 48*, 339–355.

Russell, K.K. (1992). Development of a Black Criminology and the role of the Black criminologist. *Justice Quarterly, 9*, 667–683.

Russell-Brown, K. K. (2018). Black criminology in the 21st century. In J. D. Unnever, S. L. Gabbidon, & C. Chouhy (Eds.), *Building a Black criminology: Race, theory, and crime*. New York, NY: Routledge.

Varner, D. (2018). Nineteenth century criminal geography: W.E.B. Du Bois and the Pennsylvania Prison Society. *Journal of Historical Geography, 59*, 15–26.

Wolfgang, M. E., Figlio, R. M., & Sellin, T. (1972). *Delinquency in a birth cohort*. Chicago, IL: University of Chicago Press.

Wright, E. (2002a). Using the master's tools: The Atlanta sociological laboratory and American sociology, 1896–1924. *Sociological Spectrum, 22*, 15–39.

Wright, E. (2002b). Why black people tend to shout! An earnest attempt to explain the sociological negation of the Atlanta sociological laboratory despite its possible unpleasantness. *Sociological Spectrum, 22*, 335–361.

Wright, E. (2002c). The Atlanta sociological laboratory 1896–1924: A historical account of the first American school of sociology. *The Western Journal of Black Studies, 26*, 165–174.

Wright, E. (2016). *The first American school of sociology: W.E.B. Du Bois and the Atlanta sociological laboratory*. London, UK: Routledge.

3

Beyond White Criminology

Francis T. Cullen, Cecilia Chouhy,
Leah Butler, and Heejin Lee

Our central thesis is that the founding theories of American criminology either completely ignored or downplayed the unique significance of race. This conclusion aligns with Unnever and Owusu-Bempah's (this volume) call for a "Black Criminology" in which the experiences of African Americans become the starting point for the study of Black criminal involvement. This perspective is identical to the stance taken by feminist criminologists who persuasively argued that omitting gender from criminological analysis impoverished our understanding of female and male criminology (see Messerschmidt, 1993; Miller & Mullins, 2006). None of this is to suggest that traditional criminological analysis and research are wrong or that Blacks, or women, are separate species who are immune to the criminogenic risks that affect Whites, or men. Rather, it is to assert that the failure to take race (or gender) seriously—to place it at the center of the criminological enterprise—inevitably results in an incomplete understanding of African Americans' criminality.

Criminology thus needs to move beyond White Criminology (Gabbidon, 2010). This assertion is not based on the simplistic view that criminology is a field of Whites studying Whites—that is, a field blinded by racism. If anything, criminology is a progressive or liberal academic field sympathetic to the plight of minorities. In fact, scholars have devoted an enormous amount of their research to documenting racial disparities in policing, sentencing, juvenile justice administration, and imprisonment (see, e.g., Clear, 2007; Feld, 2017; Tonry, 2011).

Why, then, the relative blindness to race in the theoretical domain? In large part, this neglect is a reflection of who most criminals were when the dominant theoretical models of American criminology were first invented. The starting point for theorists thus was not the concentration of crime in Black neighborhoods but in White, mostly immigrant or working-class neighborhoods. This starting point is understandable given the historical context in which these theories arose—though having more Black scholars might have balanced the inquiry even then (see Greene & Gabbidon, 2000).

The difficulty is the enduring legacy of these powerful theoretical traditions. These perspectives are reified and then become what are tested empirically and elaborated theoretically. Once race is omitted, it tends to be forgotten, squeezed into an analytical framework as an afterthought, or relegated to the bottom of a regression table as a control variable. The result is a White Criminology in which race endures benign neglect. The value of a Black Criminology is that it unmasks this inadvertent neglect and makes its continuation a more purposeful academic sin.

Such a broad indictment of criminology risks glossing over exceptions in which race is central to the analysis (e.g., Anderson, 1999; Miller, 2008). But exceptions are just that—exceptions—and they prove the rule. It is fair to say that the first comprehensive theory in the tradition was Unnever and Gabbidon's (2011) *A Theory of African American Offending* (see also Gabbidon, 2010). The starting point for their model is racial oppression, and it includes core factors unique to Blacks (e.g., racial socialization, racial discrimination). To use Laub's (2004) term, this book represents a turning point in American criminology in which a systematic Black Criminology has become possible.

In this context, this chapter illustrates the hegemony of White Criminology within criminological theory by examining five foundational schools of thought that give short shrift to the unique experiences of African Americans. Two of these traditions whose roots extend to the 1920s and 1930s—the Chicago school and strain theory—focused on ethnicity and social class at the expense of race. Two other perspectives—Sykes and Matza's neutralization/drift theory and Hirschi's control theory—sought to normalize delinquency and divorce it from inner-city neighborhoods and, to use Kozol's (1991) term, society's "savage inequalities." We argue as well that more contemporary perspectives have not escaped the hegemony of White Criminology (see also Gabbidon, 2010). As an illustration, we show that the most influential life-course theories have largely ignored race due to theoretical loyalties and the data used in the analyses.[1]

The Chicago School

The origins of American criminology can be traced most fully to the Chicago school and, in particular, to the social disorganization theory of Clifford Shaw and Henry McKay (1942). Their work eventually yielded cultural (or learning) theories and control theories on the micro and macro levels. Their work was subsequently formalized by Ruth Kornhauser (1978) in her spectacular analytical treatise, *Social Sources of Delinquency*. In these works, race was a negligible concern, with the racial oppression Blacks experienced during the invention of the perspective ignored. Although race has infiltrated later works in this tradition (see, e.g., Sampson & Wilson, 1995), the uniqueness of the African American experience in the United States has been pushed to the periphery of this tradition. The Chicago school thus is our first illustration of White Criminology.

Shaw and McKay's Social Disorganization Theory

In his classic life history, *The Jack-Roller: A Delinquent Boy's Own Story*, Clifford Shaw (1930) interviews Stanley, the son of Polish immigrants. White ethnic youngsters were the subjects in other life histories. Sidney Blotzman was the case study for *The Natural History of a Delinquent Career*. His "parents were of Jewish descent, and emigrated to America at the time of their marriage" (Shaw with Moore, 1931, p. 42). The parents of the subjects of *Brothers in Crime*, the five Martin brothers, were also from a "rural community in Europe" (Shaw with McKay & McDonald, 1938, p. 127). Today, of course, the likely focus of such a study would be a Black juvenile—perhaps named Jamal but certainly not Stanley or Sidney. Thus, in Alex Kotlowitz's (1991) moving account of two African American brothers growing up in Chicago's Henry Horner Homes, the youths were named Lafayette and Pharoah Rivers.

Shaw and McKay, however, were living in a different social reality. When they departed their childhood homes in rural Indiana (Shaw) and South Dakota (McKay) to attend the University of Chicago, the city was in the midst of rapid expansion, fueled mainly by the arrival of European immigrants (Snodgrass, 1976). It is not surprising that the classic account of this influx of population was W. I. Thomas and Florian Znaniecki's (1984) *The Polish Peasant in Europe and America*, a five-volume account published between 1918 and 1920. Indeed, by 1907, 360,000 Poles lived in Chicago, making it the third-largest Polish city in the world after Warsaw and Lódz (Bulmer, 1984, p. 50). At the turn of the century, half of the city's population was not native-born Americans (Wilcox, Cullen, & Feldmeyer, 2018, p. 13). As Bulmer (1984, p. 13) notes, Chicago became "an ethnic melting pot of Germans, Scandinavians, Irish, Italians, Poles, Jews, Czechs, Lithuanians, and Croats." By contrast, Blacks made up only 2% of the city's residents in 1910 and 6.9% in 1930 (Gibson & Jung, 2005). In the first part of the 1900s, African Americans were just another migrant group leaving a rural area—the American South—and newly arriving to the city.

This would change. As with other groups, Blacks were pulled to Chicago by opportunities for factory employment. But two important push factors in the South also motivated the trek northward. First, by 1890, states in the post-Reconstruction South had passed oppressive Jim Crow laws, legalizing segregation and institutionalizing discrimination. The extra-legal, terrorizing practice of lynching also was condoned. Second, by the 1940s, the mechanization of cotton picking caused the share-cropper system to collapse as the need for manual labor diminished (Lemann, 1991). In all, between 1910 and 1970 when the Great Migration slowed, six and one-half million Blacks would leave the South for the North. Notably, five million would migrate northward after 1940. In that year, 77% of African Americans still lived in the South (Lemann, 1991). By the 1970s, however, nearly half (47%) of Blacks resided outside the South (Wilkerson, 2010). By the end of the century, as Wilkerson (2010, p. 11) notes, the Black population in Chicago had "rocketed" to "more than one million." African Americans "made up a third of the city's residents, with more Blacks living in Chicago than in the entire state of Mississippi" (Wilkerson, 2010, p. 11).

Today, in Chicago and elsewhere, African Americans are not just another group moving in and out of the zone in transition. White flight and policies enforcing housing segregation have concentrated Blacks into hyper-ghettos. As members of the "truly disadvantaged," they often live in disadvantaged neighborhoods across generations (Wilson, 1987; see also Sampson, 2012). Race and crime are now inextricably mixed in reality and in stereotypes that infuse the academic and public consciousness—an identity captured by Russell-Brown's (2009) term of the "criminalblackman" (see also Wacquant, 2001). If Shaw and McKay were to invent social disorganization theory in today's Chicago, race would be central to that enterprise.

Again, the social reality of Shaw and McKay and their Chicago compatriots was different. Take the work of Harvey Zorbaugh (1929) in his classic study, *The Gold Coast and the Slum*. African Americans were portrayed as just another group who lived in a "natural area" in a human ecology produced by the ongoing process of invasion and succession. As described by Zorbaugh (1929, p. 4, emphasis added), the "slum has offered these alien people a place to live cheaply and to themselves; and wave upon wave of immigrants has swept over the area—Irish, Swedish, German, Italian, Persian, Greek, and *Negro*—forming colonies, *staying for a while*, then giving way to others." Indeed, according to Zorbaugh (1929, p. 147), the "story of this Negro invasion is an old story." To be sure, the "Sicilian has not retired before the Negro without a show of resistance," with "landowners" banding "together to keep the Negro from acquiring property" (p. 147). At school and on the playgrounds, Negro children were "mistreated and ostracized," and gang fights ensued (p. 148). But this experience is portrayed as *normal* and not attributed to a system of racial oppression. As Zorbaugh observes, these incidents merely "re-enacted the scenes of a generation ago when the Sicilian was forcing out the Swede" (p. 148).

Thus, for members of the Chicago school such as Shaw and McKay, the key issue was not *racial inequality* but *racial/ethnic heterogeneity*. Although exceptions exist in their writings, the orientation was not to single out African Americans as a uniquely oppressed people but rather to normalize their migration into Chicago's slum areas. This normalization of the Black experience constituted a rejection of racist racial theorizing attributing African American criminality to group inferiority (see, e.g., Hooton, 1939). Still, it was done at the cost of purging race as a central variable within the social disorganization model.

Admittedly, as Unnever (this volume) alerted us, Shaw and McKay had to grapple with the fact that the delinquency of African Americans— "Negroes" in their historically specific language—departed in some ways from that of Whites. In a 1949 rejoinder to a critique of their work (Jonassen, 1949), they noted that the "institutions of migrating Negroes have been singularly unsuited to the problems of urban life" (Shaw & McKay, 1949, p. 617). They also admitted that comparing White and Black delinquency is impossible because Whites do not experience the same kind of "segregation and the barriers to upward social mobility," which "combine to create for the Negro child a type of social world in which the higher rates of delinquents are not unintelligible" (1949, p. 617). But these insights failed to penetrate the core of their model. In the revised edition of *Juvenile Delinquency and Urban Areas*, they argued that "reorganization" and lower crime rates occurred in "old Negro areas" even when they were "not able to move out to other areas" (1972, p. 382; cf. Bursik & Webb, 1982). Indeed, rather than anticipate Black Criminology, they voiced an early version of the so-called racial invariance thesis that the sources of crime are the same across racial and ethnic groups (Wilcox et al., 2018):

> High or low rates of delinquents are not permanent characteristics of any ethnic or racial group. Each population group experienced high rates of delinquents when it occupied the areas of first settlement, and these rates went down as the groups either moved out to better areas *or moved toward stability in the same area.* (Shaw & McKay, 1972, p. 385, emphasis added)

The constraining influence of the Chicago school paradigm is even seen in the early writings of E. Franklin Frazier, who, according to Greene and Gabbidon (2000, p. 59), was not only a "pioneer in African American studies and sociology" but also "an outspoken militant and race man and was viewed as an 'improper Negro' for his time." Frazier received his doctorate from the University of Chicago in 1931, and his dissertation was published a year later under the title of *The Negro Family in Chicago*. In the book's chapter on delinquency, Frazier (1932, pp. 207–208) first mapped the "Distribution of Negro boys arrested" on the "South Side Negro Community." As Block (2017, p. 44) notes, "Frazier divided the Black Belt into [seven] concentric zones based on census tracts and then calculated rates of delinquency for each zone." He also replicated this analysis for adult males in county jails (Frazier, 1932, p. 210). As was true of other ethnic groups, the rates of Black crime and delinquency declined from Zone I near the Loop at Chicago's center to the more distant Zone VII. Importantly, the variation in waywardness was not attributed to racial factors, except that those migrating from the South were said to be ill prepared by their rural plantation pasts to adjust to city life. Instead, in language that could have been voiced by Shaw and McKay, Frazier (1932, p. 211) concluded that high rates of delinquency were in "those areas of the Negro community . . . characterized . . . by deterioration and social disorganization."

Equally instructive is the "Editor's Preface" to *The Negro Family in Chicago* authored by Ernest Burgess (1932). Having invented concentric zone theory (Burgess, 1925/1967), he approvingly notes the importance of "Mr. Frazier's differentiation of the different Negro zones of settlement in Chicago" (1932, p. xi). According to Burgess, this conceptual framework allows Frazier to show "quite conclusively that certain behavior popularly attributed to the Negro varies almost, if not quite, as widely within the Negro group as within the white group" (p. xi). Armed with data supportive of the invariance thesis, Burgess argues that "crime, delinquency, illegitimacy, poverty, and vice" are "not a matter so much of race as of geography" (p. xi). Indeed, the "incidence" of these "social problems . . . is not a matter of the innate traits of the Negro, but are the direct results of a community situation" (p. xi). Despite these progressive ideas, Burgess never confronts the reality of racism. What is it about their "community situation" that places African Americans at risk for crime and other challenges? Here, he gives a standard Chicago school answer that remains within the tradition of White Criminology. "The chief handicap from which the Negro suffers," observes Burgess, "is perhaps not poverty, not overcrowding . . . but the persistence of an unorganized and disorganized family life" (p. xii).

It is perhaps unfair to say that scholars of a different generation should have been more attentive to an issue—in this case racial oppression. Still, those in the Chicago school had an opportunity to grasp that newly arriving African Americans faced unique barriers. As Rothstein (2017) shows, racial segregation at that time and thereafter was produced by a range of real-estate practices (e.g., red-lining) and government policies (e.g., disparate lending, zoning). State-sanctioned violence, including in Chicago, was another tactic used to enforce segregation. Take the period of 1917 to 1921, "when the Chicago ghetto was first being rigidly defined" (2017, p. 144). According to Rothstein (2017, p. 144), "there were fifty-eight firebombings of homes in white border areas to which African Americans had moved, with no arrests or prosecutions—despite deaths of two African American residents." As Block (2017, p. 37) reports, this fact was demonstrated by a spot map created at this time showing that the "Homes Bombed in the Race Conflicts Over Housing" were largely "on the periphery of the Black Belt."

In July of 1919, a race riot occurred taking 38 lives, 23 of whom were African American (Rothstein, 2017, p. 144). As chronicled by Carl Sandburg (1919, p. 1), later to become famous as a Lincoln biographer, "a colored boy swam across an imaginary segregation line. White

boys threw rocks at him and knocked him off a raft. He was drowned."
The riot was precipitated when the police refused to make any arrests.
"Fighting," observed Sandburg (1919, p. 1), quickly "spread to all borders of the Black Belt." A commission was established to assess race
relations. As Block (2017, p. 37, fn. 3) notes, "In this period, racial
segregation was so extreme that the commission had difficulty renting
office space because its investigators included both blacks and whites."
For many years to come, observes Block, violence "remained a problem for African Americans attempting to move into still white neighborhoods" (p. 37).

The point, of course, is that the experience of African Americans was
not, as suggested by Zorbaugh (1929) and others, a mere re-enactment
of a previous ethnic invasion and succession. Race was qualitatively
different from ethnicity, a fact that the Chicago school downplayed, if
not ignored.

Kornhauser's Formalization of Social Disorganization Theory

A racially antiseptic social disorganization model was reified by
Kornhauser (1978) in *Social Sources of Delinquency*, where she formalized the components of Shaw and McKay's implicit theory. She
extracted from their writings the main sources of social disorganization:
"economic level, mobility, and heterogeneity" (1978, p. 77). For Kornhauser, heterogeneity was an analytical category that could be measured
in two ways. One approach was to create an index that "includes all
minority groups" (p. 113). In this case, "the greater the number of different groups and the higher their combined proportion in a neighborhood, the greater the heterogeneity" (p. 113). A second measure was
"the proportion of a single ethnic or racial group" (p. 113). In this case,
"heterogeneity is greatest when the group is 50% of the total" (p. 113).

This language reveals Kornhauser's quality of mind but also her
disinterest in linking social disorganization theory to the social tur-
moil gripping American society. Remember, Shaw and McKay wanted
to explain delinquency in Chicago during an era of mass immigration,
undertook life histories of youths to capture the harsh realities they
faced, and embarked on a social reform effort with the Chicago Area
Project to save wayward youths. By contrast, despite spending time at
the University of California, Berkeley in the 1960s and completing her
doctorate at the University of Chicago in the 1970s (Cullen, Wilcox,
Sampson, & Dooley, 2015), Kornhauser had no interest in using her

criminology to address the events of the day—events that included the Civil Rights Movement and urban crime and insurgency. Thus, she did not single out racial inequality as a salient condition meriting special investigation in a divided America, deciding instead to deposit it into the broader category of heterogeneity. Indeed, race does not appear in the index of *Social Sources of Delinquency.*

Kornhauser's treatment of race proved consequential for criminology. Her work formed the basis for the systemic model of crime that has had a major, enduring influence on macro-level theory and research (Wilcox et al., 2018). Most notably, her framework informed the classic diagram and test of the systemic model by Sampson and Groves (1989, p. 783). Sampson and Groves identified five exogenous sources of disorganization. These included family disruption, which Sampson (1987) had previously studied, and community variation in urbanism. The other three factors were drawn directly from Kornhauser's interpretation of Shaw and McKay's work (see Sampson & Groves, 1989, p. 780): low economic status, residential mobility, and "ethnic heterogeneity" (Sampson & Groves, 1989, p. 783). Once again, race was not seen as worthy of separate analysis. Rather, using British Crime Survey data, this classic study employed a heterogeneity index in which the sample "is distributed across five categories: white, West Indian or African black, Pakistani or Bangladeshi Indian, other non-white, and mixed" (1989, p. 784). Let us hasten to say that this methodological decision is defensible. But when writ large across the discipline, it is also why a Black Criminology is needed.[2]

Classic Strain Theory

Merton's SS&A Paradigm

Born in 1910 to Eastern European Jewish immigrant parents, Robert K. Merton was raised in the slums of south Philadelphia before eventually living the American Dream—making his way to Harvard University for his doctorate and then spending his career at Columbia University. His given name was Meyer R. Schkolnick. He took the Americanized name of "Robert King Merton" when, as a teenager, he performed an act of magic tricks at local events such as birthday parties and Sunday schools. He liked the sound of, and was known to his friends as, "Bob Merton." Not uncommon at the time, he retained the Merton name— making it legally permanent—as he pursued an undergraduate degree on scholarship at Temple University and an academic career at Harvard (Cullen & Messner, 2007). In 1938, he would publish his famous 10-page "Social Structure and Anomie." Classic strain theory refers to Merton's writings in the "SS&A paradigm"—an acronym he commonly used to refer to his model (see, e.g., Merton, 1995)—and to the classic contributions on gang subcultures of Albert Cohen (1955) and of Richard Cloward and Lloyd Ohlin (1960; see also Cloward, 1959).

Recall that Shaw and McKay, the products of the rural Midwest, viewed the city as socially disorganized. By contrast, Merton, who grew up in such a disadvantaged neighborhood, referred to it as a "benign slum" (Cullen & Messner, 2007, p. 15). There was poverty, gang rivalries, and some crime, but Merton also observed that his neighborhood had a local Carnegie Library only three blocks away from his home and did not strike him as that dangerous (2007, p. 15). In an interview with Cullen and Messner (2007, p. 16), Merton noted that "if we sociologists did more probing and were looking for that, we would get away from the generic notion that a slum environment is wholly and solely conducive to delinquency in life."

As is well known, Merton did not link crime and deviance to the daily effects of residing in the so-called zone in transition. Rather, slum life mattered to the extent that it provided differential opportunity to gain the universal goal of upward mobility—that is, the American Dream. Although not citing Marx, Merton was unmasking a central contradiction of American capitalism, which held out the false ideology of success for all but perpetuated a class structure that provided access to this goal only for some (see also Gouldner, 1973). In an important way, Merton thus brought class barriers and inequality into the criminological enterprise. As Coser (1975, p. 94) notes:

> Merton retained Durkheim's emphasis while he recast the conceptualization so as to spell out the effects of the class structure on persons variously placed within it. Through Durkheim's theory of anomie as a point of departure, and with a powerful assist from Marxian class theory, Merton arrived at a theory of differential opportunity structures leading to systematic departures from normative expectations by persons variously placed in specific class situations.

What Merton omitted in his SS&A writings, however, was a systematic analysis of race. In his original essay, Merton consigns race to a footnote. He suggests that Blacks might be partially insulated from pressures because the reality of their position in society might depress success aspirations:

> Certain elements of the Negro population have assimilated the dominant caste's values of pecuniary success and social advancement, but they also recognize that social ascent is at present restricted to their own caste almost exclusively. The pressures upon the Negro which would otherwise derive from the structural inconsistencies we have noticed are hence not identical with those upon lower class whites. (1938, p. 680, fn. 17)

His later works also do not bring race into the heart of the SS&A paradigm. Most notably, in his two essays on the theory in *Social Theory and Social Structure*, which extended 63 pages (1968, pp. 185–248), race is virtually ignored. The same is true in Merton's (1995) otherwise brilliant 75-page essay on the "sociological concept" of "opportunity structure," his last major commentary on his SS&A paradigm prior to his death in 2003 (but see Merton, 1997).

Cohen's Subcultural Theory

Albert Cohen was raised in Roxbury, then a working-class Jewish neighborhood in Boston (Laub, 1983; Young, 2010). Commuting to Harvard University each day by train, Cohen encountered in the "ancient days of 1937–38," according to Merton's (1995, p. 43) recollection of their meeting, "a young instructor" who "hesitantly delivered himself of the conceptual scheme of 'social structure and anomie' before a class of undergraduates that included Albert K. Cohen." Due to anti-Semitism, Cohen's only acceptance to graduate school came in a belated telegram from Edwin Sutherland offering him an assistantship at Indiana University, which had the serendipitous effect of leading him into criminology. After a stint in the military, he returned to Harvard for his doctorate, where he studied with Talcott Parsons. Then it was off to Indiana University for a faculty appointment (Laub, 1983; Young, 2010). His dissertation formed the basis for his classic analysis of youth subcultures, *Delinquent Boys: The Culture of the Gang* (1955).

In essence, Cohen used Merton's SS&A paradigm to explain the origin of delinquent subcultures. The Chicago school had focused on the causal importance of the transmission of cultural values but had not accounted for their creation, especially in collectives. Two insights were at the core of his explanation. First, Cohen (1955, p. 37) observed that delinquent subcultures—represented in gangs—were not spread evenly across society but were "concentrated in the male, working-class sector of the juvenile population." Second, Cohen rejected the idea that working-class neighborhoods were criminogenic because they were disorganized. Building on the work of William Foote Whyte (1943, 1955) and likely on his own experience of growing up in a working-class, urban neighborhood, Cohen argued instead that these slums were often highly organized, just in ways that differed from more affluent areas. While studying at Indiana University, he persuaded Sutherland to change the concept of social disorganization to "differential group organization," which Sutherland (1942/1956, p. 21) defined as involving "organization for criminal activities on one side and organization against criminal activities on the other side." For Cohen (1955, p. 109), the difficulty faced by many working-class youths was their location at "the bottom of the heap," which created cultural and structural barriers to achieving middle-class status. Delinquency was a solution to this status frustration.

In *Delinquent Boys*, Cohen takes us inside working-class adolescent life. Working-class youths live in a world in which they are evaluated by middle-class cultural standards and risk being frozen out of vertical mobility. He recognizes that some kids are, to use Whyte's (1955, p. 104) term, "college boys," who have "assumed middle-class behavior" and are prepared to pursue upward social mobility. But most youths are "corner boys," who will spend the rest of their lives in their slum community. Cohen perceptively notes that social class is both a "cultural setting" and a "training ground." Middle-class youths are socialized into a set of middle-class cultural values (e.g., ambition, rationality, good manners, control of physical aggression, respect for property). Whereas "working-class socialization . . . tends to be relatively easy-going," middle-class parents are anxious about their kids' achievement, leave little to chance, and socialize in a "rational, deliberate, and demanding" way (1955, pp. 98–99). A telling reality is that corner boys are ill prepared to succeed at the core institution of the school, which is an institution designed to impart "middle-class aspirations, character, skills and manners" (p. 114). They are also likely to be excluded from activities that require the "material apparatus" that they "cannot afford" (p. 109).

For Cohen (1955, p. 128), the status frustration—really, degradation— that working-class youths experience presents them with a major "problem of adjustment." Extending back to Merton's (1938) typology of individual adaptations, classic strain theorists have understood that strain can be responded to with a diversity of responses (Cullen, 1984,

1988). The essential precondition for a collective as opposed to an individual response is that a sufficient concentration of corner boys allows them to interact with one another where they can share their common grievance. In essence, the solution is to create a status universe with new criteria for assigning worth. Anticipating the work of Messerschmidt (1993), Cohen (1955, pp. 168–169) asserted that delinquency becomes a way of demonstrating masculinity for youths who "have few other avenues of distinctly masculine achievement open" to them. Most important, the content of this invented subculture constitutes a repudiation and inversion of middle-class culture—acts that are negativistic, aggressive, malicious, or wantonly destructive. The emergent subculture thus becomes a solution to a collective problem, serving two functions:

> first, of establishing a set of status criteria in terms of which the boy can more easily succeed; and second, of enabling him to retaliate against the norms at whose impact his ego has suffered, by defining merit in terms of the opposite of those norms and by sanctioning aggression against them and those who exemplify and apply them. (Cohen, 1955, p. 168)

Despite his perceptive analysis of class-based status frustration, Cohen was silent on the issue of race; the words "race" and "Negro" are not in the index of *Delinquent Boys*. Again, White ethnic neighborhoods were his social reality. Roxbury, his childhood community in Boston, would only later become predominantly African American. In 1940 and 1950, the percentage of Blacks in the city was, respectively, 3.1% and 5.0% (Gibson & Jung, 2005). Whyte's *Street Corner Society*, which had a demonstrable impact on Cohen's theorizing, was an ethnographic study of an Italian slum in the North End of Boston. And Sutherland and Merton, his intellectual mentors, would do little to emphasize the salience of race within their respective perspectives. Not surprisingly, Cohen would remain within the tradition of White Criminology.

Cloward and Ohlin's Opportunity Theory

Our discussion of Richard Cloward and Lloyd Ohlin's (1960) *Delinquency and Opportunity: A Theory of Delinquent Gangs*, in fundamental ways, differs little from the story just told about Cohen's *Delinquent Boys*. Ohlin earned his master's degree at Indiana in 1942 and, after military service, his doctorate at Chicago (Laub, 1983). Ohlin and Merton served on Cloward's dissertation committee at Columbia University.

During the Korean War, Cloward gained access to a military prison in Pennsylvania, where he served as the director of social work. Using the SS&A paradigm, he conducted a study of the impact of social control on inmate adaptations within the prison (see Cloward, 1968). Cloward's (1959) classic statement on "illegitimate means," published in the *American Sociological Review*, was a chapter in the dissertation. Cloward and Ohlin would become colleagues at Columbia's School of Social Work and coauthor *Delinquency and Opportunity*, published (as was Cohen's book) by The Free Press in 1960 (Brotherton, 2010; Merton, 1995, 1997).

Similar to Cohen, *Delinquency and Opportunity* is really two theories that are integrated into a general explanation of the location of delinquent subcultures. First, a perspective has to explain "the origin of the pressure toward deviance"—that is, why people are motivated to break norms (1960, p. 35). Although the analysis is complex, Cloward and Ohlin provide an answer that draws less from Cohen (status frustration) and more from Merton: Youths lack the opportunity to reach the culturally prescribed success goal, whether at school or beyond. Second, a perspective has to explain why a person faced with a problem of adjustment selects one solution rather than another (see also Cullen, 1984). Just as someone who wants pecuniary success cannot simply become a physician or professional athlete, a person cannot simply become a jackroller or professional thief (Shaw, 1930; Sutherland, 1937). As Cohen also understood, creating or joining a gang is differentially available across the social structure. In most contemporary middle-class neighborhoods, the parents would have to organize a "gang day" to bring their kids together and schedule in delinquent activities—Monday for tennis, Tuesday for gymnastics, Wednesday for gang day, Thursday for math tutoring! Otherwise, joining a gang is virtually impossible.

In his classic 1959 article, "Illegitimate Means, Anomie, and Deviant Behavior," Cloward merged Merton's concept of differential access to opportunity or "legitimate means" with the Chicago school's insights on how social context shapes access to criminal roles, which he called "illegitimate means" (Cullen, 1988; Merton, 1995, 1997). For Cloward, illegitimate means included what is now called "opportunity" by environmental criminologists—that is, the sheer ability to "discharge" a role (1959, p. 168). But an opportunity could not be capitalized upon unless a person also had access to a "learning structure" that provided "for the acquisition of the values and skills associated with the performance of a particular role" (p. 168). Whether legitimate or illegitimate, the "term 'means'. . . subsumes, therefore, both *learning structures* and *opportunity structures*" (1959, p. 168, emphasis in the original).

When faced with the strain of blocked success goals, why does not a juvenile become suicidal, take drugs, or perhaps secretly shoplift? Why make a collective response? One key ingredient is that a process of alienation must ensue in which allegiance to the legitimacy of conventional norms is withdrawn because failure is attributed "to the social order rather than to oneself" (Cloward & Ohlin, 1960, p. 111). The other key ingredient, which Cohen also recognized, is that any single alienated youngster must be in a location—a slum neighborhood—where he or she interacts with many similarly alienated adolescents. Unlike Cohen, however, Cloward and Ohlin (1960, p. 139) asserted that not all delinquent subcultures were the same. There was "subcultural differentiation." As such, the type of gang that arose depended on the degree of organization in the slum.

Cloward and Ohlin distinguished three subcultural forms: criminal, conflict, and retreatist (with the last populated by "double failures" who turn to drug use because they cannot reach goals through legitimate or illegitimate means, p. 181). The organized, working-class slum of Whyte (1943, 1955) and Cohen (1955) provides for an "age-graded criminal structure" in which juveniles learn criminal values and skills and that controls any violent proclivities (Cloward & Ohlin, 1960, p. 170). Thus, the illegitimate means exist for a criminal delinquent subculture to arise and persist. In "disorganized" communities, however, opportunities to create a subculture around sustained criminal enterprises do not exist. In those areas, crime also flourishes, but it is "individualistic, unorganized, petty, poorly paid, and unprotected" (1960, p. 173). Local adults, law abiding and law violating, are unable to exercise social control in this area. As a result, a "conflict" subculture arises in which status is achieved through violence.

Similar to Cohen, then, Cloward and Ohlin's analysis of delinquent subcultures is class based, though they give a more complicated analysis of variation within slum neighborhoods. But also similar to Cohen, they fail to bring race into the core of their theory. They stayed within the traditions of the Chicago school and Merton's SS&A paradigm, and thus they could not break out of the strictures of White Criminology. Even in the few instances where race is discussed, the analysis ultimately was limited.

First, Cloward and Ohlin (1960, p. 121) recognized that discrimination poses special barriers for "Negroes" and may justify their "withdrawal of attribution of legitimacy from conventional rules." These passing observations, however, did not inspire a race-specific analysis. Second, toward the end of *Delinquency and Opportunity*, they predicted that White ethnic slums would turn more disorganized and home to more conflict rather than criminal subcultures, with delinquency "becoming increasingly aggressive and violent" (1960, p. 203). One reason is that many White ethnics have assimilated into the middle class, creating "residual" slums composed of "those who have been unable to find a channel of social ascent" (p. 203). Other contributing factors that undermined local control and organization included the decline of urban political machines, the control of vice activities (e.g., gambling) by syndicates from outside the neighborhood, and "massive slum-clearance projects" that "destroy whatever vestiges of social organization remain in the slum community" (p. 209).

But what fate would African Americans suffer? Cloward and Ohlin reflected on this issue, perhaps because between 1950 and 1960 the Black population in New York City increased from 9.5% to 14% (Gibson & Jung, 2005). However, in a version of the invariance thesis, they argued that Black delinquency, until this time more conflict oriented due to neighborhood disorganization, "may change in the next decade or two" (1960, p. 199). In their local communities, observed Cloward and Ohlin (1960, pp. 201–202), the "likelihood is great that the Negro will eventually win his struggle for control of the rackets and for a greater voice in urban politics . . . the Negro's power is beginning to be felt." Whereas White slums were disintegrating, Black areas would become more organized and thus "change the character of Negro delinquency" (p. 202). As Cloward and Ohlin (1960, p. 202) optimistically predicted:

> The growth of illegal wealth and political power will probably lead to the types of neighborhood integration that provide opportunities for legitimate as well as illegitimate social ascent. We may expect, therefore, that violence will diminish in Negro neighborhoods and that criminal modes of delinquency will increase. In addition, such defeatist adaptations as widespread drug use may be on the wane.

Although Cloward and Ohlin should be credited for assessing possible race effects (even in a minimalist way), they could not escape the logic of their White Criminology, which limited their thinking to the dimension of organized and disorganized slums. They did not consider the enduring effects of a history of racial oppression and the power of discrimination and segregation to blunt Blacks' upward social mobility. As a result, they simply could not see that the urban future for poor African Americans was less social ascent and more life as the "truly disadvantaged" in inner-city hyper-ghettos (see, e.g., Wilson, 1987).

A Note on General Strain Theory

Classic strain theory was revitalized by Agnew's (1992) "general strain theory," known by its acronym "GST." Although race was virtually ignored in key statements of the theory (Agnew, 1992, 2001), the GST paradigm did evolve to consider race-specific issues. In his most comprehensive statement of the theory, *Pressured Into Crime*, Agnew (2006) moves beyond the invariance thesis by noting that social class does not fully account for race differences in crime. Building on research linking discrimination to criminal involvement, he notes that at school, at work, and by the police, "African Americans at all class levels are more likely to experience discrimination than whites" (2006, p. 147). Discrimination evokes strain and negative emotions, and it makes criminal coping more likely because this situation is seen as unjust. Brezina and Agnew (2013) also observe that racial/ethnic discrimination, including by the police, is one factor contributing to urban violence. Despite these promising insights, Agnew's project is, understandably, to fit race within his GST paradigm. He does not start with race as the organizing construct and detail fully the historical and contemporary sources of the strains faced by African Americans.

Sykes and Matza: Normalizing the Offender

As a doctoral student in sociology at Princeton University, David Matza was left without an assistantship and a mentor when his major professor took a year's leave of absence. He had the good fortune of meeting a newly hired professor, Gresham Sykes, who invited Matza to work on a grant and agreed to supervise his dissertation, though not on the labor movement as he had intended but on delinquency (Blomberg, 2018; Lemelle, 2010). They would combine to write two influential articles, one on "techniques of neutralization" (Sykes & Matza, 1957) and one on "subterranean values" (Matza & Sykes, 1961). Building on these ideas, Matza would then go on to write his classic book, *Delinquency and Drift* (1964).

Sykes and Matza (1957, p. 664) began their essay on neutralization by observing that in "attempting to uncover the roots of juvenile delinquency, the social scientist has long since ceased to search for devils in the mind or stigma in the body." Nonetheless, they noted that sociological positivism continued to differentiate delinquents from non-delinquents by arguing that they reside in slums and are inculcated by oppositional subcultural values. They challenged the empirical accuracy of this view (Benson & Cullen, 2018). Writing in post–World War II America marked by prosperity and a mass culture, their delinquent was not Stanley the jack-roller (Shaw, 1930) but Johnny the petty offender. Delinquency was not concentrated in urban slums but found across the class structure. Most important, "the world of the delinquent is embedded in the larger world of those who conform," which is why nearly all wayward youngsters remain "at least partially committed to the dominant social order" (1957, p. 666). Indeed, as Matza (1964, p. 37) pointed out, "children have a curious way of being influenced by the society of elders which frequently includes parents, almost all of whom, whatever their own proclivities, are united in their denunciation of delinquent deeds."

This connection to the dominant social order is precisely why techniques of neutralization are needed. According to Sykes and Matza, these linguistic devices allow youths to neutralize conventional normative controls in specific situations and engage in conduct that otherwise would evoke guilt or shame. For example, a youth might "appeal to the higher loyalty" of friendship to justify joining in a fight involving a peer. But this delinquent act does not "necessarily repudiate the imperatives of the dominant normative system" (Sykes & Matza, 1957, p. 669). Rather, "caught up in a dilemma that must be resolved," the youth chooses instead to follow other norms of higher value—in this case, allegiance to a friend in need (1957, p. 669).

Matza and Sykes (1961) added complexity to their analysis by also rejecting the Chicago school's portrayal of culture as neatly divided into a purely conformist side and a criminal side. In this view, this division was the source of the culture conflict that allows for differential association, with crime occurring "because of an excess of definitions favorable to violation of law over definitions unfavorable to violation of law" (Sutherland, 1947/1956, p. 9). By contrast, Sykes and Matza argued that conventional culture itself can be criminogenic because it contains not only Puritan ascetic values (e.g., espousing thrift and hard work) but also subterranean values that approve of adventure, soft but lucrative jobs, conspicuous consumption, and displays of masculinity (see Benson & Cullen, 2018). Whereas adults are sufficiently mature to hold subterranean values (e.g., desire for thrills) "in abeyance until the proper moment and circumstances for its expression arise," juveniles are prone to display these values in the wrong way, time, and place (Matza & Sykes, 1961, p. 718). As such, the "delinquent may not stand as an alien in the body of society but may represent instead a disturbing reflection or a caricature" (p. 711).

Sykes and Matza's goal thus was to *normalize* the delinquent. Good kids and bad kids are not so different. Normative consensus in American society means that all youths are more or less part of the same social order. Mass immigration that produces slum neighborhoods in the zone in transition and an inequitable class structure that provides differential access to pecuniary success can be safely ignored. In his *Delinquency and Drift*, Matza pays little attention to the broader social context, preferring instead to climb inside individuals to probe the subjective side of deviant choices. His delinquents are not driven but drifting into illegality, not constrained to offend but exercising will or human agency. Most tellingly, life-course-persistent antisocial youths receive scant theoretical consideration. His typical delinquent "is casually, intermittently, and transiently immersed in a pattern of illegal action" (1964, p. 28). The majority experience "maturational reform"—they are adolescence-limited offenders (Moffitt, 1993). Theories that emphasize "constraint and differentiation" suffer from an "embarrassment of riches" by predicting persistence; they cannot account for this pattern of widespread desistance.

Sykes and Matza were engaging in what might be called "cognitive criminology," seeking to detail the content of delinquent cognitions and the way in which the decision to offend is made (see Cullen, 2017; Giordano & Copp, 2018). But in doing so, their analysis became largely ahistorical and acontextual. By seeking to remove social class and neighborhood-based subcultures from the center of criminology, they unwittingly took a giant step away from any possibility of considering how race conditions their constructs of neutralization, subterranean values, and drift (for examples of how this might be done, see Burt, Lei, & Simons, 2017; Unnever & Gabbidon, 2011). They left unstated that the dominant culture to which all youths, delinquent or not, were tied was essentially a culture that privileged Whiteness. Issues such as segregation, cultural isolation, and the devaluing of diversity simply never came to mind. Thus, although of enduring value, Sykes and Matza's classic works contributed yet another chapter in the ongoing reification of White Criminology within the discipline.

Hirschi's Control Theories

Travis Hirschi's (1969) scholarly project was to specify a control theory and show that it was empirically superior to the reigning perspectives of his day, cultural deviance and strain perspectives. The strategy he employed in *Causes of Delinquency* (1969) has become normal science in the discipline (Cullen, 2011; Laub, 2002). Following Hirschi, investigators have conducted hundreds of theoretical tests in which they use self-report data to assess how much variance is explained by measures of rival theories (see Cullen, 2011; Weisburd & Piquero, 2008). Although Hirschi's work has proven invaluable, it also has done nothing to challenge the hegemony of White Criminology. In fact, books that focus on his control theory are virtually silent on the issue of race (see, e.g., Britt & Gottfredson, 2003; Hay & Meldrum, 2016).

As a graduate student at the University of California, Berkeley, Hirschi was influenced by Erving Goffman, David Matza, and Irving Piliavin. When preparing to undertake his dissertation, Charles Glock, his advisor, asked the Gluecks if Hirschi might use their data, a request that was denied (Laub, 2002). As an alternative, Glock arranged for him to join Alan Wilson's Richmond Youth Project, a study of more than 4,000 students "entering the eleven public junior and senior high schools of this area in the fall of 1964" (Hirschi, 1969, p. 34). This was not Hirschi's survey, but he was allowed to place items on the questionnaire (Laub, 2002). Hirschi was skilled in methods, coauthoring with Hanan Selvin *Delinquency Research* (titled *Principles of Survey Research* in the paperback edition), which would win the 1968 C. Wright Mills Award (see Hirschi & Selvin, 1967/1973). He would use the data to write a dissertation that would be published, virtually unchanged, as *Causes of Delinquency* (1969).

Importantly, Hirschi's methodological approach not only served as a research paradigm for criminology but also effectively denied him the opportunity to consider community context in his theorizing. (Alas, multilevel modeling did not exist at this time!) For Clifford Shaw, life histories were important because they captured how delinquents were enmeshed in disorganized neighborhoods. In *The Jack-Roller*, one learns about Stanley's criminal career involving the antisocial influences of his stepbrother William, about "getting educated" in crime in the St. Charles School for Boys, and about robbing drunks with his "pal" Tony. Hirschi was part of a generation of what Hagan and McCarthy (1997, p. 5) call "school criminologists" who, "armed with self-report methodologies," had schools replace "the streets as sites for data collection" (see also

Chouhy, Cullen, & Unnever, 2016). The research subject now sat at a desk and quietly filled out questionnaires, much like taking a test.

In a finding discomforting to cultural deviance and strain theories, Hirschi's data seemed to show that social class was unrelated to standard types of delinquency—offenses such as petty theft, vandalizing property, and joy riding. No question in his six-item self-report delinquency scale asked about jack-rolling (see Hirschi, 1969, p. 54). For Hirschi, the focus was on social bonds to parents, teachers, and peers and on the institutions of family and school, not the streets. Issues such as poverty and inequality, let alone racial segregation and oppression, were not part of his social bond theory and thus were not included in his analysis. In an interview, John Laub (2002, p. xxiv) "asked Hirschi if there was any sense that *Causes of Delinquency* was written in 1969 when all hell was breaking loose." Hirschi seemed proudly unaffected by the prevailing events, which included the civil rights movement and racial insurgency. Hirschi responded,

> Causes of Delinquency is a good example of the ability of people to construct intellectual products that are contrary to the spirit of the times. It is, I suppose, a 1930s book. But it wasn't out of line with what was happening on the Berkeley campus in the social sciences. It wasn't out of line with the thinking of Goffman, or Piliavin, or Matza. Not at all. (quoted in Laub, 2002, p. xxiv)

In all fairness, Hirschi recognized that African Americans experienced racial discrimination. First, the fact that race is more strongly related to arrest than self-report data, lends credence to the "official reaction hypotheses" (Hirschi, 1969, p. 79). Hirschi (1969, p. 79) noted that the police "patrol more heavily the Negro areas" and believe that Blacks are "more likely to commit criminal acts." Second, for most of the analyses reported in the *Causes of Delinquency*, Hirschi included only Whites, claiming—in a statement that one could not imagine being made today—that the Black responses were less reliable "partly stemming from their generally lower verbal skills" (1969, p. 79, fn. 23). One exception was his test of whether African American youths who blame the system (i.e., discrimination) rather than themselves for failure are, as Cloward and Ohlin proposed, more likely to offend. Contrary to the strain theory proposition, observed Hirschi (1969, p. 184), "ascription of blame is essentially unrelated to the commission of delinquent acts." All this led Hirschi (1969, p. 79) to embrace the invariance thesis, stating that "there is no reason to believe that the causes of crime among Negroes are different from those among whites."

As Unnever, Cullen, and colleagues (2009) point out, however, Hirschi missed an opportunity to reconsider his embrace of the generality of social bond theory. Generously provided the Richmond data by Hirschi, Unnever et al. discovered that the data set contained measures of perceived racial discrimination—presumably not placed on the questionnaire by Hirschi and thus not included in his study. When a multivariate analysis was conducted, these measures were significantly related to self-reported delinquency. The effects proved "robust even when numerous factors [were] controlled" and rivaled "the predictive power of the social bond measures" (Unnever et al., 2009, pp. 393–394). Given that Hirschi was aware of racial discrimination, had he thought to undertake this analysis in the 1960s, he might have articulated the need for a Black Criminology that considered the causal importance of perceived racial animus.

In their *A General Theory of Crime*, Gottfredson and Hirschi (1990) transform a social control theory into a self-control theory. The focus on the individual rather than on context intensifies. The theories are linked by their emphasis on consequences. In social bond theory, control and thus conformity are produced because people have something to lose that can impose a consequence—for example, attachments to parents or commitments to an educational future. In self-control theory, conformity is produced for those individuals who have the propensity to pay attention to consequences—those with self-control. Beyond childhood, the time when parenting inculcates self-control, context matters little. In fact, "context"—the social situations in which people find themselves—is a reflection of self-control. People are the architects of their lives. Those with low self-control create or select into problematic contexts. Crime is another bad choice, and any correlation between crime and bad contexts is spurious (Lilly, Cullen, & Ball, 2019).

According to Gottfredson and Hirschi (1990), racial differences in crime exist, but they have nothing to do with community-based structural inequality or subcultures. The "code of the street" (Anderson, 1999), for example, does not matter because "there is nothing in crime that requires the transmission of values or the support of other people" (1990, p. 151). Alas, the source of self-control and thus of crime—effective parenting—is invariant across races. African Americans just fall short more often in being good parents. "Given the potentially large differences among racial groups in the United States in the elements of child-rearing . . . (monitoring, recognizing, and correcting evidence of antisocial behavior)," observed Gottfredson and Hirschi (1990, p. 153), "it seems to us that research on racial differences should focus on differential child-rearing practices and abandon the fruitless effort to ascribe such differences to culture or strain." White Criminology is affirmed. All causes are general, and none are race specific. Once child-rearing is completed—for better or for worse—it simply does not matter if someone is Black or White. Self-control is colorblind, even if American society is not.

Developmental/Life-Course Theories

Three years following the publication of Gottfredson and Hirschi's *A General Theory of Crime*, Terrie Moffitt (1993) and Robert Sampson and John Laub (1993) published path-breaking works on crime across the life course. Suddenly, criminology had three powerful life-course theories, each of which articulated a distinct perspective. For Gottfredson and Hirschi, crime propensity in the form of self-control was established early in childhood and produced stable differences in crime from that time forward. For Moffitt, antisocial conduct was a developmental outcome, with an adolescence-limited group experiencing maturation reform and life-course-persistent group manifesting early onset of misconduct and persistence in offending deep into adulthood. Sampson and Laub (2005) rejected both lifetime stability and differential group trajectories. For them, there is continuity and change across the life course, with age-graded social bonds the main factor causing persistence in and desistance from crime (see also Laub & Sampson, 2003).

Taken together, these works ensured the founding of developmental/life-course criminology (DLCC) as a core paradigm within the discipline (Cullen, 2011). But inadvertently, these foundational DLCC works produced theoretical interest and research in which race was either ignored or discussed in passing. Believing in general or invariant effects, Gottfredson and Hirschi (1990) were not inclined to consider race-specific causes of crime. Moffitt (1993) was sensitive to how disadvantaged neighborhoods exacerbate neuro-psychological deficits, and she also noted how some interactions in poor Black neighborhoods might actually encourage abstention from crime. Still, race did not penetrate to the core of her taxonomy theory of development. One reason might be that in the Dunedin Multidisciplinary Health and Development Study—the New Zealand cite for Moffitt's research—the sample is "of predominantly white European ancestry" (Moffitt, Caspi, Rutter, & Silva, 2001, p. 11). Only a small percentage is of Maori or Pacific Islander heritage.

Similarly, Sampson and Laub (1993) discovered and analyzed Sheldon and Eleanor Gluecks' data (Laub, 2014). This remarkable achievement had one telling limitation: The Gluecks' sample consisted exclusively of Whites born in slum neighborhoods in Boston around 1930—a time when, in a city of more than 780,000, the Black population was only 2.6% (Gibson & Jung, 2005). Not surprisingly, race and factors unique to African Americans were not central to their age-graded social bond theory.

For the most part, theories within the DLCC paradigm have not escaped the strictures of White Criminology (cf. Piquero, MacDonald, & Parker, 2002). For example, cognitive or identity theories do not include race as a key construct in their models (see, e.g., Maruna, 2001; Paternoster & Bushway, 2009; for a partial exception, see Giordano, Cernkovich, & Rudolph, 2002). They do not consider whether perceived racial discrimination creates cognitions, such as a "condemnation script," that might inhibit desistance (Maruna, 2001). Similarly, the indexes to prominent books in the DLCC area contain, at most, only a few entries under "race" (see, e.g., Farrington, 2005; Thornberry & Krohn, 2003). Of course, the issue is not just whether race is mentioned, perhaps folded into a discussion of neighborhood disadvantage, but whether the analysis has a Black Criminology starting point.

Benson (2013) provides one example of how such an analysis might proceed. In his *Crime and the Life Course*, he includes a chapter based on the premise that the "structure of the life course is shaped by historical conditions and can be reshaped by social change" (2013, p. 149). Although he does not detail a complete theory, Benson discusses how not only market forces but also discriminatory government house policies created segregated ghettos, marked by large public housing projects conducive to crime and drugs (see also Rothstein, 2017). Growing up in these "segregated and disadvantaged neighborhoods," notes Benson (2013, p. 166), can "have profound effects on how children develop over the life course." To give one example discussed by Benson, African American youths in these areas are disproportionately exposed to violence, which then heightens stress hormones that are released at the sign of danger. In turn, research shows that stress hormones are related to health problems, psychological symptoms, and a propensity to use violence. Although speculative, Benson is engaging in Black Criminology because his causal chain starts with racial oppression and purposive segregation that make African Americans uniquely vulnerable to stressful circumstances and their unhealthy outcomes.

Conclusion

Our review of these major theoretical traditions is meant to illustrate a simple but consequential point: Theorizing in the discipline has been unwittingly trapped within the confines of White Criminology. Race has often been ignored in favor of related constructs such as social class, neighborhood disadvantage, and heterogeneity. The embrace of the invariance thesis at the macro and micro levels is understandable because most causes of crime are general. But trapped in traditions invented in the previous century and committed to showing that there is nothing about African Americans and their culture that is inherently criminogenic, scholars have remained blind to the fact that being Black in America is a unique, historical reality that exposes African Americans to unique subordination, injustice, and hostility, which calls forth unique socialization experiences and social adaptations (Unnever & Gabbidon, 2011). A Black Criminology starts with this realization—not in the immigrant neighborhoods of Chicago or the working-class slums of Boston, not in schools where questionnaires are passed out, and not with developmental perspectives that follow individuals across a life-course devoid of racial barriers.

None of this is to argue that criminologists are in any way racially insensitive or that existing theoretical criminology is not of enormous value. But it is to say that due to the work of James Unnever and his colleagues, it is time to move beyond White Criminology and to explore systematically the fruits that can be reaped by taking seriously the value of a Black Criminology.

Notes

1. For a systematic review of the extent to which criminological theories and related empirical research have considered race, see Gabbidon (2010).
2. Later reformulations of social disorganization theory led by Sampson incorporated the notion of race from a new perspective and made it somewhat central to their study (see, e.g., Sampson, 1987; Sampson, Morenoff, & Raudenbush, 2005; Sampson & Wilson, 1995; Sampson, Wilson, & Katz, 2018). However, Sampson's perspective on race has been criticized by the proponents of Black Criminology for his subscription to the racial invariance thesis and for his overreliance on neighborhoods as anchors of cognitions that came at the cost of virtually ignoring other experiences with oppression and discrimination that shape Black lives above and beyond neighborhood social realities (for a full discussion, see Unnever, this volume).

References

Agnew, R. (1992). Foundation for a general strain theory of crime and delinquency. *Criminology, 30*, 47–87.

70	Francis T. Cullen, Cecilia Chouhy, et al.

Agnew, R. (2001). Building on the foundation of general strain theory: Specifying the types of strain most likely to lead to crime and delinquency. *Journal of Research in Crime and Delinquency, 38*, 319–361.

Agnew, R. (2006). *Pressured into crime: An overview of general strain theory.* Los Angeles, CA: Roxbury.

Anderson, E. (1999). *Code of the street: Decency, violence, and the moral life of the inner city.* New York, NY: W. W. Norton.

Benson, M. L. (2013). *Crime and the life course: An introduction* (2nd ed.). New York, NY: Routledge.

Benson, M. L., & Cullen, F. T. (2018). Subterranean values, self-deception, and white-collar crime. In T. G. Blomberg, F. T. Cullen, C. Carlsson, & C. L. Jonson (Eds.), *Delinquency and drift revisited: The criminology of David Matza and beyond* (pp. 99–124). New York, NY: Routledge.

Block, R. (2017). The Chicago school of sociology maps crime: 1895–1931. In C. Bijleveld & P. van der aan (Eds.), *Liber Amicorum Gerben Bruinsma* (pp. 35–46). Verschijningsjaar, The Netherlands: Boom Criminologie.

Blomberg, T. G. (2018). David Matza—criminologist: With new reflections from David Matza. In T. G. Blomberg, F. T. Cullen, C. Carlsson, & C. L. Jonson (Eds.), *Delinquency and drift revisited: The criminology of David Matza and beyond* (pp. 3–11). New York, NY: Routledge.

Brezina, T., & Agnew, R. (2013). General strain and urban youth violence. In F. T. Cullen & P. Wilcox (Eds.), *The Oxford handbook of criminological theory* (pp. 145–159). New York, NY: Oxford University Press.

Britt, C. L., & Gottfredson, M. R. (Eds.). (2003). *Control theories of crime and delinquency (Advances in criminological theory*, Vol. 12). New Brunswick, NJ: Transaction.

Brotherton, D. (2010). Richard Cloward (1926–2001). In K. Hayward, S. Maruna, & J. Mooney (Eds.), *Fifty key thinkers in criminology* (pp. 147–152). London, UK: Routledge.

Bulmer, M. (1984). *The Chicago school of sociology: Institutionalization, diversity, and the rise of sociological research.* Chicago, IL: University of Chicago Press.

Burgess, E. W. (1932). Editor's preface. In E. F. Frazier (Ed.), *The Negro family in Chicago* (pp. ix–xii). Chicago, IL: University of Chicago Press.

Burgess, E. W. (1967).The growth of the city: An introduction to a research project. In R. E. Park & E. W. Burgess (Eds.), *The city: Suggestions for investigation of human behavior in the urban environment* (Reprint ed., pp. 47–62). Chicago, IL: University of Chicago Press. (Original work published in 1925.)

Bursik, R. J., Jr., & Webb, J. (1982). Community change and patterns of delinquency. *American Journal of Sociology, 88*, 24–42.

Burt, C. H., Lei, M. K., & Simons, R. L. (2017). Racial discrimination, racial socialization, and crime over time: A social schematic theory model. *Criminology, 55*, 938–979.

Chouhy, C., Cullen, F. T., & Unnever, J. D. (2016). Mean streets revisited: Assessing the generality of rival criminological theories. *Victims and Offenders, 11*, 225–250.

Clear, T. R. (2007). *Imprisoning communities: How mass incarceration makes disadvantaged neighborhoods worse.* New York, NY: Oxford University Press.

Cloward, R. A. (1959). Illegitimate means, anomie, and deviant behavior. *American Sociological Review, 24*, 164–176.

Cloward, R. A. (1968). Social control in the prison. In L. E. Hazelrigg (Ed.), *Prison within society: A reader in penology* (pp. 78–112). New York, NY: Anchor Books.

Cloward, R. A., & Ohlin, L. E. (1960). *Delinquency and opportunity: A theory of delinquent gangs.* New York, NY: Free Press.

Cohen, A. K. (1955). *Delinquent boys: The culture of the gang.* New York, NY: Free Press.

Coser, L. A. (1975). Merton's uses of the European sociological tradition. In L. A. Coser (Ed.), *The idea of social structure: Papers in honor of Robert K. Merton* (pp. 85–100). New York, NY: Harcourt Brace Jovanovich.

Cullen, F. T. (1984). *Rethinking crime and deviance theory: The emergence of a structuring tradition.* Totowa, NJ: Rowman & Allanheld.

Cullen, F. T. (1988). Were Cloward and Ohlin strain theorists? Delinquency and opportunity revisited. *Journal of Research in Crime and Delinquency, 25,* 214–241.

Cullen, F. T. (2011). Beyond adolescence-limited criminology: Choosing our future—The American Society of Criminology 2010 Sutherland address. *Criminology, 49,* 287–330.

Cullen, F. T. (2017). Choosing our criminological future: Reservations about human agency as an organizing concept. *Journal of Developmental and Life-Course Criminology, 3,* 373–379.

Cullen, F. T., & Messner, S. M. (2007). The making of criminology revisited: An oral history of Merton's anomie paradigm. *Theoretical Criminology, 11,* 5–37.

Cullen, F. T., Wilcox, P., Sampson, R. J., & Dooley, B. D. (Eds.). (2015). *Challenging criminological theory: The legacy of Ruth Rosner Kornhauser* (*Advances in criminological theory*, Vol. 19). New Brunswick, NJ: Transaction.

Farrington, D. P. (Ed.). (2005). *Integrated developmental and life-course theories of offending* (*Advances in criminological theory*, Vol. 14, pp. 183–209). New Brunswick, NJ: Transaction.

Feld, B. C. (2017). *The evolution of the juvenile court: Race, politics, and the criminalization of juvenile justice.* New York, NY: New York University Press.

Frazier, E. F. (1932). *The Negro family in Chicago.* Chicago, IL: University of Chicago Press.

Gabbidon, S. L. (2010). *Criminological perspectives on race and crime* (2nd ed.). New York, NY: Routledge.

Gibson, C., & Jung, K. (2005). *Historical census statistics on population totals by race, 1790 to 1990, and by Hispanic origin, 1970 to 1990, for large cities and other urban places in the United States.* Working Paper No. 76. Washington, DC: Population Division, U.S. Census Bureau.

Giordano, P. C., Cernkovich, S. A., & Rudolph, J. L. (2002). Gender, crime, and desistance: Toward a theory of cognitive transformation. *American Journal of Sociology, 107,* 990–1064.

Giordano, P. C., & Copp, J. (2018). Cognitions and crime: Matza's ideas in classic and contemporary context. In T. G. Blomberg, F. T. Cullen, C. Carlsson, & C. L. Jonson (Eds.), *Delinquency and drift revisited: The criminology of David Matza and beyond* (pp. 127–150). New York, NY: Routledge.

Gottfredson, M. R., & Hirschi, T. (1990). *A general theory of crime.* Stanford, CA: Stanford University Press.

Gouldner, A. W. (1973). Foreword. In I. Taylor, P. Walton, & J. Young (Eds.), *The new criminology: For a social theory of deviance* (pp. ix–xiv). London, UK: Routledge & Kegan Paul.

Greene, H. T., & Gabbidon, S. L. (2000). *African American criminological thought.* Albany, NY: State University of New York Press.

Hagan, J., & McCarthy, B. (1997). *Mean streets: Youth crime and homelessness.* Cambridge, UK: Cambridge University Press.

72   **Francis T. Cullen, Cecilia Chouhy, et al.**

Hay, C., & Meldrum, R. (2016). *Self-control and crime over the life course.* Thousand Oaks, CA: Sage.

Hirschi, T. (1969). *Causes of delinquency.* Berkeley, CA: University of California Press.

Hirschi, T., & Selvin, H. (1973). *Principles of survey analysis* (Paperback ed.). New York, NY: Free Press. (Original work published in 1967.)

Hooton, E. A. (1939). *The American criminal: An anthropological study.* Cambridge, MA: Harvard University Press.

Jonassen, C. T. (1949). A re-evaluation and critique of the logic and some methods of Shaw and McKay. *American Sociological Review, 14,* 608–614.

Kornhauser, R. R. (1978). *Social sources of delinquency: An appraisal of analytical models.* Chicago, IL: University of Chicago Press.

Kotlowitz, A. (1991). *There are no children here: The story of two boys growing up in the other America.* New York, NY: Doubleday.

Kozol, J. (1991). *Savage inequalities: Children in America's schools.* New York, NY: Crown.

Laub, J. H. (1983). *Criminology in the making: An oral history.* Boston, MA: Northeastern University Press.

Laub, J. H. (2002). Introduction: The life and work of Travis Hirschi. In T. Hirschi (Ed.), *The craft of criminology: Selected papers* (pp. xi–xlix). New Brunswick, NJ: Transaction.

Laub, J. H. (2004). The life course of criminology in the United States: The American Society of Criminology 2003 Presidential address. *Criminology, 42,* 1–26.

Laub, J. H. (2014). *Finding the Glueck data.* Unpublished manuscript. University of Maryland.

Laub, J. H., & Sampson, R. J. (2003). *Shared beginnings, divergent lives: Delinquent boys to age 70.* Cambridge, MA: Harvard University Press.

Lemann, N. (1991). *The promised land: The Great Black Migration and how it changed America.* New York, NY: Alfred A. Knopf.

Lemelle, A. J., Jr. (2010). David Matza (1930–). In K. Hayward, S. Maruna, & J. Mooney (Eds.), *Fifty key thinkers in criminology* (pp. 185–192). London, UK: Routledge.

Lilly, J. R., Cullen, F. T., & Ball, R. A. (2019). *Criminological theory: Context and consequences* (7th ed.). Thousand Oaks, CA: Sage.

Maruna, S. (2001). *Making good: How ex-convicts reform and rebuild their lives.* Washington, DC: American Psychological Association.

Matza, D. (1964). *Delinquency and drift.* New York, NY: Wiley.

Matza, D., & Sykes, G. M. (1961). Juvenile delinquency and subterranean values. *American Sociological Review, 26,* 712–719.

Merton, R. K. (1938). Social structure and anomie. *American Sociological Review, 3,* 672–682.

Merton, R. K. (1968). *Social theory and social structure* (Enlarged ed.). New York, NY: Free Press.

Merton, R. K. (1995). Opportunity structure: The emergence, diffusion, and differentiation of a sociological concept, 1930s–1950s. In F. Adler & W. S. Laufer (Eds.), *The legacy of anomie theory* (*Advances in criminological theory*, Vol. 6, pp. 3–78). New Brunswick, NJ: Transaction.

Merton, R. K. (1997). On the evolving synthesis of differential association and anomie theory: A perspective from the sociology of science. *Criminology, 35,* 517–525.

Messerschmidt, J. W. (1993). *Masculinities and crime: Critique and reconceptualization of theory*. Totowa, NJ: Rowman & Littlefield.

Miller, J. (2008). *Getting played: African American girls, urban inequality, and gendered violence*. New York, NY: New York University Press.

Miller, J., & Mullins, C. W. (2006). The status of feminist theories in criminology. In F. T. Cullen, J. P. Wright, & K. R. Blevins (Eds.), *Taking stock: The status of criminological theory* (*Advances in criminological theory*, Vol. 15, pp. 217–249). New Brunswick, NJ: Transaction.

Moffitt, T. E. (1993). Adolescence-limited and life-course—persistent antisocial behavior: A developmental taxonomy. *Psychological Review, 100*, 674–701.

Moffitt, T. E., Capsi, A., Rutter, M., & Silva, P. A. (2001). *Sex differences in antisocial behavior: Conduct disorder, delinquency, and violence in the Dunedin longitudinal study*. Cambridge, UK: Cambridge University Press.

Paternoster, R., & Bushway, S. (2009). Desistance and the feared self: Toward an identity theory of criminal desistance. *Journal of Criminal Law and Criminology, 99*, 1103–1156.

Piquero, A. R., MacDonald, J. M., & Parker, K. F. (2002). Race, local life circumstances, and criminal activity. *Social Science Quarterly, 83*, 654–670.

Rothstein, R. (2017). *The color of law: A forgotten history of how our government segregated America*. New York, NY: Liveright.

Russell-Brown, K. (2009). *The color of crime: Racial hoaxes, white fear, black protectionism, police harassment, and other microaggressions* (2nd ed.). New York, NY: New York University Press.

Sampson, R. J. (1987). Urban black violence: The effect of male joblessness and family disruption. *American Journal of Criminology, 93*, 348–382.

Sampson, R. J. (2012). *Great American city: Chicago and the enduring neighborhood effect*. Chicago, IL: University of Chicago Press.

Sampson, R. J., & Groves, W. B. (1989). Community structure and crime: Testing social-disorganization theory. *American Journal of Sociology, 94*, 774–802.

Sampson, R. J., & Laub, J. H. (1993). *Crime in the making: Pathways and turning points through life*. Cambridge, MA: Harvard University Press.

Sampson, R. J., & Laub, J. H. (2005). A general age-graded theory of crime: Lessons learned and the future of life—course criminology. In D. P. Farrington (Ed.), *Integrated developmental and life-course theories of offending* (*Advances in criminological theory*, Vol. 14, pp. 165–181). New Brunswick, NJ: Transaction.

Sampson, R. J., Morenoff, J. D., & Raudenbush, S. (2005). Social anatomy of racial and ethnic disparities in violence. *American Journal of Public Health, 95*, 224–232.

Sampson, R. J., & Wilson, W. J. (1995). Toward a theory of race, crime, and urban inequality. In J. Hagan & R. D. Peterson (Eds.), *Crime and inequality* (pp. 37–54). Stanford, CA: Stanford University Press.

Sampson, R. J., Wilson, W. J., & Katz, H. (2018). Reassessing "Toward a theory of race, crime, and urban inequality": Enduring and new challenges in 21st century America. *Du Bois Review: Social Science Research on Race, 15*, 13–34.

Sandburg, C. (1919). *The Chicago race riots*. New York, NY: Harcourt, Brace and Howe.

Shaw, C. R. (1930). *The jack-roller: A delinquent boy's own story*. Chicago, IL: University of Chicago Press.

Shaw, C. R., & McKay, H. D. (1942). *Juvenile delinquency and urban areas*. Chicago, IL: University of Chicago Press.

Shaw, C. R., & McKay, H. D. (1949). Rejoinder. *American Sociological Review, 14*, 614–617.

Shaw, C. R., & McKay, H. D. (1972). *Juvenile delinquency and urban areas* (Revised ed.). Chicago, IL: University of Chicago Press.

Shaw, C. R. with McKay, H. D. & McDonald, J. F. (1938). *Brothers in crime.* Chicago, IL: University of Chicago Press.

Shaw, C. R., with Moore, M. E. (1931). *The natural history of a delinquent career.* Chicago, IL: University of Chicago Press.

Snodgrass, J. (1976). Clifford R. Shaw and Henry D. McKay: Chicago criminologists. *British Journal of Criminology, 16,* 1–19.

Sutherland, E. H. (1937). *The professional thief: By a professional thief.* Chicago, IL: University of Chicago Press.

Sutherland, E. H. (1942/1956). Development of the theory. In A. Cohen, A. Lindesmith, & K. Schuessler (Eds.), *The Sutherland papers* (pp. 13–29). Bloomington, IN: Indiana University Press.

Sutherland, E. H. (1947/1956). A statement of the theory. In A. Cohen, A. Lindesmith, & K. Schuessler (Eds.), *The Sutherland papers* (pp. 7–12). Bloomington, IN: Indiana University Press.

Sykes, G. M., & Matza, D. (1957). Techniques of neutralization: A theory of delinquency. *American Sociological Review, 22,* 664–673.

Thomas, W. I., & Znaniecki, F. (1984). *The Polish peasant in Europe and America* (Edited and abridged by E. Zaretsky). Urbana, IL: University of Illinois Press. (Original five volumes published between 1918 and 1920.)

Thornberry, T. P., & Krohn, M. D. (Eds.). (2003). *Taking stock of delinquency: An overview of findings from contemporary longitudinal studies.* New York, NY: Kluwer Academic.

Tonry, M. (2011). *Punishing race: A continuing American dilemma.* New York, NY: Oxford University Press.

Unnever, J. D., Cullen, F. T., Mathers, S. A., McClure, T. E., & Allison, M. C. (2009). Racial discrimination and Hirschi's criminological classic: A chapter in the sociology of knowledge. *Justice Quarterly, 26,* 377–406.

Unnever, J. D., & Gabbidon, S. (2011). *A theory of African American offending: Race, racism, and crime.* New York, NY: Routledge.

Unnever, J. D. (this volume). The racial invariance thesis in criminology: Toward a Black criminology. In J. D. Unnever, S. L. Gabbidon, & C. Chouhy (Eds.), *Building a Black criminology: Race, theory, and crime* (*Advance in criminological theory,* Vol. 24, pp. 77–100). New York, NY: Routledge.

Unnever, J. D., & Owusu-Bempah, A. (this volume). Black criminology matters. In J. D. Unnever, S. L. Gabbidon, & C. Chouhy (Eds.), *Building a Black criminology: Race, theory, and crime* (*Advance in criminological theory,* Vol. 24, pp. 3–28). New York, NY: Routledge.

Wacquant, L. (2001). Deadly symbiosis: When ghetto and prison meet and mesh. *Punishment and Society, 3,* 95–134.

Weisburd, D., & Piquero, A. R. (2008). How well do criminologists explain crime? Statistical modeling in published studies. In M. Tonry (Ed.), *Crime and justice: A review of research* (Vol. 37, pp. 453–502). Chicago, IL: University of Chicago Press.

Whyte, W. F. (1943). Social organization in the slums. *American Sociological Review, 8,* 34–39.

Whyte, W. F. (1955). *Street corner society: The social structure of an Italian slum* (2nd ed.). Chicago, IL: University of Chicago Press.

Wilcox, P., Cullen, F. T., & Feldmeyer, B. (2018). *Communities and crime: An enduring American challenge*. Philadelphia, PA: Temple University Press.

Wilkerson, I. (2010). *The warmth of other suns: The epic story of America's Great Migration*. New York, NY: Vintage.

Wilson, W. J. (1987). *The truly disadvantaged: The inner city, the underclass, and public policy*. Chicago, IL: University of Chicago Press.

Young, J. (2010). Albert Cohen (1918–). In K. Hayward, S. Maruna, & J. Mooney (Eds.), *Fifty key thinkers in criminology* (pp. 105–115). London, UK: Routledge.

Zorbaugh, H. W. (1929). *The gold coast and the slum: A sociological study of Chicago's Near North side*. Chicago, IL: University of Chicago Press.

4

The Racial Invariance Thesis[*]

James D. Unnever

The "general theories of crime" generate our understanding of the causes of crime. A theory of crime is considered to be a "general theory" when it claims that its explanation generalizes across races, ethnicities, and crimes. In other words, a general theory of crime assumes that African Americans and Whites commit crimes for identical reasons regardless of the type of crimes committed. Of course, this assumption also means that studying African Americans will reveal the reasons why Whites commit crimes. Scholars refer to this foundational assumption of the general theories of crime as "the racial invariance thesis." In short, the racial invariance thesis states that there are no unique reasons why Whites or African Americans commit crime.

The racial invariance thesis is provocative. It discounts the possibility that the profound and subtle differences between superordinate groups (i.e., Whites) and subordinate groups (i.e., African Americans) produce their offending. It also dismisses the possibility that the systemic racism that flows from the U.S. being a racially stratified society is related to why some African Americans commit crime (Bonilla-Silva, 1997). This dismissal requires us to assume that the innumerable forms of racial subjugation, such as racist stereotypes and discrimination that African Americans ubiquitously encounter, have nothing to do with their likelihood of committing crimes. Similarly, the racial invariance thesis discounts the possibility that White offending is related to the power and privileges that are associated with being White, a superordinate group. In short, the racial invariance thesis argues that the differences in the power and privileges between Whites and African Americans are irrelevant for explaining why a minority of African Americans commit crimes.

However, as is well known, official statistics show that African Americans disproportionately commit more property and violent crimes than Whites do.[1] Indeed, the Uniform Crime Reports (UCR) data reveal that for two crimes, homicide and robbery, African Americans account for approximately half of those the police arrest even though they make up only about 13% of the U.S. population. This disproportionality in offending is why race is one of the strongest and most consistent correlates of crime (on par with gender). General theories of crime attempt to account for the overrepresentation of African Americans in the official arrest statistics by asserting that they are disproportionately exposed to crime-producing mechanisms. For example, social disorganization theorists account for the disproportionality in arrests found among African Americans by arguing that they are more likely to reside in areas of compounded deprivation, areas that have little collective efficacy (Sampson, 2013). Thus, social disorganization theorists speculate that if Whites and African Americans lived next door to each other in an area of compounded deprivation, they would have exactly the same likelihood of committing crimes, controlling for the factors specified by the other general theories (e.g., age, gender, low self-control, peer group affiliation, etc.).

Scholars usually assess the validity of the racial invariance thesis in two ways. First, they explore whether the measures specified by the general theories account for the direct correlation between race and crime. For example, disorganization theorists examine whether the correlation between the percentage of African Americans living in an area (e.g., a Census tract) and the area's rate of crime is fully accounted for by measures of social disorganization (e.g., economic deprivation and measures of collective efficacy). The measures of social disorganization should account for the direct effect of race on crime if the racial invariance thesis is correct. Such a finding suggests that the correlation between race and crime is spurious. African Americans have higher rates of arrests because they are disproportionally exposed to crime-producing mechanisms such as economic deprivation.

Second, researchers testing the validity of the racial invariance thesis must rule out the possibility that the effect of a particular variable or measure on crime is not the same for both African Americans and Whites (Unnever et al., 2016). This is the equivalent of splitting a sample into African Americans and Whites and assessing whether the effect of a measure of a general theory of crime (e.g., economic deprivation) on crime is equal across the two samples. If the racial invariance thesis is valid, the effect of the measures associated with the general theories on crime should be statistically equivalent for both African Americans and Whites. In sum, tests that support the racial invariance thesis must find that the effect of race on crime is insignificant after controlling for the measures of the general theories *and* that the effect of a measure on crime does not vary across race.

Social Disorganization Theory and the Racial Invariance Thesis

In what follows, I assess how the theory of social disorganization's adherence to the racial invariance thesis has affected its development and analyses of crime. I chose social disorganization theory for three reasons. First, it has a long history of being the most vocal proponent of the racial invariance thesis (Shaw & McKay, 1949; Snodgrass, 1976; Sampson, 2013). Second, social disorganization theorists have articulated the reasons why they argue that race does not matter (Kirk & Papachristos, 2011; Papachristos, Hureau, & Braga, 2013; Sampson, 2013). Third, social disorganization theorists have created a considerable body of research that tests the racial invariance thesis (Kirk & Papachristos, 2011; Papachristos et al., 2013).

Shaw and McKay

Shaw and McKay (1949) set into motion—a path dependency—the reasons why social disorganization theorists are vocal adherents and proponents of the racial invariance thesis (Sampson, 2013). Snodgrass's (1976, p. 5) historical analysis reveals that Henry McKay was obsessed with—was "haunted" by—a desire to prove that race and nationality were not related to delinquent behavior. Indeed, Snodgrass (1976) argues that social disorganization theory was created specifically in order to refute any race–crime relationship. To do so, Shaw and McKay (1949) showed that race and nationality—focusing on mostly second-generation White ethnic groups (e.g., Germans, Irish, Italians, Poles)—were not related to crime because these groups only had high rates of crime while they resided in deteriorated inner-city areas. Shaw and McKay (1949) then found that as "assimilation took place and the nationalities were dispersed to outlying areas of Chicago, their delinquency rates approximated to those of 'native Americans'" (Snodgrass,

1976, p. 5). Additionally, Shaw and McKay (1949, p. 617) found that the "outward movement of immigrant groups from the inner city areas tends to be identified with the upward movement of these groups in the status structure. As the status of ethnic groups improves, the direction of movement tends to be toward those areas where the physical characteristics symbolize enhanced status, and where rates of delinquents are low. Thus, rates of delinquents in nationality groups have tended to vary inversely with group status." In short, Shaw and McKay (1931, p. 435) argue that racial and ethnic origins are unrelated to crime because "the delinquency-producing factors are inherent in the community."

However, Shaw and McKay (1949) noted that generating a consistent argument to explain why some African Americans commit crime challenged the premises of their theory. Shaw and McKay (1949) found that Black rates of delinquency were higher than for Whites. However, they noted that the living conditions of African Americans and Whites were not comparable. Indeed, they recognized that racist segregation laws created unique living conditions for African Americans. Shaw and McKay (1949) stated, "but it cannot be said that they are higher than rates for white boys in comparable areas, since it is impossible to reproduce in white communities the circumstances under which Negro children live. Even if it were possible to parallel the low economic status and the inadequacy of institutions in the white community, it would not be possible to reproduce the effects of segregation and the barriers to upward mobility."

Shaw and McKay (1949) also recognized that racist segregation laws created conditions for African Americans that had no parallel for Whites, because these laws prevented African Americans from moving out of the inner city. As Snodgrass (1976, p. 6) argues, "Stuck in the ghetto, African Americans" had crime rates that remained high over generations. This not only threatened the generalization (of succession-assimilation), it also implicated American society. Stubbornly, trying to support his thesis in regard to African Americans as well, McKay persisted with the calculation of rates with each decennial issue of the national census. . . . When last interviewed in 1972, McKay was patiently waiting for the rates based on the 1970 census to match "native Americans." Note that had McKay lived longer, he would have found that in the inner-city areas of Chicago the rates of crime for African Americans have persistently remained higher than those for Whites.

In sum, Snodgrass's (1976) historical account reveals that three facts prevented Shaw and McKay (1949) from presenting an explanation that was consistent with their theory of social disorganization. First, as Shaw and McKay (1949) recognized, African Americans reside in inner-city neighborhoods that are distinct from those inhabited by Whites because of systemic racism (e.g., segregation laws). Second, systemic racism—segregation laws—caused African Americans to persistently live across generations in deprived areas; that is, segregation laws prevented African Americans from moving out of the inner city (succession-assimilation). Third, systemic racism blocked the opportunities for African Americans to become successful—improving their group status—regardless of where they lived. Surprisingly, despite these undeniable facts, Shaw and McKay (1949) never rejected the racial invariance thesis (Snodgrass, 1976). In other words, they continued to believe that the reason some African Americans commit crime was unrelated to their unique encounters with systemic racism.

Contemporary Social Disorganization Theory

As a result, Shaw and McKay's (1949) adherence to the racial invariance thesis has colored the thinking of contemporary social disorganization theorists. For example, Sampson (2013, p. 16) in his presidential address to the American Society of Criminology, declared that "We pursued this logic to argue that the community-level causes of violence are the same for both whites and African Americans—known in the literature as the 'racial invariance' thesis—but that racial segregation by community differentially exposes members of minority groups to violence-inducing and violence-protecting social mechanisms, explaining black-white disparities in violence." Thus, Sampson (2013), like Shaw and McKay, recognizes that systemic racism exists—it causes racially segregated communities—but denies that racism is a cause of why some African Americans commit crime. Rather, Sampson's (2013) core assumption, which allows him to deny that systemic racism causes some African Americans to commit crime, is that if Whites lived in racially segregated communities, they would have the same likelihood of offending as African Americans. In short, Sampson (2013, p. 17) argues that the impact of racism is only related to Black (and White) offending because it gives "rise to the concentration of the truly disadvantaged, which in turn leads to structural barriers and cultural adaptations that undermine social organization and ultimately the control of crime."

Sampson (2013) has articulated the racially invariant structural barriers and cultural adaptations that undermine a neighborhood's level of social organization and ultimately its capacity to control crime. These include the neighborhood's level of collective efficacy, the degree to which its residents perceive disorder, the degree to which its residents embrace legal cynicism, the level of social altruism among its residents, and the area's organizational capacity. Sampson (2013) argues that people who live in areas of economic deprivation have a greater likelihood of committing crimes because they are more likely to experience or embrace these cultural adaptations to economic deprivation. Thus, the residents of an economically deprived area who are most likely to commit crimes are the ones who embrace certain crime-producing cultural adaptations to economic deprivation.

Legal Cynicism: A Cultural Adaptation

Kirk and Papachristos (2011) use the example of legal cynicism to illustrate how cultural adaptations to economic deprivation arise in ghettos and are transmitted across generations. Social disorganization theorists define legal cynicism as occurring when "the law and the agents of its enforcement, such as the police and courts, are viewed as illegitimate, unresponsive, and ill equipped to ensure public safety." Kirk and Papachristos (2011) further argue that legal cynicism predicts an area's level of crime because "mistrust of the agents of the law may propel some individuals toward violence simply because they feel they cannot rely upon the police to help them resolve grievances" (Kirk & Papachristos, 2011, p. 1191).

Kirk and Papachristos (2011) argue that legal cynicism became historically embedded in ghettos because it is "an adaptation to neighborhood structural conditions such as concentrated poverty." They further argue that "cynicism exerts an influence on neighborhood rates of violence independent of the structural circumstances that originally produced such cynicism" (Kirk & Papachristos, 2011, p. 1192). In other words, at one point in time (decades ago?), the structural conditions associated with deteriorated inner-city areas caused their residents—African Americans and Whites—to develop a deep distrust of the criminal justice system. Once set into motion, the belief in legal cynicism becomes self-perpetuating and only currently exists in deteriorated inner-city areas because it is culturally transmitted across generations. That is, legal cynicism now has a life of its own, as each new generation of inner-city residents is socialized into embracing a deep distrust of the criminal justice system. Thus, the structural conditions that initially created a distrust in the criminal justice system are now irrelevant because it is *culturally* transmitted across generations. Kirk and Papachristos

(2011) specify that this process unfolds across generations when "individual perceptions of the law are augmented and solidified through communication and social interaction among neighborhood residents." In short, legal cynicism is a race invariant *cultural* orientation—"a lens through which individuals observe, perceive, and interpret situations" (Kirk & Papachristos, 2011, p. 1192).

Social disorganization theorists have examined whether the cultural networks that perpetuate the violence-producing mechanisms in ghettos are racially invariant. Initially, Papachristos et al. (2013) proposed to study whether endogenous network processes mediate the direct effect of race (being Black) on fatal and nonfatal shootings between gangs in Boston and Chicago.[2] However, their plans fell victim to the same empirical shortcomings that haunted Shaw and McKay's (1949) research design. First, Papachristos et al. (2013) found that nearly all of their homicide or shooting victims were nonWhite. For Chicago, "less than 1 percent involved a white homicide victim" and in "Boston, non-Hispanic African Americans accounted for 69 percent of all homicide victims during this period, Latino/Hispanics accounted for 17 percent, and non-Hispanic whites accounted for less than 11 percent" (Papachristos et al., 2013, p. 443). Second, Papachristos et al. (2013, p. 443) discovered that they could not include Whites in their analyses because in Chicago, "No white gangs or gang homicide victims were reported during the observation period and, in general, the prevalence of white gangs appears to have diminished in Chicago since the late-1980s" and "most all-white gangs in Boston are now considered defunct or else do not enter our data as victims in homicides or non-fatal gunshot injuries." Together, these findings caused Papachristos et al. (2013) to test the *racial* invariance thesis by comparing African Americans to an *ethnic* minority group, Latinos. Despite this inappropriate comparison, Papachristos et al. (2013, p. 439) concluded that their results are of "particular relevance for the racial invariance hypothesis—the underlying mechanisms associated with violence are the same across races (Sampson & Wilson, 1995). Indeed, our findings suggest that many direct effects of race are mediated by spatial and network processes."

Assessing Social Disorganization Theory's Adherence to the Racial Invariance Thesis

Social disorganization theory's contention that race does not matter is built upon three assumptions. First, social disorganization scholars assume that if there were "white urban ghettos" that were identical to

"Black inner-city ghettos," the White urban ghettos would produce the same amount of crimes as the inner-city Black ghettos. Second, social disorganization scholars assume that if African Americans and Whites lived next door to each other in a deteriorated inner-city area, their likelihood of committing crimes would be identical because their experiences would be indistinguishable.[3] Third, social disorganization scholars assume that deteriorated inner-city areas have race-invariant crime-producing culturally transmitted mechanisms that are divorced from the circumstances that originally created them.

Systemic racism undermines the validity of the first assumption; that is, African Americans and Whites reside in comparable inner-city urban areas. Segregation laws and their contemporary corollaries have created and have sustained hypersegregated inner-city Black ghettos (Drew & Bialik, 2017; Massey, 1990, 2005; Massey & Denton, 1993; Robinson, 1993; Shaw & McKay, 1949). Thus, the data show that there are no White inner city ghettos, and too few Whites live in urban Black ghettos to meaningfully test the racial invariance thesis (Peterson & Krivo, 2005, 2010; Sharkey, 2013). Furthermore, the data reveal that Black urban ghettos are unlike any other inner-city deteriorated area. Unlike most ghettos or disadvantaged neighborhoods where the population of families turns over every few years, successive generations of the same families populate Black urban ghettos.

Indeed, Sharkey (2013) found that since the 1970s, a majority of Black families have resided in the poorest quarter of inner-city neighborhoods in consecutive generations, compared to only 7% of White families. Sampson (2013) concurs with Sharkey as he states, "spatial inequality by race and place makes fair comparisons between whites and African Americans almost impossible. Almost a third of black children in Chicago live in the upper quartile of concentrated disadvantage—for whites the percentage is zero." These findings explain why Papachristos et al. (2013) could not include Whites in their analyses. White gangs in urban Black ghettos simply do not exist. Thus, the data reveal that systemic racism inhibits the ability of African Americans to move out of the urban ghettos and has blocked their opportunities to achieve a higher group status (Drew & Bialik, 2017; Doleac & Stein, 2013; Ewens, Tomlin, & Wang, 2013; Gaddis, 2014; Kuroki, 2016; Massey, 2005; Pager, 2003; Pager & Pedulla, 2015). In short, the Black experience in urban Black ghettos is unique and has no parallel among Whites.

Relatedly, Small and McDermott (2006) analyzed Department of Commerce and 2000 Census data and documented the exceptionalism of Black neighborhoods. These scholars examined whether poor neighborhoods are deinstitutionalized ghettoes—areas with a depletion of organizational resources (e.g., child-care centers, grocery stores, pharmacies)—because of market-driven economic forces or race-related effects. Small and McDermott's (2006, p. 1716) results revealed that "predominantly black neighborhoods constitute special cases," whereby the effects of segregation and institutional (and interpersonal) discrimination are strong enough to temper the effects that other differences between cities such as concentrated poverty have on the number of organizational resources. Small and McDermott (2006, p. 1716) concluded, "that de-institutionalization is associated more with segregation and depopulation than with concentrated poverty."

In addition, Small and McDermott (2006) highlight another methodological issue confronting social disorganization theorists who have mostly studied clusters or neighborhoods in Chicago. "Much of the work supporting the de-institutionalization thesis has been based on ethnographic research in predominantly black neighborhoods in Chicago. The de-institutionalization perspective argues strictly for economic, not racial, effects. However, its empirical support has stemmed from studies of African Americans, such that it was often unclear whether it applied to most poor neighborhoods or only to predominantly black ones" (Small & McDermott, 2006, p. 1716). In short, there are not enough Whites living in Black inner-city neighborhoods to generate racially invariant generalizations.

The data also do not support the second assumption that if African Americans and Whites lived next door to each other in a deteriorated inner-city area, their likelihood of committing crimes would be identical because their experiences would be indistinguishable. This assumption is a theoretical luxury that ruminates about whether Whites would respond the same way if they encountered the same conditions as African Americans. However, this reality never will occur, which makes the claim both nonfalsifiable and irrelevant. In many ways, it is like saying that there would be gender invariance in crime if patriarchy did not exist and if both men and women were the same size and had the same reproductive functions.

Furthermore, recent research completely disputes the argument that if African Americans and Whites equally resided in areas of concentrated disadvantage, they would produce identical outcomes. Chetty, Hendren, Jones, and Porter (2018) analyzed longitudinal data covering nearly the entire U.S. population from 1989 to 2015 to examine the sources of racial and ethnic disparities in income. Given their results summarily reject the racial invariance thesis; I quote what they found at length.

> Third, the black-white gap persists even among boys who grow up in the same neighborhood. Controlling for parental income, black boys have lower incomes in adulthood than white boys in 99% of Census tracts. Both black and white boys have better outcomes in low-poverty areas, but black-white gaps are larger on average for boys who grow up in such neighborhoods. The few areas in which black-white gaps are relatively small tend to be low-poverty neighborhoods with low levels of racial bias among whites and high rates of father presence among African Americans. Black males who move to such neighborhoods earlier in childhood earn more and are less likely to be incarcerated. However, fewer than 5% of black children grow up in such environments. These findings suggest that reducing the black-white income gap will require efforts whose impacts cross neighborhood and class lines and increase upward mobility specifically for black men.

Additionally, social disorganization theorists fail to integrate into their analyses the reality that by the age of 7, Black children are fully aware that their race matters and that 98% of African American adults report experiencing some form of racial discrimination in the past year (Klonoff, Landrine, & Ullman, 1999; Rogers & Meltzoff, 2016). Indeed, research indicates that Whites misperceived Black boys (ages 10–17) as older relative to peers of other races, as less innocent than children of other races, and as more culpable for their actions within a criminal justice context than peers of other races (Goff, Jackson, Di Leone, Culotta, & DiTomasso, 2014). Skorinko and Spellman (2013) note that racialized stereotypes are crime specific. African Americans were most associated with serious crimes such as mugging, rape, robbery, assault, gang involvement, and murder, while Whites were more likely to be typified with lesser crimes such as plagiarism, prescription drugs, public nudity, research fraud, stalking, credit fraud, domestic violence, driving under the influence, and embezzlement. These findings indicate that African Americans are embedded within racialized structures regardless of their age and where they live (Fish, 2017; Steele, 1997; Gates & Steele, 2009).

Social disorganization theorists also fail to integrate into their analyses the vast research that finds that racism negatively impacts the well-being of African Americans and causes them to commit crimes (Paradies et al., 2015; Pascoe & Richman, 2009). The existing research is unequivocally clear that the more African Americans perceive being discriminated against because of their race, the more likely they are to commit crimes, regardless of whether the discrimination occurs in or outside of their neighborhood (Burt, Simons, & Gibbons, 2012; Unnever, Cullen, & Barnes, 2016a, 2016b; Unnever, Cullen, Mathers, McClure, & Allison, 2009; Unnever, 2014). In addition, African Americans who perceive that they have been discriminated against in their own neighborhood because of their race are more likely to engage in externalizing behaviors (Riina, Martin, Gardner, & Brooks-Gunn, 2013). Thus, racialized areas of compounded deprivation are themselves criminogenic and may intensify the noxious consequences that racial discrimination has on why some African Americans commit crime (Brunson & Miller, 2006; Isom, 2016; Unnever & Gabbidon, 2011).

Insightfully, Chetty et al. (2018) show the deleterious consequences of racism at the macro level. They created two aggregated measures of racial bias and report that Black boys who grew up in low-income families in media markets with greater racial animus had lower incomes in adulthood, were less likely to be employed, and were more likely to be incarcerated. In sum, it is clear that regardless of where African Americans live, they have the unique additional burden of experiencing racist attitudes, stereotypes, and practices that negatively affect their well-being including compelling some down racialized pathways to crime (Herda, 2016; Unnever et al., 2016a).

The data also do not support the third assumption that there are *cultural* adaptations in Black urban ghettos that its residents transmit across generations, which are independent of the structural circumstances that originally produced them. For example, supporters of this assumption, such as Kirk and Papachristos (2011, p. 1192), argue that legal cynicism became embedded in urban ghettos because it is "an adaptation to neighborhood structural conditions such as concentrated poverty" and that it is now independent of the structural conditions that produced it. That is, legal cynicism is now a self-perpetuating crime-producing mechanism in inner-city areas because residents culturally transmitted it across generations through various social networks embedded within the areas.[4]

However, the data indicate that the deep legal cynicism presently found among African Americans, regardless of where they live, has not resulted from neighborhood structural conditions such as economic deprivation (English et al., 2017). Rather, legal cynicism is ubiquitous among African Americans because of their past and present personal and vicarious noxious experiences with the criminal justice system. For example, a 2014 Gallup poll revealed that one in four (24%) young African American men reported that the police had treated them unfairly *just in the last 30 days*, and Burt et al. (2012) report that more than half of the Black adolescents in their sample reported experiencing racial discrimination by the police within the past year (Newport, 2014). Indeed, Hagan, Shedd, and Payne (2005, p. 382) note that these findings are not aberrations but part of a Black "history of public dishonor and ritualized humiliation" by the criminal justice system. Together, these findings invalidate the social disorganization theorists' argument that the legal cynicism found in Black ghettos is a cultural phenomenon that is "culturally" reproduced. Rather, the contemporary day-to-day negative experiences that African Americans personally or vicariously have with the criminal justice system cause them to be cynical of the criminal justice system.

Scholars note that the criminal justice system has always been the knife's edge in the racial subjugation of African Americans. This leading edge of oppression originated with the role that the criminal justice system had in institutionalizing slavery (e.g., slave patrols), continued because the criminal justice system was the primary enforcers of the Jim Crow laws, and is found in the contemporary Black Lives Matter social movement (Brooks et al., 2016; Dunham & Petersen, 2017; Edwards & Harris, 2016; Skolnick, 2007; Oshinsky, 1997). Thus, because of centuries of accumulated race-specific encounters with the criminal justice system, scholars argue that African Americans are uniquely embedded with a "sea of hostility" or a "reservoir of bad will."[5] These seas of hostility— that include personal experiences of rage—undermine the moral justifications to obey the law and diminish the deterrent effects of legal proscriptions (Noble, 2006). These racialized attitudes—rage and cynicism—are revealed as African Americans discuss their feelings toward criminal justice injustices: "And with any kind of toxicity—if it sits long enough—it's going to come out as rage because it's going to have to come out. It can either come out in a constructive way or allowed on its own to be destructive" (Brooks et al., 2016, p. 353). In short, these "seas of hostility" fuel the anger, negativity, and anxiety/depressive symptoms that immediately flow from experiencing criminal justice injustices, which in turn harden one of the racialized pathways that lead to the disproportionately high levels of offending among African Americans, especially in disadvantaged areas (English et al., 2017).

The data further reveal that the persistence of legal cynicism in Black communities is a strategic adaptation to the clearly perceived reality that they or someone they know will undergo a criminal justice injustice (Bell, Hopson, Craig, & Robinson, 2014; Ng, Sze, Tamis-LeMonda, & Ruble, 2017; Nix, Campbell, Byers, & Alpert, 2017). Thus, the distrust of the criminal justice system is part of the racialized cognitive schema of what it means to be a Black person living in a racist society (Unnever, 2008).[6] Otherwise stated, the resiliency of Black America demonstrates their historically accumulated wisdom on how to overcome their subjugation (Unnever & Gabbidon, 2011).

Indeed, the research shows African Americans uniquely transmit both their legal cynicism and wisdom across generations. Scholars label this process of transmitting a racialized worldview across generations as racial socialization (Dunbar, Leerkes, Coard, Supple, & Calkins, 2016; McNeil, Reynolds, Fincham, & Beach, 2016; Saleem et al., 2016). One of the salient components of racial socialization is when Black parents prepare their children for their encounters with racism (i.e., preparation for bias). Scholars reveal that "the talk" is a particularly salient characteristic of the preparation for bias (Coates, 2015). The talk reflects the depth of the legal cynicism that African Americans uniquely continue to accumulate. However, the talk also includes their collective wisdom of how to avoid the toxic crime-producing consequences of police brutality. Brooks et al. (2016, p. 355) outline some of the wisdom transmitted during "the talk" among African Americans:

- Pull over right away (preferably in a lighted area).
- Keep both hands on the steering wheel.
- Do not make any quick or sudden moves.
- If you need your wallet or registration etc. and it is in your pocket or glove compartment . . . do not reach for it—explain to the officer where the documents are and ask permission to get them.
- If it is dark when you are pulled over, turn on the dome light so they can see you clearly.
- Watch your mouth! "Yes sir, officer. Yes, ma'am, officer." Be as polite as possible.
- Don't argue—even if you're absolutely right. Don't argue. Let them give you the ticket and dispute the case in court.

All told, the research reveals that the depth of the inimitable legal cynicism that African Americans have has not resulted from them residing in structurally disadvantaged neighborhoods. Their profound distrust of the criminal justice system is also not divorced from their past and present experiences (Noble, 2006; Tyler, 1990). Rather, their racialized legal cynicism is transmitted across generations—racial socialization—because African Americans continue to personally or vicariously experience profound racist encounters with the criminal justice system on a daily basis (e.g., stop and frisk, driving while Black, or shot while walking away) (Brunson, 2007; Brunson & Miller, 2006; Brunson & Weitzer, 2009; Unnever, Owusu-Bempah, & Deryol, 2017). In short, the peerless racialized legal cynicism among African Americans results from their incomparable grounded lived experiences with what it means to be a Black person living in a systemically racist society.

In sum, it is confounding as to why social disorganization theorists are still promoting the racial invariance thesis with neighborhood-level data when 70 years ago, Shaw and McKay acknowledged that Black ghettos are unreproducible. Social disorganization theorists may use euphemisms such as "inner-city residents" but the factual reality is that the vast majority (95%) of "residents" in these inner-city neighborhoods are African Americans. Put simply, there are no White areas of *compounded deprivation*. However, not all is lost. Contemporary social disorganization theory has illuminated the processes by which inner-city Black ghettos create higher rates of offending among African Americans while incorporating the historical reasons why Whites purposefully created these segregated areas of compounded deprivation. Thus, contemporary social disorganization theory has generated a holistic race-specific understanding of offending that is grounded in the present and past subjugation of Black America. In short, contemporary social disorganization should be considered as part of a Black Criminology because it only applies to Blacks (just as its earlier versions only applied to white immigrants).

In conclusion, in order for a theory to be a "general" theory, it must argue that the causes of crime are identical for African Americans and Whites (Unnever et al., 2009). Hirschi (1969, p. 80) clearly illustrates how general theories of crime ground their understanding of the causes of crime in the racial invariance thesis: "It follows, that we need not study Negro boys to determine the causes of their delinquency." Consequently, general theories are limited in their ability to generate holistic understandings of White and Black offending. At best, a general theory of crime can show that the effect of a particular variable (e.g., legal cynicism) increase crime among Whites and African Americans. However, analyses such as these are vacuous unless they ground their results in the interpretive frameworks that African Americans and Whites have created over centuries that give meaning to their attitudes and behaviors.

Scholars will find that in most instances, the cognitive schemas that African Americans and Whites have are "two worlds far apart" (Unnever, 2008). Furthermore, scholars will discover that policies that are grounded in the unique lived experiences of African Americans and Whites will be more efficacious.

Review of the Literature That Tests the Racial Invariance Thesis

Scholars have tested the validity of the racial invariance thesis, and a few studies potentially support the thesis. For example, Shihadeh and Shrum (2004) found that for Baton Rouge block groups, the effect of percent Black on rates of separate violent index offenses became non-significant after controlling for structural disadvantage and social disorganization. They concluded that "the association between block group racial composition and crime rates is due to an underlying association between serious crime and structural factors that are often implicated in the Black urban experience" (Shihadeh & Shrum, 2004, p. 526). Krivo and Peterson (2000), analyzing urban homicide rates, found that if African Americans and Whites held similar positions in relation to structural disadvantage, the effects of disadvantage and home ownership were relatively comparable for the two races. Bellair and McNulty (2005) found that the race effect became insignificant after they included individual-level measures (e.g., school grades, verbal ability, prior violence, use of substances, access to guns, peer group affiliations), measures of the community context (e.g., concentrated disadvantage), and family-related measures (e.g., parental education and income). Sampson (2013, p. 17), after reviewing the existing literature, declared, "it is fair to say that the evidence is supportive—there is wide variability in crime rates among white and black communities with robust similarity in key predictors (Krivo & Peterson, 2000). Neighborhood factors correlated with race also explain a significant proportion of the black-white racial gap in violence among individuals (Sampson, 2012, p. 249)."

In contrast, other researchers have found that the effect of being Black (race) on crime remained significant after controlling for other relevant correlates. Using census place-level data from California and New York, Ulmer, Harris, and Steffensmeier (2012) found that racial differences in structural disadvantage did not completely explain Black–White gaps in violent crime. Analyzing data from Chicago, Sampson, Morenoff, and Raudenbush (2005) found that the effect of race on violence (e.g., self-reports of hitting someone outside of the house, throwing objects such as rocks or bottles at people) was reduced (60%) but remained significant after controlling for a host of individual (e.g., impulsivity, age, gender, married parents) and community characteristics (e.g., concentrated disadvantage, collective efficacy). Similarly, examining the National Survey of Families and Households and the 1990 U.S. census, Benson, Wooldredge, Thistlethwaite, and Fox (2004) found that the relationship between race and engaging in domestic violence remained significant after controlling for ecological contexts and individual-level risk factors.

In addition, scholars have found that the effects of crime-producing factors are not identical for African Americans and Whites. Analyzing data from 125 cities, Ousey (1999) found that the associations between homicide and several measures of socioeconomic deprivation (e.g., poverty, unemployment, income inequality, female-headed households, and deprivation index) were stronger among Whites than they were among African Americans. Ousey and Lee (2004) report that the magnitude of the illicit drug market–homicide relationship was not racially invariant. Their results indicated that the influence on homicide rates of within-city change in the drug market was significantly stronger for African Americans than for Whites.

Furthermore, Steffensmeier, Ulmer, Feldmeyer, and Harris (2010) analyzed 1999–2001 averaged arrest data from California and New York and report that in 10 out of 15 group comparisons (Black, White, and Hispanic) of the effects of disadvantage variables (e.g., overall structural disadvantage, poverty, unemployment, low education, and female headship) on a violent crime index were significantly different. Based on these findings, Steffensmeier et al. (2010) concluded that more difference than similarity exists in the effects of structural disadvantage on White and Black overall violence. Parker, Stansfield, and McCall (2016) report that the effects of numerous social disorganization measures (e.g., economic disadvantage, industrial restructuring, a Hispanic immigration index) and macrostructural conditions (e.g., measures of incarceration rates, drug sales arrests, and police presence) on homicide rates varied unequally across African Americans and Whites.

It is also notable that the vast majority of the research that has specifically tested the racial invariance thesis has analyzed aggregate-level data. That is, there is scant research that specifically tests the racial invariance thesis with individual-level data. As an exception, Fagan and Novak (2017) analyzed prospective data from approximately 600 high-risk families in the Longitudinal Studies of Child Abuse and Neglect and found that White youth experienced a significantly greater number of adverse childhood experiences (e.g., physical and sexual abuse). However, Fagan and Novak (2017) reported that the impact of adverse childhood experiences on various forms of delinquency was statistically significant for African American adolescents in all but one model (predicting violence), but no significant relationships were found among Whites. In addition, analyzing individual-level data from Chicago (The Project on Human Development in Chicago Neighborhoods, PHDCN), Unnever et al. (2016) found that people were more likely to commit crimes when they perceived that the police discriminated against them, but the effect was greater for African Americans than Whites or Hispanics.[7] Furthermore, Walters (2018) analyzed 2,000 federal supervisees and evaluated whether race and sex were differentially associated with proactive and reactive criminal thinking. His results revealed that the instrumental aspects of crime (i.e., crime as a means to an end) motivated African Americans, particularly Black men, more than Whites. Walters (2018) concluded that cultural, structural, and motivational factors combine to produce the quantitative differences between African Americans and Whites that cause the well-known Black–White differences in crime rates.[8]

Given these limitations, in general, the research has generated little support for the racial invariance thesis. Most of the studies have found that including other crime-producing factors in the multivariate models fails to render the correlation between race and crime insignificant. Indeed, Sampson et al.'s (2005) research found that up to 40% of the race effect on crime remains unexplained after controlling for other relevant crime-producing mechanisms. This large percentage indicates that scholars need to account theoretically and empirically for the variance that remains unexplained after the measures specified by the general theories are included in the analyses. It is likely that the racialized experience that African Americans ubiquitously encounter accounts for the unexplained variance in the race–crime correlation.

As noted earlier, researchers claim support for the racial invariance thesis when they find that the race–crime correlation becomes insignificant after introducing controls or if the effect of a variable on crime is the same for African Americans and Whites. However, such findings may not support the racial invariance thesis. It is likely that the framework that African Americans and Whites use to interpret their perceptions and experiences and that causes their behaviors differs. For example, Ho, Kteily, and Chen (2017) examined whether African Americans and Whites associated Black–White multiracials more with their minority versus majority parent race and if so, why. Ho et al. (2017) found that both races were equally likely to categorize Black–White multiracials as more Black than White. However, the Whites' categorization was associated with intergroup antiegalitarianism (i.e., the desire to preserve the racialized hierarchical status quo), whereas the African Americans' classification was associated with intergroup egalitarianism. That is, African Americans associated biracials as Black because they perceived that Black–White biracials face discrimination and consequently feel a sense of linked fate with them. Thus, research can show that African Americans and Whites have the same outcomes (e.g., react with anger when perceiving being discriminated against) but have vastly different reasons and interpretations for reactions (e.g., African Americans interpret being discriminated against based upon their racialized worldview, whereas Whites are indignant because of their privileged position).

Therefore, I suggest that it is premature to declare that a factor—social bonds, strains, impulse control—is race neutral because it equally affects offending for African Americans and Whites. Scholars need to (1) explain why African Americans and Whites encounter different levels of these factors (e.g., low self-control), (2) show that the sources of these factors are identical for African Americans and Whites, and (3) provide proof that African Americans and Whites similarly interpret and react to these factors. I contend that to declare any factor—social bonds, strains, impulse control—to be race neutral, scholars must find that the interpretive frameworks that encase these factors are identical across races/ethnicities. However, I contend that the interpretive frameworks are race-specific. Therefore, scholars must generate race-specific analyses that explicate the unique interpretive frameworks that give meaning to the reasons why African Americans and Whites offend.

Conclusion

It is unfortunate that the discipline of criminology has largely relegated racial subjugation to the periphery of its analyses. It is also unfortunate that the discipline of criminology has failed to integrate into its research agenda the multifaceted ways in which systemic racism causes some African Americans to commit crime. These glaring omissions are disconcerting given that much of the general theorizing on why African Americans commit crime took place during the Jim Crow era and the tumultuous decades associated with the civil rights movement, both of which are moments in time when the full force of systemic racism was on display. It is further unfortunate and disappointing that there is no full-blown accepted Black Criminology within the discipline of criminology given that, in 1900, Du Bois (1900, p. 104) declared that "the world problem of the 20th century is the problem of the color line." Furthermore, it is incongruent that the discipline of criminology has incorporated into its fold a feminist criminology but not a Black Criminology, since women underoffend and African Americans overoffend. Just as there are gendered pathways to crime there are racialized pathways to Black offending (Unnever & Gabbidon, 2011; Unnever et al., 2016a). In short, it is understandable why the discipline of criminology has no clear understanding or policy solution as to why there are profound racial disparities in crimes and why only a minority of African Americans offend.

Notes

* I thank J.C. Barnes, Michael Benson, Frank Cullen, Shaun Gabbidon, David Kirk, Alex Piquero, Dan Mears, Akwasi Owusu-Bempah, Andrew Papachristos, Katheryn Russell-Brown, Darrell Steffensmeier, Eric Stewart, and Geoff Ward for their insightful comments on earlier drafts.
1. Note that these official rates are likely inflated because they are generated by a criminal justice system that engages in racial profiling, racially targeted policing (in poor/low-income areas), police emphasis on open-area drug markets, and low-level crimes (Russell, 1992; Unnever & Gabbidon, 2011).
2. Papachristos et al. (2013) considered four endogenous group processes: (1) reciprocity, (2) delayed reciprocity, (3) transitivity, and (4) distribution of violent ties among the observed gangs.
3. In general, if true, the racial invariance thesis implies that the individual rates of offending would be the same regardless of where African Americans and whites reside as long as they reside in the same place—advantaged or disadvantaged.
4. Kirk (2016) argues that external factors such as when a large number of released prisoners, who are distrustful of the criminal justice system, return to resource-deprived neighborhoods can alter the intergenerational cultural transmission of legal cynicism. Thus, the race-neutral culture of legal cynicism found among residents in inner cities persists "because of structural reproduction and also because of bounded rationality. As an example of the former, we suggest that mass incarceration and the repetitive churning of offenders between select inner-city neighborhoods and prisons continuously reproduces a culture of cynicism" (Kirk & Papachristos, 2017). Note, however, that Kirk (2016) fails to acknowledge that mass incarceration and the mass release of prisoners are problems that are essentially only affecting black communities.
5. It is highly unlikely that there are deep pockets of legal cynicism among Whites who reside in inner-city ghettos because Whites do not live in purposefully constructed neighborhoods designed to keep them at a structural disadvantage (Mayrl & Saperstein, 2013; Wilkins, Wellman, Babbitt, Toosi, & Schad, 2015).

6. English et al. (2017) list a variety of negative encounters that Black men reported that they had with the police including being unfairly arrested, being accused of drug-related behavior, being unfairly pulled over while driving, being unfairly stopped and searched, being assumed a thief, experiencing verbal abuse, experiencing physical abuse, and unfair treatment associated with attire.
7. In addition, scholars have found that the effects of social disorganization measures varied across whites and African Americans when examining rates of homicide victimization. Berthelot, Brown, Thomas, and Burgason (2015) report that for African Americans, low income increased victimization risk and disadvantaged communities exacerbated the association, whereas income tended to have a protective effect across levels of aggregate resource deprivation for whites.
8. Tangentially related, Kiecolt and Hughes (2017, p. 68) analyzed the General Social Survey (GSS) and report "that racial identity works somewhat differently for African Americans and whites. Closeness was somewhat more related to greater positive affect about life for African Americans than whites. More strikingly, positive ingroup evaluation and ingroup bias were related to greater positive affect about life for African Americans, but lower positive affect for whites."

References

Bell, G. C., Hopson, M. C., Craig, R., & Robinson, N. W. (2014). Exploring black and white accounts of 21st-century racial profiling: Riding and driving while black. *Qualitative Research Reports in Communication, 15*, 33–42.

Bellair, P. E., & McNulty, T. L. (2005). Beyond the bell curve: Community disadvantage and the explanation of black-white differences in adolescent violence. *Criminology, 43*, 1135–1168.

Benson, M. L., Wooldredge, J., Thistlethwaite, A. B., & Fox, G. L. (2004). The correlation between race and domestic violence is confounded with community context. *Social Problems, 51*, 326–342.

Berthelot, E. R., Brown, T. C., Thomas, S. A., & Burgason, K. A. (2016). Racial (in) variance, disadvantage, and lethal violence: A survival analysis of black homicide victimization risk in the United States. *Homicide Studies, 20*, 103–128.

Bonilla-Silva, E. (1997). Rethinking racism: Toward a structural interpretation. *American Sociological Review, 62*, 465–480.

Brooks, M., Ward, C., Euring, M., Townsend, C., White, N., & Hughes, K. L. (2016). Is there a problem officer? Exploring the lived experience of black men and their relationship with law enforcement. *Journal of African American Studies, 20*, 346–362.

Brunson, R. K. (2007). "Police don't like black people": African-American young men's accumulated police experiences. *Criminology & Public Policy, 6*, 71–101.

Brunson, R. K., & Miller, J. (2006). Young black men and urban policing in the United States. *British Journal of Criminology, 46*, 613–640.

Brunson, R. K., & Weitzer, R. (2009). Police relations with black and white youths in different urban neighborhoods. *Urban Affairs Review, 44*, 858–888.

Burt, C. H., Simons, R. L., & Gibbons, F. X. (2012). Racial discrimination, ethnic-racial socialization, and crime a micro-sociological model of risk and resilience. *American Sociological Review, 77*, 648–677.

Chetty, R., Hendren, N., Jones, M. R., & Porter, S. R. (2018). *Race and economic opportunity in the United States: An intergenerational perspective.* National Bureau of Economic Research.

Coates, T-N. (2015). *Between the world and me.* Melbourne: Text Publishing.

Doleac, J. L., & Stein, L. C. D. (2013). The visible hand: Race and online market outcomes. *The Economic Journal, 123*, F469–F492.

Drew, D., & Bialik, K. (2017). *African Americans and Hispanics face extra challenges in getting home loans.* Retrieved from www.pewresearch.org/fact-tank/2017/01/10/African Americans-and-hispanics-face-extra-challenges-in-getting-home-loans/

Du Bois, W. E. B. (1900). The present outlook for the dark races of mankind. *AME Church Review, 17*, 95–110.

Dunbar, A. S., Leerkes, E. M., Coard, S. I., Supple, A. J., & Calkins, S. (2016). An integrative conceptual model of parental racial/ethnic and emotion socialization and links to children's social-emotional development among African American families. *Child Development Perspectives, 11*, 16–22, published online.

Dunham, R. G., & Petersen, N. (2017). Making black lives matter. *Criminology & Public Policy, 16*, 341–348, published online.

Edwards, S. B., & Harris, D. (2016). *Black lives matter.* Minneapolis, MN: ABDO.

English, D., Bowleg, L., del Río-González, A. M., Tschann, J. M., Agans, R. P., & Malebranche, D. J. (2017). Measuring black men's police-based discrimination experiences: Development and validation of the Police and Law Enforcement (PLE) scale. *Cultural Diversity and Ethnic Minority Psychology, 23*, 185–199, published online.

Ewens, M., Tomlin, B., & Wang, L. C. (2013). Statistical discrimination or prejudice? A large sample field experiment. *Review of Economics and Statistics, 96*, 119–134.

Fagan, A. A., & Novak, A. (2017). Adverse childhood experiences and adolescent delinquency in a high-risk sample: A comparison of white and black youth. *Youth Violence and Juvenile Justice*, published online.

Fish, R. E. (2017). The racialized construction of exceptionality: Experimental evidence of race/ethnicity effects on teachers' interventions. *Social Science Research, 62*, 317–334.

Gaddis, S. M. (2014). Discrimination in the credential society: An audit study of race and college selectivity in the labor market. *Social Forces, 93*, 1451–1479.

Gates, H. L., & Steele, C. M. (2009). A conversation with Claude M. Steele: Stereotype threat and black achievement. *Du Bois Review: Social Science Research on Race, 6*, 251–271.

Goff, P. A., Jackson, M. C., Di Leone, B. A. L., Culotta, C. M., & DiTomasso, N. A. (2014). The essence of innocence: Consequences of dehumanizing black children. *Journal of Personality and Social Psychology, 106*, 526–545.

Hagan, J., Shedd, C., & Payne, M. R. (2005). Race, ethnicity, and youth perceptions of criminal injustice. *American Sociological Review, 70*, 381–407.

Herda, D. (2016). The specter of discrimination: Fear of interpersonal racial discrimination among adolescents in Chicago. *Social Science Research, 55*, 48–62.

Hirschi, T. (1969). *Causes of Delinquency.* Berkeley, CA: University of California Press.

Ho, A. K., Kteily, N. S., & Chen, J. M. (2017). "You're one of us": Black Americans' use of hypodescent and its association with egalitarianism. *Journal of Personality and Social Psychology, 113*, 753–768.

Isom, D. (2016). An air of injustice? An integrated approach to understanding the link between police injustices and neighborhood rates of violence. *Journal of Ethnicity in Criminal Justice, 14*, 371–392.

Kiecolt, J. K., & Hughes, M. 2017. Racial identity and the quality of life among African Americans and whites in the U.S. *Social Science Research, 67*, 59–71.

Kirk, D. S. (2016). Prisoner reentry and the reproduction of legal cynicism. *Social Problems, 63*, 222–243.

Kirk, D. S., & Papachristos, A. V. (2011). Cultural mechanisms and the persistence of neighborhood violence. *American Journal of Sociology, 116*, 1190–1233.

Kirk, D. S., & Papachristos, A. V. (2017). Concentrated disadvantage, the persistence of legal cynicism, and crime: Revisiting the conception of "culture" in criminology. In F. T. Cullen, P. Wilcox, R. J. Sampson, & B. Dooley (Eds.), *Challenging criminological theory: The legacy of Ruth Kornhauser* (pp. 259–274). New Brunswick, NJ: Transaction.

Klonoff, E. A., Landrine, H., & Ullman, J. B. (1999). Racial discrimination and psychiatric symptoms among African Americans. *Cultural Diversity and Ethnic Minority Psychology, 5*, 329–339.

Krivo, L., & Peterson, R. (2000). The structural context of homicide: accounting for racial differences in process. *American Sociological Review, 65*(4), 547–559.

Kuroki, M. (2016). An analysis of perceptions of job insecurity among white and black workers in the United States: 1977–2012. *The Review of Black Political Economy, 43*, 289–300.

Massey, D. S. (1990). American apartheid: Segregation and the making of the underclass. *American Journal of Sociology, 96*, 329–357.

Massey, D. S. (2005). Racial discrimination in housing: A moving target. *Social Problems, 52*, 148–151.

Massey, D. S., & Denton, N. A. (1993). *American apartheid: Segregation and the making of the underclass.* Cambridge, MA: Harvard University Press.

Mayrl, D., & Saperstein, A. (2013). When white people report racial discrimination: The role of region, religion, and politics. *Social Science Research, 42*, 742–754.

McNeil, S., Reynolds, J. E., Fincham, F. D., & Beach, S. R. H. (2016). Parental experiences of racial discrimination and youth racial socialization in two-parent African American families. *Cultural Diversity and Ethnic Minority Psychology, 22*, 268–276.

Newport, F. (2014). *In U.S., 24% of young black men say police dealings unfair: More likely to perceive police treatment more unfair than four other situations.* Retrieved from www.gallup.com/poll/163523/one-four-young-black-men-say-police-dealings-unfair.aspx

Ng, F. F., Sze, I. N., Tamis-LeMonda, C. S., & Ruble, D. N. (2017). Immigrant Chinese Mothers' socialization of achievement in children: A strategic adaptation to the host society. *Child Devoplment, 88*, 979–995.

Nix, J., Campbell, B. A., Byers, E. H., & Alpert, G. P. (2017). A bird's eye view of civilians killed by police in 2015. *Criminology & Public Policy, 16*, 309–340, published online.

Noble, R. (2006). *Black rage in the American prison system.* New York, NY: LFB Scholarly Publishing.

Oshinsky, D. M. (1997). *Worse than slavery.* New York, NY: Free Press.

Ousey, G. C. (1999). Homicide, structural factors, and the racial invariance assumption. *Criminology, 37*, 405–426.

Ousey, G. C., & Lee, M. R. (2004). Investigating the connections between race, illicit drug markets, and lethal violence, 1984–1997. *Journal of Research in Crime and Delinquency, 41*, 352–383.

Pager, D. (2003). The mark of a criminal record. *American Journal of Sociology, 108*, 937–975.

Pager, D., & Pedulla, D. S. (2015). Race, self-selection, and the job search process. *American Journal of Sociology, 120*, 1005–1054.

Papachristos, A. V., Hureau, D. M., & Braga, A. A. (2013). The corner and the crew: The influence of geography and social networks on gang violence. *American Sociological Review, 78*, 417–447.

Paradies, Y., Denson, B. J., Elias, N., Priest, A., Pieterse, A., Gupta, A., . . . Gee, G. (2015). Racism as a determinant of health: A systematic review and meta-analysis. *PLOS One, 10*, published online.

Parker, K. F., Stansfield, R., & McCall, P. L. (2016). Temporal changes in racial violence, 1980 to 2006: A latent trajectory approach. *Journal of Criminal Justice, 47*, 1–11.

Pascoe, E. A., & Richman, L. (2009). Perceived discrimination and health: A meta-analytic review. *Psychological Bulletin, 135*, 531–554.

Peterson, R. D., & Krivo, L. J. (2005). Macrostructural analyses of race, ethnicity, and violent crime: Recent lessons and new directions for research. *Annual Review of Sociology, 31*, 331–356.

Peterson, R. D., & Krivo, L. J. (2010). *Divergent social worlds: Neighborhood crime and the racial-spatial divide*. New York, NY: Russell Sage Foundation

Riina, E. M., Martin, A., Gardner, M., & Brooks-Gunn, J. (2013). Context matters: Links between neighborhood discrimination, neighborhood cohesion and African American adolescents' adjustment. *Journal of Youth and Adolescence, 42*, 136–146.

Robinson, C. D. (1993). The production of black violence in Chicago. In D. F. Greenberg (Ed.), *Crime and capitalism: Readings in Marxist criminology* (pp. 366–404). Philadelphia, PA: Temple University Press.

Rogers, L. O., & Meltzoff, A. N. (2016). Is gender more important and meaningful than race? An analysis of racial and gender identity among black, white, and mixed-race children. *Cultural Diversity and Ethnic Minority Psychology, 23*, 323–334, published online.

Russell, K. K. (1992). Development of a black criminology and the role of the black criminologist. *Justice Quarterly, 9*, 667–683.

Saleem, F. T., English, D., Busby, D. R., Lambert, S. F., Harrison, A., Stock, M. L., & Gibbons, F. X. (2016). The impact of African American parents' racial discrimination experiences and perceived neighborhood cohesion on their racial socialization practices. *Journal of Youth and Adolescence, 45*, 1338–1349.

Sampson, R. J. (2013). The place of context: A theory and strategy for criminology's hard problems. *Criminology, 51*, 1–31.

Sampson, R. J., Morenoff, J. D., & Raudenbush, S. (2005). Social anatomy of racial and ethnic disparities in violence. *American Journal of Public Health, 95*, 224–232.

Sharkey, P. (2013). *Stuck in place: Urban neighborhoods and the end of progress toward racial equality*. Chicago, IL: University of Chicago Press.

Shaw, C. R., & McKay, H. D. (1931). *Social factors in juvenile delinquency* (Wickersham Commission). Washington, DC: Government Press.

Shaw, C. R., & McKay, H. D. (1949). Rejoinder. *American Sociological Review, 14*, 608–617.

Shihadeh, E. S., & Shrum, W. (2004). Serious crime in urban neighborhoods: Is there a race effect? *Sociological Spectrum, 24*, 507–533.

Skolnick, J. H. (2007). Racial profiling—then and now. *Criminology & Public Policy, 6*, 65–70.

100   James D. Unnever

Skorinko, J. L., & Spellman, B. A. (2013). Stereotypic crimes: How group-crime associations affect memory and (sometimes) verdicts and sentencing. *Victims & Offenders, 8*, 278–307.

Small, M. L., & McDermott, M. (2006). The presence of organizational resources in poor urban neighborhoods: An analysis of average and contextual effects. *Social Forces, 84*, 1697–1724.

Snodgrass, J. (1976). Clifford R. Shaw and Henry D. McKay: Chicago criminologists. *The British Journal of Criminology, 16*, 1–19.

Steele, C. M. (1997). A threat "in the air": How stereotypes shape intellectual identity and performance. *American Psychologist, 52*, 613–629.

Steffensmeier, D., Ulmer, J. T., Feldmeyer, B. E. N., & Harris, C. T. (2010). Scope and conceptual issues in testing the race—crime invariance thesis: Black, white, and Hispanic comparisons. *Criminology, 48*, 1133–1169.

Tyler, T. R. (1990). *Why people obey the law: Procedural justice, legitimacy, and compliance.* New Haven, CT: Yale University Press.

Ulmer, J. T., Harris, C. T., & Steffensmeier, D. (2012). Racial and ethnic disparities in structural disadvantage and crime: White, black, and hispanic comparisons. *Social Science Quarterly, 93*, 799–819.

Unnever, J. D. (2008). Two worlds far apart: Black-white differences in beliefs about why African American men are disproportionately imprisoned. *Criminology, 46*, 511–538.

Unnever, J. D. (2014). A theory of African American offending a test of core propositions. *Race and Justice, 4*, 98–123, published online.

Unnever, J. D., Barnes, J. C., & Cullen, F. T. (2016). The racial invariance thesis revisited: Testing an African American theory of offending. *Journal of Contemporary Criminal Justice, 32*, 7–26.

Unnever, J. D., Cullen, F. T., & Barnes, J. (2016a). Racial discrimination and pathways to delinquency testing a theory of African American offending. *Race and Justice, 7*, 350–373, published online.

Unnever, J. D., Cullen, F. T., & Barnes, J. (2016b). Racial discrimination, weakened school bonds, and problematic behaviors testing a theory of African American offending. *Journal of Research in Crime and Delinquency, 53*, 139–164.

Unnever, J. D., Cullen, F. T., Mathers, S. A., McClure, T. E., & Allison, M. C. (2009). Racial discrimination and Hirschi's criminological classic: A chapter in the sociology of knowledge. *Justice Quarterly, 26*, 377–409.

Unnever, J. D., & Gabbidon, S. L. (2011). *A theory of African American offending: Race, racism, and crime.* New York, NY: Taylor & Francis.

Unnever, J. D., & Owusu-Bempah, A. (2017). A Black criminology matters. In J. D. Unnever, S. Gabbidon, & C. Chouhy (Eds.), *Building a Black criminology: Race, theory, and crime.* New York, NY: Routledge.

Unnever, J. D., Owusu-Bempah, A., & Deryol, R. (2017). A test of the differential involvement hypothesis. *Race and Justice.*

Walters, G. D. (2018). Black—white and male—female differences in criminal thinking: Examining instrumental and expressive motives for crime in federal supervisees. *The Prison Journal, 98*, 277–293, published online.

Wilkins, C. L., Wellman, J. D., Babbitt, L. G., Toosi, N. R., & Schad, K. D. (2015). You can win but I can't lose: Bias against high-status groups increases their zero-sum beliefs about discrimination. *Journal of Experimental Social Psychology, 57*, 1–14.

5

Black Criminology in the 21st Century

Katheryn Russell-Brown

When I began graduate school, I had no particular interest in focusing on how race impacts the criminal justice system. During my years of graduate study, I became increasingly intrigued with how criminologists studied race as a variable in analyzing criminal offending and the impact of race on justice system processing. By the time I completed my doctoral studies in 1992, race had become a focal point of my research, in large part because of what I learned about race and crime during graduate school.

Three observations about race and crime were salient. First, that across offense types, geography, and methodologies, race was consistently a significant predictor of involvement in criminal offending. Specifically, research findings reported a clear relationship between Blackness and criminal offending—that Blacks are disproportionately more likely to engage in criminal offending. Second, much of the research that used race as an independent variable (with gender, education, and socioeconomic status), did not present a nuanced framework for understanding race. This matters because of the salience of race as a predictor of criminal involvement. It also matters because the absence of a detailed look at how and why race matters (e.g., at individual and systemwide levels) may foster the presumption that there is a connection between Black skin and crime. Without a historical framework for understanding race, the race–crime link may unwittingly promote biological perspectives of the relationship between race and crime. Third, the empirical evaluations of race were themselves racialized. Researchers often used "race" as shorthand for "minority." And more often than not, "minority" was conflated with "Blacks." This was a notable imbalance, especially since it seemed to suggest that studying race meant studying African Americans (thereby tacitly supporting a link between Blackness and criminality). The resulting equation was unmistakable: *Race + Crime = Blacks + Crime*. This racial calculus was buttressed by the fact that there was no other racial group that could be said to be so strongly linked to crime. For instance, while there was plenty of criminological research on Blacks and crime and Black criminality, there was no robust academic interest in White criminality (Russell, 2009).

My reaction to these observations was frustration and puzzlement. I sought to articulate and analyze these concerns in my first article, "Development of a Black Criminology and the Role of the Black Criminologist" (Russell, 1992). This was my academic ode to race and criminology—more accurately, an ode to criminology's deep racial voids. The goal was to assert that Blackness matters in criminology, far beyond its use as a variable. Specifically, the call for a Black Criminology was a call for expanding the theoretical framework for race and crime research. Done properly, a Black Criminology would work the same way that feminist criminology works to fairly represent women's experiences in criminology scholarship. Theoretical approaches that would be categorized as part of a Black Criminology would include novel, African American–centered analyses designed to understand Black involvement in the justice system. The development of a Black Criminology seeks to move the discipline of criminology toward a full accounting and reckoning with the intersections of race, racism, and crime. At its core, the development of a Black Criminology requires that Black criminologists set the agenda for this scholarship. The argument is that leadership by Black criminologists is essential for both the legitimacy and longevity of a Black Criminology.

Now, more than 25 years later, this essay revisits the earlier argument for developing a Black Criminology. This discussion is divided into five sections. The first part provides an overview of the key arguments and components of the proposed Black Criminology paradigm. This includes a review of how scholars have responded to the argument for a Black Criminology and whether its development is essential to the vibrancy of criminology. The second part looks at how race matters to the discipline of criminology in contemporary times. This section explores the ways in which criminology has expanded and how this has influenced race-based analyses of the justice system. The third part assesses whether the best fit for "Black Criminology" is within an existing theoretical framework, such as critical race criminology. An alternate view is that Black Criminology should be a stand-alone theoretical approach, one with the potential to develop and expand in ways different from recognized approaches. The fourth part takes up the language of race and crime, with a specific evaluation of the impact of using "Black" to label an approach to understanding criminal offending and justice system processing of African Americans. This section looks at how language influences the receptivity to and viability of a criminological perspective. The fifth and final section identifies some key steps necessary to move Black Criminology from the margins to the center.

Key Arguments, Critiques, Adjustments, and a Note on Mainstream Silence

Over the past two decades, the idea of a Black Criminology has gained slow but steady traction. This section details the goals and structure of a Black Criminology. This is followed by the scholarly critiques offered in response and some additional considerations for revising the approach of a Black Criminology.

Key Arguments of Black Criminology

The premise of a Black Criminology is that race is a central organizing theme in understanding Black offending, Black victims, and how Blacks are processed in the criminal justice system. Its goal is to highlight Blackness in mainstream discussions of criminology and criminal justice in ways that place race at the center of the analysis. In the late 1980s and 1990s, much of the writing and research on race and the justice system examined race as an independent variable. These analyses typically did not go beyond stating that race was a significant predictor of, e.g., involvement in crime. Thus, race was highlighted as a significant and consistent predictor of criminal offending, but an understanding of how race works was limited. Scholars interested in teasing out how race matters in criminology have observed that because race is a social construct, by itself, it is insufficient to explain crime and criminal offending. Rather, it is how race interacts with other variables and the larger institutional structures that presents a fuller picture (e.g., Hawkins, McKean, White, & Martin, 2017; Owusu-Bempah, 2017). A Black Criminology addresses the need to see race not as the end of analyses of justice system processing but in some ways as a beginning point. For instance, one race-related issue that is gaining more research focus is colorism. The ultimate aim of a Black Criminology is to push the discipline to align itself with the historical realities of race and racism for African Americans in the United States.

Responses and Critiques

A number of scholars have made specific reference to the notion of a Black Criminology. These scholars embrace the idea that a Black-centered criminology is a necessary pursuit, and some have offered their own articulations of a Black Criminology and how it might move the discipline forward. In general, criminologists who have commented on the idea of developing a Black Criminology agree that there is a need for this subfield (Glynn, 2014; Kitossa, 2012).

A few journal articles responded directly to the 1990s call for developing a Black Criminology. In their 2000 piece, Ihekwoaba Onwuidwe and Michael Lynch "heed the call" for a Black Criminology. They note that although issues of race have become more popular within criminology, the discipline still employs an ahistorical analysis of crime (Onwudiwe & Lynch, 2000). This has resulted in a glaring theoretical deficit in criminology. Because the history of race and crime is organized around racist assumptions and stereotypes, investigating this history has to be part of any attempt to understand how race matters in justice system outcomes (p. 183). For instance, Onwudiwe and Lynch discuss their "fertilization of Black criminality" approach:

> It assumes that Black criminality is ingrained in the institutional practices of the justice system in particular and society in general. Fertilization of criminality holds that there are situations whereby opportunities for crime are increased by both the government's action and inaction. For example, the government inaction reflects the inability (or unwillingness) to stop the massive importation of illegal drugs in the United States, while actively incarcerating minority drug violators at a disproportionate rate. (Onwudiwe & Lynch, 2000, p. 192)

This approach offers an alternative lens through which to view drug crimes, drug laws, and race. Onwudiwe and Lynch conclude that a Black criminology is necessary and that Black criminologists should lead the way (p. 194).

In 2003, Everette Penn wrote an article supportive of the call for a Black Criminology (Penn, 2003). He argues that the discipline's reliance on stagnant theories of crime make it more susceptible to reverting to racist theories of crime causation. Penn identifies several strengths of developing a Black Criminology, primarily the fact that it supports the identification of "Black commonalities"—e.g., racial discrimination, profiling, stereotyping, etc.—as a base for investigating how these commonalities impact various sub-groups within the Black community (as victims, offenders, and individuals subject to processing in the justice system). Penn notes that a Black Criminology's explicit focus on race is a recognized strength, particularly when compared with other theories that focus on class.

As to which scholars can and should engage in developing a Black Criminology, Penn agrees that it should be open to anyone who wants to contribute. Ultimately, Penn states, "Black Criminology is not simply a body of work written by Blacks for Blacks: It is the use of sound social research practices by criminologists to grasp the unique and diverse variables associated with Blacks who commit crime" (p. 320). Noting that White criminologists study White offending, he rejects the tacit assumption by some that Black criminologists cannot objectively study Black offending. This assumption is another example of an unsupported negative racial label placed on Blacks, in this instance, Black criminologists—that they are biased and unqualified. Penn concludes by observing that a Black Criminology is designed to address the question at the root of criminology, "Why does crime occur?" (p. 325).

Other scholars have analyzed how the argument for a Black Criminology contrasts with the argument for developing a "minority perspective" in criminology (e.g., Kitossa, 2012, p. 215; Owusu-Bempah, 2017). In his 2017 article, Akwasi Owusu-Bempah argues that the longstanding debate about whether it is disproportionate offending by Blacks or racial discrimination against Blacks that explains skewed Black involvement in the justice system is due to mainstream criminology's failure to understand that these are "mutually reinforcing phenomena—both rooted in the history of American race relations" (pp. 24–25). He argues for an intersectional approach—noting that however race works in the justice system, it does not work alone. For instance, to unpack racial profiling requires an examination of the interplay between two forms of oppression, both race and class, as well as history.

James Unnever and Shaun Gabbidon's theory of Black offending offers the clearest and most detailed articulation of a theoretical approach that demonstrates the need for a Black Criminology (Unnever & Gab-bidon, 2011). In their book, *Theory of African American Offending*, they detail the construction of their theory, which they situate within a Black Criminology paradigm. A Black Criminology fills a void in the crimi-nological canon by providing a "more holistic and fuller understanding of African American offending" (p. 10). Unnever and Gabbidon situ-ate their theory under the Black Criminology umbrella. They expressly reject the idea that general theories of crime (e.g., Gottfredson & Hirs-chi, 1990) can explain why all crime happens. They note that general theories fail in particular to explain Black offending, because African Americans have racially unique experiences, such as racial subordina-tion. Under some conditions, they predict, these experiences enhance the likelihood of Black criminal involvement. To be clear, Unnever and Gabbidon do not deny that other factors play a role in criminal involve-ment, only that when discussing African Americans, considerations of the micro level impact of society's racial ranking are important. Their theory of Black offending exemplifies the type of work a Black Crimi-nology is structured to include. Their theory is novel, expands beyond mainstream criminology borders, and offers a potentially transformative approach to how racial bias interacts with Black offending patterns.

In their book *Roots of African American Violence*, Darnell Hawkins, Jerome McKean, Norman White, and Christine Martin (2017) propose a historically rooted criminological theory that explains Black offend-ing. While their work does not explicitly reference a Black Criminol-ogy, their approach represents a clear attempt to ground criminological theory in the history of race and racism. They rebuild social disorganiza-tion, a mainstream theory, and address how it should be reconstructed to account for the disproportionately high rates of Black violence. They highlight, for instance, the need to evaluate within-race cultural differ-ences between Blacks. The approach presented by Hawkins et al. rep-resents a paradigm shift in that it pushes past a monolithic Black racial box. Their work clearly exemplifies and fits within the framework of a Black Criminology.

Developing a Black Criminology has the support of criminologists outside the United States as well. In Canada and the United Kingdom, Black criminologists have embraced the idea of a Black Criminology. For instance, Martin Glynn's scholarship uses Black Criminology as a framework to examine desistance. He argues that there is a need to develop a "black criminology of desistance" (Glynn, 2014, p. 50). With his study of the choices Black men make *not* to engage in crime, Glynn presents a shift in the typical theoretical gaze placed on Blacks and crime. His research focus posits that there is as much value in understanding why people choose not to offend as there is in understanding why they choose to offend. Beyond theory, he details an "on road" method of research designed to capture Black life in action (p. 53). In discussing the work of an "on road" criminologist, Glynn states,

> I am not talking about holding focus groups in comfy constructed spaces, or handing out questionnaires in the safety of a classroom, or sitting in the comfort of an office, tape recording someone who has signed up to your research. I'm talking about dialogue that takes place in shopping centres, barber shops, bookies, car parks, street corners, and other locations within the confines of the inner cities. (Glynn, 2014, p. 53)

Notably, Du Bois described these types of practices as "car window" sociology (Du Bois, 1978).[1] Glynn's work not only details the richness of data collected when the degrees of separation between the researcher and subject disappear, but importantly, he also upholds "on road" methods as equal in rigor and heft to more mainstream forms of qualitative research. His research is precisely what the Black Criminology rubric is designed to cover.

Adjustments

As initially formulated, a Black Criminology focuses on expanding the theoretical framework for understanding how race works with criminal justice. It makes sense, however, to expand its scope beyond theory. This expansion should include the identification of research methods that will allow for new ways of thinking about race, social structures, and crime. This expansion also means that empirical tests of theories that fall under the Black Criminology rubric are also included within a Black Criminology—such as an empirical test of James Unnever and Shaun Gabbidon's theory of African American offending (Unnever, 2014).

Mainstream Academic Silence

While an enthusiastic and robust group of criminologists has embraced the idea of a Black Criminology, it has mostly been met with academic silence. The silence is likely due to several factors. One, there is silence because most criminologists are not aware of the argument for a Black Criminology. Two, perhaps more scholars are aware of the argument and are waiting for Black criminologists to "lead the way," as was argued should be the case (Russell, 1992, p. 678). Three, some criminologists may be reluctant to address race directly in their scholarship. Perhaps the academic shyness about engaging in race-based analysis results from the fact that addressing race is challenging, uncomfortable, and full of pitfalls. Some criminologists may be reluctant because they do not want to be associated with biological theories of crime—whose early theorists portrayed Blacks as subhuman and savage (e.g., Cesare Lombroso). Regardless of the reason, the discipline's silence makes a clear and unequivocal statement: The status quo approaches to understanding how race interacts with criminal justice are satisfactory and sufficient.

Changing Landscapes: Where Black Criminology Stands Today

Over the past two decades, there has been a marked increase in the criminological scholarship on race. The development of a more robust analysis of race and justice is particularly noticeable when compared with our international peers. For instance, Alpa Parmer notes that UK scholars pay little attention to research at the intersections of criminology and race (Parmar, 2017). Several factors have enhanced the presence and viability of race as a topic of serious academic inquiry scrutiny in criminology.

Salience of Race

One factor is that more researchers have taken up the subject of race as it relates to crime. Today, race and crime is considered a mainstream criminological issue. In fact, interest in crime and race has moved beyond the halls of academia. It is now a mainstream public issue. The popularity of Michelle Alexander's breakthrough book, *The New Jim Crow: Mass Incarceration in the Age of Colorblindness* (Alexander, 2010), helped to propel race and crime scholarship from the margins of criminology. In fact, there is a long list of books that tackle the intersections of race and crime (Greene, Gabbidon, & Wilson, 2017).[2] Notably, a number of these books, including Alexander's, are not authored by criminologists.[3] This attests to the broad and general interest in questions of race and justice. Another example is Ta-Nehisi Coates's book, *Between the World and Me* (Coates, 2015), which explores in part this country's history of oppressive policing against Blacks and police killings of African Americans in contemporary times.

Growing Scholarly Focus on Race and Crime

The growing number of scholars who are interested in studying how race impacts various social institutions, including the criminal justice system, is another factor in the advancement of race scholarship. Many of these scholars are African Americans (e.g., Greene, Gabbidon, & Wilson, 2017).[4] It seems reasonable to estimate that today there are a few dozen criminologists who consider themselves race and crime scholars. This includes the work of Black criminologists in other countries (e.g., Agozino, 2004; Glynn, 2014; Kitossa, 2012; Philips & Bowling, 2002.)

Increasing Ranks of Black Criminologists

A third factor is the growing number of Black criminologists. Between 1980 and 1990, 27 Blacks were awarded criminology doctoral degrees, compared with 297 Whites during the same period (Russell, 1992). In 1990, Blacks comprised 5% of the criminology doctorates (2 of the 37 doctorates that year were African American).

In their 2016 article, Meda Chesney-Lind and Nicholas Chagnon detail their research on the evolution of gender and racial diversity within criminology. They take their measure by examining the theoretical development within criminology, the gender and race of scholars in the discipline, and the types of articles published in top-ranking criminology journals. Their research analyzes the membership of the American Society of Criminology (ASC), the premier conference for criminal justice educators, researchers, practitioners, and policy makers (Chesney-Lind & Chagnon, 2016). They found that Blacks comprised 7.1% of the ASC membership.[5] Chesney-Lind and Chagnon conclude that while today there are more criminologists of color, these increases have not fundamentally altered the racial composition of who holds positions of prestige within the ASC (e.g., publications in top journals, winners of top ASC awards) and who holds rank-and-file positions (Chesney-Lind & Chagnon, 2016, p. 327).[6]

They conclude that the epistemology of criminology is both positivist and male centered, and research that does not fit into this mold is less likely to be published in top-ranked journals.[7]

In their comprehensive study of the presence of African American scholars in criminology, Helen Taylor Greene, Shaun Gabbidon, and Sean Wilson found that Blacks make up approximately 6% of all criminology professors (40 people) (Greene et al., 2017). Blacks comprise 5% of the faculty members at the top five criminology programs. They found that Black students make up 11% of all doctoral students. However, Black students comprise only 6% of the doctoral students at the top five criminology/criminal justice doctoral programs (Greene et al., 2017, pp. 8–9).[8] Their look at other measures of achievement for Black criminologists, including presence on editorial boards and receipt of discipline-wide awards, shows moderate progress. As was true for Chesney-Lind and Chagnon's research, race statistics are not consistently available across categories. However, both studies show similar racial patterns regarding the involvement of Blacks in the discipline.

As this discussion makes clear, there are many ways to assess racial progress within the discipline. Numerical diversity of scholars in the field is only one measure of racial diversity. The increasing number of scholars of color has not led to broad transformative changes in disciplinary approaches to understanding the race–crime connection. In evaluating statistics on race and gender in the discipline, Chesney-Lind and Chagnon suggest a caveat: "mere numerical inclusion of women and non-Whites within the academy does not necessarily mean better representation of these groups' intellectual perspectives" (Chesney-Lind & Chagnon, 2016, p. 329).

Expanding Scholarly Outlets

Another reason for the increased prominence of race and crime research is the growing number of scholarly outlets for this work. In recent years, various academic outlets, including journals, special issues, and book series, have highlighted race and justice scholarship.[9] Also, there are more books, edited volumes, and text readers that focus on race and justice issues.[10] Notably, most of these publications focus on African Americans and the criminal justice system.

Where's Home for Black Criminology?

As detailed in the previous section, the topography of race and criminology has changed over the past two decades. One of the major shifts has been that research examining how race impacts justice system outcomes is no longer relegated to criminology's periphery. Scores of articles, books, and reports document how race matters in the administration of justice. This research includes a look at how racial groups experience crime and justice system outcomes, (e.g., Ball & Hartlep, 2017; Urbina, 2012), how, in comparative terms, different racial groups are treated within the justice system, the direct and collateral consequences of crime policies (e.g., Turanovic, Rodriguez, & Pratt, 2012), and the theoretical explanations of how race matters in offending patterns (Unnever & Gabbidon, 2011). While the amount of race-focused research appears to have increased, race and crime research is still done mostly through mainstream theoretical and methodological approaches. Over the past decade, there has been a notable number of articles and books that apply a critical approach to examine how the framing of race and crime within society impacts perceptions of crime and, in turn, involvement in the criminal justice system.

Even with the growing interest in the topic, some foundational questions about the development of a Black Criminology remain. Specifically, where exactly does it fit within criminology's disciplinary framework? Let's examine two approaches to situating Black Criminology. Black Criminology might be framed as an approach that falls under an existing criminological paradigm. Alternatively, it could be labeled as a stand-alone theoretical perspective. This section considers arguments for both approaches.

Critical Race Criminology

In recent years, critical race criminology has emerged as one of the favored critiques of how social structures work to produce and continue to embed race discrimination within the justice system. There is a vibrant though relatively sparse criminology literature that falls under the heading "critical race criminology." Karen Glover describes this approach:

> A critical race criminology . . . places race at the fore of social analyses. It is concerned with the representations of race, crime, law, and justice specifically as they operate in the production of knowledge . . . [It] addresses traditional and contemporary examinations of race and criminology and contests the ways the discipline produces and represents race by focusing on . . . the social narrative of marginalized communities. (Glover, 2009, p. 2)

Critical or radical criminology, which emerged in the 1960s and 1970s (e.g., Taylor, Walton, & Young, 1975) and critical race theory (Crenshaw et al., 1995), which emerged in the 1980s, set the theoretical foundation for critical race criminology and related approaches, such as critical Whiteness studies. The research done using these analytical frameworks offer wholesale critiques of the ways that criminology reinforces and imposes a systemic racial hierarchy (e.g., Seigel, 2017). This work also investigates how Whiteness works as a racial shield, one that both protects racial privilege and denies its existence (e.g., Dirks, Heldman, & Zack, 2015). Most of the research that constitutes Black Criminology fits within the above description of critical race criminology. This raises a question: If the research and theorizing done under the Black Criminology rubric can fit into an already recognized sub-area, does Black Criminology need to exist as a separate subfield? With these frameworks in mind, we turn now to consider the benefits of keeping Black Criminology separate and the value of incorporating it into a larger existing framework.

Black Criminology as a Subfield Within Critical Race Criminology

Let's now consider whether including Black Criminology within critical race criminology is a preferable alternative to a separate Black Criminology. Including Black Criminology within critical race criminology has strong appeal. First, it is inclusive. Critical race criminology invites critical analyses of the impact of the criminal justice system on all racial groups, individually and combined. This inclusiveness is particularly important when we consider that race and crime research is often framed within a Black/White dichotomy. Encouraging a broader racial landscape for criminological research—one that includes a robust and not simply a tangential look at Latinos, Native Americans, Asians, and Muslims—is necessary. This broad research umbrella creates space to address contemporary manifestations of how the justice system responds to the actions of specific subgroups, for example, "Dreamers" and White supremacists, and as well, "shades of whiteness" (Smith, 2014, p. 115).

Second, critical race criminology could be seen as a fitting space for Black Criminology because it invites a critique of dominant criminological paradigms. It provides a broader framework for examining how race and racism operate than mainstream theoretical approaches. Special journal issues devoted to critical race criminology and, relatedly,

Whiteness studies, demonstrate the breadth of topics that fall under this approach.[11]

Black Criminology as a Stand-Alone Subfield

The arguments for maintaining Black Criminology as a separate subfield are most compelling. One of the express goals of developing a Black Criminology is to highlight the theoretical and empirical work of Black criminologists (Russell, 1992, p. 678). Thus, it must be noted that almost all of the research written under the heading of critical race criminology and critical Whiteness studies has been written by White academics. Justin Smith and Travis Linnemann acknowledge this concern:

> We understand the inherent contradictions here, in that a group of mostly white academics, taking up the subject of whiteness, is embedded in and runs the risk of perpetuating the same sorts of privilege we aim to critique. (Smith & Linnemann, 2015, p. 102)

Any theoretical tension between the approaches of Black Criminology and critical race criminology may lie in research emphasis rather than focus. The perception may be that critical race criminology leans more toward critical analysis of the justice system than racial analysis. While this criticism may be debated, it is reasonable to support the independent development of a Black Criminology.

A Black Criminology should primarily reflect the perspectives and paradigms developed by Black criminologists. The fact that most of the critical race criminology scholarship is authored by White academics—all of whom support a racial critique of the justice system—is another argument for allowing a Black Criminology to develop and exist as a stand-alone approach. To be clear, criminologists of any color can contribute to a Black Criminology. However, ensuring that it is Black criminologists who create the foundation for this approach, is necessary to the authenticity of the perspective. Further, allowing Black criminologists to lead the way creates empirical and theoretical space to support, encourage, and acknowledge racialized approaches that have historically been dismissed, misused, or usurped. W.E.B. Du Bois's extensive empirical research published in *The Philadelphia Negro* offers an example (Du Bois, 1899). A growing number of scholars have argued that Du Bois should be acknowledged as one of the founders of the famed Chicago school of criminology (Gabbidon, 1996, 1999; Morris, 2015). They note that his work on race and crime in Philadelphia in the late 1800s was completed before the Chicago school scholarship and that Robert Sampson—father of the Chicago school—was aware of and familiar with some of Du Bois's research. And as Unnever and Gabbidon note, in *The Philadelphia Negro*, Du Bois was "doing Black criminology" (Unnever & Gabbidon, 2011, p. 8).

Black criminologists pursuing a Black Criminology can work in conjunction with scholars of other races who are interested in examining how Blackness matters in the criminal justice system. This is a nonessentialist stance, with a proviso.[12] Black Criminology should be *led by* Black scholars who study crime. These researchers can identify, test, and apply novel and previously marginalized theories and methods to understand for instance, racial disparities in arrest. A look at the connection between colonialism and criminology has been a topic of exploration for some Black criminologists (e.g., Agozino, 2004; Kitossa, 2012; Tatum, 2000). In his 2012 piece, Tamari Kitossa questions the origins of criminology and argues that it has always had a glaring blind spot regarding the foundational role of colonialism in defining and punishing crime (Kitossa, 2012). He raises several queries:

> What is mainstream criminology's connection to colonialism and imperialism? Why has radical criminology failed to develop a thorough-going critique of racism, internal/colonialism and imperialism vis-à-vis the continued White and Western dominance of the field? (p. 205)

Further, based on the disproportionately high levels of Black involvement in the justice system, Black criminologists are more likely to know someone who is or has been involved in the justice system, know someone who knows someone who is or has been involved in the justice system, or to have had direct experience with the justice system themselves. It is reasonable to believe that this proximity to policing, court processing, and the correctional system impacts a person's viewpoint on how to interpret, study, and correct the existing criminal-legal system. For example, Black criminologists may place greater weight (than mainstream criminologists) on desistence, why some people decide not to engage in crime (e.g., Glynn, 2014).[13] Another example of a difference is that Black criminologists may be disproportionately more likely to engage in hands-on research, which may impact the framing of research questions and the ultimate research conclusions.

In light of the above arguments, Black Criminology should not be relegated to a subarea within critical race criminology. In fact, one of the problems that a Black Criminology seeks to address is the lack of a home for criminological approaches that do not fit existing frameworks. More pointedly, the objective of establishing a Black Criminology is to *build a home* for Black-focused investigations of criminal offending and justice system outcomes. The goal is not to have Black Criminology treated like a roomer who rents space in the home of another theoretical perspective.

The Language and Grammar of Race and Crime

We now turn to consider "Black Criminology" as terminology. What does "Black Criminology" mean? Does the label make a statement? In his analysis of the language of crime, Michael Coyle pushes for a consideration of the ways that language presents and shapes reality. He observes that the words we use to talk about justice create "complex and intertwined perceptions that construct 'crimes,' 'offenders,' and entire paradigms of justice" (Coyle, 2010, p. 14). For instance, in mainstream parlance, terms such as "innocent victim" and "tough on crime" are imbued with specific meanings. The former may mean a person who has been unfairly victimized and whose victimizer deserves harsh punishment, while the latter may refer to someone who measures justice by the severity of the punishment an offender receives (it is also a label assigned to conservative politicians).[14] Over time, these terms and their assigned meanings have become routinized, dominant, and culturally embedded.

There are several concerns with using the term "Black Criminology." The first is that it reinforces the association between Blackness and crime. Joining "Black" and "crime" together suggests that the two concepts are connected. Unfortunately, for many people, the presumed connection is that Blacks are more violent, more deviant, and thus in need of more control by the system. Language that links criminality with Blackness—Black Criminology—arguably reifies existing structures of racial dominance. "Black Criminology" may reinforce the dominant narrative of the *criminalblackman* (Russell-Brown, 2009, p. 2).

Over decades, psychological studies have consistently shown that there are broad and deeply held negative stereotypes about African Americans (e.g., Bobo & Charles, 2009). These stereotypical images typically link Blacks with violence and criminality (e.g., Eberhardt, Goff, Purdie, & Davies, 2004). Researchers have also determined that this stereotype is bidirectional: "[J]ust as Black faces and Black bodies can trigger thoughts of crime, thinking of crime can trigger thoughts of Black people" (p. 876).

This research raises the question of the degree to which using the label "Black Criminology" is shaped by the existing framework of justice language and terminology. In other words, is the "Black Criminology" label itself a reflection of mainstream stereotypes about the connection between Blackness and criminality? After all, "Black Criminology" fits comfortably into the existing racialized language of crime, which includes "Black crime," "Black-on-Black crime," "Black criminality," etc. The prevalence of the Black–crime link is even more apparent when we consider that mainstream criminology rarely uses racial terms to describe crime committed by Whites or that link Whiteness with criminality. For instance, "White crime" and victimization are rarely investigated as racially specific criminological phenomena (Russell-Brown, 2009, p. 128). This is true even when there are specific crimes and delinquencies portrayed in the media as having primarily White victims and offenders such as the opioid drug epidemic (e.g., Katz & Goodnough, 2017). It is important to investigate whether our "justice-related language" helps to sustain racially biased discourses and practices within the criminal justice system (Coyle, 2010, p. 15).

It is noted that there is a compelling alternative view of what the term "Black Criminology" signals. For some, it may work as a countercriminological narrative to the standard Blacks-and-crime connection. Viewed this way, "Black Criminology" reflects empowerment, self-determination, and racial resistance. In this alternative framework, Black Criminology is comparable (though on a much smaller scale) to the term "Black Power," which was widely used during the civil rights struggles of the 1960s.

A second concern with using "Black Criminology" is that it implies that Black criminality is a singular issue, one that does not intersect with other social problems or one that is not part of the much larger structural apparatus of justice administration. Black Criminology offers a big tent of approaches and perspectives. Under this tent, all manner of approaches to understanding African American offending and victimization and the racialized responses of the justice system are welcome (e.g., Agozino, 2004; Unnever & Gabbidon, 2011).

A third issue with the "Black Criminology" label is that its use may overshadow research examining the relationship between other racial groups and crime. Specifically, as already noted, there needs to be a broader look at White criminality (Russell-Brown, 2009). In fact, there is room in the Black Criminology paradigm to address White crime. The push for research on White-on-White crime and punishment is another example of how Black Criminology offers a unique perspective on race and crime studies. In this way, Black Criminology also pushes back against the normalized link between Blackness and criminal offending. There is room within Black Criminology to address other racial groups, including Latinos, Native Americans, Asians, and Whites.

A Note on "White Criminology"

Based on the above discussion, perhaps it makes sense to label this new perspective "White Criminology" rather than "Black Criminology." The theories and empirical research catalogued under Black Criminology could just as easily be placed under the heading of White Criminology. This is especially true for approaches that offer critiques of the role of race in the evolution of the dominant criminological paradigm (e.g., Kitossa, 2012) and critiques of how White privilege functions in criminology research. For instance, Kathryn Henne and Rita Shah examined over 500 criminology articles, published from 2010 to 2012, to see how Whiteness influenced the analysis. Specifically, they looked at the theoretical approach, methodological approach, type of crime being evaluated, variables examined, and whether there was a discussion of race (Henne & Shah, 2013). In studying the texts, two racialized patterns—"White methods"[15]—emerged. They found that researchers either ignored race issues or relegated race to a variable and treated it as separate from other forms of inequality. Henne and Shah conclude that standard empirical methods work to whitewash the ways in which criminological research reinforces racial hierarchies within and across the justice system.

The initial reaction to naming this subfield "White Criminology" may be to reject and dismiss this flipped racial label. As Richard Delgado has keenly observed, "No one focuses on white crime or sees it as a problem. In fact the very category, 'White Crime,' sounds funny, like some sort of 'debater's trick' (Delgado, 1995, p. 175). Perhaps though, using Whiteness as a framework to discuss Blackness would provide a much-needed jolt to the race and crime discourse.

Next Steps for Building a Black Criminology

A concerted effort is required to push Black Criminology forward. Here are five proposed steps that would raise awareness about a Black Criminology—what it is, why it matters, and where it fits within criminological theory and research. If followed, each will help push Black Criminology from the margins and a little closer to the mainstream of criminology.

1. *Identifying Black Criminology.* Whenever criminologists and sociologists publish work that they consider part of Black Criminology, they should state this explicitly. Black Criminology should be explicitly claimed by scholars in their work.
2. *Teaching Black Criminology in Theory and Race-Related Criminology Courses.* Instructors who teach courses that address criminological theory and/or ones that specifically focus on race and crime should include a discussion of Black Criminology.
3. *Increasing Availability of Race Courses in Criminology/Criminal Justice Doctoral Programs.* The increased attention on race and justice issues should be met with an increased availability of race and crime courses within criminology programs. Ideally, all doctoral programs in criminology should offer a course that substantively addresses issues of race (e.g., Race and Crime or Gender, Race, and Crime). Race and crime literacy should be part of the training and skill set required for a doctorate in criminology (Russell-Brown, 2009).
4. *Increasing Black Criminology Scholarship.* Journal editors and publishers, ASC, and Academy of Criminal Justice Sciences (ACJS) leadership should be encouraged to produce more scholarship that highlights, unpacks, and applies the tenets of Black Criminology.
5. *Expanding Black Criminology Within Professional Societies.*
    a. To my knowledge, the 2016 ASC meetings marked the first time that there was an entire panel session devoted to Black Criminology. Going forward, panel sessions on the broad topic of Black Criminology should be standard for the ASC and other criminology conferences.
    b. Both ASC and ACJS members should consider creating a Black Criminology division. The ASC has a Division on People of Color and Crime (DPCC). However, a separate division on Black Criminology would bring together and provide a platform for scholars, educators, and policy makers who wish to focus on the development and dissemination of Black Criminology. In this way, a Black Criminology division would be comparable to existing divisions within the ASC, such as the Critical Criminology and Policing Divisions.

Conclusion

The time for a broad, developed, vibrant, and widely embraced Black Criminology is now. The concept and worth of a Black Criminology have deep-seated roots. Over a century ago, Du Bois's work planted the seeds for a Black-centered criminology. While the need for a Black Criminology persists, it has yet to take firm root within criminology and criminal justice studies. The potential impact of a Black Criminology is far reaching. Disciplinewide acknowledgment and application of Black Criminology approaches would likely expand the range of research methods and the resulting policy prescriptions. It is possible that research conducted using a Black Criminology approach will offer new and successful ways of addressing longstanding crime and justice issues. It may also offer more "ground-up" prescriptions—new processes and practices identified by the people directly involved in the system (victims, arrestees, and offenders) that address justice system–related flaws. In this way, Black Criminology may reduce the perceived illegitimacy of the justice system (Tyler, 2006). The integration of Black Criminology into mainstream criminology would signal greater openness to a holistic, historically based understanding of crime, specifically, how the evolution of crime and justice in the U.S. has historically (and thus contemporarily) been entangled with race.

This chapter reaffirms the argument that developing a Black Criminology is essential to the legitimacy and vibrancy of criminology scholarship. The development of this field, which includes both theory and methods, needs to be directed by Black criminologists, with the support and involvement of criminologists of all racial backgrounds. It is important that Black Criminology continues to grow as a stand-alone approach. While a Black Criminology approach overlaps with other perspectives (e.g., critical criminology and critical race criminology), it needs to develop organically and should not be limited by existing frameworks for race and justice studies. Important questions remain about the language of Black Criminology, including whether the label reinforces widely held stereotypes linking Blackness and crime. Due consideration should be given to whether a "White criminology" label or something else is preferable. The work of developing, implementing, and integrating a Black Criminology is vast. Black Criminology has not yet rattled the mainstream ranks of criminology. Individual criminologists and criminal justice researchers, as well as national and regional criminological associations, can in some way support the development of a Black Criminology. Together, we will determine whether the idea of a Black Criminology is relegated to a criminological footnote or something much more.

Notes

1. Du Bois used the term to describe people who "while attempting to understand the South or Black Americans, spent a few leisurely hours on holiday, riding in a Pullman car through the South, generally not venturing into communities" (Du Bois, 1938, p. 38).
2. Additional works by Black criminologists include Johnson, D., Warren, P. Y., & Farrell, A. (Eds.). (2015). *Deadly injustice: Trayvon Martin, race, and the criminal justice system* and Peterson, R., Krivo, R., & Russell-Brown, K. (Eds.). (2018). Color matters: Race, ethnicity, crime and justice in uncertain times. *The Du Bois Review*, *15*(1).
3. E.g., Davis, A. J. (Ed.). (2017). *Policing the Black man: Arrest, prosecution and imprisonment* and Butler, P. (2017). *Chokehold: Policing Black men*. New York, NY: The New Press.
4. One gauge of the increased interest in criminology is the number of race- and crime-related texts on display at academic conferences, such as the American Society of Criminology and the Academy of Criminal Justice Sciences.
5. Chesney-Lind and Chagnon note that they were unable to determine a race code for about one-third of the sample. They consider (and dismiss) the likelihood that if available, the numbers would show that Blacks are represented at proportionate or disproportionately high percentages.
6. Chesney-Lind and Chagnon (2016) state:

   Although criminology has made strides in terms of gender inclusion, the same cannot be said in terms of the racial/ethnic makeup of the field. Although our data are partial, they strongly suggest that Whites occupy not only the top positions within this hierarchically arranged field, such as those influential authors and award winners, but also nearly all positions. On the contrary, people of color are almost a nonpresence in criminology, with a few key exceptions (p. 327).

7. Chesney-Lind and Chagnon (2016) offer a detailed discussion of how criminology works to consistently marginalize nonpositivist perspectives (such as those that would fall within a Black Criminology paradigm):

   . . . [T]he hegemony of positivism within criminology is not a novel phenomenon . . . Anyone familiar with the history of the social sciences would identify the dominance of positivism as a historically persistent phenomenon, rather than an emergent one . . .

   [S]uch dominance is highly resonant with the academic neoliberal logics that promote scientist research over other forms of research producing influence that is less ostensibly quantifiable. Put simply positivistic bias predates the neoliberal turn, but it is only logical to assume that it is exacerbated by broader cultural saturation characterized by the valuation of quantification, calculability, and means-ends rationality. Thus, academic neoliberalism and the dominance of positivism are interrelated, and mutually strengthening phenomena, which constitute a significant and growing obstacle to the ascendance of feminist research, and, as well, culturally diverse research (p. 328).

   It is noted that Meda Chesney-Lind is the 81st president of the American Society of Criminology and its seventh woman president.

8. The representation of Latinos and Asians is low as well. In 2015, Latinos com-prised 3% of the faculty in criminology and criminal justice programs. The same percentage existed for Asians. The percentage of Latino students in top-tier criminology programs was 8%, compared with just under 3% for Asians (Greene, Gabbidon, & Wilson, 2017).

   They found that in some years prior to 2015, Blacks had higher rates of rep-resentation as criminology professors and doctoral students.

9. For instance, the journal *Race and Justice* (SAGE) and Palgrave's book series Critical Race Criminology (Springer). See also *Du Bois Review* (2018), Vol. 15 (1) (symposium on color matters and crime) and *Contemporary Justice Review* (2015), Vol. 18(2) (symposium on critical White studies).

10. See, e.g., Peterson, R. D., Krivo, L. J., & Hagan, J. (2006). *The many colors of crime: Inequalities of race, ethnicity, and crime in America.* New York, NY: New York University Press; Gabbidon and Greene. (2018). *Race and crime.* Belmont, CA: Sage; Ball, D., & Hartlep, N. D. (2017). *Asian/Americans, edu-cation and crime.* Lanham, MD: Lexington Books; Glynn, M. (2014). *Black men, invisibility, and crime.* London: Routledge.

11. See *Contemporary Justice Review* (2015), *18*(2), J. Smith & T. Linnemann (Eds.); *Western Criminology Journal* (2010), *11*(1), K. Glover, C. Curtis, & S. Hall (Special Eds.).

12. There has been discussion and debate about whether a "Black Criminology" promotes an essentialist—Black-only—stance (e.g., Kitossa, 2012).

13. Glynn argues for a "Black Criminology of desistance."

14. In his article, "The dilemma of 'racial profiling': an abolitionist police history" Micol Seigel (2017) offers an incisive critique of the term "racial profiling." The piece examines how the term both individualizes and minimizes the prac-tice of police profiling on basis of race.

15. Henne and Shah borrow this term popularized by Eduardo Bonilla-Silva and Tukufu Zuberi (2008).

References

Agozino, B. (2004). Imperialism, crime and criminology: Towards the decoloniza-tion of criminology. *Crime, Law and Social Change, 41*, 343–358.

Alexander, M. (2010). *The New Jim Crow: Colorblindness in an age of mass incar-ceration.* New York, NY: The New Press.

Ball, D., & Hartlep, N. D. (2017). *Asian/Americans, education and crime.* Lanham, MD: Lexington Books.

Bobo, L. D., & Charles, C. Z. (2009). Race in the American mind: From the Moyni-han report to the Obama candidacy. *The Annals of the American Academy of Political and Social Science, 612*, 243–259.

Bonilla-Silva, E., & Zuberi, T. (2008). Toward a definition of white logic and white methods. In T. Zuberi & E. Bonilla-Silva (Eds.), *White logic, white methods: Racism and Methodology* (pp. 3–27). Lanham, MD: Rowman & Littlefield.

Chesney-Lind, M., & Chagnon, N. (2016). Criminology, gender, and race: A case study of privilege in the academy. *Feminist Criminology, 11*, 311–333.

Coates, T. (2015). *Between the world and me.* New York, NY: Spiegel & Grau.

Coyle, M. (2010). Notes on the study of language: Towards critical race criminol-ogy. *Western Criminology Review, 11*(1), 11–19.

Crenshaw, K., Gotanda, N., Peller, G., & Thomas, K. (1995). *Critical race theory: The key writings that formed the movement.* New York, NY: The New Press.

Davis, A. J. (Ed.). (2017). *Policing the Black man: Arrest, prosecution, and imprisonment*. New York, NY: Random House.

Delgado, R. (1995). *The Rodrigo Chronicles: Conversations about America and race*. New York, NY: New York University Press.

Dirks, D., Heldman, C., & Zack, E. (2015). "She's white and she's hot, so she can't be guilty": Female criminality, penal spectatorship, and white protectionism. *Contemporary Justice Review, 18*, 160–177.

Du Bois, W. E. B. (1899). *The Philadelphia Negro: A social study*. New York, NY: Schocken Books.

Du Bois, W. E. B. (1978). *On sociology and the Black community*. Chicago, IL: University of Chicago Press.

Eberhardt, J., Goff, A., Purdie, V., & Davies, P. (2004). Seeing black: Race, crime and visual processing. *Journal of Personality and Social Psychology, 87*, 876–893.

Gabbidon, S. L. (1996). An argument for the inclusion of W. E. B. Du Bois in the criminology/criminal justice literature. *Journal of Criminal Justice Education, 7*, 99–112.

Gabbidon, S. L. (1999). W. E. B. Du Bois and the "Atlanta School" of social scientific research, 1897–1913. *Journal of Criminal Justice Education, 10*, 21–38.

Glover, K. (2009). *Racial profiling: Research, racism, and resistance*. Lanham, MD: Rowman & Littlefield.

Glynn, M. (2014). *Black men, invisibility and crime*. London, UK: Routledge.

Gottfredson, M., & Hirschi, T. (1990). *A general theory of crime*. Stanford, CA: Stanford University Press.

Greene, H. T., Gabbidon, S. L., & Wilson, S. (2018). Included? The status of African American scholars in the discipline of criminology and criminal justice since 2004. *Journal of Criminal Justice Education, 29*, 96–115.

Hawkins, D. F. McKean, J. B., White, N. A., & Martin, C. (2017). *Roots of African American violence: Ethnocentrism, cultural diversity, and racism*. Boulder, CO: Lynne Rienner.

Henne, K., & Shah, R. (2013). Unveiling white logic in criminological research: An intertextual analysis. *Contemporary Criminal Justice, 18*, 105–120.

Johnson, D., Farrell, A., & Warren, P. Y. (Eds.). (2015). *Deadly injustice: Trayvon Martin, race, and the criminal justice system*. New York, NY: New York University Press.

Katz, J., & Goodnough, A. (2017). The opioid crisis is getting worse, particularly for Black Americans. *New York Times*, December 22, p. A1.

Kitossa, T. (2012). Criminology and colonialism: Counter colonial criminology and the Canadian context. *Journal of Pan African Studies, 4*, 204–226.

Morris, A. (2015). *The scholar denied: W.E.B. Du Bois and the birth of modern sociology*. Berkeley, CA: University of California Press.

Onwudiwe, I. D., & Lynch, M. J. (2000). Reopening the debate: A reexamination of the need for a black criminology. *Social Pathology: A Journal of Reviews, 6*, 182–198.

Owusu-Bempah, A. (2017). Race and policing in historical context: Dehumanization and the policing of Black people in the 21st century. *Theoretical Criminology, 21*, 23–34.

Parmar, A. (2017). Intersectionality, British criminology and race: Are we there yet? *Theoretical Criminology, 21*, 35–45.

Penn, E. B. (2003). On black criminology: Past, present, and future. *Criminal Justice Studies, 16*, 317–327.

Philips, C., & Bowling, B. (2002). *Racism, race and justice*. Harlow, UK: Longman.

Russell, K. K. (1992). Development of a black criminology and the role of the black criminologist. *Justice Quarterly, 9*, 667–683.

Russell-Brown, K. (2009). *The color of crime* (2nd ed.). New York, NY: New York University Press.

Seigel, M. (2017). The dilemma of "racial profiling": An abolitionist history. *Contemporary Justice Review, 20*, 474–490.

Smith, J. (2014). Interrogating whiteness within criminology. *Sociology Compass, 8*, 107–118.

Smith, J., & Linnemann, T. (2015). Whiteness and critical white studies in crime and Justice. *Contemporary Justice Review, 18*, 101–104.

Tatum, B. (2000). Toward a neocolonial model of adolescent crime and violence. *Journal of Contemporary Criminal Justice, 16*, 157–170.

Taylor, I. R., Walton, P., & Young, J. (Eds.). (1975). *Critical criminology*. London, UK: Routledge & Kegan Paul.

Turanovic, J., Rodriguez, N., & Pratt, D. (2012). The collateral consequences of incarceration revisited: A qualitative analysis of the effect on caregivers of children of incarcerated parents. *Criminology, 50*, 913–959.

Tyler, T. R. (2006). *Why people obey the law*. Princeton, NJ: Princeton University Press.

Unnever, J. (2014). A theory of African American offending: A test of core propositions. *Race and Justice, 4*, 93–123.

Unnever, J., & Gabbidon, S. L. (2011). *A theory of African American offending: Race, racism, and crime*. New York, NY: Routledge.

Urbina, M. G. (Ed.). (2012). *Hispanics in the U.S. criminal justice system: The new American demography*. Springfield, IL: Charles C. Thomas.

Part II

Explaining Crime

6

The Cost of Racial Inequality Revisited: An Excursion in the Sociology of Knowledge

Steven F. Messner and Brian J. Stults

Approximately 35 years ago, Judith and Peter Blau (1982) published their seminal article in the *American Sociological Review* (*ASR*) entitled "The Cost of Inequality: Metropolitan Structure and Violent Crime." This research had a highly significant influence on the macro-level study of crime among American criminologists, setting the stage for a series of studies that were intended to replicate, extend, or challenge the conclusions advanced by the Blaus. The distinctive feature of the Blaus' work was not the proposition that is aptly captured in the title of the article—the proposition that inequality might have undesirable consequences for society, i.e., an identifiable "cost." This general notion had long been considered by scholars. Rather, the Blaus' lasting contribution was to direct attention to the criminogenic consequences of inequality rooted in ascribed characteristics and, more specifically, to racial inequality.

In this chapter, we revisit the pioneering research by the Blaus. We begin by placing their work in intellectual context, noting the long-standing interest in the potential impacts of economic conditions such as inequality on crime among social thinkers and explicating the foundations of the Blaus' analyses in general sociological theory. We then review the Blaus' research and the theoretical and empirical controversies directly stimulated by it and survey selected aspects of the evolution of criminological research on the cost of racial inequality over the following decades. Our discussion of the subsequent legacy of the Blaus' work directs particular attention to the growing recognition of the importance of the racialized hierarchy of place in American society.

The Intellectual Setting

At least since the time of antiquity, scholars have been cognizant of the possibility that social inequality in general and unequal economic conditions in particular might have profound consequences for society. For example, Aristotle (1962, p. 192) singled out inequality as one of the "fundamental causes" of revolutions, and he cited economic need as a factor leading to some property crimes, although he placed greater emphasis on the presumed natural human tendency for excessive desires (see McDonald, 1976, p. 29). In the 19th century, the pioneering "moral statisticians" André-Michel Guerry and Adolphe Quetelet conducted systematic empirical inquiry into the relationship between economic conditions and crime (Taylor, Walton, & Young, 1973, p. 37). Guerry created ecological maps to identify the social correlates of crime rates in different areas of France and concluded that, contrary to widely held views, crime rates were influenced less by poverty than by the opportunities for crime in wealthy areas. Quetelet conducted similar analyses with data for France, Belgium, and Holland. While also acknowledging a role for opportunity in understanding crime, Quetelet directed attention to inequality as well, citing the ways in which "wealth and poverty in the same place excites passions and provokes temptations of all kinds" (Vold & Bernard, 1986, p. 132). The "most fundamental and uncompromising" claims about the linkages of economic conditions and crime can be found in Marxist approaches, which depict all social problems, including crime, as manifestations of the underlying mode of production in society and the concomitant social inequalities (Radzino-wicz, 1971, p. 420).

In the years immediately preceding the publication of the Blaus' article in the *American Sociological Review*, the empirical connections between economic conditions and crime rates had already become a prominent topic of inquiry among American criminologists. Much of this research was concerned with differentiating the effects of poverty and economic inequality on crime rates. Poverty was typically related to criminal activity via processes associated with "absolute deprivation," whereas the connection between inequality and crime was theorized through various processes associated with "relative deprivation."

The results of these studies were largely inconclusive and sometimes contradictory.[1]

The Blaus were thus trespassing on well-traveled terrain when embarking on their efforts to identify crime as a "cost" of inequality. They initially approached the topic, however, from a vantage point quite distinct from that adopted by any of the scholars preceding them. They set out to derive their overarching prediction about inequality and crime from a macro-sociological theory that had recently appeared in Peter Blau's (1977) book, *Inequality and Heterogeneity: A Primitive Theory of Social Structure*. Blau characterized his theory as "primitive" not in the sense that it was in some way lacking in sophistication.[2] Rather, he wanted to call attention to the "formal" character of his theory—the arguments and propositions contained in the theory could be arrived at deductively from explicit definitions of the major terms and a set of core, basic assumptions and axioms.[3] One of the most important of the core assumptions that gives the theory its distinctive flavor is the virtual truism that actual social associations ultimately depend on opportunities for contact (Blau, 1977).

Blau (1977) adopted a quantitative conceptualization of social structure according to which social structure refers to the distributions of the population among social positions. These distributions can be understood with reference to two "parameters" of social structure—nominal parameters and graduated parameters. Nominal parameters divide the population into subgroups that have no inherent rank order (e.g., sex, religion, race), whereas graduated parameters differentiate the population with respect to some type of status rank-order (e.g., prestige, income) (Blau, 1977). The distributions of the population along these parameters are the bases of the major forms of social differentiation that are referred to in the title of Blau's book—inequality and heterogeneity. Differentiation with respect to graduated parameters is the basis of inequality; differentiation with respect to nominal parameters is the basis of heterogeneity.

Blau's principal substantive concern was with the implications of these forms of differentiation for macro-social integration, which he defined in terms of actual face-to-face associations (Blau, 1977). A social structure with a high degree of macro-social integration is one in which there are extensive associations between persons situated in different social positions. From his concepts, assumptions, and axioms, Blau deduced a number of theorems or propositions about how the various forms of social differentiation might promote or impede macro-social integration. Of greatest relevance for present purposes is Blau's proposition concerning the implications of the correlation or "consolidation" between a nominal parameter and a graduated parameter. Blau reasoned that when group membership (differentiation with respect to a nominal parameter) is correlated with some status distribution (differentiation with respect to a graduated parameter), group boundaries are reinforced (Blau, 1977; see also Blau & Schwartz, 1984). This consolidation of parameters of social structure in turn limits the opportunities for random contacts between members of different groups, thereby inhibiting the emergence of intergroup associations. Racial inequality can thus be conceptualized as one instance of the more general concept of consolidated parameters, but it is likely to be a particularly consequential instance because of the salience of race in American society.

Blau thus introduced an abstract, highly original theory of social structure. Blau and Blau took this theory as a point of departure for developing their arguments about the ways in which crime can be understood as a cost of inequality, and especially as a cost of racial inequality. As we explain in what follows, these arguments incorporated intervening processes that were drawn from wide-ranging perspectives, and as a result, these arguments ultimately roamed far afield from the originating macro-structural theory.

Theoretical Extensions, Empirical Findings, and Further Assessments

The Blaus (1982, p. 117) introduced their theoretical arguments in the *ASR* article with the explicit statement that "the objective of this study is to test a hypothesis about inequality and violence which is derived from a general macro-sociological theory (Blau, 1977)." They explained that to accomplish this task, they needed to extend the theory in two ways. On the one hand, whereas the original theory focused primarily on "positive" or cordial social relations, such as marriage and friendship, their substantive focus was " 'negative' social relations, notably interpersonal conflict" (Blau & Blau, 1982, p. 118). The thrust of their theorizing was devoted to establishing linkages initially between racial inequality and conflict, and ultimately between racial inequality and violent crime.

The Blaus' also emphasized in a footnote a second extension of the macro-sociological theory. They pointed out that "the original theory dealt with influences on the positive social relations between members of *different groups* [original emphasis] whereas this paper deals with negative social relations (conflict) between persons regardless of whether they belong to the same or to different groups" (1982, p. 120). They justified this shift in substantive focus on the grounds of data availability, but they recognized that it presupposed a departure from the basic logic underlying the original theory. As we noted above, the macro-structural theory was specifically developed to be a formal theory, and as such, the hypotheses were supposed to follow from the axioms and assumptions by purely deductive logic. The hypothesis that can be deduced directly from the macro-structural theory pertaining to racial inequality is that this structural condition should be negatively associated with rates of *interracial* crime. This follows because consolidated parameters are theorized to impede opportunities for random contacts between members of different groups, and such opportunities are the prerequisites for the establishment of meaningful social associations. Applying the theory to develop the hypothesis that violent crime *in general* is a cost of racial inequality required the Blaus to formulate "extensions" that, as they acknowledged, were "more conjectural and inferential" (1982, p. 120).[4]

To facilitate such conjectures and inferences, the Blaus reasoned that economic inequality generates the potential for violence because it stimulates conflict over the distribution of economic resources. They further proposed that such potential for conflict and violence varies for different forms of inequality. The form of inequality that is most likely to create such potential is inequality that is "experienced as illegitimate" and thus serves as a "source of aggression" (1982, p. 118). Moreover, the prevailing institutional order in society determines what forms of inequality are experienced as illegitimate. In a democratic society, the Blaus argued, inequalities that are "inborn" in the sense of being tied to group membership (such as ethnicity or race) are "feudal survivals" and thus are "condemned as illegitimate" (1982, p. 118). This line of reasoning undergirds the overarching hypothesis inferred by the Blaus that "socioeconomic inequalities that are associated with ascribed positions, thereby consolidating and reinforcing ethnic and class differences, engender pervasive conflict in a democracy" (1982, pp. 118–119).

The next step for the Blaus was to link racial inequality with the specific phenomenon of crime. They initially proposed a linkage that borrowed the concept of "nonrealistic conflict" from Coser (1968). The main idea here is that when conflicts of interest cannot be expressed in ways that are "realistic" in the sense that they can potentially resolve the conflicts, the conflicts are frequently expressed nonrealistically in the form of "diffuse aggression" or "hostility." The Blaus (1982, p. 119) accordingly hypothesized that ascribed inequalities (such as racial inequality) lead to criminal violence in part via the mechanism of diffuse hostility.

The Blaus invoked additional, diverse sociological and social psychological processes that might connect racial inequality with violent crime. They hypothesized that the reinforcement of in-group boundaries and the accompanying conflict associated with ascribed inequality leads to "much social disorganization." They further called attention to the tendency for ascribed inequality to generate "much resentment, frustration, hopelessness, and alienation." They characterized such a state of affairs as one "akin to Durkheim's state of anomie," but with less emphasis on normative deregulation and more emphasis on "the prevalent disorganization, sense of injustice, discontent, and distrust generated by the apparent contradiction between proclaimed values and norms, on the one hand, and social experiences, on the other" (1982, p. 119).

Having developed their hypothesis relating racial inequality to violent crime, the Blaus implemented a modeling strategy designed to engage the ongoing debates referred to above over the relative importance of absolute deprivation, as reflected in poverty, and relative deprivation, as reflected in inequality. They based their empirical analyses on data for a sample of the 125 largest metropolitan areas in the U.S. The dependent variables were the violent index crimes from the FBI's *Uniform Crime Reports* considered separately and as the aggregated violent crime rate. Poverty was measured with the poverty index from the Social Security Administration, while income inequality was measured with the Gini coefficient of family income. The strategic independent variable was *racial* inequality, operationalized as "the difference in average socioeconomic statuses between non-whites and whites based on Duncan's . . . SEI scores" (1982, p. 121). Conventional control variables were included in the empirical analyses as well.

In a series of regression models, the Blaus reported that poverty had nonsignificant effects on violent crime rates when income inequality was controlled and that racial SES inequality had effects on violent crime rates net of those of income inequality. Both income inequality and racial SES inequality emerged as significant predictors of violent crime rates in the fully specified models, with some variation by offense. The results thus indicated that inequalities of both forms were important, although the Blaus placed particular emphasis on racial inequality. To quote their overarching conclusion:

> High rates of criminal violence are apparently the price of racial and economic inequalities. In a society founded on the principle that "all men are created equal" economic inequalities rooted in ascribed positions violate the spirit of democracy and are likely to create alienation, despair, and conflict. The hypothesis derived from this assumption, which is also deducible from a general sociological theory, is that racial socioeconomic inequalities are a major source of much criminal violence. (1982, p. 126)

The Blaus' essay in *ASR* managed to reach a wide audience, and it stimulated a number of efforts to assess further the claim of a distinctive effect of *racial* inequality on violent crime and crime more generally.[5] The results of this literature were highly inconsistent, reflecting to some extent methodological issues that served as the launching pad for challenges and extensions. For example, research by Williams (1984) and by Blau and Schwartz (1984) modified the original models of the Blaus by estimating various nonlinear forms with logarithmic transformations for samples of metropolitan areas. The results from both studies reaffirmed the Blaus' earlier findings about the positive relationship between racial inequality and violent crime while arriving at opposing conclusions about the effects of poverty. Simpson (1985) introduced the methodological modification of using logits to represent percentage-type variables. His results failed to support the Blaus' claim that criminal violence can be regarded as a cost of either racial inequality or general levels of income inequality.[6] Substituting U.S. cities for metropolitan statistical areas as units of analysis, studies by Carroll and Jackson (1983) and by Jackson (1984) reported nonsignificant effects of racial inequality on crime rates once other city characteristics were controlled. In the study by Carroll and Jackson (1983), the coefficients for racial inequality were actually negative for rates of robbery and burglary.

In an effort to resolve some of the empirical inconsistencies in the literature and to further the Blaus' research agenda more generally, Messner and Golden (1992) introduced two new points of departure. They built upon a recently published article by Land et al. (1990) that had confronted the issue of inconsistencies in the homicide literature more generally. Land et al. argued that the highly inconsistent results across studies could be attributed largely to multicollinearity, and they recommended that researchers alleviate this statistical problem by simplifying the dimensional structure of covariates with principal components factor analysis. Land et al. constructed composite measures of social structural characteristics based on such procedures, and they reported theoretically meaningful relationships in models predicting homicide rates across multiple levels of aggregation (cities, metropolitan areas, and states in the U.S.). Messner and Golden (1992, p. 422) adopted this general methodological strategy in an effort to construct a measure of racial inequality that would be "sufficiently distinct from other aspects of social structure to permit reliable estimation of its effects on . . . homicide rates."

Messner and Golden also set out to begin the task of probing into the underlying mechanisms that might link levels of racial inequality with rates of criminal violence. As we explained above, the Blaus had invoked a diverse array of social processes in their theoretical arguments, yet their analyses of the violent crime rates for metropolitan areas offered no evidence that could help distinguish which, if any, of these intervening processes might actually be operating. Messner and Golden proposed that examining racially disaggregated homicide offending rates, along with the aggregated rates, could provide some leverage for identifying causal processes.

Recall that Blau and Blau had cited social disorganization and anomie as possible intervening mechanisms that might generate positive associations between racial inequality and criminal violence. Messner and Golden drew upon this part of their theoretical arguments to derive the following hypotheses:

> Insofar as this process does in fact operate, racial inequality should have a positive effect on the total homicide rate; it should also have positive effects on the offending behavior of racial subgroups. These predictions follow because social disorganization and anomie presumably have an impact on all segments of the population. (1992, p. 423)

Other parts of the Blaus' theorizing imply differing relationships for the race-specific offending rates. The various social psychological states that are theorized to be criminogenic (e.g., diffuse hostility, resentment, frustration, etc.) are presumably most likely to be experienced by the racial minority, the group that is relatively deprived. Insofar as these intervening processes are at work, racial inequality should exhibit a significant positive effect on Blacks, the racially disadvantaged group. In contrast, given that Whites derive benefits from conditions of racial inequality, it is plausible to speculate, using the same general logic as that for the "relative deprivation of the racial minority," that Whites experience relative gratification from high levels of racial inequality. This reasoning leads to the hypothesis that "the level of racial inequality should be *inversely* [original emphasis] related to the offending rate of whites" (1992, p. 424).[7]

Messner and Golden collected data on total and racially disaggregated homicide rates, along with data for indicators of racial differentials in socioeconomic status (income, education, employment opportunities, and residential patterns) and measures of conventional control variables for a sample of 154 large U.S. cities. They constructed a factor scale for racial socioeconomic inequality that proved to be empirically distinct from other social structural covariates, thereby circumventing the common problem of multicollinearity. The results of their regression analyses revealed that racial inequality exhibited significant positive effects on the total homicide rates and on both race-specific homicide rates as well. Messner and Golden concluded that the hypothesis of "relative gratification" for Whites was clearly disconfirmed by the positive rather than negative coefficient for the White homicide offending rate. Although the positive coefficients for the total homicide rate and the Black homicide rate were consistent with both the social disorganization/anomie and relative deprivation/disadvantage hypotheses, Messner and Golden (1992, p. 440) concluded that:

> The explanation that is most compatible with the full range of results is thus the social disorganization/anomie explanation. Racial inequality evidently affects the social order in some generalized way that increases criminogenic pressures on the entire population.

Around the same time as the study by Messner and Golden (1992), a similar call for racially disaggregated tests of the Blaus' hypotheses was made by Harer and Steffensmeier (1992). Additionally, they argued that a complete evaluation of the impact of racial inequality required not only a test of the effects of total and interracial inequality but also intraracial inequality. This was motivated by social psychological research showing that members of a racial group are more likely to use same-race group members as a comparative reference than members of other racial groups. Therefore, in addition to including the typical Gini coefficient for overall inequality and the Black–White ratio of median income for interracial inequality, Harer and Steffensmeier also included a race-specific Gini coefficient as a measure of intraracial inequality. Their analysis of the largest 125 metropolitan areas in 1980 revealed that, contrary to the Blaus' expectations and the findings by Messner and Golden, interracial inequality was not related to rates of offending or arrest, and this was true regardless of whether crime was aggregated to the total population or racially disaggregated for Whites and Blacks. Moreover, Harer and Steffensmeier found no support for their own expectation that intraracial inequality would be positively associated with Black arrest rates. Indeed, only White arrest rates were significantly affected by inequality, as evidenced by effects of both total inequality and White-specific inequality on White arrest rates for all measured forms of crime.

Throughout the remainder of the decade and beyond, macrosocial criminologists continued to examine racially disaggregated rates of offending and arrest, with many of them including measures of racial inequality as predictors, though inequality was not always the primary focus of the study. The findings of this body of research were similarly mixed, with some finding support for the expectation that racial inequality leads to higher rates of crime (e.g., Corzine & Huff-Corzine, 1992; Hipp, Tita, & Boggess, 2009; Jacobs & Wood, 1999; McCall & Parker, 2005; Parker, 2001; Parker & McCall, 1999; Ulmer, Harris, & Steffensmeier, 2012), while others found no significant effect of racial inequality (Eitle, 2009; Krivo & Peterson, 2000; Ousey & Augustine, 2001; Stolzenberg, Eitle, & D'Alessio, 2006; Wadsworth & Kubrin, 2004).

In addition to advocating for the use of racially disaggregated measures of crime and inequality, this body of research has raised a number of other methodological and theoretical questions in an effort to provide better-specified models, more closely align the methods of measurement with the theoretical concepts, and expand the scope of the theory. One concern has been determining the appropriate unit of analysis for testing the tenets of the theory. Researchers have employed a variety of units including states (Loftin & Hill, 1974), metropolitan areas (Eitle, 2009; Harer & Steffensmeier, 1992; Messner & Golden, 1992), counties (Reisig, Bales, Hay, & Wang, 2007), cities (Krivo & Peterson, 2000; Peterson & Krivo, 1993; Parker & McCall, 1999; Stolzenberg et al., 2006), and neighborhoods (Hipp, 2007; Hipp et al., 2009; Messner & Tardiff, 1986). Though no single unit is clearly superior to the others, some have argued that the pattern of findings might be associated with the particular unit of analysis that is used. There is some consensus that states are too large a unit and almost certainly obscure a substantial amount of heterogeneity within units and that they do not provide a meaningful context within which individuals can experience inequality through interaction with others (Bailey, 1984; Parker, 1989; Hipp, 2007; Hipp et al., 2009; Williams, 1984; Vieraitis, 2000). For example, Messner (1982) argued that states are rather arbitrary aggregations and that metropolitan areas may be a more meaningful unit of analysis, though after finding weak support for racial inequality, he conceded that metropolitan areas may also not provide relevant frames of reference. Bailey (1984) also concluded that metropolitan areas are too large because they conceal potential differences between cities and suburbs, arguing instead for the use of cities. Messner and Tardiff (1986) went a step further and argued for analysis at the level of neighborhoods, arguing that people learn about income differences through interaction with others and are unlikely to gain knowledge about inequality at large aggregate levels such as metropolitan areas or cities. More recently, Hipp (2007, p. 666) echoed these claims, stating that because "the mechanisms explaining the relationship between race and class distributions and crime rates require interaction among residents, measuring the distribution of race and class for such a large unit of analysis arguably does not capture the construct of interest." Indeed, studies at smaller levels of aggregation have found support for the effect of inequality on crime rates, though the results are more supportive for the effect of overall inequality than for racial inequality (Chamberlain & Hipp, 2015; Hipp, 2007; Messner & Tardiff, 1986; Vieraitis, 2000).

Finally, a small number of recent studies have examined the effect of racial inequality in a contextual or multilevel framework. For example, Hipp and Kane (2017) found that both the inequality of the city and inequality in the broader county have independent effects on city crime rates. They also detected a multiplicative effect whereby cities with high levels of inequality tend to experience particularly large increases in crime when they are located in a county with low levels of inequality (see also Roberts & LaFree, 2004). Others have extended the unit of analysis down to the individual level, while also expanding the scope of research beyond crime rates, by examining whether living in a context of racial inequality increases the likelihood of reoffending among individual offenders released from prison, with mostly supportive results (Reisig et al., 2007; Wright, Turanovic, & Rodriguez, 2016). For example, Wright et al. (2016) found that racial inequality at the zip code level increases the likelihood of reoffending among Black at-risk youth, though opposite effects are found for Latino youth. Likewise, Reisig et al. (2007) reported that Black prisoners released to counties with higher levels of racial inequality are more likely to be convicted of a new felony within 2 years.

The Subsequent Evolution of Research on Racial Inequality and Criminal Violence

In recent years, evaluations of racial inequality and crime rates in the tradition of Blau and Blau have declined. Inconsistent findings throughout prior decades may have contributed to this, but two theoretical developments in macrosocial criminology may be at least as important in precipitating the decline. First, the re-emergence of social disorganization theory beginning in the latter part of the 1980s has directed much scholarly attention toward concepts such as concentrated disadvantage, social ties, collective efficacy, and informal social control, often relegating racial inequality to the status of control variable if it is included at all. While resource deprivation is a fundamental concept in social disorganization theory, with strong and consistent empirical support, it is generally measured as absolute deprivation using indicators such as the overall poverty rate of an area or a composite index comprised of factors such as poverty, unemployment, education levels, and other economic conditions of places. Despite the many studies discussed above that illustrated the importance of examining relative deprivation in addition to absolute deprivation, many macro-level studies of crime in recent decades do not consider the importance of inequality, and especially racial inequality, alongside other forms of disadvantage.

Another development in macrosocial criminological theory, which has redirected research on racial inequality away from the tradition of Blau and Blau, also grew out of this reemergence of the social disorganization perspective. In 1995, Sampson and Wilson proposed a theory of race and crime that emphasizes the extent to which increasing social isolation and concentrated disadvantage undermine community social organization and lead to increasing crime rates (Sampson & Wilson, 1995; Sampson & Bean, 2006). A fundamental contention of their theory is that the causes of crime are the same for Blacks and Whites and that racial variation in crime rates can instead be explained by differential exposure to the ecological conditions that are associated with crime. This has come to be called the "racial invariance hypothesis," and it has received extensive attention in the literature on communities and crime.

We do not provide a review of this literature, given that other chapters in the current volume are dedicated to it (Unnever, this volume). We note, however, that several reviews have claimed strong support for the notion that a handful of key concepts, such as concentrated disadvantage and family disruption, are consistent predictors of both White and Black crime rates (Peterson & Krivo, 2005; Pratt & Cullen, 2005), with Sampson and Bean (2006, p. 11) stating that the "data are now in and confirm the wide variability in crime rates across White and Black communities along with robust similarity in their basic predictors at the community level."

While a careful evaluation of the evidence pertaining to the racial invariance hypothesis reveals nothing to invalidate the claim that racial inequality leads to crime, the name "racial invariance" itself might seem to suggest that racial inequality and racial invariance cannot both serve as valid explanations of community crime rates (see especially Unnever's chapter in the current volume). If the causes of crime are the same in Black and White communities, with variation in crime rates due only to racial differences in exposure to those structural factors, how can racial inequality be a predictor of crime rates in the fashion hypothesized by Blau and Blau given that Whites do not experience the negative side of racial inequality at an aggregate level?

Of course, any nuanced version of the racial invariance hypothesis does not require that the factors contributing similarly to White and Black rates of crime are the *only* factors contributing to crime rates. It is also important to note that while many community-level causes of crime have been shown to operate similarly in Black and White communities, there is often so little overlap in the ecological distribution of structural characteristics across racially segregated neighborhoods that analyses of "comparable" Black and White areas typically leave out large numbers of advantaged White communities and disadvantaged Black communities. Sampson, Wilson, and others who have contributed to the development of the racial invariance hypothesis have attempted to make this clear, but many tests of the hypothesis emphasize the similarities in causal effects without also highlighting the gross racial differences—indeed, *racial inequality*—in the underlying distributions of those common causal factors. For reasons we outline below, oversimplified arguments in support of racial invariance may seem to undercut the importance of racial inequality, but careful attention to its emphasis on racial differences in exposure to structural characteristics, when combined with much of the influential theoretical and empirical work on communities and crime that has developed in recent decades, strongly supports the notion that racial inequality is a key factor in explaining community levels of crime.

Recent theory and research on communities and crime has increasingly emphasized the importance of racial inequality in the *spatial distribution* of resources. Peterson and Krivo (2010) described this as the "racial–spatial divide" resulting from persistently high levels of racial residential segregation in cities and metropolitan areas. Though rates of residential segregation may have declined over the past couple decades, much of that decline has occurred in areas where relatively few Blacks reside (Logan & Stults, 2011; Logan, Stults, & Farley, 2004). Moreover, the sorting processes that led to these levels of segregation, including discriminatory practices in real-estate and mortgage lending, have resulted in neighborhoods that are not only separate for Whites and Blacks but also largely unequal. Thus, Black and White neighborhoods are not randomly distributed across urban space but rather are organized along a spatial hierarchy where Black neighborhoods tend to be located in areas characterized by inferior city services, weaker institutions, and higher rates of crime (Peterson & Krivo, 2010). Research finds that this racial inequality in neighborhood resources persists for poor Blacks and Whites but also for the middle class and affluent even when they have socioeconomic and demographic profiles similar to their White counterparts (Alba, Logan, & Stults, 2000; Logan & Stults, 1999; Pais, South, & Crowder, 2012; Sampson & Bean, 2006).

This racial residential disadvantage is compounded by the fact that Black residents are not only disproportionately located in disadvantaged neighborhoods, but also their neighborhoods tend to be situated within broader clusters of disadvantage. For example, using data from the city of Chicago, Sampson (2012, p. 249) found that "even white working-class areas do better than the highest-income Black neighborhoods when it comes to the economic status of near neighbors" (see also Sharkey, 2014). He also discovered that White neighborhoods, regardless of their own structural characteristics, are predominantly situated adjacent to neighborhoods with high levels of collective efficacy—a key form of social control that inhibits crime—while Black neighborhoods—even those with high collective efficacy—tend to be surrounded by neighborhoods with low collective efficacy. Likewise, Peterson and Krivo (2010) found that Black neighborhoods are far worse off than White neighborhoods with regard to levels of disadvantage, mortgage lending, and violent crime in surrounding neighborhoods. It also appears that this racial disparity in the spatial clustering of disadvantage has changed very little over time (Sharkey, 2014).

In addition to this rapidly expanding literature documenting the spatial disadvantage faced by Blacks, studies over the past decade or so have also provided consistent evidence that this clustering of disadvantage is strongly associated with neighborhood crime rates independent of the characteristics of focal neighborhoods themselves. For example, in an early study examining the spatial dynamics of violence, Morenoff, Sampson, and Raudenbush (2001) reported that rates of violence in surrounding neighborhoods are strongly related to homicide rates in the focal tract even after controlling for a wide array of internal neighborhood characteristics. Similarly, using data for census tracts from a nationally representative sample of U.S. cities, Peterson and Krivo (2009, 2010) found that surrounding levels of economic disadvantage, population instability, and White percentage are significantly associated with crime rates in focal neighborhoods and that this explains a large proportion of the variation in crime rates across White, Black, and Latino neighborhoods. Summarizing this literature, Sampson (2012, p. 259) concluded that "analyses here and in related papers are consistent in supporting the idea that the social characteristics of a 'neighborhood's' neighbors independently explain variation in the outcome of a focal neighborhood."

This racial–spatial stratification has at least two implications for assessing the evolving role of racial inequality in explaining variation in crime rates. First, inequality between the races comes not only in the form of racial disparities in characteristics such as household income and unemployment rates, but also in the form of severe racial inequality in the characteristics of neighborhoods and their surrounding areas. Given that Black neighborhoods are far more likely than White neighborhoods to be situated within broad clusters of disadvantage, the spatial distribution of resources itself represents a persistent form of racial inequality that transcends aggregate racial disparities in socioeconomic characteristics. Second, though there may be racial invariance in the direction and significance of key predictors of crime rates such as concentrated disadvantage and collective efficacy, Whites simply do not experience aggregate levels of deprivation relative to other racial groups, and this is especially true with regard to the characteristics of neighborhoods and their surrounding areas. As noted above, there is often very little overlap in the distributions of disadvantageous characteristics for White and Black neighborhoods—a condition that McNulty (2001) described as the "problem of restricted distributions." Results from several studies show that even the most advantaged Black neighborhoods are comparable with just the average White neighborhood, and the most disadvantaged White neighborhoods tend to be far above the average Black neighborhood (Krivo & Peterson, 1996; McNulty, 2001; Peterson & Krivo, 2005, 2010; Sampson, 2012; Sampson & Bean, 2006). Thus, the effect of racial–spatial inequality on neighborhood crime rates highlights a limitation of the racial invariance hypothesis narrowly understood because few if any comparable White and Black neighborhoods exist at the lower end of the distribution of clustered neighborhood disadvantage. As Sampson (2012, p. 249) aptly concludes:

> A paradox of sorts thus emerges—where studies have compared appropriate points in the ecological distribution where blacks and whites are similarly situated, there is little evidence that the neighborhood causes of violence are distinctly different. But these comparisons camouflage the larger reality of how race organizes the spatial dynamics of neighborhood inequality in the metropolitan system.

In short, even when Whites live in relatively disadvantaged areas or in neighborhoods with weak collective efficacy or low levels of informal social control, they tend to live adjacent to neighborhoods that are much better off, and this racialized hierarchy of place seems to be strongly related to racial differences in neighborhood crime rates.

Conclusion

All things considered, where does the "cost of inequality" stand as a contribution to our understanding of the social sources of crime and violence? It seems clear upon careful scrutiny that the Blaus were unsuccessful in their efforts to instill a new, distinctive, and innovative theoretical framework—Peter Blau's macro-sociological theory—to inform and guide research on the longstanding issue of inequality and crime. In essence, they adopted the *terminology* of the theory, i.e., that of "consolidated parameters," to characterize racial inequality. However, as explained above, virtually nothing else in the theory is incorporated in the Blaus' substantive arguments pertaining to the linkages between racial inequality and criminal violence. At various points, the potpourri of hypothesized variables that were cited as possible mediators between racial inequality and violent crime includes social psychological states (diffuse hostility, resentment, frustration, hopelessness, and alienation), features of social organization (or the lack thereof—prevalent social disorganization), and the vitality of the normative order (anomie). Each of these mechanisms has a degree of plausibility and a foundation in the scholarly literature, but none reflects in any meaningful way the core concepts and processes of the macro-sociological theory.

We suggest that the fault here lies less in the creativity of the Blaus than in fundamental limitations of this theory itself. Peter Blau characterized his theory as "primitive" in the sense that its content could be derived deductively from a small set of axioms and assumptions. Moreover, he adopted an explicitly narrow conceptualization of social structure, a conceptualization "stripped . . . to its core properties, its primitive meaning" (1977, p. ix). Social structure conceptualized in this manner encompasses simply the quantitative distributions of persons among the social positions in a society. This quest for parsimony is admirable to a degree, but the resulting vision is indeed a very narrow one. It allows for no significant role of culture and history—features of social reality that are indispensable for comprehending the profound influence of race in American society. Accordingly, there is no systematic attention to *racism*, its manifestations in cultural prejudices, in institutional arrangements, in the spatial configurations of communities, nor to the ways in which these manifestations promote criminal violence.

Notwithstanding these criticisms, the "cost of inequality" without question served the discipline quite well in a number of important respects. Over 40 years ago, Stephen Cole (1975) published a study tracing the influence of Robert Merton's theory of social structure and anomie (SS&A) by analyzing citation counts. Cole reported that Merton's variant of anomie theory enjoyed something of a golden age, but then it faded in prominence. Cole further argued that in retrospect, the most significant contribution of Merton's introduction of SS&A to the scholarly community was not to establish indisputable evidence supportive of its distinctive hypotheses about crime and deviance. Rather, it succeeded in creating "puzzles for research." The same can certainly be said for the Blaus' article on the cost of inequality. It too followed a life course of ascending and then declining influence. Along the way, it generated numerous "puzzles" that inspired fruitful research. It enhanced awareness of and serious concerns about a host of important methodological issues. These include the implications of multicollinearity, the importance of attending to the functional form of statistical relationships, the modifiable areal unit problem (MAUP), and the utility of disaggregating measures of both inequality and crime by race to elucidate underlying social processes. Building on while extending this work, contemporary researchers have developed the analytic framework referred to earlier, a "racialized hierarchy of place," that has been applied effectively in the empirical literature.

Perhaps most important of all, the Blaus sensitized the criminological community to a form of inequality that, for whatever reason, had not previously played a particularly important role in theory and research on levels of criminal violence. In his presidential address to the American Society of Criminology in 1991, John Hagan (1991) lamented a tendency on the part of many criminologists at the time to dismiss the centrality of social class in the study of crime. He cautioned that "the omission of class would lead to an impoverished criminology" (1992, p. 1). Blau and Blau's original article and the body of research inspired by it has helped criminologists appreciate that the omission of racial inequality from studies of crime would similarly lead to an impoverished criminology. Such a legacy is surely worth acknowledging and commending.

Notes

1. See Vold and Bernard (1986, pp. 140–141) for a review of this literature.
2. For linguistic convenience, "Blau," in contrast with "Blau and Blau," refers to Peter Blau throughout our discussion.
3. Blau's approach to theorizing is stated as follows in a subsequent book coauthored with Schwartz: "The fundamental requirement for constructing a scientific theory is to formulate a deductive system of propositions in which definitions of primitive terms and postulated assumptions imply less general synthetic propositions, which are the theorems and, on a still general level, empirical predictions of the theory" (Blau & Schwartz, 1984, p. 5).
4. For examples of empirical assessments of the proposition derived from Blau's macro-structural theory that racial inequality is inversely related to rates of interracial crime, see Messner and South (1986, 1992) and South and Messner (1986). Sampson (1984) assessed hypotheses derived from Blau's theory pertaining to group size, heterogeneity, and intergroup victimization. See also O'Brien (1987) for an analysis of the racial character of violent crime that is also informed by a structuralist orientation.
5. Braithwaite (1979) had published a study prior to the Blaus' *ASR* article reporting no relationship between racial inequality and crime rates for metropolitan areas. The Blaus cited this research in their article (1982) but challenged it on the grounds of potential collinearity between Braithwaite's measures of racial inequality and overall inequality.
6. See Balkwell (1990) for an example of an effort to incorporate ethnic groups, as well as racial groups, in the study of group-based inequality and homicide.
7. Messner and Golden also derived and assessed the prediction that can be derived from Blau's macro-structural theory of an inverse relationship between racial inequality and interracial homicide rates. Their results failed to support the

hypothesis, but they acknowledged that their assessment departed from conventional approaches by examining interracial rates of homicide rather than conditional probabilities. See Messner and Golden (1992).

References

Alba, R. D., Logan, J. R., & Stults, B. J. (2000). The changing neighborhood contexts of the immigrant metropolis. *Social Forces, 79*, 587–621.

Aristotle. (1962). *The politics* (T. J. Saunders, Ed., T. A. Sinclair, Trans., Revised ed.). Harmondsworth, UK and New York, NY: Penguin Classics.

Bailey, W. C. (1984). Poverty, inequality, and city homicide rates. *Criminology, 22*, 531–550.

Balkwell, J. W. (1990). Ethnic inequality and the rate of homicide. *Social Forces, 69*, 53–70.

Blau, J. R., & Blau, P. M. (1982). The cost of inequality: Metropolitan structure and violent crime. *American Sociological Review, 47*, 114–129.

Blau, P. (1977). *Inequality and heterogeneity: A primitive theory of social structure* (1st ed.). New York, NY: Free Press.

Blau, P. M., & Schwartz, J. E. (1984). *Crosscutting social circles: Testing a macrostructural theory of intergroup relations.* Orlando: Academic Press.

Braithwaite, J. (1979). *Inequality, crime, and public policy.* London: Routledge and Kegan Paul.

Carroll, L., & Jackson, P. I. (1983). Inequality, opportunity, and crime rates in central cities. *Criminology, 21*, 178–194.

Chamberlain, A. W., & Hipp, J. R. (2015). It's all relative: Concentrated disadvantage within and across neighborhoods and communities, and the consequences for neighborhood crime. *Journal of Criminal Justice, 43*, 431–443.

Cole, S. (1975). The growth of scientific knowledge: Theories of deviance as a case study. In L. A. Coser (Ed.), *The idea of social structure: Papers in honor of Robert K. Merton* (pp. 175–220). New York, NY: Harcourt Brace Jovanovich.

Corzine, J., & Huff-Corzine, L. (1992). Racial inequality and black homicide: An analysis of felony, nonfelony and total rates. *Journal of Contemporary Criminal Justice, 8*, 150–165.

Coser, L. A. (1968). *Conflict: Social aspects.* Chicago, IL: Crowell Collier.

Eitle, D. (2009). Dimensions of racial segregation, hypersegregation, and black homicide rates. *Journal of Criminal Justice, 37*, 28–36.

Hagan, J. (1992). The poverty of a classless criminology—the American Society of Criminology Address. *Criminology, 30*, 1–19.

Harer, M. D., & Steffensmeier, D. (1992). The differing effects of economic inequality on black and white rates of violence. *Social Forces, 70*, 1035–1054.

Hipp, J. R. (2007). Income inequality, race, and place: Does the distribution of race and class within neighborhoods affect crime rates? *Criminology, 45*, 665–697.

Hipp, J. R., & Kane, K. (2017). Cities and the larger context: What explains changing levels of crime? *Journal of Criminal Justice, 49*, 32–44.

Hipp, J. R., Tita, G. E., & Boggess, L. N. (2009). Intergroup and intragroup violence: Is violent crime an expression of group conflict or social disorganization? *Criminology, 47*, 521–564.

Jackson, P. (1984). Opportunity and crime: A function of city size. *Sociology & Social Research, 68*, 172–193.

Jacobs, D., & Wood, K. (1999). Interracial conflict and interracial homicide: Do political and economic rivalries explain white killings of blacks or black killings of whites? *American Journal of Sociology, 105,* 157–190.

Krivo, L. J., & Peterson, R. D. (1996). Extremely disadvantaged neighborhoods and urban crime. *Social Forces, 75,* 619–648.

Krivo, L. J., & Peterson, R. D. (2000). The structural context of homicide: Accounting for racial differences in process. *American Sociological Review, 65,* 547–559.

Land, K. C., McCall, P. L., & Cohen, L. E. (1990). Structural covariates of homicide rates: Are there any invariances across time and social space? *American Journal of Sociology, 95,* 922–963.

Loftin, C., & Hill, R. H. (1974). Regional subculture and homicide: An examination of the Gastil-Hackney thesis. *American Sociological Review, 39,* 714–724.

Logan, J. R., & Stults, B. (2011). *The persistence of segregation in the metropolis: New findings from the 2010 census.* Census Brief prepared for Project US2010. Retrieved from www.s4.brown.edu/us2010

Logan, J. R., & Stults, B. J. (1999). Racial differences in exposure to crime: The city and suburbs of Cleveland in 1990. *Criminology, 37,* 251–276.

Logan, J. R., Stults, B. J., & Farley, R. (2004). Segregation of minorities in the metropolis: Two decades of change. *Demography, 41,* 1–22.

McCall, P. L., & Parker, K. F. (2005). A dynamic model of racial competition, racial inequality, and interracial violence. *Sociological Inquiry, 75,* 273–293.

McDonald, L. (1976). *Sociology of law and order.* London, UK: Faber & Faber.

McNulty, T. L. (2001). Assessing the race-violence relationship at the macro level: The assumption of racial invariance and the problem of restricted distributions. *Criminology, 39,* 467–490.

Messner, S. F. (1982). Poverty, inequality, and the urban homicide rate: Some unexpected findings. *Criminology, 20,* 103–114.

Messner, S. F., & Golden, R. M. (1992). Racial inequality and racially disaggregated homicide rates: An assessment of alternative theoretical explanations. *Criminology, 30,* 421–448.

Messner, S. F., & South, S. J. (1986). Economic deprivation, opportunity structure, and robbery victimization: Intra- and interracial patterns. *Social Forces, 64,* 975–991.

Messner, S. F., & South, S. J. (1992). Interracial homicide: A macrostructural-opportunity perspective. *Sociological Forum, 7,* 517–536.

Messner, S. F., & Tardiff, K. (1986). Economic inequality and levels of homicide: An analysis of urban neighborhoods. *Criminology, 24,* 297–316.

Morenoff, J. D., Sampson, R. J., & Raudenbush, S. W. (2001). Neighborhood inequality, collective efficacy, and the spatial dynamics of urban violence. *Criminology, 39,* 517–558.

O'Brien, R. M. (1987). The interracial nature of violent crimes: A reexamination. *American Journal of Sociology, 92,* 817–835.

Ousey, G. C., & Augustine, M. C. (2001). Young guns: Examining alternative explanations of juvenile firearm homicide rates. *Criminology, 39,* 933–968.

Pais, J., South, S. J., & Crowder, K. (2012). Metropolitan heterogeneity and minority neighborhood attainment: Spatial assimilation or place stratification? *Social Problems, 59,* 258–281.

Parker, K. F. (2001). A move toward specificity: Examining urban disadvantage and race-and relationship-specific homicide rates. *Journal of Quantitative Criminology, 17,* 89–110.

Parker, K. F., & McCall, P. L. (1999). Structural conditions and racial homicide patterns: A look at the multiple disadvantages in urban areas. *Criminology, 37,* 447–478.

Parker, R. N. (1989). Poverty, subculture of violence, and type of homicide. *Social Forces, 67,* 983–1007.

Peterson, R. D., & Krivo, L. J. (1993). Racial segregation and black urban homicide. *Social Forces, 71,* 1001–1026.

Peterson, R. D., & Krivo, L. J. (2009). Segregated spatial locations, race-ethnic composition, and neighborhood violent crime. *The Annals of the American Academy of Political and Social Science, 623,* 93–107.

Peterson, R. D., & Krivo, L. J. (2005). Macrostructural analyses of race, ethnicity, and violent crime: Recent lessons and new directions for research. *Annual Review of Sociology, 31,* 331–356.

Peterson, R. D., & Krivo, L. J. (2010). *Divergent social worlds: Neighborhood crime and the racial-spatial divide.* New York, NY: Russell Sage Foundation.

Pratt, T. C., & Cullen, F. T. (2005). Assessing macro-level predictors and theories of crime: A meta-analysis. *Crime and Justice, 32,* 373–450.

Radzinowicz, L. (1971). Economic pressures. In L. Radzinowicz & M. E. Wolfgang (Eds.). *Crime and Justice. Vol. 1, The Criminal in Society* (pp. 420–442). New York: Basic Books.

Reisig, M. D., Bales, W. D., Hay, C., & Wang, X. (2007). The effect of racial inequality on black male recidivism. *Justice Quarterly, 24,* 408–434.

Roberts, A., & Lafree, G. (2004). Explaining Japan's postwar violent crime trends. *Criminology, 42,* 179–210.

Sampson, R., & Bean, L. (2006). Cultural mechanisms and killing fields: A revised theory of community-level racial inequality. In R. Peterson, L. Krivo, & J. Hagan (Eds.), *The many colors of crime: Inequalities of race, ethnicity and crime in America* (pp. 8–36). New York, NY: New York University Press.

Sampson, R. J. (1984). Group size, heterogeneity, and intergroup conflict: A test of Blau's inequality and heterogeneity. *Social Forces, 62,* 618–639.

Sampson, R. J. (2012). *Great American city: Chicago and the enduring neighborhood effect.* Chicago, IL: University of Chicago Press.

Sampson, R. J., & Wilson, W. J. (1995). Toward a theory of race, crime, and urban inequality. In J. Hagan & R. Peterson (Eds.), *Crime and inequality* (pp. 37–56). Stanford, CA: Stanford University.

Sharkey, P. (2014). Spatial segmentation and the black middle class. *American Journal of Sociology, 119,* 903–954.

Simpson, M. E. (1985). Violent crime, income inequality, and regional culture: Another look. *Sociological Focus, 18,* 199–208.

South, S. J., & Messner, S. F. (1986). Structural determinants of intergroup association: Interracial marriage and crime. *American Journal of Sociology, 91,* 1409–1430.

Stolzenberg, L., Eitle, D., & D'Alessio, S. J. (2006). Race, economic inequality, and violent crime. *Journal of Criminal Justice, 34,* 303–316.

Taylor, I., Walton, P., & Young, J. (1973). *The new criminology: For a social theory of deviance* (1st ed.). London, UK: Routledge.

Ulmer, J. T., Harris, C. T., & Steffensmeier, D. (2012). Racial and ethnic disparities in structural disadvantage and crime: White, black, and Hispanic comparisons. *Social Science Quarterly, 93,* 799–819.

Unnever, J. D. (this volume). The racial invariance thesis. In J. D. Unnever, S. L. Gabbidon, & C. Chouhy (Eds.), *Building a Black criminology: Race, theory, and crime (Advance in criminological theory,* Vol. 24, pp. 77–100). New York, NY: Routledge.

Vold, G. B., & Bernard, T. J. (1986). *Theoretical Criminology* (3rd ed.). New York: Oxford University Press.

Vieraitis, L. M. (2000). Income inequality, poverty, and violent crime: A review of the empirical evidence. *Social Pathology, 6,* 24–45.

Wadsworth, T., & Kubrin, C. E. (2004). Structural factors and black interracial homicide: A new examination of the causal process. *Criminology, 42,* 647–672.

Williams, K. R. (1984). Economic sources of homicide: Reestimating the effects of poverty and inequality. *American Sociological Review, 49,* 283–289.

Wright, K. A., Turanovic, J. J., & Rodriguez, N. (2016). Racial inequality, ethnic inequality, and the system involvement of at-risk youth: Implications for the racial invariance and Latino paradox theses. *Justice Quarterly, 33,* 863–889.

7

Code of the Street: Elijah Anderson and Beyond

Kristin Swartz and Pamela Wilcox

As other chapters in this book have illustrated, the vast majority of criminological theories do not emphasize the role of Blacks' unique experiences, including racial discrimination, as underlying causes of crime (e.g., see Cullen et al., this volume; Unnever & Owusu-Bempah, this volume; see also Unnever & Gabbidon, 2011). Further, many criminological theories have been formulated with economically challenged White neighborhoods as the frame of reference, tested with data from predominantly or exclusively White samples, or based on an implicit or explicit assumption that the causal factors behind crime are racially invariant.

Ironically, this general problem even extends to cultural perspectives that are inherently well poised to consider unique experiences of certain segments of the population. Cultural theories in criminology—the focus of this chapter—are often oriented toward poor or working-class White youths and assume that culture exerts "racially invariant" effects— effects that explain both White and Black crime equally (e.g., Cloward & Ohlin, 1960; Cohen, 1955; Kornhauser, 1978; Shaw & McKay, 1942; see also Unnever, this volume). Other cultural theories focus more fully on Blacks, but in the process, they engage in racial stereotyping and suggest an autonomous "Black subculture of violence," divorced from the unique historical and structural conditions experienced by Blacks (e.g., Curtis, 1975; Wolfgang & Ferracuti, 1967). Still other cultural theories thoughtfully articulate the unique historical and structural experiences of Blacks yet still push the causal significance of these experiences to the periphery and promote "racially-invariant" causal explanations of crime instead (Sampson & Wilson, 1995; Sampson, Wilson, & Katz, in press).

However, in the past several decades, some scholars have begun to put "front-and-center" the unique structurally induced cultural experiences of African Americans trapped in highly disadvantaged urban ghettos. Though not the only work of this genre, perhaps that most emblematic of this trend is Elijah Anderson's (1999) *Code of the Street: Decency, Violence, and the Moral Life of the Inner City*. In this important ethnographic study, Anderson describes how the unique experience of living in poor, Black inner-city North Philadelphia neighborhoods in the 1980s and 1990s included adherence to a "code of the street" which, ultimately, affected involvement in crime. While Anderson's "code of the street thesis" is not explicitly framed within a Black Criminology, it departs importantly from most other cultural work in that it does identify racial discrimination suffered by Blacks as a starting point—and one which leads them, seemingly uniquely, to adopt a set of codes or rules that dictate interpersonal interactions and violent actions. Additionally, embedded within Anderson's "code of the street thesis" is a discussion of decent versus street socialization of youth. This discussion dovetails in important ways with Black Criminology's notion of racial socialization.

This chapter develops the argument that Anderson's *Code of the Street* is implicitly compatible with a Black Criminology, and, as such, there is opportunity for Black Criminology and the "code of the street thesis" to each draw upon the other for continued development. We begin the chapter by providing a brief overview of "early American" cultural perspectives in criminology. These early cultural perspectives were developed from a White-centric vantage point, with few discussions of race per se and implicit assumptions of racially invariant causes of crime. Next, we provide a brief review of mid-century, conservative theories suggesting an autonomous Black subculture of violence. We then review late-twentieth-century work that highlights the unique disadvantage experienced by Black Americans yet still suggests a racially invariant effect of attenuated culture on crime. The remainder of the chapter focuses on contemporary cultural theory, emerging at the dawn of the new millennium, which recognizes the causal significance of the unique cultural experiences of African

Americans in truly disadvantaged contexts. With a particular spotlight on Anderson's work, we describe the "code of the street and its implications for crime and explore the overlap between this perspective and Black Criminology.

The Early Subcultural Tradition in Criminology: A (Largely White) Adaptation to Disorganization and Strain

The foundational work on crime developed within the Chicago School discussed the important roles of both structural disadvantage and the inter-generational transmission of cultural values. For example, in *Juvenile Delinquency and Urban Areas*, Shaw and McKay argued that neighborhoods characterized by economic disadvantage, ethnic heterogeneity, and residential instability fostered social disorganization, which, in turn, led to high rates of crime. Importantly, Shaw and McKay (1942, p. 120) observed that disorganized communities not only had structural deficits in that they lacked legitimate opportunities and strong institutional and informal controls but also had "systems of competing and conflicting moral values"—in essence, "deviant subcultures." They based such theory in part on case studies detailing the life histories of delinquent boys such as Stanley (The Jack-Roller), whose family immigrated to Chicago from Poland (Shaw, 1930). Life histories of boys like Stanley revealed that the immigrant youths growing up in impoverished, unstable, ethnically heterogeneous neighborhoods in Chicago in the early 1900s were exposed to attitudes that approved of delinquency and that these criminogenic attitudes were then passed on to successive generations of children through social learning. In much of Shaw and McKay's work, the experiences of the various White immigrant youths and the Black youths in disorganized neighborhoods were not detailed as unique, suggesting that the crime-causing processes of weak control and subcultural transmission of values were thus racially invariant (see also Cullen et al., this volume). Though Shaw and McKay did acknowledge unique segregation faced by African Americans, in reference to some of their analyses (Shaw & McKay, 1949; see also Sampson et al., in press; Unnever & Owusu-Bempah, this volume), there was no in-depth attempt to racialize the theory— to suggest, for example, that racial inequality experienced by Blacks was the key source of social disorganization and crime.

Beyond Shaw and McKay, other criminological work in the mid-twentieth century attempted to understand the spatial patterning of crime by invoking subcultural influences that were presumed responses to class-based, not race-related, strain. Such work is represented perhaps most famously by Cohen (1955) and Cloward and Ohlin (1960). Their ideas undoubtedly emerged from thinking about early-20th-century working- and lower-class urban environments with which they were familiar—cities such as Boston or New York City, which, like Chicago, consisted of largely White ethnic neighborhoods (see Cullen et al., this volume).

For example, Albert Cohen's famous 1955 book, *Delinquent Boys: The Culture of the Gang*, suggested that delinquent subcultures in the form of male gangs were collective responses to "status frustration" among working-class boys. With little attention to race, Cohen detailed how (presumably White) working-class boys were frustrated in the school context, in particular, as they were unable to readily measure up to the values that were prized in that setting: independence, self-control, asceticism, and rationality. Gangs provided these frustrated boys with an alternative cultural context—one in which working-class boys could achieve status by exhibiting aggression, impulsiveness, and disrespect for property.

In *Delinquency and Opportunity: A Theory of Delinquent Gangs*, Cloward and Ohlin (1960) provided another example of a theory that emphasized the emergence of unique subcultures within poorer communities where young men experienced collective strain. Their theory, once again, largely ignored racial inequality and oppression as sources of strain and subcultural formation. Cloward and Ohlin suggested that strain resulted from the inability to achieve economic success through legitimate avenues—because those legitimate avenues were inaccessible. Thus, similar to Cohen, Cloward and Ohlin saw strain as class based rather than race based. Also similar to Cohen, Cloward and Ohlin posited that the collective response to class-based strain was gang formation. However, unlike Cohen's *Delinquent Boys*, Cloward and Ohlin emphasized that values and behaviors of gangs varied. Some gangs focused on instrumental criminal enterprises, some emphasized violence, and others centered on drug use. These different forms of gangs were referred to as "criminal," "conflict," and "retreatist" gangs, respectively. Cloward and Ohlin noted that poor communities were differentially organized, with the level of organization shaping the availability of illegitimate opportunities and thus the nature of collective responses to strain (i.e., the type of gang that would emerge).

Thus, Cloward and Ohlin also suggested that *illegitimate* means were also available to some but blocked for others (see also Cloward, 1959). Socially cohesive poor neighborhoods fostered criminal gangs, which demanded an organized network structure that could offer access to experienced offenders for "apprenticeship" purposes, access to co-offenders, and access to illicit markets. In contrast, neighborhoods that lacked integrated social networks were thus more likely to breed conflict gangs. Since youths in such neighborhoods lacked a readily accessible network that would allow them to address their problems of adjustment through criminal enterprise, the gangs that emerged focused on resolving strain by linking status and violence instead. Finally, retreatist gangs, emphasizing drug use, emerged in both organized and disorganized communities among youths who were unsuccessful at exercising crime or violence, thus eliminating the option of gaining status from such behaviors. For the most part, differential experiences on the basis of long-standing racial discrimination and oppression were ignored in Cloward and Ohlin's theory, as "class" and "differential organization" took center stage as key in understanding variable access to legitimate and illegitimate opportunities, and in an implicitly racially invariant way.[1]

A Mid-Century Autonomous (and Perhaps Black) Subculture

In contrast to Cohen and Cloward and Ohlin's adaptive view of gang delinquency (i.e., an adaptation or reaction to class-based strain), other mid-20th-century perspectives linked crime more directly to a class- or race-based deviant subcultures. These subcultures were seen as less tethered to structural disadvantage and therefore more autonomous than the previously discussed perspectives. For example, Walter Miller (1958) suggested that delinquent values followed more directly from a pervasive "lower class culture." Miller delineated six "focal concerns" that characterized lower-class culture and promoted crime among those within its milieu: trouble, toughness, smartness, excitement, fate, and autonomy. Through these focal concerns, Miller claimed that lower-class culture conferred status on those who engaged in fighting, stealing, drinking, drug use, gambling, con games, sexual promiscuity, and general defiance of authority. From Miller's perspective, crime was a natural outcome of socialization within lower-class culture.

Wolfgang and Ferracuti's (1967) *The Subculture of Violence* was similar to Miller's work in that it attempted to explain high rates of crime in urban, disadvantaged environments as a function of subcultural concerns. However, it differed in that it focused on the subcultural sources of *violent* crime—especially *expressive homicide*. Wolfgang and Ferracuti suggested that residents in poor urban areas were taught to respond to responses to slights and conflicts with violence. In fact, those who did not display violence in certain situations would be scorned and possibly ostracized. Youth exposed to such pro-violent definitions and reinforcements were thought to internalize them, thus perpetuating the high rates of violence across generations.

While Wolfgang and Ferracuti's subculture of violence originally aimed to understand higher rates of crime in poor, urban areas, it was also embraced as a way to account for differential rates of crime across racial and geographic groups within the United States. In particular, the notion of a race-based subculture of violence was used to explain higher rates of violence among African Americans (e.g., Curtis, 1975). Thus, in the late 1960s and early 1970s, cultural perspectives on crime moved away from discussing community dynamics—such as disorganization and strain—that fueled the formation of gangs. They became instead straight-up *class-* and *race*-based subcultural theories that implied the existence of a common set of criminal values across people who did not necessarily know or interact with one another but who shared a particular sociodemographic characteristic (Kornhauser, 1978). Though these theories had their appeal, in the mid-century context of social and cultural conservatism, they grew less popular into the mid- to late 1960s, when such approaches to crime were challenged as dangerous in their stereotyping and shortsighted in their silence on structural inequality—essentially blaming the victims of inequality in the process (see Wilcox, Cullen, & Feldmeyer, 2018, for review).

Deindustrialization, the Truly Disadvantaged, and Racially Invariant Attenuated Culture

As race- and class-based subcultural perspectives in criminology waned in the 1970s and 1980s, control perspectives flourished. This included Kornhauser's (1978) reconceptualization of Shaw and McKay's social disorganization theory as a macro-level "pure" control theory—one that was devoid of the idea that deviant subcultures took root in disorganized communities. Rather, Kornhauser's version of social disorganization theory suggested that structural and cultural disorganization were the key concepts behind community rates of crime. Structural disorganization referred to institutional and network instability. Cultural disorganization (also termed "cultural attenuation") referred to the instability or irrelevance of conventional culture—but it did not refer to the *embracement* of deviant subcultural values. Both structural and cultural disorganization were believed to weaken informal social control of crime. In reformulating social disorganization theory as a macro-level control theory, Kornhauser followed in the footsteps of Shaw and McKay (1942) and micro-level control theories (Hirschi, 1969) in that she largely ignored the inequality faced by Black communities as a unique causal force in the process of social and cultural disorganization. Instead, she posited that neighborhoods characterized by economic disadvantage, ethnic *heterogeneity*, and residential instability fostered social and cultural disorganization, which, in turn, led to high rates of crime. There was an underlying assumption that this process operated in a racially invariant way.

Building upon Kornhauser's macro-level control theory, Sampson and Wilson (1995) combined the notions of structural and cultural disorganization to explain higher rates of crime in African American communities most specifically. As such, they paid much more explicit attention to race—and to the disadvantages faced by Black communities in particular. They theorized that extracommunity political economic forces were behind the creation of Black "hyper-ghettos" in the 1980s. More specifically, the massive loss of inner-city jobs to deindustrialization, the out-migration of Whites and middle-class Blacks from the inner city, and discriminatory and segregationist decisions about housing fueled a truly disadvantaged existence in many increasingly Black inner-city neighborhoods (see also Wilson, 1987). Sampson and Wilson (1995) suggest further that this "concentrated disadvantage" created both structural and cultural disorganization.

Regarding structural disadvantage, Sampson and Wilson suggest that contexts of concentrated disadvantage undermine key crime-controlling systems of private and parochial ties. Regarding cultural disorganization, they argued that contexts of concentrated disadvantage shape norms regarding appropriate standards of conduct—what they term "cognitive landscapes." They note, "crime, disorder, and drug use are less than fervently condemned and hence expected as a part of everyday life" in truly disadvantaged communities (p. 50). Sampson and

Wilson claim that such behaviors are tolerated and accepted because mainstream behaviors, in extremely disadvantaged contexts, are "existentially irrelevant" (p. 51). Sampson and Wilson thus stress the point that relaxed norms regarding appropriate conduct and tolerance of deviance are adaptations to a truly disadvantaged context rather than representing the underlying values of a monolithic subculture (see also Sampson & Bartusch, 1998). Still, this cultural disorganization is a key part of weakened social control, and it thus serves to foster further deviance. Specifically, tolerance of unconventional behavior opens the door for the behaviors to be seen more frequently, and when unconventional behaviors are frequently observed, "the transmission of these modes of behavior by precept, as in role modeling, is more easily facilitated" (Sampson & Wilson, 1995, p. 51).

Despite paying great attention to the unique plight of Black communities in the postindustrial era, Sampson and Wilson argued explicitly that their structural-cultural integrative framework was a racially invariant explanation (see also Sampson et al., in press). Concentrated disadvantage and resultant structural and cultural disorganization were the presumed cause of crime in both Black and White communities. Underlying this explanation was the assumption that if Whites and Blacks experienced equivalent levels of community disadvantage and isolation, then racial differences in structural disorganization, cultural attenuation, and crime would disappear. Thus, the experiences of Blacks were not thought of as playing a unique causal role. That is, Sampson and Wilson essentially focused on what is socially common between Whites and Blacks and not their dissimilarities.

Black Communities and Crime at the Dawn of the New Millennium

Important ethnographic scholarship and journalism in the late 1990s and early 2000s focused more concretely on the implications of unique experiences of Black Americans for understanding crime (e.g., Anderson, 1990; Kotlowitz, 1991; Miller, 2008). For example, Mary Pattillo studied the Chicago Southside Black middle-class neighborhood of Groveland (Pattillo, 1998; Pattillo-McCoy, 1999). Her work challenged the applicability of prevailing community-level explanations for crime, such as those assuming racially invariant effects of structural and cultural disorganization described above. Such theory would suggest that a stable, middle-class neighborhood like Groveland would have little crime. Yet Groveland had an "extensively organized and visible criminal element" (Pattillo, 1998 p. 750).

Pattillo provided a portrait of the unique challenges faced by Black middle-class communities such as Groveland (compared to White middle-class communities). She points out that "[g]eographically, black middle-class neighborhoods tend to be nestled between areas that are less economically stable and have higher crime rates" (1998, p. 751). In other words, while White middle-class neighborhoods are typically located within suburban areas with rich resources, Black middle-class communities often remain in urban areas, on the periphery of poorer minority neighborhoods (see also Peterson & Krivo, 2012). Pattillo posited that this unique "urban racial geography" was a key exogenous factor in understanding the control of crime in Groveland. The poorer, more crime-ridden areas proximal to Groveland represented "a dangerous training ground for Groveland's youth who are not confined to the small area of the neighborhood" (1998, p. 752). Thus, racialized geography affected the social networks formed among Groveland residents—specifically, it fostered the development of dense social ties *among criminal and noncriminal adults*. The overlapping licit and illicit network structure, in turn, served to attenuate structural and cultural organization. As Pattillo (1998, p. 755) poignantly suggests, "living in a black middle-class neighborhood requires that law-abiding residents compromise some of their attitudes . . . for the achievement of a 'quiet neighborhood.'"

While Pattillo's work served as a key step in the movement toward Black-focused work on culture and crime, Elijah Anderson's *Code of the Street: Decency, Violence, and the Moral Life of the Inner City* is arguably the most influential work in this regard. The remainder of this chapter focuses specifically on Anderson's work and attempts to draw linkages between such work and several of the key premises of Black Criminology—that racial stratification and oppression have created a contemporary racialized experience for inner-city Blacks that is criminogenic and that racial socialization is related to individual difference in resiliency/offending.

Anderson's *Code of the Street* and Black Criminology

Through his in-depth ethnographic analysis of a poor, urban, Black North Philadelphia neighborhood, Elijah Anderson provides a depiction of the unique social and cultural dynamics that exist in this context. Anderson's work is often interpreted as proposing that the variation in crime rates across neighborhoods is due to the degree to which residents adhere to what he refers to as a "code of the street." The code of the street is a set of rules and norms that guides residents' interpersonal interactions in public. Many of these rules and norms counter mainstream culture and often promote the use of violence and other types of criminal behavior in order to gain respect or provide self-protection. Anderson (1999) identifies that "the violence springs from the circumstances of life among the ghetto poor—the lack of jobs that pay a living wage, limited basic services . . . the stigma of race, the fallout from rampant drug use and drug trafficking, and the resulting alienation and absence of hope for the future" (p. 32). Therefore, according to Anderson, the code and the violence that results are adaptations to entrenched poverty, alienation from wider society, and relentless racial discrimination.

Anderson goes on to describe how individuals living in these conditions often cannot obtain success, status, and respect through conventional means recognized by broader society. It is through this conflict that "the need for being in physical control of at least a portion of one's environment becomes internalized, and the germ of the code of the street emerges" (Anderson, 1999, p. 68). Ultimately, individual faced with this dilemma place extreme importance on respect gained in the streets. An emphasis is placed on gaining respect through physical toughness, and violent retaliation is expected in response to verbal transgressions and any other form of disrespect. While having already gained respect can deter transgressions, there is no guarantee. Others fighting for respect may challenge an individual with a tough reputation so that they too can gain respect in the streets. In this sense, the campaign for respect is a challenging game, one that is competitive, aggressive, and potentially dangerous.

With this brief overview of Anderson's work as the backdrop, the following sections of this chapter illustrate and discuss the overlap between some of the major elements of Anderson's code of the street and Black Criminology. First, we suggest that Anderson's account of a North Philadelphian neighborhood provides a vivid depiction of the unique consequences for inner-city Blacks due to racial stratification and oppression. Second, we offer the interpretation that, through his discussion of the orientations of "decent" and "street," Anderson identifies that racial socialization is related to individual differences in resiliency and, as a byproduct, differences in offending.

Racial Stratification and Oppression on Germantown Avenue

Anderson begins his ethnographic work in North Philadelphia by describing Germantown Avenue, a main artery into downtown Philadelphia. Through this description, Anderson illustrates a continuum not only of physical decay and disorder but also "a natural continuum characterized by a code of civility at one end and a code of conduct regulated by threat of violence—the code of the street—at the other" (Anderson, 1999, pp. 15–16). Starting in the northwest corner of Philadelphia, in the neighborhood of Chestnut Hill, Germantown Avenue is lined with large homes and well-manicured lawns; it is occupied predominately by White, well-educated, and affluent individuals. The business and shopping district is bustling with people who have come from all over the city. As Anderson moves southeast along Germantown Avenue, buildings become older but still well maintained, and the neighborhood becomes more racially integrated. Couples walk hand in hand, people make eye contact, and people seem at ease.

Continuing further down Germantown Avenue, the racial makeup of the neighborhoods transitions from racially integrated to predominately Black, and the residences and other buildings exhibit significant decline. The types of businesses change from high-end boutiques to liquor stores, pawn shops, and barber shops. Buildings' windows have bars on them, and riot gates can be seen on many front doors. As Anderson reaches the complete opposite end of Germantown Avenue from where he started, he is surrounded by boarded-up buildings, empty lots, and other lots full of trash or abandoned cars. It is near this end of Germantown Avenue that the code of the street is pervasive. It is here that residents have a profound lack of trust and faith in the police and where they rely upon themselves to achieve street justice. As Anderson (1999, p. 34) famously notes, "the code of the street thus emerges where the influence of the police ends and where personal responsibility for one's safety is felt to begin."

According to Anderson, the code of the street displayed at this end of Germantown Avenue is an adaptation to several historical and social forces, such as deindustrialization, segregation of the housing markets and White flight, racial discrimination, and neglect on the part of city services. Similar to what was originally described by Wilson (1987), Anderson describes how these forces coalesced to create an increasingly poor, predominantly Black, and socially isolated inner-city community—a truly disadvantaged community.

With deindustrialization, many jobs vacated the area. Those residents that could afford to do so or those residents who were not inhibited by a racially segregated housing market followed the jobs out of the city. The residents who remained were the poorest and likely to be Black. It was the profound social isolation that ensued allowing for the code of the street—with its emphasis on respect through displays of toughness and violence in interpersonal public encounters—to prevail and persist. Respect is a highly sought-after commodity but one that is difficult to achieve through conventional means at the far end of Germantown Avenue, where social and cultural capital is desperately lacking. Here, respect is instead largely based on the individual's reputation on the street. Respect on the street is a source of self-esteem where other options for self-expression are limited. Navigating public interactions in a neighborhood with the presence of the code that dictates the terms of respect is challenging because, as Anderson (1999, p. 36) describes,

> life in public often features an intense competition for scarce social goods in which "winners" totally dominate "losers" and in which losing can be a fate worse than death. So one must be on one's guard constantly. One is not always able to trust others fully, in part because so much is at stake socially, but also because everyone else is understood to be so deprived. In these circumstances, violence is quite prevalent—in families, in schools, and in the streets—becoming a way of public life that is effectively governed by the code of the street.

Thus, due to their experience of racially patterned concentrated disadvantage, street-based respect is often all the individuals at the far end of Germantown Avenue feel that they have. Gaining respect through mainstream avenues such as the level of formal education obtained, possession of professional jobs, or the ownership of a home are typically out of reach. In an attempt to adapt to this situation, individuals emphasize the level of respect that they have in the street. Unfortunately, usually the means of obtaining more respect in the street involves committing crime, the use of violence, or, at a minimum, holding values that counter prosocial, mainstream society values.

But beyond the experience of racially patterned concentrated disadvantage, Anderson also suggests that the code emerges and persists due to racial oppression at the hands of police. Anderson describes that residents of this disadvantaged, predominantly Black end of Germantown Avenue feel as though they have been mistreated and abandoned by the public authorities and are thus responsible for their personal defense. As such, code-based respect is also seen as a means for self-protection.

> The criminal justice system is widely perceived as beset with a double standard: one for blacks and one for whites, resulting in a profound distrust in this institution. In the most socially isolated pockets of the inner city, this situation has given rise to a kind of people's law based on a peculiar form of social exchange that is perhaps best understood as a perversion of the Golden Rule, whose by-product in this case is respect and whose caveat is vengeance, or payback. Given its value and its practical implications, respect is fought for and held and challenged as much as honor was in the age of chivalry. (Anderson, 1999, p. 66)

Overall, Anderson's description aligns with Black Criminology in that racial stratification and oppression have created a unique racialized experience for the inner-city Blacks he studied that can be criminogenic. That is, racial discrimination is described as underlying both the concentrated disadvantage and the alienation from mainstream institutions (including police) that are experienced by the residents of North Philadelphia under study. These residents cope with their unique racialized experience by adopting the code of the street. Subsequently, because the code of the street emphasizes respect gained through a tough street reputation and consists of values that promote the use of violence and other criminal behavior, high rates of offending are observed. Therefore, Anderson's work could be interpreted as describing a unique rather than racially invariant causal force for criminal offending among residents in Black communities like those at the southeast end of Germantown Avenue.

Racial Socialization and Resiliency: Decent Versus Street

While most residents living in the area observed by Anderson suffer from the racially patterned concentrated disadvantage and alienation from police, the degree to which they are detached from mainstream society varies; and therefore, the degree to which they adopt the code does as well. In short, Anderson describes systemic oppression, but he also observes that there is individual variation in the response to that systemic oppression.

According to Anderson, there are two orientations—"decent" and "street"—that exist within these neighborhoods, and the role the code plays for each orientation is very different. Further, most residents are not purely "decent" or "street." Rather, they exist somewhere on a continuum from decent to street. While most individuals are generally decent, it is those that are intimately associated with the criminal element that are the most street.

Those who fall more toward the decent end of the continuum are more likely to value mainstream norms, have a strong work ethic, exhibit personal responsibility, and display a sense of hope for the future. For decent parents, it is a primary goal to pass these values and behavioral norms on to their children. Importantly, though decent individuals are not socialized to internalize the values of the code, knowledge and an understanding of the code are necessary for survival. Familiarity with the code provides a defense for decent individuals, and it allows them to navigate through the neighborhood where others follow and live by the code of the street. Thus, decent families have a very difficult balancing act to execute in the sense that they want their children to internalize prosocial values, but at the same time, they do not want their children to be disrespected or taken advantage of on the street. In response to this dilemma, a primary strategy used by decent residents is referred to as "code switching." Code switching consists of acting "street" or adhering to the code in certain situations when acting "street" serves as a means for self-protection or as a means to achieve a goal.

On the other hand, individuals falling more toward the street end of the continuum are more likely to be socialized to internalize and follow the values of the code. These individuals were often born into "street" families that execute sporadic, superficial, or overly aggressive parenting. These families often tend to experience frustrations regarding unemployment, finances, and housing. They have a propensity toward self-destructive behaviors such as drugs and alcohol, and they are likely to have an ingrained bitterness towards the justice system. Street parents may judge others based on the code and may even socialize their children into the code in a "normative" way (Anderson, 1999, p. 45).

Frequently, extended families are mixed with both decent and street members. The culture conflict between decent and street family members causes tension and divides within the family. Individuals who are striving to achieve upward mobility are often viewed as being disrespectful to their community and seen as a threat. For example, family members who are more street-oriented might view a decent relative as a "sell-out" or "acting white," and sometimes violence is used in retaliation to this perception of disrespect (p. 65).

Anderson's discussion of decent and street overlaps with the Black Criminology in regards to the perspective's notion of racial socialization and its role in resiliency (Unnever & Owusu-Bempah, this volume; see also Burt & Simons, this volume). From a Black Criminology perspective, it is insufficient to study the relationship between race and crime focusing only on macro-level forces, such as concentrated disadvantage and social isolation, since most racial discrimination is experienced at the individual level. Further, paralleling the individual variation in response to concentrated disadvantage and alienation from police that was observed by Anderson, a Black Criminology assumes substantial variation exists in how individual Blacks perceive, interpret, and respond to racial oppression (Unnever & Owusu-Bempah, this volume). The idea of *racial socialization* provides a mechanism for understanding such individual variation (Burt, Simons, & Gibbons, 2012), and we argue that some degree of racial socialization is evident in Anderson's description of decent versus street families.

Racial-ethnic socialization on the part of minority families is one micro-level adaptation to the oppressive reality of macro-level racial stratification and discrimination in the U.S. (Hughes, 2003; Neblett et al., 2008). Racial socialization refers to a socialization process of adults instilling pride and esteem in their racial group to children and preparing children for encountering biases regarding their race and/or ethnicity (Hughes, 2003; Hughes et al., 2006; Neblett et al., 2008). Racial/ethnic socialization has been associated with several positive outcomes such as higher levels of self-esteem (Stevenson, Reed, Bodison, & Bishop, 1997), higher academic achievement (Smith, Walker, Fields, Brookins, & Seay, 1999), and lower levels of externalizing behaviors (Bynum, Burton, & Best, 2007).

More closely related to Anderson's work, racial socialization has also been shown to be a protective factor against offending. For example, Burt et al. (2012) demonstrated, first, that interpersonal racial discrimination is associated with increases in offending and that the majority of this relationship is explained by possessing hostile views of relationships, disengaging from conventional norms, and depression. Second, they found that racial/ethnic socialization, through preparing for bias, reduced the effects of discrimination on disengaging from conventional norms, and it reduced the effect of emotional distress, hostile views, and disengaging from conventional norms on offending. However, in certain family contexts, preparing for bias actually had a direct positive effect on hostile views. That is, preparation for bias that occurred in a family context absent of supportive parenting and/or cultural socialization (building pride and esteem regarding racial group) was associated with an increase in hostile views of relationships. Third, cultural socialization served as a protective factor against the criminogenic effect of discrimination by decreasing the rejection of conventional norms. Overall, literature such as this suggests that the effects of various parenting practices, including racial socialization, are conditioned by the general caregiving context (Burt et al., 2012; McHale et al., 2006).

From this perspective, children that Anderson would have identified as street are those that, while they might have been prepared for bias, were prepared for bias in the absence of cultural socialization, in the absence of family support and warmth, or in the presence of parental authoritativeness or aggression. The racial socialization literature would suggest that the effects of preparation for bias in these familial contexts might lead youths to perceive relationships as hostile, to disengage from conventional norms, and to be at increased risk of offending. In fact, within *Code of the Street*, Anderson describes how children of street families are likely to perceive relationships as hostile, have a distrust of others, and reject conventional norms. Even more specifically, he describes street families as socializing their children to be particularly distrustful of the police, leading to legal cynicism and more likely to adapt to the community's alienation from police by adopting the code of the street, ultimately increasing offending behaviors.

On the other hand, Anderson's description of decent families suggests that the parents in such families not only prepare their children for bias but also do so in combination with cultural socialization and a relatively more nurturing parenting style. Further, this sort of socialization did appear to protect the children from a general distrust of others, including the police. In the decent familial context described by Anderson, the preparation for bias appeared to mediate the effects of discrimination on disengagement from conventional norms, just as the racial socialization thesis predicts (Burt et al., 2012). That is, even though decent children at the far end of Germantown Avenue experienced racial discrimination, their preparation for bias in a decent family environment made them less likely to cope with this discrimination by full-fledged adoption of the code of the street. At most, decent kids appeared to code-switch and adhere to the code situationally.

Below we provide a depiction of how Anderson's Code of the Street might look through a Black Criminology lens. Here, we highlight that it is the unique experiences of racial oppression and discrimination

Figure 7.1
Anderson's *Code of the Street* through a Black Criminology Lens

leading parents to prepare their children through the process of racial socialization. In decent families, this racial socialization may lead to resiliency and an acceptance of conventional norms, ultimately leading to lower levels of offending (much of which is situational offending). On the other hand, if the racial socialization occurs in the absence of warmth and care, it may lead to hostility, legal cynicism, and disengagement from conventional norms. This situation would likely lead to more persistent offending.

In sum, compatible with Black Criminology, Anderson's s discussion of decent and street can be viewed as suggesting that the criminogenic effects of racial discrimination can be combatted, at the individual level, through decent family socialization—by decent parents executing racial socialization in a supportive environment. This effective racial socialization on the part of decent families served to prepare their children for bias, yet in a manner that left them less hostile, less distrustful of the police, less likely to internalize the code of the street, and ultimately less likely to offend in relation to their "street" counterparts.

Conclusion

Cultural perspectives on crime have largely ignored the unique criminogenic experiences of Blacks. However, as shown above, cultural perspectives are amenable to the Black Criminology perspective. Specifically, this chapter has focused on how Anderson's *Code of the Street* overlaps with Black Criminology. We by no means claim that Anderson attempted to put forth a Black Criminological theory; however, our goal was to highlight its compatibility with key aspects of the Black

Criminology perspective nonetheless and to demonstrate that it could potentially be viewed through a Black Criminology lens.

In particular, we highlighted how Anderson's depiction of Northern Philadelphia provided an example of the racial stratification and oppression that has created a contemporary racialized experience for inner-city Blacks in the U.S. That is, crime in Black, urban communities is a product of racial oppression, including hypersegregation. As a result of this racialized experience, the code of the street is adopted which is ultimately criminogenic. Furthermore, the code's tether to racial oppression does not necessarily preclude a cultural explanation for offending within a Black Criminology framework in our way of thinking. We also used Anderson's orientations of street and decent to draw parallels between Anderson's work and the role of racial socialization in Black Criminology. Here we articulated that racial socialization, within certain familial contexts (decent, as opposed to street), is capable of dampening the detrimental effects of racial discrimination on hostility, disengagement from conventional values, and offending. In contrast, racial socialization within street familial contexts can foster the persistence of the code (and associated behaviors), even in light of structural improvements, especially if fueled by entrenched legal cynicism (see also Kirk & Papachristos, 2015).

There are additional emerging cultural theories that overlap with Anderson's *Code of the Street* and that are also likely overlapping with Black Criminology. For example, the concept of legal cynicism was embedded in Anderson's work (i.e., alienation from police fueled the code), yet the concept has since evolved into a theory in its own right based largely on the more contemporary work of David Kirk and Andrew Papachristos. Kirk and Papachristos (2011) define legal cynicism as a cultural orientation in which the law and agents of the criminal justice system are perceived as being illegitimate, ineffective, and unresponsive. Unjust and racialized criminal justice system practices—including harsh policing practices and disproportionate minority confinement in prisons and jails—are considered a precursor to legal cynicism (Kirk & Papachristos, 2015). In turn, residents in communities in which legal cynicism is entrenched are less likely to call upon the police when a crime occurs or when a broader crime problem exists that needs to be addressed (Kirk & Matsuda, 2011; Kirk & Papachristos, 2011, 2015). More specifically, legal cynicism, and the distrust in police that it entails, constrains the choices available for resolving grievances or for self-protection. Therefore, this may lead to residents policing themselves—using aggression and sometimes violence to handle disputes. Legal cynicism theory is still evolving, and some versions appear to articulate a racially invariant theory (see Unnever, this volume). Still, the linkages between the theory's key construct—legal cynicism—and highly racialized experiences with the criminal justice system are undeniable. Racialized patterns of incarceration and negative encounters with police would suggest that racial discrimination and oppression is a viable starting point for legal cynicism theory, therefore making it compatible with Black Criminology.

In conclusion, Black Criminology suggests that racial subordination underlies Black offending and that at least some offending cannot be separated from racial subordination (Unnever & Owusu-Bempah, this volume). Addressing this assumption cannot be accomplished with racially invariant theories. Anderson's *Code of the Street* is one of the few criminological works focused on culture that appears to *not* propose a racially invariant one but to, instead, begin with the unique experiences of Blacks and the effects of those unique experiences on offending. Perhaps a code of the street can emerge in areas different from the slice of North Philadelphia that Anderson observed, but our read of his work does not suggest that. Many scholars (including the authors of this chapter) have ignored this important aspect of Anderson's work and have attempted to test his ideas regarding a code of the street on general samples without any measures of racial discrimination or racial socialization. In doing so, perhaps we have missed the point.

Note

1. As thoroughly detailed in Cullen et al. (this volume), Cloward and Ohlin do give some consideration to how race might affect the emergence of criminal versus conflict gangs in White versus Black communities in the future (i.e., moving into the mid- and late 1960s and beyond). In a racially invariant application of theory, Cloward and Ohlin predicted greater power, greater organization, and thus more opportunity for criminal enterprise (as opposed to conflict gangs) in the poor Black communities of the future.

References

Anderson, E. (1990). *Streetwise: Race, class and change in an urban community.* Chicago, IL: University of Chicago Press.

Anderson, E. (1999). *Code of the street: Decency, violence, and the moral life of the inner city.* New York, NY: W. W. Norton.

Burt, C. H., Simons, R. L., & Gibbons, F. X. (2012). Racial discrimination, ethnic-racial socialization, and crime a micro-sociological model of risk and resilience. *American Sociological Review, 77,* 648–677.

Bynum, M. S., Burton, E. T., & Best, C. (2007). Racism experiences and psychological functioning in African American college freshman: Is racial socialization a buffer? *Cultural Diversity and Ethnic Minority Psychology, 13*, 64–71.

Cloward, R. A. (1959). Illegitimate means, anomie, and deviant behavior. *American Sociological Review, 24*, 164–176.

Cloward, R. A., & Ohlin, L. E. (1960). *Delinquency and opportunity: A theory of delinquent gangs.* New York, NY: Free Press.

Cohen, A. K. (1955). *Delinquent boys: The culture of the gang.* New York, NY: Free Press.

Cullen, F. T., Chouhy, C., Butler, L., & Lee, H. (this volume). Beyond white criminology. In J. D. Unnever, S. L. Gabbidon, & C. Chouhy (Eds.), *Building a Black criminology: Race, theory, and crime* (*Advances in criminological theory*, Vol. 24, pp. 45–75). New York, NY: Routledge.

Curtis, L. A. (1975). *Violence, race, and culture.* New York, NY: Lexington Books.

Hirschi, T. (1969). *Causes of delinquency.* Berkeley, CA: University of California Press.

Hughes, D. (2003). Correlates of African American and Latino parents' messages to children about ethnicity and race: A comparative study of racial socialization. *American Journal of Community Psychology, 31*, 15–33.

Hughes, D., Rodriguez, J., Smith, E. P., Johnson, D. J., Stevenson, H. C., & Spicer, P. (2006). Parents' ethnic-racial socialization practices: A review of research and directions for future study. *American Psychological Association, 42*, 747–770.

Kirk, D. S., & Matsuda, M. (2011). Legal cynicism, collective efficacy, and the ecology of arrest. *Criminology, 49*, 443–472.

Kirk, D. S., & Papachristos, A. V. (2011). Cultural mechanisms and the persistence of neighborhood violence. *American Journal of Sociology, 116*, 1190–1233.

Kirk, D. S., & Papachristos, A. V. (2015). Concentrated disadvantage, the persistence of legal cynicism, and crime: Revisiting the conception of "culture" in criminology. In F. T. Cullen, P. Wilcox, & B. D. Dooley (Eds.), *Challenging criminology: The legacy of Ruth Rosner Kornhauser.* Advances in criminological theory (Vol. 19, pp. 259–274). New York, NY: Routledge.

Kornhauser, R. R. (1978). *Social sources of delinquency: An appraisal of analytical models.* Chicago, IL: University of Chicago Press.

Kotlowitz, A. (1991). *There are no children here.* New York, NY: Doubleday.

McHale, S., Crouter, A., Kim, J., Burton, L., Davis, K., Dotterer, A., & Swanson, D. (2006). Mothers' and fathers' racial socialization in African American families: Implications for youth. *Child Development, 77*, 1387–1402.

Miller, J. (2008). *Getting played: African American girls, urban inequality, and gendered violence.* New York, NY: New York University Press.

Miller, W. B. (1958). Lower class culture as a generating milieu of gang delinquency. *Journal of Social Issues, 14*(3), 5–19.

Neblett, E., White, R., Ford, K., Philip, C., Nguyen, H., & Sellers, R. (2008). Patterns of racial socialization and psychological adjustment: Can parental communications about race reduce the impact of racial discrimination. *Journal of Research on Adolescence, 18*, 477–515.

Pattillo, M. E. (1998). Sweet mothers and gangbangers: Managing crime in a Black middle-class neighborhood. *Social Forces, 76*, 747–774.

Pattillo-McCoy, M. (1999). *Black picket fences: Privilege and peril among the Black middle class.* Chicago, IL: University of Chicago Press.

Peterson, R. D., & Krivo, L. J. (2012). *Divergent social worlds: Neighborhood crime and the racial-spatial divide*. New York, NY: Russell Sage Foundation.

Sampson, R. J., & Bartusch, D. J. (1998). Legal cynicism and (subcultural?) tolerance of deviance: The neighborhood context of racial differences. *Law and Society Review, 32*, 777–804.

Sampson, R. J., & Wilson, W. J. (1995). Toward a theory of race, crime, and urban inequality. In J. Hagan & R. D. Peterson (Eds.), *Crime and inequality* (pp. 37–54). Stanford, CA: Stanford University Press.

Sampson, R. J., Wilson, W. J., & Katz, H. (in press). Reassessing "Toward a theory of race, crime, and urban inequality": Enduring and new challenges in 21st century America. *Du Bois Review: Social Science Research on Race, 15*, 13–34.

Shaw, C. R. (1930). *The jack-roller: A delinquent boy's own story*. Chicago, IL: University of Chicago Press.

Shaw, C. R., & McKay, H. D. (1942/1969). *Juvenile delinquency and urban areas*. Chicago, IL: University of Chicago Press.

Shaw, C. R., & McKay, H. D. (1949). Rejoinder. *American Sociological Review, 14*, 608–617.

Smith, E, Walker, K., Fields, L., Brookins, C., & Seay, R. (1999). Ethnic identity and its relationship to self-esteem, perceived efficacy and prosocial attitudes in early adolescence. *Journal of Adolescence, 33*, 867–880.

Stevenson, H. C., Reed, J., Bodison, P., & Bishop, A. (1997). Racism stress management: Racial socialization beliefs and the experience of depression and anger in African American Youth. *Youth and Society, 29*, 197–222.

Unnever, J. D. (this volume). The racial invariance thesis in criminology: Toward a Black criminology. In J. D. Unnever, S. L. Gabbidon, & C. Chouhy (Eds.), *Building a Black criminology: Race, theory, and crime (Advance in criminological theory*, Vol. 24, pp. 77–100). New York, NY: Routledge.

Unnever, J. D., & Gabbidon, S. (2011). *A theory of African American offending: Race, racism, and crime*. New York, NY: Routledge.

Unnever, J. D., & Owusu-Bempah, A. (this volume). Black criminology matters. In J. D. Unnever, S. L. Gabbidon, & C. Chouhy (Eds.), *Building a Black criminology: Race, theory, and crime (Advance in criminological theory*, Vol. 24, pp. 3–28). New York, NY: Routledge.

Wilcox, P., Cullen, F. T., & Feldmeyer, B. (2018). *Communities and crime: An enduring American challenge*. Philadelphia, PA: Temple University Press.

Wilson, W. J. (1987). *The truly disadvantaged: The inner city, the underclass, and public policy*. Chicago, IL: University of Chicago Press.

Wolfgang, M. E., & Ferracuti, F. (Eds.). (1967). *The subculture of violence: Towards an integrated theory in criminology*. London, UK: Social Science Paperbacks.

8

Race, Place Management, and Crime

John E. Eck

In recent months, a police informant made a dozen drug buys at a sprawling apartment complex that sits on the northern edge of Baldwin Village. In the last few years, authorities seized half a dozen firearms there and investigated multiple shootings and robberies.

Los Angeles prosecutors say the Chesapeake Apartments, a 425-unit complex spread over more than 17 acres, is a longtime stronghold for a street gang called the Black P-Stones and has been plagued by violent crime for decades. The gang is so deeply entrenched in the neighborhood, officials said, that its members have tattoos that reference the property.

Now, prosecutors are targeting the property's owners and managers to curb the crime. In a lawsuit announced Monday, City Atty. Mike Feuer alleged that their mismanagement has resulted in a "serious threat" to public safety and created an environment in which anyone who comes near the property is at risk of being a crime victim.

Feuer thinks that the head of the complex, Swaranjit Nijjar, should be ordered to live on the property until the problems are resolved. The lawsuit says Nijjar is the CEO of the company that's the sole general partner of Pama V Properties LP, which owns the property. (Tchekmedyian, 2017)

This chapter is about how behaviors of property owners create crime opportunities in poor Black neighborhoods and the reasons property owners in these neighborhoods have less incentive to control crime than they would in affluent White neighborhoods. The extended quote above, from the *Los Angeles Times*, illustrates key features of my argument. This chapter is not about how being Black influences criminality (why youths join the Black P-Stones, for example). Its focus is on place managers (the owner of the Chesapeake Apartments, for example). Place managers are people and institutions that own and operate homes, rental property, businesses, and other facilities. Place managers are important because they are a source of social control in all neighborhoods. Oddly, given their rather prominent and obvious roles, they have received almost no attention in criminology. And unlike more commonly discussed sources of nonstate control, there are strong policy levers the state can be apply to them (City Attorney Feuer's lawsuit, for example); levers that researchers have demonstrated to be effective (Eck, 2002; Eck & Guerette, 2012). Place managers are important because race can influence their behavior.

In this chapter, I answer an old question: Why do some neighborhoods have far more crime than others? For readers steeped in the traditions of standard criminology and unfamiliar with environmental criminology, my argument may seem strange. So I begin by making my basic assumptions obvious. First, people are reasonably rational. They are not as rational as economists often assume, but then even economists often do not believe in extreme rationality: it just facilitates effective modeling (Friedman, 1953). Rather, people are approximately rational even if they do make mistakes (Simon, 1955; Kahneman, 2011). For the purposes of my argument, all we need to agree upon is that "rational" means people have some vague idea of what they want in the moment, that they make decisions based on these ideas in light of cues in their proximate environments, and they respond to these cues relatively consistently (i.e., not randomly or arbitrarily) (Coyne & Eck, 2015). Readers uncomfortable with the notion that offenders are reasonably rational can relax; my focus is not on offenders but on property owners.

Second, the environmental cues to which people respond are created by opportunity structures (Clarke, 1995). If we were interested in offenders, we would be interested in the opportunity structure for burglary or drug dealing or sexual assault. These opportunity structures involve both physical and social conditions that make crime easy or hard, rewarding or unrewarding, safe or risky, excusable or inexcusable, and provoked or suppressed (Clarke, 2005). In the *Los Angeles Times* example, the prosecutor is contending that the place manager has created an opportunity structure for a street gang, which results in considerable crime.

In short, an opportunity structure is a description of the environmental sources of temptation. Though environmental criminologists are very interested in crime opportunity structures, the concept applies to non-crimes as well. A rug store creates opportunity structures to buy rugs. Bars provide opportunity structures for drinking. Bowling alleys provide opportunity structures to bowl. I will discuss two sorts of opportunity structures: those created by place managers that influence possible offenders and those created by governments, financial institutions, and social norms that influence place managers.

The theory I propose covers multiple levels of analysis. At one extreme, there are crime events. These events may occur at the same places, my second level. In my theory, the places that matter are addresses, or property parcels. My third level is the place manager. A small proportion of place managers have properties with a larger proportion of crime because they own more places with high crime volumes. So far, the levels nest like a Russian doll: events in places and places in managers. Not so with the fourth level. High-crime place owners are unlikely to concentrate in high-crime neighborhoods. They will live elsewhere. But high-crime addresses tend to cluster in some neighborhoods and are relatively infrequent in most other neighborhoods. Finally, there is a vague fifth level. Here we have an assortment of private and public institutions that influence businesses and real-estate decisions in various neighborhoods through their influence on place managers. These institutions can have citywide, statewide, countrywide, or even international reach.

Figure 8.1 provides a schematic of these relationships and provides a skeletal structure for the theory that follows. Given what I just said, the figure should be relatively clear. Two points are worth emphasizing, however. Place managers often do not live on their properties. This is obvious for stores but applies to apartment buildings as well (note that the prosecutor is asking the court to force the place manager to live on his property). There is some research on this topic. The further an owner lives from her apartment complex, the less repair she will make in her buildings (Sternlieb, 1966) and the more crime there will be at these buildings (Rephann, 2009). Just as important, place managers have power over the physical and social conditions of neighborhoods within which they do not reside. Standard theories of neighborhood crime usually assume neighborhood residents have control, or could have control, over their environments, and they overlook property owners and their influence (Wilcox, Cullen, & Feldmeyer, 2018). In contrast, I focus on property owners and assume that power over one's environment depends a great deal on legal ownership rights. Wilcox and Tillyer (2018) are absolutely correct in calling for a place in neighborhood perspective. However, the hierarchical arrangements involve more than two levels, these levels are

Figure 8.1
Hierarchies of Crime and Place

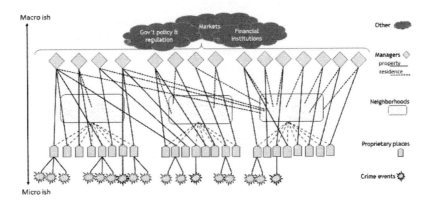

not nested, and the causal mechanism of control may be quite different than assumed by the off-spring of the Chicago school of crime communities.

Having described the elements of my theory from the bottom up, I will now give a summary working from the top of Figure 8.1 downward. The economic, social, and political institutions influence investments by place managers at places within different neighborhoods. This variation in incentives across neighborhoods influences how place managers behave: in high- and low-income neighborhoods; in White and Black neighborhoods; and in high-political-power and low-political-power neighborhoods. My theory suggests that in low income, Black, and politically disconnected neighborhoods, place managers will have weaker incentives to provide the quality services they would provide if their properties were in higher-income, White, and politically connected neighborhoods. These incentives describe the opportunity structure for bad place management. This opportunity structure is not uniform within a neighborhood: location matters. And not all place managers will respond in the same way. In fact, most place managers, in any neighborhood, do not operate their property in a way that facilitates chronic misbehavior. But it does give rise to more high-crime locations in a few neighborhoods relative to other areas. It is the clustering of high-crime places that gives rise to neighborhood crime levels.

I unfold my theory in nine steps, starting with the crime events and their concentration at places at the bottom of Figure 8.1. I will work up to institutions that incentivize bad place management. This is, roughly, how the evidence came to be discovered. At each step, I describe the theory and evidence. In the first four steps, the evidence is largely quantitative, and we can rely on systematic reviews. After the fourth step, we enter the field of urban history, and the nature of the evidence changes. Rather than being quantitative, it is based on documents and historical investigation. The fifth step examines the economics of places in low-income areas. The six step introduces race and the history of methods for racial discrimination against Blacks that create the segregated neighborhoods we see today. The methods of discrimination vary over time, as does the economics of inner-city places: the focus of the seventh step. In the eighth step, I look at variation among place managers in how they respond to the opportunity structure of places in low-income Black neighborhoods. I illustrate why it does not take many badly managed places to spoil a neighborhood. The last step describes my theory's conclusions. The final section of this chapter deals with implications for theory and practice.

Crime Is Concentrated at Places

Until the end of the 1980s, it was possible to think of neighborhood factors as being the drivers of crime. Then two studies appeared, one as a large report that went mostly unnoticed (Pierce et al., 1988) and the other in the journal *Criminology*, which did receive considerable attention (Sherman et al., 1989). They showed the same thing. A few addresses and street corners have a great deal of crime, but most addresses have no crime. This was true in Boston, Massachusetts, (Pierce et al., 1988) and in Minneapolis, Minnesota (Sherman et al., 1989). Importantly, both studies showed that even in high-crime neighborhoods, this was true. In fact, high-crime neighborhoods were comprised mostly of non- and low-crime places, just like other neighborhoods.

Following these two groundbreaking studies, places—tiny spaces within neighborhoods—start to look like drivers of crime. Over a quarter of a century later, there are at least 44 empirical studies of the crime distribution across places, and they all showed the same thing: most places have little or no crime, but a few places have most of the crime (Lee et al., 2017). The systematic review and meta-analysis Lee and colleagues conducted of the crime–place connection does not count those studies of a single place type: studies of bars, apartment buildings, banks, or other facilities. When places are divided into homogeneous groups the research also shows that a few risky facilities in each group have most of the crime, and the majority of the facilities in the group have little or no crime (Eck, Clarke, & Guerette, 2007). The place literature overlaps with the repeat victimization literature, particularly for crimes within homes or businesses, such as burglary or store robbery. Here too, a few are victimized repeatedly, but most have no victimization experience. Based on a systematic review and meta-analysis conducted by O and her colleagues, we know that the distributions of crime in these place-based victimization studies is similar to the distributions of reported crime in police data (O, Martinez, Lee, & Eck, 2017).

At this point, it is important that I define places. The term "place" is used in a number of ways: as an address, street corner, or property parcel; as a street segment (both sides of a street, from intersection to intersection); or as an area. These are all reasonable definitions, as long as we do not mix them up. For that reason, Tamara Madensen and I proposed a classification scheme. Proprietary places are of the first type. A proprietary place has a single owner who can control the location. The owner might delegate control in any of a number of ways: to employees, as in a store; to tenants, as in an apartment building; to businesses, as in shopping malls; and in many other ways (Madensen & Eck, 2013). This chapter is largely about these types of places.

Proximal places are street segments. A street segment usually has a number of proprietary places, some lined up on one side of the street and the others lined up on the other side. Typically, proximal places do not have a single owner. David Weisburd, Elizabeth Groff, and Sue-Min Yang (2013) have pioneered the study of these types of places. They are not the subject of this chapter because they do not have a single owner who can be held accountable for crime.

Finally, pooled places are areas comprising multiple proximal places. Neighborhoods are a type of pooled place. With rare exception, there is not a single owner of a neighborhood. Often there are hundreds of place managers. As I will show, neighborhoods matter because they are prominent in the minds of real-estate agents, property investors, financial institutions, and government agencies. Past decisions by these actors and institutions created the neighborhoods we see today, including the racially segregated nature of the urban and suburban landscape (Massey & Denton, 1993; Rothstein, 2017).

Crime clusters at all three types of places. But it is more clustered at among proprietary places (Andresen & Malleson, 2010; Eck et al., 2017; Johnson, 2010; Steenbeek & Weisburd, 2016). The concentration of crime at proprietary places is not controversial: it is well established.

The only questions are how this occurs and what one can do about it. We will discuss how under step four and what one can do about it at the end of the chapter.

Crime Is Clustered Among Owners

Criminologists are used to thinking about neighborhoods and crime, and they have become increasingly interested in places and crime. Crimes, places, and neighborhoods can be put on maps and their geographic arrangement scrutinized. There is another way crime and places cluster, however. That is at the level of place managers. If one's idea of a place is a single-family home, this might not be apparent. But if you are a renter or are seeking a place to rent, you realize that many apartment buildings scattered across a neighborhood or city have the same owner or management firm. And if you shift your gaze from facilities where people live to places where people work, shop, and eat, you quickly realize that many addresses have the same owner. An owner of many properties can be considered a virtual neighborhood, and you can visualize this by listing all property owners in a city and writing down all the addresses each owns.

In 2007, Troy Payne and I did this for Cincinnati apartment buildings (Payne & Eck, 2007) and found that about 8% of the owners owned about 51% of the rental apartment complexes. SooHyun O and YongJei Lee followed this up using 2009 Cincinnati data for all properties (O, Lee, & Eck, 2017). They report that 7% of the owners control 28% of the places. This is not a new finding; Michael Stegman (1972, p. 25) noted over 40 years ago, "over one-fourth of the private inner-city rental inventory is owned or controlled by about 50 professionals." Gilderbloom (1989: see also Gilderbloom & Appelbaum, 1988, pp. 58–59) reviewed the literature on the concentration of ownership for rental units. He cites six studies in seven cities and shows that relatively few owners control a substantial portion of the rental units in an area. These findings are consistent with evidence about business in general: a few businesses dominate, either in terms of people employed, market share, or other criteria (Axtel, 2001; Ijiri & Simon, 2013).

The Cincinnati findings may underestimate of concentration. That is because ownership is difficult to pin down. The ownership records we had access to, from county departments that keep property records, list individuals, companies, and limited liability corporations (LLCs). An individual may own multiple LLCs, one for each apartment building.

And LLCs maybe owned by other legal entities, which might in turn be owned by others. However, the county records only show the first-level owner (e.g., an LLC) but not higher-level owners (e.g., the LLC that owns the recorded LLC).

But even knowing we underestimated owner concentration, we find that crime is concentrated at the owner level. This is true if we look only at apartment buildings (Payne & Eck, 2007) or if we look at all places (O, Lee, & Eck, 2017).

From other research, we know that in low-income neighborhoods, owners of rental property live elsewhere (Reiss & Aldrich, 1971). This too makes sense. These owners have higher incomes and wealth than neighborhood residents and can afford to live elsewhere. There is some evidence that absentee owners are less attentive to property repairs and upkeep (Sternlieb, 1966), and their places have more crime on average (Rephann, 2009). Desmond (2016) suggests there are owners of rental property who specialize in renting to the poor, just as there are specialists in serving the well off.

Place Management Influences Crime

This brings us to the point where we can answer the question, why do some proprietary places have far more crime than other proprietary places, including nearby places? The short answer is differences in place management. Places with very high numbers of crime are managed differently from those similarly situated places that have little or no crime.

Place management theory is an extension of Routine Activity Theory (Cohen & Felson, 1979). I created it because Routine Activity Theory was not able to explain why some proprietary places were so desirable to drug dealers. Guardianship was not the answer, as neither party involved in a drug transaction had any interest in preventing it (although guardianship would be useful to prevent rip-offs) (Eck, 1994). Only the person or institution who owned the place or those to whom the owner delegated authority (e.g., an apartment superintendent, a property management firm, a janitor, and so forth) had an interest in and the authority to prevent drug dealing. If some place managers were ineffective, then this would explain why drug dealing was at some locations in a neighborhood known for drug dealing and not at most locations in that neighborhood. Pressuring place managers to change their practices could reduce drug dealing. Subsequent experiments validated that hypothesis (Eck & Wartell, 1998; Green, 1996; Mazerolle et al., 1998).

Other studies and experiments demonstrated that place managers had control over crime at their places (for apartments, Clarke & Bichler-Robertson, 1998; for motels, Bichler et al., 2013; for bars, Graham & Homel, 2008; for large retailers, Zidar et al., 2017).

The ability to manipulate something and create predicted outcomes is the soundest evidence for a theory, far superior to correlations, even with numerous controls. The latest systematic review of place-based prevention shows that we can experimentally manipulate place managers and get the predicted results (Eck & Guerette, 2012). Consequently, we can be certain, (a) that place managers exist and (b) they have the ability to control crime.

Tamara Madensen (2007) spelled out the mechanisms by which place managers influence crime and disorder on their properties. She described a set of influences, operating over different time scales and including feedback,that could explain how place management for bars blocks or creates opportunities for violence. At the shortest time scale, place managers respond to positive and negative incidents at the bar in minutes or hours. At longer time scales, they alter how they attract customers, change planned events (e.g., music and entertainment), and train employees and set expectations. At the longest time scales, they alter the physical structure itself, rebrand the location, switch locations, or even go out of business. Numerous outside influences affect these decisions: markets, regulators, business networks, and so forth.

The core of place management is the carrying out of four functions, summarized by the acronym ORCA (Madensen, 2007). Organizing the physical environment is the first function. This includes anything related to the physical environment of the property—walls, windows, doors, furnishing, decorations, and landscaping, for example. Any crime prevention through environmental design is included in this function. The second function is the regulation of conduct. This includes promoting desired behaviors as well as suppressing undesired behaviors. So stores promote shopping and the purchasing of specific products. Advertising and product placement encourage purchases. Stores also try to discourage theft through various forms of guardianship. Sometimes they emphasize the former more than the latter, and a place can become a magnet for thieves and a crime hot spot (see Zidar, Schaffer, & Eck, 2017 for an example).

The third function is control of access. Opening and closing hours are a primary example. Access varies across different types of places (i.e., facilities). A convenience store is very open relative to an office building. Like the other two functions, access control has a dual nature. All place managers want to be open to specific users but to deny access to others. The law sometimes dictates how much control a place manager can exert. In the 1950s and 1960s, Blacks demanded access to racially segregated businesses and public facilities—segregation being a form of access control. Legislation and court ruling restrict place managers' abilities to discriminate. But much access control is not so obvious: prices, for example, influence who enters and who does not.

Finally, all place managers are concerned about the acquisition of resources. This is obvious for businesses, which must generate a revenue stream in excess of their operating costs. But it is also true of nonprofits. Churches, for example, have to pass the collection plate. The "free" museum relies on the patronage of rich donors. Public buildings rely on elected officials to provide tax revenue. When place managers cannot acquire sufficient resources, they have to cut costs. And this influences their abilities to carry out the other three functions.

Madensen's work provides a clear, simple, and straightforward explanation for why some places have a great deal of crime and others do not. Whereas the experimental evidence provides a strong empirical link between place management and crime, Madensen's theory describes how this occurs. Recently, she and I have shown how all other explanations for why some places have far more crime than others—number of targets, number of offenders, informal social control, and others—may be the consequence of place management decisions (Eck & Madensen, 2018).

Crime Places Are Clustered in Some Neighborhoods

Crime place researchers have advocated for pulling back on the neighborhood focus of criminology and pushing forward on a place focus (Sherman et al., 1989; Weisburd et al., 2013, 2016). The rationale is simple. Neighborhood-level processes, such as those considered in the social disorganization framework (Shaw & McKay, 1942; Wilcox et al., 2018), imply reasonably even levels of crime across neighborhoods. The discovery of extreme differences in crime across places within the most crime-prone neighborhoods suggests this is wrong. Rather, crime-generating processes must be operating at places rather than larger areas.

Though I am very sympathetic with this critique, it goes too far. A large number of studies have shown that high-crime places concentrate within high-crime neighborhoods. Sherman, Gartin, and Buerger (1989) pointed this out at the beginning of the crime–place revolution. Since then, at least six studies have shown this (Eck, Gersh, & Taylor, 2000; Groff, Weisburd, & Yang, 2010; Payne & Gallagher, 2016; Sherman & Weisburd, 1995; Trickett, Osborn, Seymour, & Pease, 1992, 1995). In two papers, Alan Trickett and colleagues (1992, 1995) showed that repeat victimization, much of it at places, drives area-level crime. Areas where repeated victimization is high have high levels of crime. Areas with few repeat victimizations have far less crime.

Intuitively this makes sense. A neighborhood with 10 high-crime places and 100 no-crime locations is likely to have more crime than a neighborhood with one high-crime place and 109 no-crime locations. Though intuitive, it is not necessarily true. The one high-crime place in the second neighborhood could have 60 crimes and each of the 10 places in the first neighborhood could have only five each. So Trickett's findings are not tautological; they are empirical.

Based on these studies, it is reasonable to conclude that high-crime neighborhoods differ from low-crime neighborhoods in the number of high-crime places they contain. This conclusion then suggests that we need to look to neighborhoods for an explanation of the concentration of high-crime places. What could explain why a few neighborhoods have more high-crime places than others? The next sections address this question.

The Economics of Poor Areas Incentivizes Poor Place Management

The key to understanding why high-crime places cluster is to recall the functions of place managers, particularly the fourth function, acquisition of resources. All places must be economically viable. That is, the costs of maintaining and operating the place cannot exceed, for very long, the resources acquired. For a single-family home, those resources usually come from outside employment. For commercial places, the revenue comes from sales and services. In neighborhoods where residents have high incomes, maintaining large houses is seldom a problem. The businesses in such neighborhoods will also do well. In low-income neighborhoods, property owners have greater difficulty on average. A greater proportion of residents will have difficulty paying their mortgages. A greater proportion of those who rent will have difficulty paying their rents (Joint Center, 2013). Landlords will face similar problems, and so will many retail and service businesses. A place manager in these circumstances will have a greater incentive to keep down maintenance, repair, and crime-prevention costs relative to a place manager in a neighborhood with higher incomes. As Sandra Newman (2005, p. 16) has pointed out, "If landlords are unable to charge enough rent to cover debt service, taxes, insurance, ongoing maintenance and repair, and a fair return on their investment, the most discretionary of these expenditures will be the most expendable." This is also true of public agencies such as public housing authorities (Bloom, 2008; Hunt, 2009)

Compounding the difficulties faced by place managers in neighborhoods with low incomes is the fact that the physical structures of the buildings owned, rented, and leased will need more attention. The poor are very seldom provided with the newest buildings. Rather, they typically inherit the older, less desirable buildings of others who have moved elsewhere (Drake & Cayton, 1945).

Over the last few decades, environmentalists and public health practitioners have brought attention to toxic materials that builders used in older buildings: lead paint, lead pipes, asbestos, and other hazards. Though no longer allowed in new construction, where people of higher incomes can live, play, and work, they are common in older neighborhood structures (Sampson & Winter, 2016). Removing or remediating these hazards is very costly (EPA, 1990; Jacobs et al., 2002).

Operating older structures can be more costly than operating newer buildings unless someone substantially rehabilitates them. Their heating plants may be inefficient, thus making it more costly to keep the interior at a habitable temperature in the winter. Compounding this are leaking windows and poor or absent insulation. The electrical system may not be sufficient to power modern appliances, and the wiring itself may be worn and hazardous. Old iron or lead plumbing may require replacement. An old roof may require routine maintenance that the owner would not need to perform on a modern roof.

Consequently, place managers are caught between having fewer resources and higher operating costs. Though many owners of such properties can make a living (Desmond, 2016; Stegman, 1972; Sternlieb, 1966), they can only do so by being very cost conscious. Repairs may be delayed or made with shortcuts and lower-quality materials. Vermin eradication may be less punctual and thorough. Crime prevention may be less available and effective. In some circumstances, landlords will be willing to overlook criminal activity such as drug dealing, prostitution, and other seemingly consensual crimes (Eck, 1994). In extreme circumstances, they might encourage it.

In neighborhoods with place users with more means, a place manager will lose customers if she does not keep up her property. Crime prevention is often displayed as an amenity, which allows the owner to charge higher rents. Consequently, such a neighborhood will have far fewer high-crime locations compared to the poor neighborhood across town.[1]

Economics alone may be sufficient to explain differences in the frequency of high-crime places among neighborhoods, even without accounting for the prevalence of offenders. If poverty is linked to the proportion of a population who are willing to engage in crime, then this will compound the problem: we will now have more offenders in poor areas with more opportunities to offend. If the economics of real estate does not increase the incentives for place managers to tolerate crime, then the greater number of possible offenders might not make much difference. The prospective offenders would face fewer opportunities, they would offend less, and neighborhood crime differences would be smaller. As Felson and Clarke (1998) remind us, opportunity makes the thief.

Race Influences Place Management

By itself, economics would predict more hot crime places in chronically poor neighborhoods than in middle-class and wealthy neighborhoods. However, economics is insufficient for explaining the number of hot crime places in poor Black neighborhoods. In this section, I explain why White racial attitudes toward Blacks interact with poverty to increase the number of hot crime places.

There is a long, well-documented history of discrimination against Blacks with regard to property ownership and use. Table 8.1 summarizes the numerous methods by which public officials, real-estate agents, financial institutions, and White residents restricted where and under what circumstances Blacks could buy and rent property. I have listed these mechanisms in a rough chronological order, though they often overlap temporally. They also overlap in function: blight, urban renewal, and expulsive zoning are a package, as are exclusive zoning, restrictive covenants, red-lining, financial exclusion, and contract buying. The variety of mechanisms is testament to the tenacity of White decision makers in creating new tools for discrimination as courts and other institutions struck down earlier tools.

There are two reasons these mechanisms are important for understanding crime patterns in U.S. cities. First, the mechanisms reflect an enduring and pervasive racial prejudice against Blacks that may influence how place managers operate. For example, although the National Association of Real-Estate Boards removed its anti-Black language from its code of conduct in the 1950s, there is still evidence of discrimination against Blacks by real-estate agents (Galster & Godfrey, 2005). Discrimination against Blacks did not end with the Supreme Court's nullifying the use of restrictive covenants in 1948. Though the mechanisms changed, the resistance did not end in the late 1940s or early 1950s. Historians cited in Table 8.1 demonstrate continued White resistance to Black movement into White areas. Indeed, Freund (2007) makes the case that this is when resistance to integration in the North began.

Second, even policies and practices that have been long ago abandoned may have influences on place management today. Historians, urban researchers, and economists have studied the red-lining maps, created by the Home Owners Loan Corporation (HOLC) and used by the Federal Housing Administration (FHA) and Veterans Administration (VA) (Rothstein, 2017). Social scientists at HOLC created these in the 1930s. FHA also wrote a detailed guidance for appraisers, which discriminated against Blacks. The FHA and VA used the guidance and maps at least to the 1950s. The FHA resisted efforts to eliminate race as a consideration but did not eliminate racially discriminatory language in its policies until the 1960s, when Congress folded the FHA into the newly created U.S. Department of Housing and Urban Development (Boyer, 1973; Rothstein, 2017). It was not until 1977 that the U.S. Congress passed legislation outlawing red-lining by banks (Tomes, 1991).

Recently, economists from the Federal Reserve Bank of Chicago examined whether the 1930s maps continued to have an influence on housing prices. They found that areas scored as high risk in the 1930s became increasingly segregated up through the 1970s. Although segregation declined subsequently, it persisted, as did lower rates of home ownership, property values, and credit scores. They conclude, "Our results provide strongly suggestive evidence that the HOLC maps had a causal and persistent effect on the development of neighborhoods through credit access" (Aaronson et al., 2017, p. 1). Thus, even if place managers of today were race neutral, the lasting impact of discriminatory policies could influence their decisions. The economics of property has racial prejudice baked into the calculus, regardless of the personal feelings of the place manager toward Blacks. Though separating economic and social influences on place managers may be helpful to understanding why we have clusters of high-crime places, in practice the two intertwine.

The critical point is that race continues to influence those who have power over property. Not to everyone, or to the same degree, but to some in some degree. A landlord who rents property in a Black neighborhood will be aware that his clients are vulnerable to discrimination. Therefore, there will be a rational temptation to exploit them. Exploitation can take a number of forms, including charging higher rents than the landlord would for the same apartment in a White neighborhood and not servicing the building to the same degree. Ignoring crime at the building and offenders operating out of the building will be far more likely in low-income Black neighborhoods than other areas. Although both White and Black poor neighborhoods will suffer from greater frequency of high-crime sites, compared to wealthier neighborhoods, the Black neighborhood will suffer more due to race. As Unnever (in this volume) has stated, we almost never have poor urban White neighborhoods to compare to poor urban Black neighborhoods in the U.S. The singular history of Blacks accounts for this. Even though some Whites did experience some of the mechanisms described in Table 8.1—examples include displacement of White families due to urban renewal (Zipp, 2010) and Jews discriminated against by restrictive covenants (Pietila, 2010)—they did not experience them all over such a long period. Low-income Black neighborhoods have a distinct history of racial pressure that we must address in any theory of neighborhood crime.

Neighborhoods Change

Neighborhoods in U.S. cities are not static. From 1900 through today, it might be useful to think of three overlapping periods, which I will call restriction (1900s–1950s), release (1950s–1980s), and reinvestment (1990s–present). Restriction is characterized by business and government-enforced segregation and begins before the great Black migration to the North (Lemann, 1991; Wilkerson, 2011) starting around World War I. According to Massey and Denton (1993), until this migration, cities in the U.S. were far less segregated than today, and there were no concentrated poor Black neighborhoods. With the northern migration, White resistance forced Blacks into particular areas and restricted their movement out (Massey & Denton, 1993). Under restriction, place managers operated in a sellers' market because Black renters had so few options.

Table 8.1

Mechanisms for Segregation

Mechanism	How It Works	Sources
Zoning restrictions	Local governments used zoning to keep Blacks from moving into neighborhoods. In 1917, the U.S. Supreme Court ruled such zoning by government unconstitutional in *Buchanan v. Warley*.	Freund, 2007; Pietila, 2010; Silver, 1997
Restrictive covenants	After *Buchanan v. Warley*. Restrictions against selling or renting to Blacks and other minorities were written into property deeds. In 1948, the U.S. Supreme Court ruled restrictive covenants unenforceable by courts in *Shelley v. Kraemer*. But use persisted until outlawed in 1968.	Brooks & Rose, 2013; Freund, 2007; Gotham, 2000; Pietila, 2010
Violence	A versatile tool used in the Jim Crow South. It became prominent in northern cities when the migration of Blacks increased Black populations. The removal of restrictive covenants increased its salience.	Baker, 1908; Freund, 2007; Grimshaw, 1960; Hirsch, 1983
Policies of the real-estate industry	From 1917 through 1950, the National Association of Real Estate Board's code of ethics held that it was a violation of professional ethics for a real-estate agent to sell a home to a Black client in a White neighborhood. This severely curtailed Black movement out of established Black neighborhoods. Even after the code was removed, the attitudes reflected in the code continued to be reflected in the behaviors and values expressed by real-estate agents.	Helper, 1969; Mehlhorn, 1998; Rothstein, 2017
Financial exclusion	Denial of bank financing for home purchases by Blacks, codified by the Federal Housing Administration (FHA) in the 1930s and adopted by the Veterans Administration (VA) after World War II. Despite efforts to curb this policy, it was not until the mid-1960s that it was outlawed.	Bradford, 1979; Rothstein, 2017
Red-lining	Related to financial exclusion, it involved denial of federally insured loans for purchases of property in neighborhoods where Blacks lived. It was codified in FHA policy until the 1960s. Since it was hard to finance property purchases in these areas, there was less of a market for property, and prices were suppressed, reinforcing disinvestment.	Hillier, 2003; Jackson, 1980; Rothstein, 2017

Contract buying	Capitalizing on Blacks' exclusion from standard mortgages, real-estate agents would finance purchases. The Black purchaser would pay the mortgage, but the seller would retain the deed. If payments were missed, the seller would evict the buyer and could resell the home. Unscrupulous agents could resell the same house multiple times.	Satter, 2009; *Yale Law Journal*, 1971
White flight	Movement of White homeowners from cities to suburbs, particularly after World War II, due to a number of circumstances: government highway construction, better home financing in suburbs, and fear of Black neighbors created by real-estate "block-busters" who would buy properties cheap from fleeing Whites and sell it high to incoming Blacks.	Jackson, 1980; Satter, 2009; Vitcheck & Balk, 1962
Fight blight	The depression and World War II reduced investment in U.S. cities, and the White Flight to the suburbs worsened the problem. Urban planners and city governments sought to improve downtowns by declaring areas "blighted," seizing the property, and razing buildings. Many of the areas were Black neighborhoods, and many had little serious deterioration. This reduced the available housing stock for poor Blacks. "Blight" was usually undefined, thus it became a flexible tool for urban renewal.	Hirsch, 1983; Pritchett, 2003
Urban renewal	Areas where housing was razed were turned over to developers or used for public infrastructure such as universities and highways. Sometimes public housing was created for displaced residents. Much urban renewal was facilitated with federal government subsidies.	Anderson, 1964; Jacobs, 1961; Zipp, 2010)
Exclusive zoning	Restrictions on the characteristics of places in an area resulted in the exclusion of people with low or moderate incomes—large building lots, distances between buildings, and required amenities, for example—meant that only the wealthy could afford to purchase and live in an area. This is still a common practice.	Claeys, 2004; Freund, 2007

(Continued)

Table 8.1

(Continued)

Mechanism	How It Works	Sources
Expulsive zoning	Rezoning an area from residential to other uses with the result that residents must leave. Highway construction and commercial development during and after urban renewal often resulted in Blacks being forced out of their neighborhoods.	Mohl, 1989; Rabin, 1989
Racial steering	Real-estate agents show clients homes in different neighborhoods, depending on client's race. Two clients, one Black and one White, will see different homes available for purchase, even when they have the same income and preferences.	Galster, 1990; Galster & Godfrey, 2005; Helper, 1969
Discriminatory pricing	Charging Blacks seeking homes or rental apartments more than Whites. This reduces housing mobility and preserves segregated neighborhoods.	Bayer, Casey, Ferreira, & McMillan, 2012; List, 2004; Turner et al., 2012
Subprime lending	Marketing low-quality homes to low-income people who are at high risk of defaulting. Most prominent in the 2000s, but similar practices were common in the late 1960s, leading to the FHA scandals. This too reduces the ability of Blacks to move and to create wealth.	Boyer, 1973; Crump et al., 2008; Rugh & Massey, 2010

This restriction began to erode following World War II with the civil rights movement.

As courts and legislators eliminated the most formal forms of segregation, the U.S. entered the period of release. White and middle-class Black flight from the old housing stock of the urban cores created economic difficulties for place managers in these neighborhoods. During release, making money from property in the Black inner city became more difficult due to out-migration and concentration of impoverished residents left behind. Thus, in the 1960s and 1970s, New York, Baltimore, Detroit, and other cities saw housing abandonment skyrocket. Local and federal policies exacerbated this disinvestment (Boyer, 1973; Pinto, 2013). Then, beginning perhaps in the 1990s and accelerating after, inner-city neighborhoods become attractive to a new generation and reinvestment begins. We live in a period of reinvestment.

These periods overlap and cities do not enter and exit these periods in lockstep. The 1950s had elements of both restriction and release. Some neighborhoods in some cities today maybe transitioning from release to reinvestment, while others will be lagging and some further into reinvestment.

It is during release that high-crime places became most common. That is because the economic value of places in poor Black neighborhoods is at its lowest. Before release, the places had more value, though racial exploitation was common. After release, reinvestment makes it possible to sell properties that were crime ridden. The new investors either rehabilitated them for higher-income users or knocked them down and replaced them with new buildings for different place users. New property owners in these areas have less tolerance for nearby high-crime properties than the old property owners. If it were possible to count high-crime places over many decades, we should see that during restriction the numbers of these places would be at a moderate level. The number of these places would increase dramatically during release. And as reinvestment takes hold, the numbers would decline, perhaps to levels far below restriction.

If this sketch is roughly correct, then it could explain some of the crime surge of the 1960s and the crime drop of the 1990s and beyond.[2] The collapse of housing markets in inner cities incentivized some property owners to ignore crime to maintain profits. The fact that the local residents were Black made this much easier than if the neighborhoods had contained poor Whites. Once inner-city properties became valuable again, facilitating crime was no longer advantageous to property owners. The presence of many poor Blacks made it easier to displace residents so people of means could move in.

Even small changes in place management can have big consequences. Weisburd and colleagues (2004) have noted that the improvement of only a small proportion of Seattle's street segments can account for most of the crime drop in that city during the 1990s. Crime is unlikely to be distributed evenly along a segment but is likely to concentrate on a few addresses in the block (Lee, 2017). The improved segments did not have to improve at every address for crime to decline: only a small proportion of a segment's places need to flip from a crime hot spot to crime resistant (I come back to this point in the next section). Thus, in the 1960s, the deterioration of a small proportion of addresses due to bad place management could account for most of the crime rise. In the 1990s and after, the improvement in place management in a small proportion of addresses could account for the drop in crime.

Place Management Varies

The general neighborhood opportunity structure for place management explains why some neighborhoods have more high-crime locations than others. From a rational choice perspective (Clarke, 2005), the economic and social-political environment influence place managers' perceived rewards and risks for providing security as well as property maintenance. The opportunity structure influences the perceived difficulty of such decisions as well as provocations and excuses. This may give the impression that all, or nearly all, places in low-income Black neighborhoods will be crime infested, which clearly contradicts the evidence: a few are, but most are not. So given the general incentives for bad place management, why is bad place management relatively rare in low-income Black neighborhoods?

Consider a convenience store with numerous robberies. Every customer enters the same opportunity structure for robbery—the poster-covered windows, the single clerk after dark, the availability of cash, the easy escape from the parking lot to the highway, and so forth—yet extremely few customers rob the store. More rob this store than other convenience stores, to be sure, but as a percentage of the total customer volume, the number will be very low. The same is true of high-crime neighborhoods: most places have decent management, but a few do not. There are just more of these badly managed places than in other neighborhoods.

I will illustrate the power of a relatively few places to create a high-crime neighborhood using four fictitious neighborhoods of 1000 places each. For simplicity's sake, I will divide crime into two categories: systematic and random. Systematic crime comes from poorly managed places. To keep things simple, I assume each poorly managed place generates five crimes in a given time period. The four neighborhoods vary in their proportions of places that are badly managed, as shown in Table 8.2. This produces systematic crime variation across the neighborhoods. The random crimes occur throughout a neighborhood. In this simple example, the number of such crimes is a constant 10 across neighborhoods.

The highest crime neighborhood has over 17 times the crime as the safest neighborhood, even though not many places in any neighborhood are badly managed (at most, 5%). Though this example is too simplistic to characterize crime patterns overall, it does illustrate that we do not need many place managers to succumb to the opportunity structure I have described. If a few place managers operate several badly managed places, the number of individuals or firms creating the crime problems can be quite small.

Why would not more places be bad in a low-income Black neighborhood, given the conditions I have described? The answer is that places, their managers, and their immediate environments are not homogeneous. There is variation in the characteristics of place managers. There are variations in the places themselves. And there is variation in places' proximal environments.

Table 8.2

Hypothetical Example of How a Few Badly Managed Places Can Create Large Crime Differences among Neighborhoods

	Neighborhoods			
	A	B	C	D
Number of Places	1000	1000	1000	1000
Proportion of Places Badly Managed	0.001	0.010	0.020	0.050
Number of Badly Managed Places	1	10	20	50
Crimes per Badly Managed Place	5	5	5	5
Systematic Crimes from Bad Places	5	50	100	250
Random Crimes	10	10	10	10
Total Crimes	15	60	110	260

Variations Among Place Managers

A number of studies have noted that large landlords—those owning many properties—are advantaged relative to smaller landlords (Bogdon & Ling, 1998; Stegman, 1972; Newman, 2005). Larger landlords can afford to have an apartment unit remain vacant longer, be more selective in their tenants, have lower maintenance costs (even controlling for building age and design), and have better access to capital. Although smaller landlords may dominate in terms of the numbers of place managers, the larger landlords control a higher fraction of apartment units. Over two decades ago, I found that drug dealing in San Diego was more likely in smaller apartment buildings than larger ones. I suggested that one reason is that owners of a building with few units are less able to withstand vacancies than owners of a large building with many units (1 vacancy out of 10 units represents a 10% drop in revenue, compared to 2% drop for the owner of 50-unit buildings) (Eck, 1994). However, there is evidence from New York that smaller buildings with resident landlords are in better condition than units in other buildings (Furman Center, 2013).

Place managers also vary in their management capabilities. Stegman (1972) asserts, based on surveys and interviews with Baltimore landlords, that management capabilities are critical for understanding business success. Landlords owning few properties are less likely to have the management expertise necessary (Newman, 2005; Stegman, 1972). This influences place managers' abilities to attract and hold good tenants. Stegman (1972) suggests that bad management attracts bad tenants, and vice versa, over time.

There are other characteristics of place managers that vary and influence how they manage their property. Distance the place manager lives from the property, for example, has been noted as influencing management (Sternlieb, 1966; Stegman, 1972; Rephann, 2009). Stegman (1972) observed that older landlords had more difficulty than younger landlords, perhaps because their earlier experiences were less relevant to current conditions. Sternlieb (1966) suggests that Black landlords were better at working with tenants than White landlords. In 1995, the U.S. Department of Housing and Urban Development commissioned the Bureau of the Census to survey owners of rental property. The survey shows that the reasons for owning and operating rental property vary: smaller landlords, for example, were more likely to own property for the rents paid, whereas larger landlords often stated that capital gains was a major factor in their decision (Savage, 1998).

Variation Among Places

In addition to place manager variation, there are variations in the characteristics of the places. Physical characteristics such as design may matter. Newman (1972) and Jeffery (1977) have pointed this out. Building age influences state of deterioration and maintenance costs. Although the average building in a low-income Black neighborhood is likely to be substantially older than buildings in White higher-income neighborhoods, this does not mean that all buildings are of the same age in a neighborhood or constructed to the same standards. Deterioration affects the costs the place manager must pay and the manager's ability to implement security against crime.

Variation Among Place Environments

In addition to the characteristics of the place, there are the characteristics of the place's immediate environment. Here I am referring to very proximal context. The street segment, proposed as a useful unit of analysis by Weisburd, Groff, and Yang (2013), is a good approximation for this sort of context. An apartment building situated on a major thoroughfare, near vacant buildings, and a poorly managed corner store might be more attractive to offenders than a building of the same design and age located two blocks away on a side street.

Tamara Madensen and Maris Herold have proposed that crime places can be networked, with different places in the network fulfilling different functions for the offenders (crime sites, stash locations, places to sell stolen items, and places to meet other offenders) (Madensen et al., 2017). Although little research has been conducted on this new idea, the Cincinnati Police Department have applied the networked place idea to several high-crime spots and have used place management interventions to reduce violence in the small areas enveloping the place networks (Madensen et al., 2017). The network idea implies that some high-crime locations would not have as much crime if they were located farther away from the other places in the network.

Most of the sources I have found for variation in places and place management are from studies of the physical condition of buildings and financial abilities of managers. There are extremely few studies of place managers and management practices and crime in low-income areas. Researchers interested in housing issues pay little attention to crime (except vandalism), and researchers interested in crime pay little attention to property management in apartments or other places. It seems sensible to assume that the same factors that influence the repairs of roofs, elevators, electrical systems, plumbing, and broken windows also influence crime prevention. But as reasonable as this assumption appears, there is a need for empirical validation. There are good reasons to suppose that the correlation between physical deterioration and crime might be modest. This is because the relationship between crime and physical disorder maybe spurious: they stem from the same source but are not themselves causally connected. If place managers can trade off repairs for crime prevention (or the opposite), then the aggregate correlation will be weak. A landlord living on her property might decide to invest more in security than paint, for example. A landlord threatened by code enforcement may forgo crime prevention to address physical conditions if code officials pay less attention to security than to electrical or other safety hazards. The landlord has limited resources and may have to decide between different objectives. Finally, as just noted, the proximate environment of a place may influence crime, so a building that is unsuitable for criminal activity will have little crime but could be in poor physical condition.

Neighborhood Crime Levels Have Their Sources in Place Management

Criminologists tend to avoid discussions of money, except as something offenders like to steal. They usually avoid discussing finance, except when discussing corruption or white-collar criminals. They eschew mentioning property ownership, except when criticizing capitalism for producing the circumstances that lead to oppression. With the exception of environmental criminologists, they largely ignore opportunities for crime. And criminologists tend to overlook urban history.

In contrast, I argue that crime in neighborhoods stems from the intersection of these elements with race. I argue that crime is not, mostly, about how residents fail to come to some informal arrangements to curb misbehavior and minor deviancy. Rather than ask why informal social controls break-down or failed to arise, this chapter asks, "How do some owners manage their property in ways that facilitate crime and disorder?" Rather than bewailing broken windows and demanding police attention, I have asked, "Who owns that broken window and why don't they fix it?"

I argue that most control of misbehavior arises not through an emergent and largely mysterious natural process but through the overt actions—subtle or blatant—of property owners. The problem is not how to address juveniles hanging out on street corners but how to prevent serious crime that begins within definable property boundaries. I argue that race matters for the production of crime, not because of the characteristics of the people who commit crimes but because some property owners (as well as others) perceive the people who live, work, and play in particular neighborhoods as being exploitable. High-crime places are created, in part, by economics of real estate, in part by attitudes that create racial discrimination, and in part by political influence.

The reasons low-income Black neighborhoods have more crime than other neighborhoods is that they have more high-crime addresses. They have more of these because they have more places where place management is weak or ineffectual. These types of places concentrate in low-income Black neighborhoods because of the interaction of economics and racial segregation.

Limitations

I have made little mention of politics. Segregation in the United States was not merely the result of thousands of individual decisions by Whites and Blacks in a political vacuum. It was the result of deliberate government policy at the federal, state, and local levels (Freund, 2007; Massey & Denton, 1993; Pietila, 2010; Rothstein, 2017; Sugrue, 1996). Moreover, the relaxation of segregationist policies was largely governmental. The decisions regarding urban renewal and blight removal were political, as were numerous other policies that influenced the availability, prices, and quality of places in Black neighborhoods (Boyer, 1973; Hirsch, 1983; Pinto, 2013; Zipp, 2010). One area where I have not been able to find systemic information is on the interaction among property owners, local governmental regulators (e.g., health and safety or code enforcement), and local elected officials. For example, a number of authors note how government policies toward "blight" and the use of code enforcement influence place management decisions, but I have not found a systematic discussion of how property owners try to influence government decisions (in contrast, there are many descriptions of the give and take between community groups and local government). Consequently, I have not discussed how politics may enter into place managers' decision making in low-income Black neighborhoods. This, however, does not mean that it does not.

I have not said much about how poverty and discrimination may influence the production of criminality. Criminologists have written so much on this topic that it is impossible to cite a few authoritative sources (consult your favorite criminology text). Mostly, I have ignored criminal propensity for this reason. I also have ignored it because regardless of how poverty and racism may push some people toward crime, very few crimes could be committed without the appropriate opportunities to act on criminal temptations. However, if one imagines a confluence of increased crime opportunities (my topic) and increased criminality (the topic of colleagues), it is not difficult to see how crime might surge geographically and temporally.

Related to this is another of my omissions: employment discrimination and the creation and maintenance of poverty. Here too many people have written on this topic, and I have nothing new to say about it. I have taken "low-income" as given, as if low-income Black neighborhoods have two separable characteristics. The economics of employment is no more separable from race in the United States than is the economics of housing. For both, it is rather like discussing a car's engine separate from its transmission: they can be diagrammed separately, but when the car is moving, both work together. Adding employment discrimination to my discussion could only increase the importance of race in the creation of opportunity structures for bad place management.

My theory points out two mechanisms by which race influences place management and how place management influences crime. The first mechanism involves the day-to-day decisions of the place manager: "Should I address the complaints of my tenants about gang members using one of the units?" Here, a place manager might ignore race and decide based on her budget, fears of retribution, and sense of what is the right decision. Or race can enter into the calculus. The second mechanism began operating long before such decisions. Race structured the economics of the neighborhood, the availability of tenants who pay their rent on time and leave their units in good shape. As Aaronson, Hartley, and Mazumder (2017) documented, red-lining decisions decades old leave a record in housing prices (see also Fishback, 2014; and Hillier, 2005). Thus, the race-neutral place manager, attempting to do the best for his clients in a low-income Black neighborhood while maintaining his business, is operating in an economic environment created by earlier decisions based at least in part upon race.

Implications

For Theory.   Criminologists should become historical. While preparing this chapter, I recalled my graduate school courses in criminology, their primary reading materials, and the current discussions in our journal articles and conferences. I also consulted with some of my colleagues about what I was reading in relatively old books and some volumes that were newly published. The urban history of Black people does not get serious treatment. In the context of history—how neighborhoods developed, changed, grew, deteriorated, stagnated, and then regrew—some of criminology's favorite concepts do not make much sense.

It is also clear that criminologists pay too much attention to the ecological analogies of the Chicago School. Particularly troublesome is the unquestioned assumption that neighborhood safety is something that evolves spontaneously from social interaction. The most crime-ridden neighborhoods in urban areas did not develop because of millions of tiny social interactions, nor from the lack of such interactions. A reading of history suggests the opposite: government agencies, developers, and financiers created and destroyed neighborhoods. It seems far more likely that crime and social interaction are outcomes of the decisions of these unmentioned others, who live and work outside the neighborhoods where crime is frequent.

It is hard, for example, to assert that deterioration of residents' social organization, the increase in broken windows, or the fraying of collective efficacy produced the burning of the South Bronx in the 1970s and early 1980s (Jonnes, 2002). The same might be said for the abandonment of large swaths of Baltimore (Pietila, 2010) or Detroit (Sugrue, 1996). In the Bronx, scholars have pointed out that the city's housing authority (a place manager) gave tenants displaced by fire top priority for coveted public housing units. This incentivized some tenants to set fires in buildings that were substandard due to neglect by their owners. Declining property values and increasing costs of operation, coupled with insurance companies that did not question suspicious claims, also gave property owners incentives to burn their property (Jonnes, 2002). And reallocation of fire stations from the South Bronx allowed those fires to burn longer and destroy more. Fewer arson investigations and regulatory inspections removed incentives of owners to prevent fires

(Flood, 2010). No doubt, the fires destroyed much of the informal social control in these neighborhoods, created thousands of broken windows, and decimated collective efficacy. Nevertheless, the fires were the result of bad place management.

Broken windows theory deserves special attention (Wilson & Kelling, 1982). It could have been called "blight" theory instead. This would have been a term familiar to Jane Jacobs (1961), as blight was often used as the rationale for the urban renewal activities flattening neighborhoods across the United States. Like "disorder" or "incivilities," blight had no clear definition (Gordon, 2003; Zipp, 2010), and this flexibility allowed it to be used to erase Black neighborhoods for highways, civic structures, public housing, and private development. The first author of broken windows theory, James Q. Wilson, would have known all of this. He edited a well-known book on urban renewal in which blight is repeatedly mentioned (Wilson, 1966). Wilson and Kelling might have produced a more innovative theory if they had asked two simple questions: "Who owns that window? And why haven't they fixed it?" If they had asked these two questions, they might have identified a critical source of social order: the place manager. Instead, they returned to one of the criminologist's favorite targets, urban residents, and they perpetuated the canard of natural neighborhood processes creating criminogenic areas.

Urban people with means buy social order. They purchase and manage their homes. Or they select the apartments and condominiums where order is assured by management. They shop at places where managers produce order so they can market goods and services. They work at places where the building owner creates order. Those of us who are fortunate enough to have decent incomes and who live, work, and play in cities can easily ignore the role of place managers in our lives. This is true for those readers who own homes in the suburbs. This is far less true of those with fewer means.

Those interested in the production or prevention of crime should pay much more attention to place management. Once one is aware of it, one finds it everywhere. Unlike forms of informal social control, it has an unambiguous source of power: property rights enforceable through the courts. Unlike many forms of informal social control, researchers and police have demonstrated that it is possible to manipulate place management and obtain desired outcomes. Although I have been uncharitable in my discussions of resident-based theories of order—be it social disorganization, collective efficacy, or broken windows—I am not against continued research into these areas. However, without accounting for how places are managed, such research is likely to be of little practical use and distorts our understanding of crime.

For Policy.   My theory points a finger at those who own and manage property. Often these are landlords controlling rental housing, but they also control stores, bars, restaurants, parking lots, and other facilities. It would be a colossal mistake to assume that all place managers are troublesome. All the evidence suggests otherwise: the vast majority of places have little or no crime, even in high-crime areas, and the vast majority of property owners do not own high-crime locations (Eck, Clarke, & Guerette, 2007). We should not create an analogue to "stop-question-frisk" for place managers. Policies toward place managers should be governed by three principles: focus on places with the most crime, try cooperative actions first, and as a last resort use the powers of government against the recalcitrant. The story that began this chapter is an example of the sort of policy local governments should consider. Another policy is training for property owners so they know how to fight crime at their places (Campbell, 2000). Low-interest loans to assist struggling landlords and businesses might be useful as well. These and other highly targeted policies are best done by local governments.

Research demonstrating that crime is highly concentrated in small areas spurred the development of hot spot policing. Evidence shows it does reduce disorder and crime (Braga, Papachristos, & Hureau, 2014). However, evidence for effectiveness is not a sufficient condition for widespread continuous use. If poor place management creates these hot spots, then focusing on the managers is likely to have more impact at less cost than repeatedly shooing away possible miscreants. Local regulation of place managers who create crime hot spots is a potentially useful approach. There are numerous regulatory instruments local governments can tailor to a variety of crime–place conditions (Eck & Eck, 2012).

The study of 20th century urban policy is depressing. Not only did much of it fail, many policies made things worse. Red-lining was a national policy to assist financial institutions in deciding which areas should be excluded from consideration for loans. One result was to starve Black neighborhoods of financing. Urban renewal and blight abatement were funded by the federal government. One result was the destruction of functioning neighborhoods and the removal of places for business and residence. Federal largess underwrote high-rise public housing complexes. One consequence was segregated, concentrated, impoverished crime havens. The creation of the national highway system gutted urban areas, promoted suburban sprawl, and increased racial segregation. Consequently, I am highly skeptical of any federal policy toward promoting better place management unless local decision makers can focus funding on the specific places that need help and can provide assistance without aggravating racial inequities.

Notes

1. On occasion, researchers test the effectiveness of crime prevention measures by correlating their presence with crime. If effective, then the correlation should be negative, after controlling for other attributes of the location. A positive correlation is possible and can be easily misinterpreted as iatrogenic (i.e., the measure caused the crime). An iatrogenic interpretation is inadvisable when the evaluator cannot establish the temporal ordering of the prevention's implementation and the crime rise. A more plausible explanation is that the property owner, to save costs, failed to introduce the prevention measure until sufficient crimes had accumulated. At that time, the need was obvious or government pressure on him to do something became too difficult to bear. In short, the positive correlation may indicate that crime causes prevention activity.
2. I say "some" for a very specific reason. The increase in crime in the United States from the mid-1960s to the mid-1970s was not unique to the United States. Canada and Western European countries also saw an increase during this period (Pinker, 2011, pp. 116–118). It is possible that all countries had collapses in the market for places in their poorest urban areas. If so, my description might be a powerful explanation for this crime surge. I am dubious. Rather, I suspect the problems of the release period in the U.S. augmented or interacted with other conditions that were more general to the world.

References

Aaronson, D., Hartley, D., & Mazumder, B. (2017, August 3). *The effects of the 1930s HOLC "redlining" maps.* Working Paper WP 2017-12. Chicago, IL: Federal Reserve Bank of Chicago.

Anderson, M. (1964). *The federal bulldozer.* Cambridge, MA: MIT Press.

Andresen, M. A., & Malleson, N. (2010). Testing the stability of crime patterns: Implications for theory and policy. *Journal of Research in Crime and Delinquency, 48,* 58–82.

Axtell, R. L. (2001). Zipf distribution of U.S. firm sizes. *Science, 293,* 1818–20.

Baker, R. S. (1908). *Following the color line: An account of Negro citizenship in the American democracy.* New York, NY: Doubleday.

Bayer, P., Casey, M. D., Ferreira, F., & McMillan, R. (2012). *Price discrimination in the housing market.* Working Paper 18069. NBER Working Paper Series. Cambridge, MA: National Bureau of Economic Research.

Bichler, G., Schmerler, K., & Enriquez, J. (2013). Curbing nuisance motels: An evaluation of police as place regulators. *Policing: An International Journal of Police Strategies & Management, 36,* 437–462.

Bloom, N. D. (2008). *Public housing that worked: New York in the twentieth century*. Philadelphia, PA: University of Philadelphia Press.

Bogdon, A. S., & Ling, D. C. (1998, February). The effects of property, owner, location, and tenant characteristics on multifamily profitability. *Journal of Housing Research*, *9*, 285–316.

Boyer, B. D. (1973). *Cities destroyed for cash: The FHA scandal at HUD*. Chicago, IL: Follett.

Bradford, C. (1979, March). Financing home ownership: The federal role in neighborhood decline. *Urban Affairs Quarterly*, 313–335.

Braga, A. A., Papachristos, A. V., & Hureau, D. M. (2014). The effects of hot spots policing on crime: An updated systematic review and meta-analysis. *Justice Quarterly*, *31*(4), 633–63.

Brooks, R. R. W., & Rose, C. M. (2013). Saving the neighborhood: Racially restrictive covenants, law, and social norms. Cambridge, MA: Harvard University Press.

Campbell, J. (2000). *Keeping illegal activities out of rental property: A police guide for establishing landlord training programs*. Washington, DC: Bureau of Justice Assistance.

Claeys, E. R. (2004). Euclid lives? The uneasy legacy of progressivism in zoning. *Fordham Law Review*, *73*(2), 731–770.

Clarke, R. V. (1995). Situational crime prevention. In M. Tonry & D. Farrington (Eds.), *Building a safer society: Strategic approaches to crime prevention* (Vol. 19, pp. 91–150). Chicago, IL: University of Chicago Press.

Clarke, R. V. (2005). Seven misconceptions of situational crime prevention. In N. Tilley (Ed.), *Handbook of crime prevention and community safety* (pp. 35–70). Cullompton, UK: Willan.

Clarke, R. V., & Bichler-Robertson, G. (1998). Place managers, slumlords and crime in low rent apartment buildings. *Security Journal*, *11*(1), 11–19.

Cohen, L. E., & Felson, M. (1979). Social change and crime rate trends: A routine activity approach. *American Sociological Review*, *44*, 588–608.

Coyne, M. A., & Eck, J. E. (2015). Choice and crime: Offender rationality, bounded rationality, and situational choices. *Journal of Contemporary Criminal Justice*, *31*(1), 12–29.

Crump, J., Newman, K., Belsky, E. S., Ashton, P., Kaplan, D. H., Hammel, D. J., & Wyly, E. (2008). Cities destroyed (again) for cash: Forum on the U.S. foreclosure crisis. *Urban Geography*, *29*(8), 745–784.

Desmond, M. (2016). *Evicted: Poverty and profit in the American city*. New York, NY: Crown.

Drake, S. C., & Cayton, H. R. (1945). *Black metropolis: A study of Negro life in a northern city*. New York, NY: Harcourt Brace & Co.

Eck, J. E. (1994). *Drug markets and drug places: A case-control study of the spatial structure of illicit drug dealing* (Dissertation). College Park, MD: University of Maryland.

Eck, J. E. (2002). Preventing crime at places. In L. W. Sherman, D. Farrington, & B. Welsh (Eds.), *Evidence-based crime prevention* (pp. 241–294). New York, NY: Routledge.

Eck, J. E., Clarke, R. V., & Guerette, R. T. (2007). Risky facilities: Crime concentration in homogeneous sets of establishments and facilities. In G. Farrell, K. J. Bowers, S. D. Johnson, & M. Townsley (Eds.), *Imagination for crime prevention*, Crime prevention studies (pp. 225–264). Monsey, NY: Criminal Justice Press.

Eck, J. E., & Eck, E. B. (2012). Crime place and pollution: Expanding crime reduction options through a regulatory approach. *Criminology & Public Policy, 11*(2), 281–316.

Eck, J. E., Gersh, J. S., & Taylor, C. (2000). Finding crime hot spots through repeat address mapping. In V. Goldsmith, P. G. McGuire, J. H. Mollenkopf, & T. A. Ross (Eds.), *Analyzing crime patterns: Frontiers of practice* (pp. 49–64). Thousand Oaks, CA: Sage.

Eck, J. E., & Guerette, R. T. (2012). Place-based crime prevention: Theory, evidence, and policy. In B. Welsh & D. P. Farrington (Eds.), *The Oxford handbook of crime prevention* (pp. 354–382). New York, NY: Oxford University Press.

Eck, J. E., Lee, Y. J., Martinez, N., & O, S. H. (2017). Compared to what? Estimating the relative concentration of crime at places using systematic and other reviews. *Crime Science, 6.* doi:10.1186/s40163-017-0070-4

Eck, J. E., & Madensen, T. D. (2018). Place management. In G. Bruinsma & S. Johnson (Eds.), *Oxford handbook of environmental criminology*. New York, NY: Oxford University Press. doi:10.1093/oxfordhb/9780190279707.013.22

Eck, J. E., & Wartell, J. (1998). Improving the management of rental properties with drug problems: A randomized experiment. In L. G. Mazerolle & J. Roehl (Eds.), *Civil remedies and crime prevention* (*Crime prevention studies*, Vol. 9, pp. 161–185). Monsey, NY: Criminal Justice Press.

Environmental Protection Agency (EPA). (1990). *Managing asbestos in place: A building owner's guide to operations and maintenance programs for asbestos-containing materials*. Washington, DC: United States Environmental Protection Agency.

Felson, M., & Clarke, R. V. (1998). *Opportunity makes the thief: Practical theory for crime prevention*. Police Research Series Paper 98. London: Home Office, Policing and Reducing Crime Unit.

Fishback, P. (2014). Panel discussion on saving the neighborhood: Part III. *Arizona Law Review, 56*(3), 39–49.

Flood, J. (2010). *The fires: How a computer formula, big ideas, and the best of intentions burned down New York City—and determined the future of cities*. New York, NY: Riverhead Books.

Freund, D. M. P. (2007). *Colored property: State policy and white racial politics in suburban America*. Chicago, IL: University of Chicago Press.

Friedman, M. (1953). The methodology of positive economics. In M. Friedman (Ed.), *Essays in positive economics* (Vol. II, pp. 3–43). Chicago, IL: University of Chicago Press.

Furman Center for Real Estate & Urban Policy. (2013). *Maintenance and investment in small rental properties: Findings from New York City and Baltimore*. New York, NY: Furman Center for Real Estate and Urban Policy, New York University & Johns Hopkins, Institute for Policy Studies.

Galster, G. (1990). Racial steering in urban housing markets: A review of the audit evidence. *The Review of Black Political Economy, 19*(1), 105–129.

Galster, G., & Godfrey, E. (2005). By words and deeds: Racial steering by real estate agents in the U.S. in 2000. *Journal of the American Planning Association, 71*(3), 251–268.

Gilderbloom, J. I. (1989). Socioeconomic influences on rentals for us urban housing: Assumptions of open access to a perfectly competitive "free market" are confronted with the facts. *American Journal of Economics and Sociology, 48*(3), 273–292.

Gilderbloom, J. I., & Appelbaum, R. P. (1988). *Rethinking rental housing*. Philadelphia, PA: Temple University Press.

Gordon, C. (2003). Blighting the way: Urban renewal, economic development, and the elusive definition of blight. *Fordham Urban Law Journal, 31*(2), 305–337.

Gotham, K. F. (2000). Urban space, restrictive covenants and the origins of racial residential segregation in a US city, 1900–50. *International Journal of Urban and Regional Research, 24*(3), 616–633.

Graham, K., & Homel, R. (2008). *Raising the bar: Preventing aggression in and around bars, clubs and pubs*. Cullompton, UK: Willan.

Green, L. (1996). *Policing places with drug problems*. Thousand Oaks, CA: Sage.

Grimshaw, A. D. (1960). Urban racial violence in the United States changing ecological considerations. *American Journal of Sociology, 66*(2), 109–119.

Groff, E. R., Weisburd, D., & Yang, S. M. (2010). Is it important to examine crime trends at a local "micro" level? A longitudinal analysis of street to street variability in crime trajectories. *Journal of Quantitative Criminology, 26*(1), 7–32.

Helper, R. (1969). *Racial policies and practices of real estate brokers*. Minneapolis, MN: University of Minnesota Press.

Hillier, A. E. (2003). Redlining and the home owners' loan corporation. *Urban History, 29*(4), 394–420.

Hillier, A. E. (2005). Residential security maps and neighborhood appraisals: The home owners' loan corporation and the case of Philadelphia. *Social Science History, 29*(2), 207–233.

Hirsch, A. R. (1983). *Making the second ghetto: Race and housing in Chicago, 1940–1960*. New York, NY: Cambridge University Press.

Hunt, D. B. (2009). *Blueprint for disaster: The unraveling of Chicago public housing*. Chicago, IL: University of Chicago Press.

Ijiri, Y., & Simon, H. A. (2013). Interpretations of departures from the Pareto curve firm-size distributions. *Journal of Political Economy, 82*, 315–331.

Jackson, K. T. (1980). Race, ethnicity, and real estate appraisal: The Home Owners Loan Corporation and the Federal Housing Administration. *Journal of Urban History, 6*(4), 419–452.

Jacobs, D. E., Clickner, R. P., Zhou, J. Y., Viet, S. M., Marker, D. A., Rogers, J. W., . . . Friedman, W. (2002). The prevalence of lead-based paint hazards in U.S. housing. *Environmental Health Perspectives, 110*(10), A599–A606.

Jacobs, J. (1961). *The death and life of great American cities*. New York, NY: Vintage.

Jeffery, C. R. (1977). *Crime prevention through environmental design*. Thousand Oaks, CA: Sage.

Johnson, S. D. (2010). A brief history of the analysis of crime concentration. *European Journal of Applied Mathematics, 21*, 349–370.

Joint Center for Housing Studies of Harvard University. (2013). *America's rental housing: Evolving markets and needs*. Cambridge, MA: Harvard Graduate School of Design and Harvard Kennedy School.

Jonnes, J. (2002). *South Bronx rising: The rise, fall, and resurrection of an American city*. New York, NY: Fordham University Press.

Kahneman, D. (2011). *Thinking fast and slow*. New York, NY: Farrar, Straus, and Giroux.

Lee, Y. J. (2017). *Comparing measures of the concentration of crime at places and times* (Ph.D. Dissertation). Cincinnati, OH: University of Cincinnati, School of Criminal Justice.

204   John E. Eck

Lee, Y. J., Eck, J. E., O, S. H., & Martinez, N. (2017). How concentrated is crime at places? A systematic review from 1970 to 2015. *Crime Science*, *6*. doi:10.1186/s40163-017-0069-x.

Lemann, N. (1991). *The promised land: The great black migration and how it changed America*. New York, NY: Vintage.

List, J. A. (2004). The nature and extent of discrimination in the marketplace: Evidence from the field. *Quarterly Journal of Economics*, *119*(1), 49–89.

Madensen, T. D. (2007). *Bar management and crime: Toward a dynamic theory of place management and crime hotspots* (Dissertation). Cincinnati, OH: University of Cincinnati.

Madensen, T. D., & Eck, J. E. (2013). Crime place and place management. In P. Wilcox & F. Cullen (Eds.), *The Oxford handbook of crime theory* (pp. 554–578). New York, NY: Oxford University Press.

Madensen, T. D., Herold, M., Hammer, M. G., & Christenson, B. R. (2017). Research in brief: Place-based investigations to disrupt crime place networks. *The Police Chief*, *84*(4), 14–16.

Massey, D. S., & Denton, N. A. (1993). *American apartheid: Segregation and the making of the underclass*. Cambridge, MA: Harvard University Press.

Mazerolle, L. G., Roehl, J., & Kadleck, C. (1998). Controlling social disorder using civil remedies: Results for a randomized field experiment in Oakland, California. In L. G. Mazerolle & J. Roehl (Eds.), *Civil remedies and crime prevention* (*Crime prevention studies*, Vol. 9, pp. 141–159). Monsey, NY: Criminal Justice Press.

Mehlhorn, D. (1998). A requiem for blockbusting: Law, economics, and race-based real estate speculation. *Fordham Law Review*, *67*(3), 1145–1192.

Mohl, R. A. (1989). Shadows in the sunshine: Race and ethnicity in Miami. *Tequesta: The Journal of the Historical Association of Southern Florida*, *XLIX*, 63–80.

Newman, O. (1972). *Defensible space: Crime prevention through urban design*. New York, NY: Macmillan.

Newman, S. J. (2005). *Low-end rental housing: The forgotten story in Baltimore's housing boom*. Washington, DC: The Urban Institute.

O, S. H., Lee, Y. J., & Eck, J. E. (2017). *Testing the impact of place management on crime across different land uses*. Paper delivered at the American Society of Criminology Meeting, Philadelphia, PA, November 15–18.

O, S. H., Martinez, N., Lee, Y. J., & Eck, J. E. (2017). How concentrated is crime among victims? A systematic review from 1977 to 2014. *Crime Science*, *6*. doi:10.1186/s40163-017-0071-3.

Payne, T., & Eck, J. E. (2007). *Who owns crime?* Paper delivered at the Annual Meeting of the American Society of Criminology, Atlanta, GA, November 14–17.

Payne, T. C., & Gallagher, K. (2016). The importance of small units of aggregation: Trajectories of crime at addresses in Cincinnati, Ohio, 1998–2012. *Criminology, Criminal Justice Law, and Society*, *17*(1), 20–36.

Pierce, G., Spaar, S., & Briggs, L. R. (1988). *The character of police work: Strategic and tactical implications*. Boston, MA: Center for Applied Social Research, Northeastern University.

Pietila, A. (2010). *Not in my neighborhood: How bigotry shaped a great American city*. Chicago, IL: Ivan R. Dee.

Pinker, S. (2011). *The better angels of our nature: Why violence has declined*. New York, NY: Penguin Classics.

Pinto, E. J. (2013, February 6). *Examining the proper role of the federal housing administration in our Mortgage Insurance Market.* Statement before the Committee on Financial Services U.S. House of Representatives. Washington, DC: American Enterprise Institute for Public Policy Research.

Pritchett, W. E. (2003). The "Public menace" of blight: Urban renewal and the private uses of eminent domain. *Yale Law & Policy Review, 21*(1), 1–52.

Rabin, Y. (1989). Expulsive zoning: The inequitable legacy of Euclid. In C. Haar & J. Kayden (Eds.), *Zoning and the American dream: Promises still to keep* (pp. 101–121). Chicago, IL: Planners Press, American Planning Association.

Reiss, A. J., & Aldrich, H. E. (1971). Absentee ownership and management in the black ghetto: Social and economic consequences. *Social Problems, 18,* 319–339.

Rephann, T. J. (2009). Rental housing and crime: The role of property ownership and management. *Annals of Regional Science, 43,* 435–451.

Rothstein, R. (2017). *The color of law: A forgotten history of how our government segregated America.* New York, NY: Liveright.

Rugh, J. S., & Massey, D. S. (2010). Racial segregation and the American foreclosure crisis. *American Sociological Review, 75*(5), 629–651.

Sampson, R. J., & Winter, A. S. (2016). The racial ecology of lead poisoning: Toxic inequality in Chicago neighborhoods, 1995–2013. *DuBois Review: Social Science Research on Race.* 13, 261–283.

Satter, B. (2009). *Family properties: Race, real estate, and the exploitation of black urban America.* New York, NY: Metropolitan Books.

Savage, H. (1998). *What we have learned about properties, owners, and tenants from the 1995 property owners and managers survey.* Washington, DC: U.S. Department of Commerce, Bureau of the Census.

Shaw, C. R., & McKay, H. D. (1942). *Juvenile delinquency and urban areas: A study of delinquents in relation to differential characteristics of local communities in American cities.* Chicago, IL: University of Chicago Press.

Sherman, L. W., Gartin, P. R., & Buerger, M. E. (1989). Hot spots of predatory crime: Routine activities and the criminology of place. *Criminology, 27,* 27–55.

Sherman, L. W., & Weisburd, D. (1995). General deterrent effect of police patrol in crime "hot spots": A randomized, controlled, trial. *Justice Quarterly, 12*(4), 625–648.

Silver, C. (1997). The racial origins of zoning in American cities. In J. M. Thomas & M. Ritzdorf (Eds.), *Urban planning and the African American community: In the shadows* (pp. 23–42). Thousand Oaks, CA: Sage.

Simon, H. A. (1955). A behavioral model of rational choice. *Quarterly Journal of Economics, 69,* 99–118.

Steenbeek, W., & Weisburd, D. (2016). Where the action is in crime? An examination of variability of crime across different spatial units in The Hague, 2001–2009. *Journal of Quantitative Criminology, 32,* 449–469.

Stegman, M. A. (1972). *Housing investment in the inner city: The dynamics of decline; A study of Baltimore, Maryland, 1968–1970.* Cambridge, MA: MIT Press.

Sternlieb, G. (1966). *The tenement landlord.* New Brunswick, NJ: Rutgers University Press.

Sugrue, T. (1996). *The origins of the urban crisis: Race and inequality in postwar Detroit.* Princeton, NJ: Princeton University Press.

Tchekmedyian, A. (2017). Prosecutors say this housing complex is a hotbed for gang crime, and they think its owner should live there. *Los Angeles Times,*

November 27. Retrieved December 5, 2017, from https://www.latimes.com/local/lanow/la-me-ln-baldwin-village-lawsuit-20171127-story.html

Tomes, J. P. (1991). Community in the community reinvestment act: A term in search of a definition community in CRA. *The Annual Review of Banking Law*, *10*, 225–249.

Trickett, A., Ellingworth, D., Hope, T., & Pease, K. (1995). Crime victimization in the eighties: Changes in area and regional inequality. *British Journal of Criminology*, *35*, 343–359.

Trickett, A., Osborn, D. R., Seymour, J., & Pease, K. (1992). What is different about high crime areas? *British Journal of Criminology*, *31*(1), 81–89.

Turner, M. A., Santos, R., Levy, D. K., Wissoker, D., Aranda, C., & Pitingolo, R. (2013). *Housing discrimination against racial and ethnic minorities, 2012.* Washington, DC: US Department of Housing and Urban Development.

Vitcheck, N., & Balk, A. (1962). Confessions of a block-buster. *The Saturday Evening Post*, 15–19. Indianapolis, IN.

Weisburd, D., Eck, J. E., Braga, A., Telep, C., Cave, B., Bowers, K., . . . Yang, S-M. (2016). *Place matters: Criminology for the 21st century*. New York, NY: Cambridge University Press.

Weisburd, D., Bushway, S., Lum, C., & Yang, S-M. (2004). Trajectories of crime at places: A longitudinal study of street segments in the city of Seattle. *Criminology*, *42*(2), 283–321.

Weisburd, D., Groff, E. R., & Yang, S.-M. (2013). *The criminology of place: Street segments and our understanding of the crime problem*. New York, NY: Oxford University Press.

Wilcox, P., Cullen, F. T., & Feldmeyer, B. (2018). *Communities and crime: An enduring American challenge*. Philadelphia, PA: Temple University Press.

Wilcox, P., & Tillyer, M. (2018). Place and neighborhood contexts. In D. Weisburd & J. E. Eck (Eds.), *Unraveling the crime place connection: New directions in theory and policy* (Advances in criminological theory, Vol. 22, pp. 121–144). New York, NY: Routledge.

Wilkerson, I. (2011). *The warmth of other suns: The epic story of America's great migration*. New York, NY: Vintage.

Wilson, J. Q. (1966). *Urban renewal: The record and the controversy*. Cambridge, MA: MIT Press.

Wilson, J. Q., & Kelling, G. L. (1982). Broken windows: The police and neighborhood safety. *The Atlantic Monthly*, *249*(3), 29–38.

Yale Law Journal. (1971). Discriminatory housing markets, racial unconscionability, and section 1988 : The contract buyers' league. *The Yale Law Journal*, *80*(3), 516–566.

Zidar, M., Schaffer, J., & Eck, J. E. (2017). Reframing an obvious police problem: Discovery, analysis, and response to a manufactured problem in a small city. *Policing: A Journal of Policy and Practice*. https://doi.org/10.1093/police/pax085

Zipp, S. (2010). *Manhattan projects: The rise and fall of urban renewal in cold war New York*. New York, NY: Oxford University Press.

9

Racial Discrimination and Cultural Adaptations: An Evolutionary Developmental Approach

Callie H. Burt

In her incisive critique, Russell (1992) spotlighted criminology's "failure to provide a well-developed, vibrant and cohesive subfield that seeks to explain crime committed by blacks," which she termed a "Black criminology."[1] Establishing her argument, Russell emphasized the paucity of theoretical research on (and the dearth of criminologists devoting their attention to) the race–crime relationship despite its significance. In her call for the development of such a subfield, Russell urged criminologists to move beyond the "simple observation . . . that blacks are disproportionately involved in crime . . . to the development of theory that seeks to explain black criminality" (pp. 667–668). Her article charted a path for the development of such a subfield, highlighting significant gaps in knowledge and potential challenges.

Whether a response to her clarion call and/or a consequence of a broader shift in the sociopolitical winds, the theoretical neglect of race and racism in criminology is no more. In the roughly 25 years surrounding and subsequent to Russell's (1992) challenge, theoretical research on racial disparities has burgeoned and greatly enhanced our understanding of the race–crime relationship. Moreover, scholars and scholarship focused on issues related to race, crime, and criminal justice have become organized into a rather cohesive subfield, with new specialized journals, professional associations, and conferences focused on the very issues raised by Russell and echoed by many others (e.g., Peterson, 2017; Peterson, Krivo, & Hagan, 2006; Phillips & Bowling, 2003).

Although significant strides have been made in our understanding of the race–crime relationship (and these important contributions should be lauded), much more work remains to be done to enhance knowledge on the causes of racial disparities in street crime. The grounds for a Black Criminology remain compelling and the products of this labor valuable. This is especially the case as the sociopolitical winds around race and racism are once again being whipped up by competing social developments, including the emboldening of White racists in their defense of White supremacy and the ascendance of the Black Lives Matter movement (Wilson & Katz, 2018). At this time of heightened awareness of racial disproportionalities and pervasive dissatisfaction with the status quo in the criminal justice system (CJS) (Beckett, 2018; Gottschalk, 2015), profound change is a realistic possibility; thus, a Black Criminology is as important as ever.

In this chapter, I examine the connections between racial discrimination, cultural adaptations, including racial socialization, and crime. I explicate the criminogenic effects of anti-Black racism through a racialized theory, the social schematic theory of street crime (Simons & Burt, 2011; Burt, Lei, & Simons, 2017a). I expound on the evolutionary developmental underpinnings of the theory to elucidate the nature and logic of cultural adaptions, aiming to fill a gap in heretofore undertheorized yet salient structure-shapes-culture arguments in criminology (Sampson & Bean, 2006; Wilson, 2009). The aim is to unite findings and reframe them within an approach that focuses on harsh, unpredictable environments and contextually appropriate adaptations with an underlying evolutionary *developmental* logic. The result is a framework that links racial discrimination and "race-neutral" risk factors (profoundly shaped by racism) to psychosocial orientations that tend to increase the risk of street crime and other behaviors that can reinforce disadvantage through their consequences. Before moving to this racialized theory, I first say a few words on a Black Criminology.

A Black Criminology

A Black Criminology, most basically, involves incorporating a consideration of race (specifically of Blackness) as a core dimension of stratification into criminological theorizing (Russell, 1992). This entails not only putting Blacks and their contemporary lived experiences at the center of intellectual inquiry but also being sensitive to the historical and social group dynamics of racial subordination (Hawkins, 1983; Unnever & Gabbidon, 2011). Like a feminist criminology, a Black Criminology is not a monolithic worldview or a theory; instead it encompasses a diverse set of approaches that collectively share general assumptions about race and racism. Communal assumptions include (but are not limited to) the following: (1) that race is not a natural (biological) fact, but a fluid, complex social, historical, and cultural creation; (2) that ours is a racialized social system[2], and race orders social life (along with other ascribed statuses such as sex/gender and age); (3) that racial relations and racial groupings are not symmetrical but are based on an organizing principle of White supremacy (ours is not a "value-free system of racial classification" Covington, 1995, p. 548); and (4) that contemporary racism has a material and ideological foundation (racism not only is a matter of ideas but also has a structural foundation).[3]

In terms of its explanatory foci, a Black Criminology addresses three broad themes: (1) racialized or racially specific contexts, conditions, or experiences as risk factors for crime; (2) the criminalization of Blackness, which highlights White privilege/power/racism in the making of criminal definitions such that definitions of crime (legislation) are racialized; and (3) racialized law enforcement (from policing, to the courts, to penal punishments) generating a racially biased CJS. The racially specific or racialized risk factors that fall under the first theme comprise etiological factors shaping racial differences in offending, while the factors falling into the second and third categories produce racial disparities in penal control, net of differences in behavior (although these factors can and do become racialized risk factors, as involvement in the CJS tends to increase the likelihood of later crime). Altogether, these three intertwining processes undergird racial disparities in street crimes and CJS responses, which amplify initial differences (e.g., associations between race and racially-invariant risk factors), thereby increasing the risk of crime and CJS involvement among Blacks. This, in turn, reifies problematic stereotypes about Blackness and crime, including "that there is something about black skin that represents deviance and criminality" (Russell-Brown, 2009, p. 34).

As one piece of this effort to further the development of Black Criminology (as part of both this volume and the larger efforts), this chapter addresses the first theme: racialized experiences as risk factors for offending (underlying differences in behavior). In so doing, however,

I do not mean to downplay the other racially-specific or racialized factors, thereby "[minimizing] a consideration of the extent to which the criminal justice system operates as a mechanism of individual and group social control and subordination" (Hawkins, 1995, p. 11). Relatedly, my attention is explicitly on racialized risk factors shaping disparities in *street crime*. Although the concept of street crime is somewhat imprecise, it generally includes those crimes such as murder, robbery, rape, aggravated assault, burglary, and theft (LaFree, 1998). I am neither exploring nor assuming racial disparities in "crime" (as in the universe of all illegal acts, including white-collar crimes or suite crimes), nor am I treating "street crime" as a measure of general misconduct or harmful acts. Instead, I focus on street crime as a subset of all crimes and a subset of harmful acts and ask how and why racialized experiences may contribute to observed racial disparities in offending and victimization among African Americans (compared to Whites). In short, I seek to contribute to knowledge on the racialized factors contributing to the higher incidence of "street crime" among African Americans without implying that either "crime" or the larger subset of "harmful behaviors" is higher among Blacks than Whites.[4]

Developing a Racialized Theory

In this chapter, I explore racialized experiences as risk factors for crime in the context of a *racialized* general theory of crime, the social schematic theory (SST). I use the term "racialized" in the sense of "to put in a racial context," namely that of our racialized social system.[5] I focus on interpersonal racial discrimination as a minority-specific risk factor for crime and racial socialization as a cultural source of resilience among Blacks. Although some scholars have cogently argued that the inimitable experiences of Blacks require a unique theory of crime (e.g., Unnever & Gabbidon, 2011), while respecting this argument and recognizing that African Americans have distinctively pernicious experiences of racial subjugation in the U.S., I adopt a different (racialized) stance for several reasons.

First, in my reading, the accumulated evidence suggests prevailing similarity in the effects of (race-neutral) risk factors on street crime at both the macro and the micro levels (e.g., Farrington, Loeber, & Stouthamer-Loeber, 2003; McNulty & Bellair, 2003; Peterson & Krivo, 2005; see Wilson & Katz, 2018). Although emphasizing that Blacks face additional risk factors (i.e., interpersonal racial discrimination),

I propose that the individual mechanisms linking these experiences to offending are racially invariant. In other words, racialized risk factors (e.g., interpersonal racial discrimination), like race-neutral risk factors (e.g., harsh parenting), influence general psychosocial mechanisms that increase the risk of crime regardless of race. To be sure, I am not arguing that no racial differences in psychosocial orientation or cultural frames exist; rather, I argue that the key proximal (psychosocial) mechanisms linking race to crime are not racially specific. Second, despite being well entrenched, the Black-versus-White dichotomy does not neatly capture monolithic racial categories identified by common historical experiences. Americans who identify as Black come from diverse countries (e.g., African, South American, Caribbean nations; Russell-Brown, 2009), and racial classifications remain ambiguous. Indeed, the racial classification of the last U.S. president is unsettled among the U.S. public. (A recent Pew survey revealed that only a minority of Americans described President Obama as "Black"; the majority classified him as "mixed-race.") Racially specific theories thus necessarily reify bifurcations of race and racial group memberships that are technically more fluid and contextually dependent. For these reasons, I propose a racialized theory that emphasizes differences in degree.

In contrast to race-specific approaches as well as those that merely treat race as a control variable, the racialized perspective I adopt occupies a middle ground that acknowledges similarities in risk factors, mechanisms, and processes shaping criminal propensity and crime across racial groups while also emphasizing the need to incorporate how the legacy of historical and contemporary racial discrimination shapes exposure to traditional (race-neutral) risk factors as well as exposure to unique structural and cultural risk and protective factors. A guiding assumption of this approach is that "race is not a direct cause of violence but rather a marker for the cluster of social and material disadvantages that both follow from and constitute racial status in America" (Wilson & Katz, 2018, p. 5; see also Sampson, 2012). Before moving to the specifics of the racialized theory, I first briefly review the research on race and crime in an admittedly broad-brush manner that is selective in emphasis out of necessity.

Race and Street Crime

Although greatly magnified by biases in the CJS, official statistics, victimization studies, and, to a lesser extent, self-report surveys reveal that Blacks disproportionately commit (and are victimized by) street crimes compared to Whites. Explaining racial disparities in street crimes, and especially violence, has long been a focus of criminological scholarship. Early social explanations centered on the existence of ostensibly unique aspects of "ghetto-slum" (read: poor Black) culture that subvert conventional behavior and encourage crime and violence (Curtis, 1975; Miller, 1958; Wolfgang & Ferracuti, 1967). Despite the fact that many of these unflattering depictions were accompanied by declarations that structure shapes subcultural responses, the emphasis was explicitly on describing the ostensibly pathological cultural elements.[6] For better or worse, the (admittedly meager) acknowledgements of the structural bedrocks of the "ghetto subculture" were largely ignored, and these approaches were excoriated for blaming the victims and reinforcing the belief that poor inner-city residents are responsible for their circumstances, including elevated rates of crime and poverty. Although dominating race and crime scholarship for a number of years, this subcultural or "kinds-of-people" approach waned due in large part to its inadequate explanatory scheme, particularly the neglect of structural influences and inattention to the origin of subcultural adjustments and variation (e.g., Hawkins, 2003; Sampson & Wilson, 1995).

For a number of years after the demise of these cultural-deficit explanations, the study of race and crime was, as Sampson and Wilson (1995, p. 37) famously described it, "mired in an unproductive mix of controversy and silence." Beginning in the 1980s and picking up steam into the 1990s, the classic works of Blau and Blau (1982), Sampson (1987), and later Massey and Denton (1993) and Sampson and Wilson (1995), among others (Crutchfield, 1989; Hawkins, 1983) alongside Russell's (1992) instigating Black Criminology essay, reignited scholarly research on racial disparities and crime and replaced the cultural (deficit) emphasis with a racialized structural approach. Although differing in several important respects, these explanations all examined the study of race and crime from contextual lenses, focusing on variations in crime rates across communities that vary in racial composition and levels of inequality.[7] Here, race is "a marker for the constellation of social contexts" in which individuals are embedded (Sampson & Bean, 2006, p. 8). These "kinds-of-places" perspectives emphasize racialized structural forces, such as employment and housing discrimination, which converge to produce hypersegregated, economically disadvantaged neighborhoods. The social isolation and concentrated disadvantage of these communities impair social organization, which weakens community social control (e.g., collective efficacy), and is conducive to the emergence of a deviant culture either tolerating or justifying criminal behavior (Massey & Denton, 1993; Sampson & Wilson, 1995). Wilson (2009, p. 147), for example, points to "cultural traits that emerge from patterns of intergroup interaction in settings created by racial segregation and discrimination." Elevated crime rates in areas with higher concentrations of African American residents are the result.

Over the past several decades, there has been a veritable explosion in the research on race and crime testing these racialized structural explanations (see Peterson & Krivo, 2005; Wilson & Katz, 2018). This research shows that the structural influences of racial segregation and concentrated disadvantage play important roles in explaining differences in crime rates across racialized space, and ethnographic studies of disadvantaged, inner-city communities have identified and described the existence of cultural codes or cognitive landscapes tolerating or justifying street crimes (ostensibly adaptations to structural disadvantages; Anderson, 1999; Berg et al., 2016; Harding, 2010; Jones, 2010; Kirk & Papachristos, 2011; Miller, 2008; Oliver, 1994). However, a number of questions remain unexplained, especially related to within-place variations in offending; after all, even in the most highly disadvantaged neighborhoods, there is tremendous variation in offending (Rosenblatt, Edin, & Zhu, 2016).

In recent years, scholars have pointed to situational stratification and the need to compliment macro-level explanations with a consideration of the way that racial stratification is instantiated in interactional processes (e.g., Bruce, Roscigno, & McCall, 1998; Burt, Simons, & Gibbons, 2012; Unnever, Cullen, Mathers, McClure, & Allison, 2009). Fully understanding the effects of race on street crime requires that we go beyond macro-level social facts to address the practice and lived reality of racism. Given their contextual lenses, macro-level explanations of racial disparities overlook a key interactional risk factor associated with race: *interpersonal racial discrimination* (IRD)—the blatant, subtle, and covert actions, verbal messages, and signals that are supported by White racism and malign, mistreat, or otherwise harm members of racial minorities (Essed, 1991; Feagin, 1991).

Interpersonal Racial Discrimination (IRD)

Although the notion that the contemporary U.S. is a colorblind/postracial society and that racism as well as its manifestations in racially discriminatory interactions are a thing of the past gained traction among a segment of the public during the years of the Obama presidency, such beliefs are unsound. A wealth of research on racial minorities using a variety of techniques demonstrates not only that IRD persists but that it is pervasive (see Ayres, 2002; Bobo & Charles, 2009; Feagin, 2010; Pager & Shepherd, 2008). Numerous surveys document African Americans' frequent experiences with IRD (as unfair, disparate treatment based on racial status) in everyday social settings using a variety of perceived discrimination measures. (Perceptual measures ask respondents to report whether they have experienced one or more negative acts because, from their perspective, they are Black or African American or "because of [their] race or ethnicity.") For example, in their study of Black adults, Klonoff and Landrine (1999) found that 96% reported experiencing IRD in the past year, including discrimination from waiters and store clerks (83%), being called a racist slur (50%), and being hit, shoved, harmed, or threatened with physical harm (~50%). Moreover, IRD is widely experienced not only by adults but also by Black adolescents and children (Burt et al., 2012; Gibbons, Gerrard, Cleveland, Wills, & Brody, 2004; Sellers, Copeland-Linder, Martin, & Lewis, 2006). For example, in Sellers et al.'s (2006) study of Black youth, 20% reported experiencing *all* of the 17 measured racial hassles, and 93% reported at least 1 incident in the past year. Although some incidents might be considered subtle or mundane, some are decidedly not. A community study of Black adolescents found that more than 14% reported experiencing threatened physical harm because of their race in the past year (Burt et al., 2012). In short, African Americans perceive IRD in everyday life as "ubiquitous, expected, [and] integrated into the subtleties of interaction" because it is (Essed, 1991, p. 108).

Importantly, evidence of the persistence and pervasiveness of IRD is not limited to perceptual measures but is also found in experimental studies. For example, audit studies document compelling evidence of racial discrimination in important life contexts, including car sales (Ayres & Siegelman, 1995), insurance (Squires, 2003; Wissoker, Zimmerman, & Galster, 1998), housing searches (Yinger, 1995), home mortgages (Rugh & Massey, 2010; Bayer, Ferreira, & Ross, 2014), employment (Agan & Starr, 2017; Pager, 2007), and medical care (Nelson, 2002; Schulman et al., 1999). Evidence from field experiments confirms that racial discrimination exists even in such ordinary experiences as hailing a taxi (Ridley, Bayton, & Outtz, 1989). Moreover, studies of legal records from formal discrimination claims provide detailed documentation of racial discrimination across a wide range of social domains (Harris, Henderson, & Williams, 2005; Roscigno, 2007), and studies that interview "potential discriminators" (e.g., employers) document the existence of racial preferences and biases in hiring along with the persistence of racial stereotypes in shaping employment decisions (e.g., Holzer, 1996; Kirschenman & Neckerman, 1991; Wilson, 1996). Finally, contrary to claims that racial discrimination is decreasing, a recent meta-analysis showed *no change* in levels of racial discrimination against African Americans since 1989 (Quillian, Pager, Hexel, & Midtbøen, 2017). In sum, racial discrimination persists and influences the life chances and routine situations of everyday life for African Americans.

Interpersonal Racial Discrimination and Street Crime

Although the idea that interpersonal racial discrimination was implicated in offending was presented as early as 1899 by Du Bois, for nearly a century, the idea that IRD is criminogenic was largely neglected. Roughly 100 years after Du Bois's insights, McCord and Ensminger's (1997, 2003, p. 322) landmark research on African Americans identified "perceived racial discrimination as a form of victimization" and a risk factor for violence. Using a sample of African Americans tracked from age 6 to age 32, they found that respondents who reported ever having been a victim of at least one of six types of racial discrimination (80% of males and 56% of females had) were more likely to have an official record for violence. McCord and Ensminger's (2003, p. 329) research was the first to demonstrate empirically that "in addition to the more traditionally acknowledged sources of violence, exposure to racial discrimination is a risk factor."

McCord and Ensminger's pioneering work alongside the resurgence of micro-level strain theory in criminology spawned a new approach to racial disparities in offending investigating IRD as an adverse, stressful, and criminogenic experience. Over the past two decades, more than 20 studies have linked IRD to increases in street crime or similar behaviors, including self-reported violence (Caldwell, Kohn-Wood, Schmeelk-Cone, Chavous, & Zimmerman, 2004; Simons et al., 2006; Stewart & Simons, 2006), conduct problems or behavioral problems (Brody et al., 2006; DuBois, Burk-Braxton, Swenson, Tevendale, & Hardesty, 2002; Nyborg & Curry, 2003; Simons, Chen, Stewart, & Brody, 2003; Unnever, Cullen, & Barnes, 2016), and delinquency (Burt et al., 2012;

Martin et al., 2011; Unnever et al., 2009; Unnever, Cullen, & Barnes, 2017), as well as official reports of arrest (McCord & Ensminger, 1997, 2003). This work indicates that IRD is associated with increased offending whether examined cross-sectionally or longitudinally, and among youth as well as adults.

Although two rich datasets have predominated in these studies (the Family and Community Health Study [FACHS] and the Project on Human Development in Chicago Neighborhoods [PHDCN]), nationally representative surveys (e.g., the National Survey of American Life [NSAL]; Unnever, 2014) and other community-based surveys (e.g., Richmond Youth Study; Unnever et al., 2009; Flint Adolescent Study; Caldwell et al., 2004; Maryland Adolescents in Context Study; Wong, Eccles, & Sameroff, 2003) also indicate that IRD increases the risk of street crime. Furthermore, findings are robust to variation in perceptual measures of IRD, including variegated prompts, item wording, and measured life domains (e.g., in the school, community, and/or workplace). Given the high prevalence of IRD among African Americans, most studies employ multiple-item instruments, which are summed or averaged to create a scale measuring frequency of exposure to different types of IRD over some time period (usually 12 months; see, e.g., Burt et al., 2012; Caldwell et al., 2004; DuBois et al., 2002; Unnever et al., 2017).

For illustration, a common IRD instrument, and one used in the FACHS, is the Schedule of Racist Events (SRE; Landrine & Klonoff, 1996). In the FACHS, the SRE was revised in response to feedback from African American focus groups to make the items designed for adults more relevant to youth experiences (Brody et al., 2006). Respondents were presented with 11 questions about their experiences following this prompt: "Racial discrimination occurs when someone is treated in a negative or unfair way just because of their race or ethnic background. I want to ask you some questions about whether you have experienced racial discrimination. For each statement, please tell me if this situation has happened to you never, once or twice, a few times, or several times" over the past year. Assessed experiences include: "How often has someone said something insulting to you because of your race or ethnic background?"; "How often has someone yelled a racial slur or racial insult at you . . .?"; and "How often has someone threatened to harm you physically . . .?" Consonant with other racial discrimination surveys, this study found IRD to be pervasive among respondents; yet considerable variation existed. For example, in wave 4, when the youths were aged 18 to 20, 13%

reported experiencing none of the 11 racially discriminatory acts in the past year, and 6% reported experiencing all at least once. The most common racially discriminatory event was having someone say something insulting to you just because of your race or ethnic background (68% experienced this at least once). The least prevalent experience was having someone threaten to harm you physically; 14% reported experiencing this at least once, and this was significantly more common among males (see Burt & Simons, 2015).

Importantly, given the perceptual nature of these measures, studies have investigated valid concerns about the possibility of reverse or reciprocal causation. Specifically, researchers have probed findings in longitudinal models to test whether individuals who have behavioral problems are more likely to attract, perceive, and/or be victimized by later racial discrimination and that this reverse causal process accounts for the relationship between IRD and crime. In the first exploration of this idea, McCord and Ensminger (2003) noted that if being a victim of racial discrimination was a response to a disruptive orientation, then disruptive children would report more experiences with racial discrimination as adults. Contrary to this temporal sequence, they found no evidence that disruptive behavior presaged reports of IRD. In a later study using cross-lagged models separated by 2 years, Brody and colleagues (2006) showed that although a measure of problem behaviors was significantly associated with later IRD, this effect size was dwarfed by the effects of earlier IRD on later problem behaviors. Subsequent explorations using cross-lagged models and criminal outcomes revealed that discrimination influenced offending outcomes, whereas earlier offending had weak, nonsignificant effects on later racial discrimination (e.g., Burt et al., 2012, 2017a). Thus, although some analyses suggest that problematic behavior is associated with later experiences with racial discrimination, the evidence indicates that the bulk of the effect is from racial discrimination to later problematic behavioral outcomes rather than the reverse.

Altogether, the accumulated evidence is clear: IRD increases the risk of offending, influences within-race variations in offending, and, as a pernicious risk factor unique to racial minorities, contributes to racial disparities in offending (Burt et al., 2012; Unnever & Gabbidon, 2011). Consequently, most recent scholarship has focused on understanding the processes through which IRD increases the likelihood of street crime. The challenge is explaining how—through what psychosocial mechanisms—discrimination augments the risk of general offending, not limited to immediate backlash against the perpetrator(s). Addressing this challenge, scholars have developed both racially specific (i.e., Unnever & Gabbidon, 2011) and racialized explanations (Burt et al., 2012; Kaufman, Rebellon, Thaxton, & Agnew, 2008; Simons & Burt, 2011).

As noted, I link IRD to offending via a racialized theory, the social schematic theory (SST). In contrast to some theories that have been racialized after their creation, SST was initially developed as a racialized theory and utilized to explain variation in offending among a sample of African Americans (Simons & Burt, 2011). Thus, like Sampson and Wilson's thesis of racial invariance, the role of racial subordination was central to the genesis and development of this theory. SST explicitly prioritizes the role of racist structural arrangements—especially White racism instantiated in discriminatory interactions—as a causal force setting in motion a developmental cascade that may increase the likelihood of offending. As I elaborate below, this model identifies (nonconscious) cognitive adaptations that promote survival, fitness, and/or "fitness proxies" in the face of harsh, unpredictable situations such as IRD. Importantly, as a racialized theory, SST does *not* conceive of these cognitive adaptations as unique to racial minorities. In other words, SST does not posit the existence of a unique Black psychology or distinct personality traits resulting from racism. As I discuss, SST focuses on the development of criminogenic social schemas that result from internalizing the lessons inherent in harsh, unpredictable social experiences— racist and nonracist in origin (Burt, Lei, & Simons, 2017b).

The Social Schematic Theory of (Street) Crime

SST is a life-course, evolutionary developmental learning theory that elucidates the social psychological processes through which exposures to social adversities and supports (patterned by social position) influence individual differences in propensities to offend (criminality; Simons & Burt, 2011). SST starts from the assumption, consistent with research on human morality, that individuals are born with innate capacities to be fair, cooperative, and sympathetic, as well as to be egoistic, coercive, and sometimes aggressive (e.g., de Waal, 2006; Haidt, 2007; Hauser, 2006). Rather than being naturally good, bad, or empty vessels into which society pours its views of morality, SST assumes that we are born with the wiring to adapt our orientations to the world to fit our environments. Throughout our long phylogenetic history, we have evolved to survive in a variety of contexts, which vary in the degree to which they are predictably supportive versus dangerous, unpredictable, and resource limited, and these different contexts require different competencies for survival and fitness (Del Giudice, 2009; Ellis et al., 2012). For example, in high-risk environments (e.g., impoverished, high-crime neighborhoods) where resources are scarce and future rewards are substantially more uncertain than immediate ones, a preference for immediate rewards and enhanced abilities to shift attention (at the cost of inhibitory control) may allow individuals to take advantage of fleeting opportunities and identify unpredictable threats (Ellis, Bianchi, Griskevicius, & Frankenhuis, 2017). Similarly, in dangerous environments, where it is especially crucial to detect and predict threats, heightened attentional vigilance and enhanced memory for threatening information (e.g., remembering individuals who pose a threat) can enhance safety (Frankenhuis & de Weerth, 2013). Thus, rather than assuming—as most perspectives do—that orientations and capacities that foster health and "success" in safe, supportive, predictable environments are universally better or adaptive across all environments, this evolutionary developmental perspective recognizes that competencies increasing developmental "success" in safe environments may actually be maladaptive in high-risk contexts (and vice versa).

Furthermore, and central to this evolutionary *developmental* framework, contexts and circumstances can and do change over the course of humans' long life spans. As Chisholm (1999) explains:

> The perennial adaptive problem for any species, but especially our slowly developing, long-lived, highly intelligent, and intensely social species, is that of environmental uncertainty. This is the problem of obtaining sufficient information to make our way through complex social space in the face of virtually continuous sociocultural change. No environment is free of uncertainty, but such uncertainty has been a chronic, defining problem for our species because of an ultimate sort of environmental uncertainty that Plotkin (1994) calls the "uncertain futures problem." (p. 19)

The "uncertain futures problem" is rooted in the biological reality of "generational deadtime" (Plotkin, 1994). Coined by Konrad Lorenz (1966), this term refers to the fact that we are born with a set of biological resources for development (e.g., genes) that worked well (enough) for our ancestors' survival and fitness. Yet, because contexts and circumstances change across all levels of space (species-wide, community-level, individual-level), these biological resources may no longer be a fit to the varying contexts of development in which we find ourselves. The essence of the uncertain futures problem is that developmental "success" (safety, resources and status, procurement of mates) depends on an adaptive match between the organism and its environment, but genetic resources are received all at once based on past conditions; development takes time; and the environment is changing and uncertain (Chisholm, 1999; West-Eberhard, 2003). Thus, we have evolved mechanisms facilitating *adaptive developmental plasticity*, or environmentally induced malleability.[8] This capacity includes both the ability to assess local context and relative condition and to adapt (physical, psychological, and/ or behavioral phenotypes) in response to these cues to optimize fitness or "proxies of fitness" (Chisholm, 1999; Mishra, 2014). Proxies of fitness include resources reliably associated with survival and reproductive success, principally material resources, social status and respect, and quality mates (Daly & Wilson, 2001). Notably, to "optimize fitness" is not to create the best outcome imaginable but to create the best conditional match to the social environment given individuals' relative state and resources (e.g., food, safety, physical strength, health, and so on; Ellis et al., 2012).

Importantly, although we are immensely social creatures with complex, technologically advanced structures and cultures, this framework emphasizes that adaptations (learning, development) are still for survival and reproduction (Chisholm, 1999; Daly & Wilson, 2001). Thus, phenotype plasticity did not evolve to promote "success" in any Western cultural sense but to facilitate continuance (Belsky, 2012; Ellis et al., 2012). Evolutionary developmental frameworks thus shed light on allegedly dysfunctional cognitive biases and ostensibly pathological behaviors (such as crime) in response to high-risk environments by acknowledging their adaptive logic (underlying fitness-relevant motivations) or contextually appropriate rationale.[9] In other words, harsh, unpredictable environments *shape* rather than exclusively impair development (Ellis & Del Giudice, 2014), as "individuals become developmentally adapted ('specialized' and potentially enhanced) for solving problems that are ecologically relevant in such environments" (Ellis et al., 2017, p. 562; Frankenhuis & de Weerth, 2013). This view contrasts with prevailing deficit approaches (e.g., Gottfredson & Hirschi, 1990; Mani, Mullainathan, Shafir, & Zhao, 2013; Shonkoff et al., 2012), which imply that stress-adapted individuals are ill or broken and need to be treated or fixed (e.g., improved attention, delaying gratification, following rules, and trusting others; Ellis et al., 2017). This is important because it suggests that rather than being a result of individual, familial, or cultural failings, environmentally-induced compensations, such as attentional shifting and hostile attribution biases, can be seen as specialized skills that maximize fitness and minimize risks in harsh environments (Fawcett, McNamara, & Houston, 2012; Griskevicius, Tybur, Gangestad, Perea, & Kenrick, 2009).

SST adopts these developmental-evolutionary assumptions (supported by a wealth of research from multiple species) that development is above all for survival and then reproduction; that phenotype plasticity evolved to allow organisms to optimize fitness in response to social-environmental cues during development; and that given the long generational deadtime and the "virtually continuous sociocultural change" experienced by our extremely social species, we have evolved a relatively expansive capacity for developmental plasticity. The idea is that our minds, our moral sentiments, and our psychosocial characteristics are calibrated by cues about social-environmental risk and uncertainty, and that in addition to other social behaviors that risk harm (often delayed) for more immediate rewards,[10] street crimes—often characterized as offering immediate gratification at the expense of delayed or uncertain punishments—are made more likely by developmental adaptations to harsh, unpredictable environments. Why this is the case requires a bit more explication.

A developmental-evolutionary approach views *life as a knowledge-gaining process*, with adaptations as environmental information that has become embodied or represented in phenotypes (Plotkin, 1994). In this view, learning itself is an adaptation for actively extracting information from the environment in order to develop mental models of reality to predict the future (minimize risk and uncertainty) and facilitate optimal decision making (Chisholm, 1999; Plotkin, 1994). As Chisholm (1999, p. 65) articulated, "Plasticity . . . implies the contingent development of various kinds of learning biases or predispositions—which are evaluative or motivational phenomena." SST focuses on the internalization of the life lessons relevant to crime and the enduring influence of these lessons on meaning making, decision making, and behavioral trajectories in the form of *social schemas*. Also referred to as cognitive schemas or more broadly as psychosocial orientations, social schemas are cognitive representations of the patterns in social interaction that influence future behavior by specifying the import and meaning of various social stimuli and the probable consequences of various lines of action (see Crick &

Dodge, 1994; see also Bourdieu, 1990; Mead, 1934). Social schemas are integral to all social action, as they allow us to move more efficiently through life—attending to relevant cues, interpreting these cues in light of past experience and contextual information, and responding in ways that facilitate our aims—based on prior experiences (themselves shaped by our existing schemas). Through these invariably nonconscious processes, individuals develop environmentally calibrated heuristics composed of lessons from past experiences that reflect a deep evolutionary logic (Mishra, 2014).

Focusing on racial disparities, in our racialized social system, racial status patterns exposure to harsh, dangerous, unpredictable environments. Due to the legacy of historical and ongoing IRD and institutional discrimination, Blacks are more likely to have lower SES and reside in segregated, disadvantaged contexts (e.g., Reardon & Bischoff, 2011; Sampson, 2012; Sharkey, 2013). As Wilson (2016, p. 1452) averred, "residents in high jobless inner-city black neighborhoods . . . live under constraints and face challenges that most people in the larger society do not experience, or *cannot even imagine*" (emphasis added). In short, being Black is, without question, associated with increased risk of exposure to ("race-neutral") harsh, unpredictable environments, including neighborhood danger (crime/victimization); harsh parenting; low-quality child care; bad housing conditions characterized by noise, crowding, and violence; residential instability; peer and school difficulties; family disruption; resource scarcity; morbidity-mortality; incarceration; adult joblessness; and the like (e.g., Conley, 1999; Duncan & Brooks-Gunn, 2000; McLoyd, 1990; Sharkey, 2013). African Americans have the additional burden of IRD—clearly demonstrated to be a harsh, unpredictable experience (Clark, Anderson, Clark, & Williams, 1999; Harrell, 2000; Sellers, Caldwell, Schmeelk-Cone, & Zimmerman, 2003). Indeed, whether it's driving while Black, shopping while Black, or walking while Black, simply *being* Black in the U.S. is dangerous and unpredictable (Russell-Brown, 2009), leading Gabbidon and Peterson (2006) to coin the phrase "living while Black" to capture this stressful reality. Notably, experimental research on the phenomenology of discrimination demonstrates that IRD is experienced as psycho-biologically threatening (activating our primal fight-or-flight system), and because of its prevalence and severity, one must be on guard constantly (e.g., Essed, 1991; Feagin, 1991).

SST proposes that harsh, unpredictable interactions and environments foster *three key ("race-neutral") lessons*: that delayed rewards rarely or inequitably materialize; that the world is a hostile, unpredictable place; and that social rules and punishments do not apply equally to everyone (Burt & Simons, 2015; Simons & Burt, 2011). These lessons are stored as (and correspond to) three key *criminogenic social schemas*: present orientation (also called immediate gratification or low self-control; e.g., Gottfredson & Hirschi, 1990), hostile views of relationships (e.g., Anderson, 1999; Dodge, 2006), and disengagement from conventional norms (e.g., Akers, 1985; Hirschi, 1969). Simons and Burt (2011) contend that these criminogenic schemas are rooted in the same set of social conditions (harshness and unpredictability), which communicate similar lessons about the world, namely that the world is unpredictably unfair, delaying gratification can result in the absence of gratification, and following social conventions (e.g., keeping one's word, respecting norms, eschewing violence) does not result in predictably (or overall) better outcomes. Consequently, these three cognitive schemas coalesce into a higher-order mental model, designated a *criminogenic knowledge structure* (CKS) that operates as dynamic unity in making situational definitions compelling or legitimating crime more likely.

A wealth of research suggests that harsh, unpredictable, segregated environments increase immediate gratification, insecure attachment, more reactive responses to threat, defensive hostility, and a here-and-now attitude (e.g., Brezina, Tekin, & Topalli, 2009; Gardner, 1993; Griskevicius et al., 2009; Hill, Ross, & Low, 1997; Sharkey & Sampson, 2015; Sharkey, Tirado-Strayer, Papachristos, & Raver, 2012; Wilson & Daly, 1997). As Curtis (1975, p. 19) discerned some 40 years ago, in neighborhoods where resources are scarce and unpredictable, "the choice is not necessarily seen as one between immediate and deferred gratification, but probably more accurately as between immediate gratification and no gratification at all." Even more bluntly, Brezina et al.'s (2009, p. 1116) respondent "Blue Eyes," proclaimed, "I say fuck tomorrow. It's all about today. Might not be a tomorrow. Might get shot. Might get hit by a bus. So get it now. Now, now, now. Next week might as well be next century. Fuck next week. Fuck tomorrow (Blue Eyes, age 23)." Ethnographic studies of segregated, inner-city communities also document the cynicism and institutional distrust engendered by harsh, racially biased conditions: "Theirs is a cynical outlook, and trust of others is severely lacking, even trust of those they are close to. Consistently, they tend to approach all persons and situations as part of life's obstacles, as things to subdue or even to 'get over'" (Anderson, 1999, p. 37; see also Goffman, 2014; Hannerz, 1969; Oliver, 1994, 2003).

Similarly, Anderson (1999, p. 67) documented: "As a means of *survival*, [a child] often learns the value of having a 'name,' a reputation for being willing and able to fight" (my emphasis).

Moreover, focusing explicitly on IRD, research, noted earlier, reveals that cumulative exposures to IRD increase immediate gratification, hostile views, and disengagement from norms (e.g., Burt, Simons, & Gibbons, 2012; Burt, Lei, & Simons, 2017a; Unnever, Cullen, & Barnes, 2016, 2017). In short, a compelling body of research suggests that harsh, unpredictable conditions and experiences, including IRD, produce more opportunistic, risky, and short-term worldviews or orientations to life, consistent with the CKS in SST.

Notably, this framework is not merely a rational choice model cloaked in evolutionary reasoning and ultimate aims; rather, these adaptations—manifest in an individual's preferences, desires, and behaviors—are usually made unconsciously and reflect a deep evolutionary logic (Chisholm, 1999; Ellis et al., 2012). Furthermore, as is hopefully clear by now, despite increasing the risk of offending, these schemas are not viewed as pathological or maladaptive but rather as contextually appropriate. For example, all else equal, risky behaviors that can enhance resources and status (and thus facilitate access to mates) in the present are objectively more valuable when life expectancies are shorter, resources are scarce, and local status hierarchies are known and/or easily discernable through symbolic displays (Anderson, 1999; Ellis et al., 2012). Similarly, when expected profits from safe choices are negligible (e.g., low-wage, insecure employment), choosing high-risk, high-reward strategies (spending scarce funds on lottery tickets; engaging in illicit activity such as drug trafficking) can be an optimal strategy (Griskevicius, Tybur, Delton, & Robertson, 2011). Likewise, enhanced ability in attention shifting and working memory can promote the detection of threats and fleeting opportunities in harsh, unpredictable environments, even as these enhanced skills may come at the expense of impulse control (Mittal, Griskevicius, Simpson, Sung, & Young, 2015).

Conceptualizing interpersonal approaches as adaptations involves recognizing that in dangerous environments, heightened vigilance, hostile attribution biases, and lower levels of trust and cooperation can enhance fitness and/or status, even if they impose significant costs on the individual and society. In other words, individuals with those traits are (or were) more likely to avoid fitness-damaging outcomes (compared with nonvigilant, trusting individuals in the same context), even if such psychological responses are unpleasant and physiologically costly

(Ellis et al., 2017; Griskevicius et al., 2009; Simpson & Belsky, 2008). For example, as Anderson (1999) and others have documented, developing a reputation for violence is valuable for deterring predation or attacks in contexts where legal authority is weak or unreliable (see also Cooney, 1998; Nisbett & Cohen, 1996). In sum, this approach emphasizes that these temporal, interpersonal, and normative approaches to the world are not irrational or reflections of individual deficits or dysfunctions; rather, animal and human research suggests that these reflect ecological rationality (Pepper & Nettle, 2017; Ellis et al., 2012, 2017).

Extant Research on IRD From an SST Perspective

Although currently limited to studies utilizing the FACHS, research testing SST's predictions about the effects of IRD on street crime has been largely supportive. Cross sectional studies of Black adolescents indicate that IRD increases street crime largely through the CKS (~ 80% of the effects of IRD on crime are mediated by the CKS), including both violent and nonviolent crimes, and for both males and females; Burt & Simons, 2015). Notably, the effect of IRD on the CKS is stronger for males than females, and IRD is more strongly linked to violent than nonviolent crimes (Burt et al., 2012, Burt & Simons, 2015). Importantly, analyses reveal that IRD increases all component schemas of the CKS (immediate gratification, hostile views, and disengagement from norms) in a similar manner (Burt et al., 2017a).

Research has also explored the effects of cumulative exposures to IRD in childhood and adolescence on offending in emerging adulthood in a life-course model (Burt et al., 2017a). Consistent with SST, this work revealed that childhood experiences with IRD are associated with emerging adulthood offending in large part through the CKS, which is maintained over time through processes of cumulative and interactional continuity. In other words, both the cumulative negative consequences of a high CKS as well as the evocative responses to such worldviews, individuals' local ecologies, and situational circumstances tend to remain relatively stable over time (e.g., Caspi, Bem, & Elder, 1989; Sampson & Laub, 1995; Sharkey, 2013). This life-course SST model conceptualizes a higher CKS more broadly as 'self-limiting social dispositions' (Wilson, 2006) or 'socioemotional capacities' (Heckman, 2008), which are rooted in structural circumstances and hinder success in conventional institutions and relationships (schools, jobs, romantic relationships) in addition to increasing crime. This broader conceptualization not only facilitates identifying a "behavioral constellation of deprivation" (behaviors reflecting more opportunistic, risky, and short-term views of life; Pepper & Nettle, 2017) shaping life opportunities and outcomes but also enables mapping the psychosocial pathways undergirding the persistence of inequalities. After all, hostile views, impulsivity, and disengagement from conventional norms (e.g., resolving conflicts without violence, remaining faithful to one's partner; being on time) are not conducive to successful or positive experiences in the school, on the job, or in one's relationship. To this end, Burt et al. (2017a) found that the criminogenic effects of childhood IRD were maintained (or augmented) over time through the CKS and its interactional social effects (decreasing the likelihood of satisfactory involvement in supportive institutions and relationships, specifically education, employment, and romantic relationships). In the SST model, relationships and institutional involvements are theoretically significant, as they represent aggregates of situations that vary in predictability and support. These longitudinal findings are consistent with research elucidating the perpetuation of inequality through socioemotional capacities shaped by low-SES ("high-risk") backgrounds (Hackman et al., 2014; Jones, Greenberg, & Crowley, 2015; Mani et al., 2013) as well as criminological research using other samples that links IRD to crime through weakened attachment to conventional institutions (the school; Unnever et al., 2016, 2017) as well as low self-control, anger, and increased substance use (Unnever, 2014). Finally, this life-course SST model is also consonant with research indicating that harsh, unpredictable environments (shaped by racial inequality, e.g., exposure to violent crime) decrease impulse control in the classroom and impede academic achievement (Sharkey et al., 2012; Sharkey & Sampson, 2015). Altogether, this work suggests that by shaping social schemas, IRD in concert with other harsh, unpredictable environments patterned by racial status decrease the likelihood of success in conventional domains, with consequences that accumulate and amplify initial disadvantages.

Importantly in longitudinal tests of SST where IRD predicts offending several years later, not all of racial discrimination's effects on street crime are mediated by the CKS. Instead, as Simons, Burt, Barr, Lei, and Stewart (2014) found in their test of SST (focusing on cumulative continuity through selection into criminogenic contexts and risky activities), IRD has a direct effect on criminogenic situational definitions. Contrary to this finding, SST predicts that the effects of harsh, unpredictable developmental environments on criminogenic situational definitions should be mediated by the CKS. At this point, we can only speculate why IRD, unlike other measured harsh, unpredictable experiences, such as harsh parenting and community crime, has a direct effect on criminogenic situational definitions. Whether these findings are due to inherent limitations in using longitudinal surveys to capture complex cognitive processes underlying decision making or this remaining direct effect indicates that a general theory cannot fully capture the effects of racial status and IRD and on crime remains to be seen. Consonant with the latter view, Unnever and colleagues (2009, 2016; Unnever & Gabbidon, 2011) have argued that Whites' systematic sociopolitical domination can undermine Blacks' bonds to historically White-dominated institutions in general. And, more specifically, pernicious racially biased treatment by police and the justice system will foster unique criminogenic worldviews, including cultural frames of legal cynicism, among Blacks. Although, as I have noted, I am hesitant to postulate the existence of qualitative differences between Blacks and Whites in psychosocial orientations, I concur with Unnever and Gabbidon's (2011) argument that the historical and continuing legacy of racialized control and subordination by the U.S. CJS has almost certainly fostered a shared cultural belief that the CJS is unjust and racially biased and shaped perceptions of racist threats by the police among Blacks. However, our analyses with the FACHS youth suggest that stronger agreement with a scale measuring racial biases in the CJS does not mediate the remaining direct effects of IRD on increased crime. In fact, this measure of CJS racial biases is not even related to criminal offending among Black youth in the FACHS. This is perhaps due to the fact that most Black youth believe that the CJS is racially biased (see Unnever & Gabbidon, 2011), and thus the effects of this shared cultural frame on increased offending are only observed in between-group comparisons between Blacks and other racial groups. In any case, the point remains that in longitudinal models, the CKS does not fully explain the effects of IRD on later offending, and more research on this remaining direct effect is needed.

Altogether, research converges in demonstrating that IRD is a harsh (stressful, threatening), unpredictable experience that increases criminogenic psychosocial schemas (immediate gratification, hostile views, and disengagement from norms), which come together as a higher-order CKS increasing crime and other purportedly dysfunctional behaviors (substance use, risky sex). Of course, it is clear that despite being subject to considerable adversity and unfair treatment, most African Americans manage to successfully negotiate the deleterious consequences of

IRD and avoid sustained, serious involvement in street crime. To better understand how most African Americans manage not only to survive but also to generate meaningful lives in the face of extraordinarily harsh, racially oppressive conditions not of their own making (Billingsley, 1988; Hill, 1972; Miller & MacIntosh, 1999), scholars have focused on a salient source of resilience among African American cultures—racial socialization.

Before moving on to resilience, however, I want to briefly address a significant theoretical question, noted above, that remains undertheorized: How does structure shape culture and influence individual offending, given that structural aggregates do not commit street crime. In my view, the ease of equating cultural "pathologies" or "lifestyles" with innate deficits and moral decadence is rooted in the collective failure to clearly explain how these cultural traits represent adaptations to structural inequalities. I propose an evolutionary developmental framework can shed light on the structure–culture link. Specifically, such a framework can elucidate how humans' universally shared evolutionary goals (survival and continuance) can produce quite divergent psychosocial orientations in response to (sometimes "unimaginably") different ecological contexts and social conditions.

Structural-Cultural Mechanisms: A Theoretical Lacuna

As noted above, most current macro-level research on race and crime theorizes culture as an adaptation to structural circumstances (e.g., Massey & Denton, 1993; Sampson & Wilson, 1995). Culture is thus endogenous to structure, "a mediating mechanism that shapes individuals' subjective experiences and responses" to their conditions of existence (Sampson & Bean, 2006, p. 22). In general, these models assume a consensus view of culture (that of mainstream "prosocial" culture) and propose that structural disadvantages exacerbated by social isolation foster cultural attenuation as weakened adherence to societal values (Kornhauser, 1978; Sampson & Wilson, 1995). In these conditions, individuals may learn that in some situations, it is expedient or necessary to engage in violence, drug use and selling, and other street crimes as "ecologically structured tolerances" of deviance (Sampson & Wilson, 1995). These tolerances are passed along to children through role modeling and operant conditioning, and the acceptance of violence and street crime becomes part of the cognitive landscape of everyday life (Sampson & Bean, 2006; Sampson & Wilson, 1995; Wilson, 2006).

Importantly, although the proximal cause of crime is cultural attenuation, the causal emphasis of these theories is on the role of racialized structural forces (high unemployment, concentrated poverty, housing discrimination, and concomitant family disruption), with the implication that reducing structural inequality would change culture (reduce cultural attenuation; Sampson & Wilson, 1995; Wilson, 2006, 2009).

Despite the clear theoretical linkages between structure and culture and thick ethnographic descriptions of cultural conditions in these underclass neighborhoods (Anderson, 1978, 1999; Fader, 2013; Hannerz, 1969; Harding, 2010; Goffman, 2014; Jones, 2010; Young, 2006), *how* structure shapes cultural adaptations is not well understood theoretically (Sampson & Bean, 2006; Wilson, 2006).[11] For example, Wilson (2006, p. 115) noted,

> Patterns of behavior in the inner city often represent particular cultural adaptations to the systemic blockage of opportunities in the environment of the inner city and the society as a whole. These adaptations are reflected in the habits, skills, styles, and attitudes that are shaped over time.

But how? Through what psychosocial mechanisms do structural conditions shape individual attitudes, habits, styles, and skills (hereafter cultural traits)?[12]

Addressing this gap, I submit that SST provides mechanistic insights into how structure shapes cultural adaptations and propose the CKS as a conceptual (social-psychological) bridge linking the two. Moreover, the depiction of these cultural traits as dysfunctional or counterproductive is countered with a contextually appropriate evolutionary characterization. But first, a caveat is in order; what I offer is a preliminary consideration to integrate bodies of literature and competing analytical approaches to fill gaps in explanatory models into a more general theoretical whole. This is an ambitious approach, in that I try to cover a lot of important ground in a short space; if the grounds covered here seem fruitful, later work can add depth and tighten theoretical strands.

Structural Influences, Social Schemas, and Cultural Frames

Culture is an elusive concept; it is often left undefined or is simply described vaguely in terms of a group's values, attitudes, and behavior, with the former often deduced from the latter. This lack of sophistication impedes our understanding of within-group variations in cultural factors and confounds attempts to link structure to culture as an intermediary mechanism (Lamont & Small, 2006). However, work by cultural sociologists has refined traditional conceptions of culture facilitating the incorporation of cultural concepts in a richer, more heterogeneous manner. These refined approaches discard misguided assumptions that social groups have inherent cultural traits (such as "Jewish frugality" or "Asian work ethic") and thereby avoid tautological reasoning that shirks explanation while reifying cultural stereotypes (see Lamont & Small, 2006; Patterson, 2014; Young, 2006).

Drawing on this rich cultural array, I adopt a broad relational definition of culture as a shared mental reality that is place and position based and which includes habits, skills, styles, outlooks, meanings, and the like (Hannerz, 1969; Wilson, 2009 Swidler, 1986). Culture is shared because it is both communicated between individuals in processes of communication and grounded in navigating similar conditions of experience (e.g., Cohen, 1955; Liebow, 1967).[13] Culture can be conceived as communal information—ideas, knowledge, skills—about the world and about addressing recurrent problems of existence, information that is embodied in human brains.[14] In this approach, "[i]nstead of having a culture, individuals exist in the midst of, respond to, use and create cultural symbols" (Lamont & Small, 2006, p. 79).

The social-developmental processes by which such "cultural traits" may develop are more complicated than the canonical model of social learning via intergenerational transmission (Cohen, 1955; Kirk & Papachristos, 2011). Instead, there are two theoretically distinct yet practically overlapping modes of cultural learning, producing two prototypical cultural traits: transmitted and evoked. *Transmitted cultural traits* refer to those that are rooted in socialization practices and involve the transmission of social knowledge from one mind to another via modeling or teaching. For example, many Americans are taught at an early age that green means go while red means stop; pumpkins signify Halloween and candy; and sticks with tiny bristles plus paste are used to clean teeth (and clean teeth are desirable). In contrast, *evoked cultural traits* are cultural factors engendered by shared conditions of existence. In other words, given that we have evolved to optimize fitness in various conditions, shared exposure to such conditions produces similar patterns of adaptation. In my view, earlier conceptions of culture were of limited utility in part because the focus was almost solely on transmitted culture (with an emphasis on values); transmitted culture is only a small part of the story, and maybe not even the most important part.

A long legacy of sociological scholarship on culture and crime has explored and described cultural properties observed in impoverished, segregated inner-city neighborhoods (previously referred to as "culture of poverty," "black poverty subculture," "delinquent subculture"; for reviews, see Curtis, 1975; Oliver, 2003; Young, 2006). Even though these (especially early) works tend to misguidedly assume subcultural consensus with a limited focus on values, patterns identified among low-income individuals (usually minority men) in "ghetto-slums" are insightful. In particular, several cultural leitmotifs emerge from these urban ethnographies, including themes of present orientation, low motivation or persistence in conventional domains of school and work, a heightened propensity to violence, sexual promiscuity, thrill seeking or change versus sameness or routines, verbal ability, shrewdness or street smarts, and among men an emphasis on toughness and sexual conquest (e.g., Anderson, 1978, 1999; Cohen, 1955; Curtis, 1975, Fader, 2013, Hannerz, 1969; Miller, 1958; Rainwater, 1970; Oliver, 1994; Patterson, 2016).[15] These vivid accounts of the everyday lives of low-income men suggest that such cultural traits, which are sometimes derogatorily referred to as "poor lifestyles" or a "culture of poverty," are present and palpable in certain "ghetto-slum" areas. But why and how? Why do some of the most disadvantaged people in society who face challenging life circumstances often respond with attitudes and behaviors that seem to merely exacerbate their situations? As discussed at length above, when people lack the social and material resources required to hold danger and uncertainty at bay, they are evolutionarily predisposed to develop in ways that prioritize immediate survival and reproduction, including adopting a present and opportunistic orientation as well as a cautious, mistrusting view of others (Chisholm, 1999; Ellis et al., 2009, 2012). Among these responses are "traits" or social schemas related to time perspective, views of relationships and attachment styles, and beliefs about fairness and the wisdom and value of following social rules as evocative responses to the conditions of existence. Although often worsening situations from a Western mainstream cultural perspective, these traits can foster (or did foster) evolutionary "success" as survival and fitness.[16]

The implications of this perspective for bridging the structure–culture divide are hopefully clear. Given that social schemas—as mental models of reality and ways of approaching the world—are rooted in similar conditions of experience, insofar as these are shared among a group or community experiencing the same conditions, these schemas are cultural (see also Patterson, 2014).[17] I propose that by virtue of their grounding in shared conditions of experience based in both place (highly disadvantaged, dangerous) and position (racial minority, low SES), the "criminogenic social schemas" identified in SST are to some extent communal among members of "ghetto-slum" neighborhoods, providing a bedrock on which other cultural traits, more specific frames, and culturally transmitted information are configured. In other words, these structurally evoked cultural schemas, as mental models of the world shaping perception, meaning making, and decision making, are crucially implicated not only in behavior but also in attitudes, motivations, and priorities as well (Bourdieu, 1990; Wilson, 2009; Young, 2006).

Previously, (avowedly inchoate) scholarly efforts to bridge the structure–culture divide at the social psychological level pointed to "self-limiting social dispositions" fostered by social isolation among the highly disadvantaged underclass (Wilson, 1987, 2006). For example, Wilson (2009, pp. 147–148) argued that structure shapes

> cultural traits that . . . are embodied in the micro-level processes of meaning making and decision making—that is, the way that individuals in segregated communities develop an understanding of how the world works and make decisions and choices that reflect that understanding.

Similarly, scholarship focused on racial disparities in educational achievement highlights the salient role of "socioemotional characteristics," alternatively called "soft skills" or "character" in shaping individuals' abilities to succeed in conventional domains (Heckman, Humphries, & Kautz, 2014; Heckman, 2008). I submit that widely documented shared experiences among residents of "ghetto-slum" neighborhoods—including community crime, low collective efficacy, residential instability, resource scarcity, poor child care, high unemployment, and low-wage employment—foster a higher CKS as "socioemotional capacities," which serve as "self-limiting social dispositions" (self-limiting from a mainstream [low-risk] perspective) influencing life chances and thus so-called "lifestyles" through their effects on decision making. In concert with the structural constraints and hardships that engender their development, these criminogenic social schemas influence the reproduction of inequality through their effects. As noted, consonant with this idea, a recent study showed that a higher CKS (shaped by cumulative exposures to IRD in childhood) not only increased the likelihood of crime in adulthood but also decreased the likelihood of success in conventional domains and thereby fostered the social conditions that served to perpetuate a higher CKS (Burt et al., 2017a).

In sum, I propose that SST, with its developmental-evolutionary assumptions, provides mechanistic insights into the effects of racialized structural influences on cultural adaptations shaping offending as well as a host of other outcomes as a "behavioral constellation of disadvantage." In so doing, SST sheds light on the evolutionary logic of seemingly "maladaptive" cultural traits, conceptualizing individuals' minds and behaviors as adaptations to local contexts. The disparate ecological distributions of "race-neutral" harsh, unpredictable conditions by race along with IRD pattern racial differences in social schemas, as cultural mechanisms, that serve to reinforce structural disadvantages. Of course, a feature of this approach is a recognition of within-group and within-place variations in cultural traits qua adaptations, which includes a recognition of other influences—from family and school to peers and random experiences (e.g., natural disasters, random victimizations, fantastic inspiring teacher). To be clear, my argument is not that social schemas as contextually appropriate responses undergirding shared worldviews and orientations constitute "culture" writ large nor imply homogeneity in schemas among individuals in segregated communities (as a "culture of poverty").[18] Other cultural elements interact with and are built upon these psychosocial orientations. These include transmitted culture, such as "cultural framing designed to fend off insults that promotes strong feelings of racial pride within the community" (Wilson, 2009, p. 56). To a consideration of another cultural element, salient among African American families, I now turn.

Racial Socialization

Prominent cultural analysts have highlighted the way individuals use culture to navigate their social worlds "not by providing the ultimate values toward which action is oriented but by shaping a repertoire or 'tool kit' of habits, skills, and styles from which people construct 'strategies of action'" (Swidler, 1986, p. 273; Hannerz, 1969; Lamont & Small, 2006). Recognizing the strength of Black communities in the face of racial hostilities and tacitly adopting this conception of culture, research identifies racial socialization—"the process through which children come to understand their own and others' identities, roles, and positions vis-à-vis race in various contexts, and how race will function in their lives" (Winkler, 2010, p. 274)—as a salient transmitted cultural practice that fosters resilience to anti-Black racial discrimination (e.g., Bowman & Howard, 1985; Essed, 1991; Hughes et al., 2006). Racial socialization includes verbal, nonverbal, deliberate, and unintended racial messages and lessons (Thornton, Chatters, Taylor, & Allen, 1990). Although youth receive racial socialization messages from numerous sources (e.g., peers, media, school agents), scholarship identifies *familial* racial socialization as a key cultural resource equipping minority youth with competencies (e.g., skills and scripts) for navigating our racialized social system in ways that mitigate the harms of racism and promote well-being (e.g., Bowman & Howard, 1985; Hughes et al., 2006; Stevenson, 2003).

Although most African American caregivers engage in racial socialization with their children (e.g., Hughes et al., 2006), and many report that it is an important component of their parenting (Peters, 1985), both the content and the frequency of these messages vary (Hughes et al., 2006; Peters, 1985; Thompson, 1994). Scholars have developed specific typologies representing different racial socialization content messages that racial minority parents transmit to their children (see Coard & Sellers, 2005; Hughes et al., 2006). Two forms of racial socialization have been identified as particularly salient among Black families in fostering resilience: *preparation for bias*, defined as the various actions by which adults warn youth about and discuss discrimination and provide skills and strategies ("tools") for coping with and overcoming racial barriers (Hughes et al., 2006), and *cultural socialization*, which includes messages and practices that emphasize racial heritage and promote cultural customs and traditions and thereby nurture youths' racial pride and sense of belonging (Stevenson, 1995). Research reveals the beneficial role of racial socialization in nurturing positive youth development through tacit and explicit messages that foster, among other things, the ability to maintain self-esteem and racial pride in the face of racial hostilities, to attribute race-based maltreatment appropriately to external sources, and to cope with and overcome racism in healthy ways (see Hughes et al., 2006; Peters, 1985). Through these practices, Black youth learn to place specific social occurrences in a general context of race relations and develop strategies to resist racism (Essed, 1991; Peters, 1985).

A growing body of research highlights the resilience effects of preparation for bias and cultural socialization on psychological well-being, racial identity, self-esteem, and academic outcomes (Bynum, Burton, & Best, 2007; Fischer & Shaw, 1999; Harris-Britt, Valrie, Kurtz-Costes, &

Rowley, 2007; Neblett et al., 2008; Stevenson, Reed, Bodison, & Bishop, 1997; see reviews in Hughes et al., 2006; Unnever & Gabbidon, 2011). Moreover, several recent studies show that these two forms of racial socialization provide resilience to the *criminogenic* effects of racial discrimination by compensating for and buffering the effects of IRD on offending (Burt et al., 2012, Burt & Simons 2015). Specifically, research adopting the SST model suggests that racial socialization compensates for the effects of IRD on the CKS and buffers the effects of IRD on the CKS in contemporaneous assessments (Burt & Simons, 2015, Burt et al., 2017b). Moreover, consistent with the conceptualization of racial socialization as a cultural practice that provides resources for constructing strategies of action to solve recurring problems is the idea that these cultural tools shape behavior over time, especially if they are effective. Consistent with this idea, Burt et al. (2017a) found that familial racial socialization provided enduring resilience to the deleterious effects of childhood racial discrimination on adult crime. Specifically, racial socialization not only compensated for and buffered the effects of racial discrimination on the CKS in childhood but also reduced the effect of IRD's deleterious effects on involvement in supportive social fields (and thus crime) in emerging adulthood. Altogether, these studies of racial socialization contravene earlier misguided ideas about "cultural deficiencies" or "maladaptive cultures," demonstrating that adaptive transmitted cultural practices contribute to a variety of domains that influence life satisfaction and well-being, including reducing the criminogenic effects of racial discrimination and attenuating discrimination's negative effects on socioemotional capacities conducive to success in "mainstream" institutions.

Discussion

In this chapter, I have addressed the role of anti-Black racism and cultural adaptations in theorizing about racial disparities in street crime. In so doing, I have adopted a racialized perspective, which points to African Americans' increased exposure to race-neutral risk factors (due to the legacy of and continued racism and institutional discrimination) as well as a race-specific risk factor (IRD) and links these racialized criminogenic risk factors to an increased risk of street crime through race-neutral processes. I have expounded on the evolutionary underpinnings of SST, arguing, following others, that it elucidates why certain seemingly irrational or counterproductive attitudes and behaviors persist under harsh, unpredictable conditions (e.g., Ellis et al., 2012; Pepper & Nettle, 2017). I have explicated how criminogenic social schemas (higher CKS) represent a contextually appropriate response to structural constraints and harsh experiences rather than a pathology, deficit, or failure of willpower.

At first glance, using evolutionary and cultural ideas to shed light on racial disparities in offending and a broader behavioral constellation of disadvantage may seem like the worst idea ever. Most evolutionary and cultural explanations for racial disparities have been excoriated for their racist and blaming-the-victim overtones. However, drawing on recent elaborations of an evolutionary *developmental* perspective, which emphasizes that individuals' minds and psychosocial orientations are environmentally calibrated, and linking these to an emergent (structurally induced) cultural landscape avoids the misguided (and racist) trappings of earlier approaches while uniting structural hardships to cultural adaptations. Overlaid and interwoven with these evoked environmental adaptations are familial racial socialization practices, which are transmitted cultural practices fostering skills, scripts, and even frames dealing with and overcoming anti-Black racism. The end result is a framework that links harsh, unpredictable environments profoundly shaped by racism to social schemas that tend to increase the risk of street crime and other behaviors that can perpetuate disadvantage through their consequences. These psychosocial orientations are contextually appropriate in the sense that they, however imperfectly, evolved to make the best of a bad situation for fitness outcomes (including fitness proxies of status and resources). Thus, seemingly inexplicable and counterproductive behaviors and attitudes (from the perspective of low-risk environments) are united and imbued with ultimate (fitness) logic.

Here I have only sketched the broad contours of this model, as I have tried to cover main themes in a relatively short space, but a few additional features deserve mention. First, although evidence does suggest that we have an expansive capacity for adaptive developmental plasticity, we are not, of course, infinitely malleable in response to social-environmental conditions. Complicating matters further, individuals vary in the extent to which they are susceptible to environmental influences; in other words, developmental plasticity is itself a trait that varies between individuals (see Belsky, Bakermans-Kranenburg, & Van IJzendoorn, 2007; Ellis et al., 2011). Given this, SST—like all other social scientific models—only identifies a pattern. Individuals reared in harsh, unpredictable environments *tend* to develop higher CKSs, all else equal. However, we know all else is not equal, and environments are complex and multilayered; thus, when speaking in cultural terms about these traits, we should consider these as "sociocultural configurations," recognizing considerable heterogeneity in culture even among relatively small, seemingly homogenous groups (Patterson, 2014).

Additionally, this model of evoked culture is but one piece of the expansive array of the cultural ensemble. Although we view this facet of culture as particularly influential given its elementary role in perception, decision making, and response, other features of culture can mold these unconscious, foundational tendencies into different configurations (e.g., religious beliefs and practices). Finally, it should be noted that in addition to recognizing the life-long malleability of the human mind (even as sensitive periods in childhood and adolescence have been identified), this framework can also incorporate human agency and change (or indeterminism). As Dupre (2001, p. 158) has noted, "causal order is everywhere partial and incomplete . . . the significance of recognizing indeterminism is not at all to show that human actions are unreliable or random. It is rather to show that . . . humans, are, sometimes causally efficacious in the world around them." In short, humans are not simply cultural or structural dupes programmed to act without any modicum of causal efficacy. This is true in the boardroom and in the "ghetto-slum" and everywhere in between.

Implications

In addition to deepening our theoretical understanding of the processes through which racial and socioeconomic inequalities shape psychosocial adaptations and cognitive landscapes and can become amplified and embedded, this framework also has implications for policies, programs, and practices to reduce harm and suffering (including crime and victimization) for the benefit of Black communities and the wider society (regardless of the evolutionary adaptiveness of the behavior). Importantly, despite the current focus on contextual appropriateness, it is the case that harsh conditions do injure individuals and some adaptations to "make the best of a bad situation" increase behaviors (including crime) that are harmful for everyone. Perhaps the most obvious implication from this model is that criminogenic social schemas are not fixed but instead are plastic responses that reflect environmental experiences rooted in structural inequalities. To be sure, the broad implications of this model are in many ways similar to those of other frameworks: to effect serious and sustained change it is necessary to improve environmental conditions and life experiences, ideally eradicating the edifice of White supremacy and providing a basic living wage, high-quality child care, social cushions for those who are experiencing hardships so they do not face degrading, unpredictable, dangerous realities of isolated, impoverished neighborhoods (e.g., Wilson, 2009).

In some sense, it is difficult to believe that policies to dismantle the edifice of White supremacy will ever gain any traction on the mainstream agenda, as White privilege has remained militantly resistant to subversion. However, the ability to challenge dominant narratives and mainstream ideologies has been facilitated by recent technological advances, especially social networking capacities. With online networking and communication, personal and local struggles and assaults (e.g., police killings) can now be connected with ease to build more public awareness of violent racist realities and unite those who endeavor to challenge the racist social order. We are currently witnessing the most overt, sustained critique of White supremacy and structural racism in over a generation. African Americans and allies are engaging in an avalanche of protests and collective actions to shift the political narrative and marshal agency for change under the banner of the Black Lives Matter movement.

Even so, it is unlikely that racism and racial material inequalities will substantially diminish in the near future, and efforts to identify, challenge, and dismantle White privilege and ongoing White racism (the harsh, unpredictable racial edifice) will no doubt meet resistance. As these struggles continue, efforts to target the distinctive challenges faced by youth in impoverished, segregated communities working *with* rather than *against* environmentally induced adaptations may help support without denigrating stress-adapted individuals (Ellis et al., 2012, 2017). More than just a culturally sensitive approach (but it should be culturally sensitive), this implies a reformulation of our institutionalized racist and classist methods of training and interventions as well as a reevaluation of the mainstream hierarchy of human socioemotional capacities, which privileges skills and capacities fostered in low-risk environments. In other words, interventions can work with the strengths of stress-adapted children (Ellis et al., 2012, 2017). For example, the environment of the classroom (quiet, predictable, emphasizing certain skills) might be varied. After all, the classroom is an artificial environment, and one that does not match the reality of most jobs. Allegedly maladaptive stress compensations that enhance the ability to facility switch between tasks, to readily identify threats and make quick decisions, and operate calmly in high-pressure situations are, in reality, quite valuable skills across many occupational domains. Harnessing such skills and providing opportunities for movement up the socioeconomic ladder and into more predictably supportive environments should provide the means to effect sustained change. Although research on the enhanced skills and abilities that are ecologically relevant in harsh, unpredictable environments is still in early stages, initial findings are promising (Mittal et al., 2015; Young, Griskevicius, Simpson, Waters, & Mittal, 2018). Better understanding the "hidden talents" of stress-adapted individuals while supporting them in a culturally sensitive manner might enable the design of classroom environments, community centers, job training, and employment opportunities (that pay a living, respectable wage) that draw upon the capacities of stress-adapted individuals while providing them with supportive, predictable contexts to hone further skills and effect greater change (see Ellis et al., 2017 for excellent, detailed examples of interventions).

Conclusions

In the end, we believe that careful consideration of the ways that exposure to racialized risks shapes individual differences not from a deficit model but from a contextually appropriate racialized framework is theoretically valuable (see Ellis et al., 2012; Pepper & Nettle, 2017). Even so, as we have emphasized, adaptive compensations to harsh, unpredictable environments can still be costly to the individual, their groups, and society. Black Americans have been incredibly disadvantaged and injured by anti-Black racism and its institutional and interpersonal manifestations, including higher rates of crime, victimization, and racially biased CJS responses. The remedy to this situation will not be found in asking or supporting individuals to make conscious changes in their culture or "better" decisions. We are all products of our social environments, trying to make the best of our situations while acting and interacting with unconsciously evolved motives that we did not choose and that are resistant to change (without environmental change).

At the same time, acknowledging that structure shapes culture and "structure trumps culture" does not imply that we can simply ignore cultural mechanisms as insignificant epiphenomena (Wilson, 2009). This is true not only because "cultural mechanisms are embedded in reinforcing cycles of structural disadvantage" but also because we would neglect "the role of cultural mechanisms that operate among non-poor and that serve to perpetuate poverty" (Sampson, 2016, pp. 205, 226). Thus, transcending the misguided, harmful cultural deficit frame posited by Lewis with a contextually appropriate structural-cultural model can enhance explanations of the persistence of racial disparities while offering new insights for policies and interventions (without blaming victims). The harms our racialized system has perpetrated on Black Americans—including elevated rates of offending and victimization—are too severe and the possibilities for change too great to settle for partial, fragmentary understandings (Patterson, 2016).

Notes

1. Importantly, Russell outlined two crises facing criminology; the other, related to the first, was the lack of Black scholars in the field. Although out of the scope of this chapter, it should be noted that although there certainly remains room for improvement, over the past 25 years, there have been significant increases in the number and prominence of Black criminologists (see Greene, Gabbidon, & Wilson, 2018; Peterson, 2017).
2. "This term refers to societies in which economic, political, social, and ideological levels are partially structured by the placement of actors in racial categories or races" (Bonilla-Silva, 1997, p. 469).
3. This list is modeled on Daly and Chesney-Lind's (1988) list for feminist criminology, and the latter point is indebted to Bonilla-Silva's (1997) theorizing.
4. In the absence of measures of the incidence and prevalence of all forms of crimes, especially those committed by the powerful, and absent any measurement protocol for "harmful acts" or their impact, whether the likelihood of crime or the prevalence of harmful acts is higher among Whites or Blacks is an unanswerable question. However, some scholars persuasively argue that, in part because they occur on a much larger scale than interpersonal crimes, elite crimes (committed likely disproportionately by Whites) cause substantially more harm than street crimes (committed disproportionately by Blacks; e.g., Reiman, 1979).
5. The terms "racialize" and "racialization" have also been used in a critical sense to refer to the practice of imposing typologies on or cataloguing differences in culture, temperaments, motivations, and behaviors by race (Covington, 1995; Webster, 1992). Here my focus is on racializing in the sense of purposefully incorporating differential experiences that both flow from and embody racial status in explaining differences in behavior.
6. For example, Curtis (1975, p. 2) noted that he sought to "build a general interpretive framework in which culture is viewed as a variable intervening between more basic structural determinants of poor black behaviors and violent criminal outcomes." Moreover, in my reading, Curtis seems to agree with significant criticisms levied by Black scholars (and others) against "maladaptive black subculture explanations" (e.g., Billingsly, 1968; Hill, 1972), noting, for example, "Thus, what many white scholars perceive in their value subjectivity as pathological disorganization can from another posture be interpreted as *functional*

responsiveness to environmental circumstances" (p. 6; emphasis added). To be sure, some works adopted an explicitly cultural determinist model to conclude that the poor (and Blacks) have only themselves to blame (Banfield, 1970; Lewis, 1966; Mead, 1986).

7. Among these, Sampson and Wilson's (1995) racialized theory, which has been labeled the thesis of "racial invariance," has received perhaps the most scholarly attention. The theory is racialized through its incorporation of the pivotal role of historical and continuing racial discrimination in the formation and perpetuation of segregated, disadvantaged inner-city neighborhoods. The thesis is deemed "racially invariant" due to its guiding proposition of equivalence in the community-level sources of street crime.

8. Acknowledging the existence of phenotype plasticity in a social scientific context is akin to telling a dairy farmer that lactating cows can be milked; however, my discussion of developmental plasticity is not aimed at explaining the obvious reality of environmentally induced variation but rather that such variation can be understood within an evolutionary framework.

9. To say that a behavior is adaptive in an evolutionary sense is to suggest that it maximizes (or did maximize in ancestral environments) Darwinian fitness. Given that not all environmentally induced variation is strictly adaptive and rapid changes in society over the past several centuries (invention and development of guns, cars, the internet) have altered features of our environments, this does not imply that all behaviors necessarily maximize fitness in contemporary social environments; some enhance fitness proxies, which may not translate to actual fitness advantages, and others may be by-products, side effects, or simply antiquated in current environments. However, the important point is that plasticity exists with the function of differentially tailoring individuals to their social environments for the evolutionary goal of continuance (Ellis et al., 2012; Pepper & Nettle, 2017).

10. In recent work, Pepper and Nettle (2017) refer to such a class of shortsighted behaviors as a "behavioral constellation of deprivation."

11. A notable exception is William Oliver's (2003, p. 291) body of research linking structure to "dysfunctional cultural adaptations" that influence high levels of violent offending and victimization among Black males, including: "1) the lack of an affirming cultural agenda and 2) dysfunctional definitions of manhood." We build on Oliver's insights, but recast them in a more general evolutionary-developmental model that links inequality to more general psychological mechanisms and highlights their contextually appropriate nature. Oliver's (1984, 1994, 2003) insights and theorizing about the "black compulsive masculinity alternative" are compatible with the SST model, even as the lens and emphases are distinct.

12. To be sure, addressing these ostensibly perplexing adaptations is intricate, not only because these adaptations seem from a conventional perspective to be anything but adaptive (in the sense that they seem to be antithetical to health and "success," as defined in "mainstream" terms; Wilson, 2006) but also because a focus on these mechanisms risks losing sight of their structural foundation (and thus blaming the victim). Ultimately, however, the validity of these structural-cultural theories hinges on the central supposition that culture is, in fact, endogenous to structure, such that changing structural conditions (reducing racial inequality) is the causal key to the problem of street crime (racial

disparities in offending). Therefore, understanding how structure shapes culture is paramount.

13. Importantly, this conception of culture does not imply place-based homogeneity in values, skills, frames, or ideas due to the fact that even within the most highly segregated neighborhoods, there exists considerable variation in ecological exposures and situational experiences (e.g., neighborhood, school, peer groups, family, media exposures), all of which influence social schemas.

14. In addition to being shared, culture is also relational in several senses. Cultural processes exist in relations between individuals (Lamont & Small, 2006); social-environmental knowledge that becomes embodied in shared cognitive schemas can be said to represent the relation between individuals and their social environment; and cultural schemas relate the past to the future through their effects on perception and evaluation of alternative courses of action (decision making).

15. It is no wonder that such scholarship has traditionally been precarious in the U.S. context; invoking cultural explanations entails identifying "deficient" or "maladaptive" characteristics, which can be harmful and racist if unmoored from the structural conditions of existence and applied monolithically. One might also note that every social group or milieu contains unflattering cultural properties that would be discerned in an in-depth study.

16. In a penetrating discussion, Jeremy Freese (2017) recently acknowledged that academics should be more aware of the "perch" from which they observe behaviors, noting, "In truth, we—not poor people—are the weird ones. From an evolutionary perspective, many commonplace high-SES behaviors in developed societies from long-delayed first pregnancy to voluntary low fertility to regular recreational exercise to deliberately abstemious diets, are downright peculiar" (p. 26).

17. Notably, cognitive cultural traits can be highly specific to certain situations (e.g., cultural frames shaping perceptions and action responses involving police encounters among minority males in "ghetto areas"; Goffman, 2015; Stuart, 2016), more broadly applied to specific places (e.g., shaping presentation of self and responses to others out on the street; e.g., Anderson, 1999; Young, 2006); or most generally the perceptual lens with which one views and interprets the world at large. Although several important works have focused on cultural habits, styles, and skills in specific situations and places, the focus of SST and its relevance for bridging the structure–culture divide concerns the latter broad worldviews.

18. As Patterson and Fosse (2016, p. 4) note: "The simple truth of the matter is that there is no such thing as *the* culture of poverty. Poor people all over America and the world adapt to their socioeconomic, physical, and political environments in a wide variety of ways" (emphasis in original).

References

Agan, A., & Starr, S. (2017). The effect of criminal records on access to employment. *American Economic Review, 107*(5), 560–564.

Akers, R. L. (1985). *Deviant behavior: A social learning approach*. Belmont, CA: Thompson Wadsworth.

Anderson, E. (1978). *Place on the corner*. Chicago, IL: University of Chicago Press.

Anderson, E. (1999). *Code of the street: Decency, violence, and the moral life of the inner city.* New York, NY: W. W. Norton.

Ayres. I. (2002). *Pervasive prejudice: Unconventional evidence of race and gender discrimination.* Chicago, IL: University of Chicago Press.

Ayres, I., & Siegelman, P. (1995). Race and gender discrimination in bargaining for a new car. *The American Economic Review, 304*–321.

Banfield, E. (1970). *The unheavenly city: The nature and future of our urban crisis.* Boston, MA: Little, Brown & Co.

Bayer, P., Ferreira, F., & Ross, S. L. (2014, December). *Race, ethnicity and high-cost mortgage lending.* Working Paper. National Bureau of Economic Research. Retrieved December 19, 2017, from www.nber.org/papers/w20762

Beckett, K. (2018). The politics, promise, and peril of criminal justice reform in the context of mass incarceration. *Annual Review of Criminology, 1*, 235–259.

Belsky, J. (2012). The development of human reproductive strategies: Progress and prospects. *Current Directions in Psychological Science, 21*(5), 310–316.

Belsky, J., Bakermans-Kranenburg, M. J., & Van IJzendoorn, M. H. (2007). For better and for worse: Differential susceptibility to environmental influences. *Current Directions in Psychological Science, 16*(6), 300–304.

Berg, M. T., Burt, C. H., Lei, M. Simons, L. G., Stewart, E. A., & Simons, R. L. (2016). Neighborhood social processes and adolescent sexual partnering: A multilevel appraisal of Anderson's player hypothesis. *Social Forces, 94*, 1823–1846.

Billingsley, A. (1968). *Black families in white America.* Englewood Cliffs, NJ: Prentice-Hall.

Blau, J., & Blau, P. (1982). The cost of inequality: Metropolitan structure and violent crime. *American Sociological Review, 47*, 114–129.

Bobo, L. D., & Charles, C. Z. (2009). Race in the American mind: From the Moynihan report to the Obama candidacy. *The Annals of the American Academy of Political and Social Science, 621*(1), 243–259.

Bonilla-Silva, E. (1997). Rethinking racism: Toward a structural foundation. *American Sociological Review, 62*, 465–480.

Bourdieu, P. (1990). *The logic of practice.* Stanford, CA: Stanford University Press.

Bowman, P. J., & Howard, C. (1985). Race-related socialization, motivation, and academic achievement: A study of Black youths in three-generation families. *Journal of the American Academy of Child Psychiatry, 24*(2), 134–141.

Brezina, T., Tekin, E., & Topalli, V. (2009). "Might not be a tomorrow": A multimethods approach to anticipated early death and youth crime. *Criminology, 47*(4), 1091–1129.

Brody, G. H., Chen, Y. F., Murry, V. M., Ge, X., Simons, R. L., Gibbons, F. X., . . . Cutrona, C. E. (2006). Perceived discrimination and the adjustment of African American youths: A five-year longitudinal analysis with contextual moderation effects. *Child Development, 77*(5), 1170–1189.

Bruce, M. A., Roscigno, V. J., & McCall, P. L. (1998). Structure, context, and agency in the reproduction of black-on-black violence. *Theoretical Criminology, 2*(1), 29–55.

Burt, C. H., Lei, M. K., & Simons, R. L. (2017a). Racial discrimination, racial socialization, and crime over time: A social schematic theory model. *Criminology, 55*(4), 938–979.

Burt, C. H., Lei, M. K., & Simons, R. L. (2017b). Racial discrimination, racial socialization, and crime: Understanding mechanisms of resilience. *Social Problems, 64*(3), 414–438.

Burt, C. H., & Simons, R. L. (2015). Interpersonal racial discrimination, ethnic-racial socialization, and offending: Risk and resilience among African American females. *Justice Quarterly, 32*(3), 532–570.

Burt, C. H., Simons, R. L., & Gibbons, F. X. (2012). Racial discrimination, ethnic-racial socialization, and crime: A micro-sociological model of risk and resilience. *American Sociological Review, 77*(4), 648–677.

Bynum, M. S., Burton, E. T., & Best, C. (2007). Racism experiences and psychological functioning in African American college freshmen: Is racial socialization a buffer? *Cultural Diversity and Ethnic Minority Psychology, 13*(1), 64.

Caldwell, C. H., Kohn-Wood, L. P., Schmeelk-Cone, K. H., Chavous, T. M., & Zimmerman, M. A. (2004). Racial discrimination and racial identity as risk or protective factors for violent behaviors in African American young adults. *American Journal of Community Psychology, 33*(1–2), 91–105.

Caspi, A., Bem, D. J., & Elder, G. H. (1989). Continuities and consequences of interactional styles across the life course. *Journal of Personality, 57*(2), 375–406.

Chisholm, J. S. (1999). *Death, hope and sex: Steps to an evolutionary ecology of mind and morality.* Cambridge: Cambridge University Press.

Clark, R., Anderson, N. B., Clark, V. R., & Williams, D. R. (1999). Racism as a stressor for African Americans: A biopsychosocial model. *American Psychologist, 54*(10), 805.

Coard, S. I., & Sellers, R. M. (2005). African American families as a context for racial socialization. In N. E. Hill & V. McLoyd (Eds.), *African American family life: Ecological and cultural diversity* (pp. 264–284). New York: Guilford Press.

Cohen, A. (1955). *Delinquent boys.* New York, NY: Free Press.

Conley, D. (1999). *Being black, living in the red: Race, wealth, and social policy in the United States.* Berkeley, CA: University of California Press.

Cooney, M. (Ed.). (1998). *Warriors and peacemakers: How third parties shape violence.* New York, NY: New York University Press.

Covington, J. (1995). Racial classification in criminology: The reproduction of racialized crime. *Sociological Forum, 10*, 547–68.

Crick, N. R., & Dodge, K. A. (1994). A review and reformulation of social information-processing mechanisms in children's social adjustment. *Psychological Bulletin, 115*(1), 74.

Crutchfield, R. D. (1989). Labor stratification and violent crime. *Social Forces, 68*, 489–512.

Curtis, L. A. (1975). *Violence, race, and culture.* Washington, DC: Health and Company.

Daly, K., & Chesney-Lind, M. (1988). Feminism and criminology. *Justice Quarterly, 5*, 497–538.

Daly, M., & Wilson, M. (2001). Risk taking, intrasexual competition, and homicide. *Nebraska Symposium on Motivation, 47*, 1–36.

de Waal, F. (2006). *Primates and philosophers: How morality evolved.* Princeton, NJ: Princeton University Press.

Del Giudice, M. (2009). Sex, attachment, and the development of reproductive strategies. *Behavioral and Brain Sciences, 32*(1), 1–21.

Dodge, K. A. (2006). Translational science in action: Hostile attributional style and the development of aggressive behavior problems. *Development and Psychopathology, 18*(3), 791–814.

Du Bois, W. E. B. (1899). *The Philadelphia Negro: A social study.* Philadelphia, PA: University of Pennsylvania Press.

DuBois, D. L., Burk-Braxton, C., Swenson, L. P., Tevendale, H. D., & Hardesty, J. L. (2002). Race and gender influences on adjustment in early adolescence: Investigation of an integrative model. *Child Development*, *73*(5), 1573–1592.

Duncan, G. J., & Brooks-Gunn, J. (2000). Family poverty, welfare reform, and child development. *Child Development*, *71*, 188–196. doi:10.1111/1467-8624.00133

Dupre, J. (2001). *Human nature and the limits of science*. Oxford: Oxford University Press.

Ellis, B. J., Boyce, W. T., Belsky, J., Bakermans-Kranenburg, M. J., & Van IJzendoorn, M. H. (2011). Differential susceptibility to the environment: An evolutionary—neurodevelopmental theory. *Development and Psychopathology*, *23*(1), 7–28.

Ellis, B. J., Bianchi, J., Griskevicius, V., & Frankenhuis, W. E. (2017). Beyond risk and protective factors: An adaptation-based approach to resilience. *Perspectives on Psychological Science*, *12*(4), 561–587.

Ellis, B. J., & Del Giudice, M. (2014). Beyond allostatic load: Rethinking the role of stress in regulating human development. *Development and Psychopathology*, *26*(1), 1–20.

Ellis, B. J., Del Giudice, M., Dishion, T. J., Figueredo, A. J., Gray, P., Griskevicius, V., . . . Wilson, D. S. (2012). The evolutionary basis of risky adolescent behavior: Implications for science, policy, and practice. *Developmental Psychology*, *48*(3), 598.

Ellis, B. J., Figueredo, A. J., Brumbach, B. H., & Schlomer, G. L. (2009). Fundamental dimensions of environmental risk. *Human Nature*, *20*(2), 204–268.Essed, P. (1991). *Understanding everyday racism: An interdisciplinary theory*. Newbury Park, CA: Sage.

Fader, J. J. (2013). *Falling back: Incarceration and transitions to adulthood among urban youth*. New Brunswick, NJ: Rutgers University Press.

Farrington, D. P., Loeber, R., & Stouthamer-Loeber, M. (2003). How can the relationship between race and violence be explained? In D. F. Hawkins (Ed.), *Violent crime: Assessing race and ethnic differences* (pp. 213–237). Cambridge: Cambridge University Press.

Fawcett, T. W., McNamara, J. M., & Houston, A. I. (2012). When is it adaptive to be patient? A general framework for evaluating delayed rewards. *Behavioural Processes*, *89*(2), 128–136.

Feagin, J. R. (1991). The continuing significance of race: Antiblack discrimination in public places. *American Sociological Review*, 101–116.

Feagin, J. R. (2010). *Racist America: Roots, current realities, and future reparations*. New York, NY: Routledge.

Fischer, A. R., & Shaw, C. M. (1999). African Americans' mental health and perceptions of racist discrimination: The moderating effects of racial socialization experiences and self-esteem. *Journal of Counseling Psychology*, *46*(3), 395.

Frankenhuis, W. E., & de Weerth, C. (2013). Does early-life exposure to stress shape or impair cognition? *Current Directions in Psychological Science*, *22*(5), 407–412.

Freese, J. (2017). What about the behavioral constellation of advantage? *Behavioral and Brain Sciences*, e326. doi:10.1017/S0140525X17000966

Gabbidon, S. L., & Peterson, S. A. (2006). Living while Black: A state-level analysis of the influence of select social stressors on the quality of life among Black Americans. *Journal of Black Studies*, *37*(1), 83–102.

Gardner, W. (1993). A life-span rational-choice theory of risk taking. In *Adolescent risk taking*. Newbury Park, CA: Sage.

Gibbons, F. X., Gerrard, M., Cleveland, M. J., Wills, T. A., & Brody, G. (2004). Perceived discrimination and substance use in African American parents and their children: A panel study. *Journal of Personality and Social Psychology, 86*(4), 517.

Goffman, A. (2014). *On the run: Fugitive life in an American city*. Chicago: University of Chicago Press.

Gottfredson, M. R., & Hirschi, T. (1990). *A general theory of crime*. Stanford, CA: Stanford University Press.

Gottschalk, M. (2015). *Caught: The prison state and the lockdown of American politics*. Princeton, NJ: Princeton University Press.

Greene, H. T., Gabbidon, S. L., & Wilson, S. K. (2018). Included? The status of African American scholars in the discipline of criminology and criminal justice since 2004. *Journal of Criminal Justice Education, 29*, 96–115.

Griskevicius, V., Tybur, J. M., Delton, A. W., & Robertson, T. E. (2011). The influence of mortality and socioeconomic status on risk and delayed rewards: A life history theory approach. *Journal of Personality and Social Psychology, 100*(6), 1015.

Griskevicius, V., Tybur, T. M., Gangestad, S. T., Perea, E. F., & Kenrick, D. T. (2009). Aggress to impress: Hostility as an evolved context-dependent strategy. *Journal of Personality and social Psychology, 96*(5), 980–994.

Hackman, D. A., Betancourt, L. M., Gallop, R., Romer, D., Brodsky, N. L., Hurt, H., & Farah, M. J. (2014). Mapping the trajectory of socioeconomic disparity in working memory: Parental and neighborhood factors. *Child Development, 85*(4), 1433–1445.

Haidt, J. (2007). The new synthesis in moral psychology. *Science, 316*(5827), 998–1002.

Hannerz, U. (1969). *Soulside: Inquiries into ghetto culture and community*. Columbia: Columbia University Press.

Harding, D. J. (2010). *Living the drama: Community, culture, and conflict among inner-city boys*. Chicago, IL: University of Chicago Press.

Harrell, S. P. (2000). A multidimensional conceptualization of racism-related stress: Implications for the well-being of people of color. *American Journal of Orthopsychiatry, 70*(1), 42.

Harris-Britt, A., Valrie, C. R., Kurtz-Costes, B., & Rowley, S. J. (2007). Perceived racial discrimination and self-esteem in African American youth: Racial socialization as a protective factor. *Journal of Research on Adolescence, 17*(4), 669–682.

Harris, A. M. G., Henderson, G. R., & Williams, J. D. (2005). Courting customers: Assessing consumer racial profiling and other marketplace discrimination. *Journal of Public Policy & Marketing, 24*(1), 163–171.Hauser, M. (2006). *Moral minds: How nature designed our universal sense of right and wrong*. New York, NY: Ecco/HarperCollins Publishers.

Hawkins, D. F. (1983). *Homicide among Black Americans*. Lanham, MD: University Press of America.

Hawkins, D. F. (1995). "Ethnicity, race, and crime: A review of selected studies." In D. F. Hawkins (Ed.), Ethnicity, race, and crime: Perspectives across time and place (pp. 11–45). Cambridge: Cambridge University Press.

Hawkins, D. F. (Ed.) (2003). *Violent crime: Assessing race and ethnic differences*. New York: Cambridge University Press.

Heckman, J. J. (2008). Schools, skills, and synapses. *Economic Inquiry, 46*(3), 289–324.

Heckman, J. J., Humphries, J. E., & Kautz, T. (Eds.). (2014). *The myth of achieve-ment tests: The GED and the role of character in American life.* Chicago, IL: University of Chicago Press.

Hill, E. M., Ross, L. T., & Low, B. S. (1997). The role of future unpredictability in human risk-taking. *Human Nature, 8*(4), 287.

Hill, R. (1972). *The strength of black families.* New York, NY: Emerson Hall.Hirs-chi, T. (1969). *Causes of delinquency.* Berkeley, CA: University of California Press.

Holzer, H. J. (1996). *What employers want: Job prospects for less-educated work-ers.* New York, NY: Russell Sage Foundation.

Hughes, D., Rodriguez, J., Smith, E. P., Johnson, D. J., Stevenson, H. C., & Spicer, P. (2006). Parents' ethnic-racial socialization practices: A review of research and directions for future study. *Developmental Psychology, 42*(5), 747.

Jones, D. E., Greenberg, M., & Crowley, M. (2015). Early social-emotional function-ing and public health: The relationship between kindergarten social competence and future wellness. *American Journal of Public Health, 105*(11), 2283–2290.

Jones, N. (2010). *Between good and ghetto: African American girls and inner-city violence.* New Brunswick, NJ: Rutgers University Press.

Kaufman, J. M., Rebellon, C. J., Thaxton, S., & Agnew, R. (2008). A general strain theory of racial differences in criminal offending. *Australian & New Zealand Journal of Criminology, 41*(3), 421–437.

Kirk, D. S., & Papachristos, A. V. (2011). Cultural mechanisms and the persistence of neighborhood violence. *American Journal of Sociology, 116*(4), 1190–1233.

Kirschenman, J., & Neckerman, K. M. (1991). We'd love to hire them, but . . .: The meaning of race for employers. In C. Jencks & P. E. Peterson (Eds.), *The urban underclass* (pp. 203–234). Washington, DC: Brookings Institution.

Klonoff, E. A., & Landrine, H. (1999). Cross-validation of the schedule of racist events. *Journal of Black Psychology, 25*(2), 231–254.

Konrad, L. (1966). *On aggression* (M. K. Wilson, trans.). New York, NY: Harcourt, Brace & World.

Kornhauser, R. R. (1978). *Social sources of delinquency: An appraisal of analytic models.* Chicago, IL: University of Chicago Press.

LaFree, G. (1998). *Losing legitimacy: Street crime and the decline of social institu-tions in America.* Boulder, CO: Westview Press.

Lamont, M., & Small, M. L. (2006). How culture matters for poverty: Thicken-ing our understanding. In *The colors of poverty.* New York, NY: Russell Sage Foundation.

Landrine, H., & Klonoff, E. A. (1996). The schedule of racist events: A measure of racial discrimination and a study of its negative physical and mental health consequences. *Journal of Black Psychology, 22*(2), 144–168.

Lewis, O. (1966). The culture of poverty. *Scientific American, 215,* 19–25.

Liebow, E. (1967). *Tally's corner.* Oxford: Little, Brown & Co.

Mani, A., Mullainathan, S., Shafir, E., & Zhao, J. (2013). Poverty impedes cognitive function. *Science, 341,* 976–980. doi:10.1126/science.1238041

Martin, M. J., McCarthy, B., Conger, R. D., Gibbons, F. X., Simons, R. L., Cutrona, C. E., & Brody, G. H. (2011). The enduring significance of racism: Discrimi-nation and delinquency among Black American youth. *Journal of Research on Adolescence, 21*(3), 662–676.

Massey, D. S., & Denton, N. (1993). *American apartheid: Segregation and the mak-ing of an underclass.* Cambridge, MA: Harvard University Press.

McCord, J., & Ensminger, M. E. (1997). Multiple risks and comorbidity in an African-American population. *Criminal Behaviour and Mental Health*, 7(4), 339–352.

McCord, J., & Ensminger, M. E. (2003). Racial discrimination and violence: A longitudinal perspective. In D. F. Hawkins (Ed.), *Violent crime: Assessing race and ethnic differences* (pp. 319–330).New York: Cambridge University Press.

McLoyd, V. C. (1990). The impact of economic hardship on Black families and children: Psychological distress, parenting, and socioemotional development. *Child Development*, 61(2), 311–346.McNulty, T. L., & Bellair, P. E. (2003). Explaining racial and ethnic differences in serious adolescent violent behavior. *Criminology*, 41, 709–48.

Mead, G. H. (1934). *Mind, self and society* (Vol. 111). Chicago, IL: University of Chicago Press.

Mead, L. (1986). *Beyond entitlement: The social obligations of citizenship*. New York, NY: Free Press.

Miller, D. B., & MacIntosh, R. (1999). Promoting resilience in urban African American adolescents: Racial socialization and identity as protective factors. *Social Work Research*, 23(3), 159–169.

Miller, J. (2008). *Getting played: African American girls, urban inequality, and gendered violence*. New York, NY: New York University Press.

Miller, W. B. (1958). Lower class culture as a generating milieu of gang delinquency. *Journal of Social Issues*, 14(3), 5–19.

Mishra, S. (2014). Decision-making under risk: Integrating perspectives from biology, economics, and psychology. *Personality and Social Psychology Review*, 18(3), 280–307.

Mittal, C., Griskevicius, V., Simpson, J. A., Sung, S., & Young, E. S. (2015). Cognitive adaptations to stressful environments: When childhood adversity enhances adult executive function. *Journal of Personality and Social Psychology*, 109(4), 604.

Neblett, E. W., White, R. L., Ford, K. R., Philip, C. L., Nguyen, H. X., & Sellers, R. M. (2008). Patterns of racial socialization and psychological adjustment: Can parental communications about race reduce the impact of racial discrimination? *Journal of Research on Adolescence*, 18(3), 477–515.

Nelson, A. (2002). Unequal treatment: Confronting racial and ethnic disparities in health care. *Journal of the National Medical Association*, 94(8), 666.

Nisbett, R. E., & Cohen, D. (1996). *Culture of honor: The psychology of violence in the South*. London, UK: Hachette UK.

Nyborg, V. M., & Curry, J. F. (2003). The impact of perceived racism: Psychological symptoms among African American boys. *Journal of Clinical Child and Adolescent Psychology*, 32(2), 258–266.

Oliver, W. (1984). Black males and the tough guy image: A dysfunctional compensatory adaptation. *The Western Journal of Black Studies*, 8(4), 199.

Oliver, W. (1994). *The violent social world of black men*. New York, NY: Lexington Books.

Oliver, W. (2003). The structural-cultural perspective: A theory of Black male violence. In D. F. Hawkins (Ed.), *Violent crime: Assessing race and ethnic differences* (pp. 280–302). New York: Cambridge University Press.

Pager, D. (2007). *Marked: Race, crime, and finding work in an era of mass incarceration*. Chicago, IL: University of Chicago Press.

Pager, D., & Shepherd, H. (2008). The sociology of discrimination: Racial discrimination in employment, housing, credit, and consumer markets. *Annual Review of Sociology*, 34, 181–209.

Patterson, O. (2014). Making sense of culture. *Annual Review of Sociology, 40,* 1–30.

Patterson, O. (2016). The nature and dynamics of cultural processes. In O. Patterson & E. Fosse (Eds.), *The cultural matrix: Understanding black youth* (pp. 25–44). Cambridge, MA: Harvard University Press.

Patterson, O., & Fosse, E. (2016), The cultural matrix: Understanding black youth. Cambridge, MA: Harvard University Press.

Pepper, G. V., & Nettle, D. (2017). The behavioural constellation of deprivation: Causes and consequences. *Behavioral and Brain Sciences, 40.*

Peters, M. F. (1985). Racial socialization of young Black children. In H. P. McAdoo & J. L. McAdoo (Eds.), *Black children: Social, educational, and parental environments* (pp. 159–173). Thousand Oaks, CA: Sage.

Peterson, R. D. (2017). Interrogating race, crime, and justice in a time of unease and racial tension. *Criminology, 55,* 245–272.

Peterson, R. D., & Krivo, L. J. (2005). Macrostructural analyses of race, ethnicity, and violent crime: Recent lessons and new directions for research. *Annual Review of Sociology, 31,* 331–356.

Peterson, R. D., Krivo, L. J., & Hagan, J. (Eds.). (2006). *The many colors of crime: Inequalities of race, ethnicity, and crime in America.* New York: New York University Press.

Phillips, C., & Bowling, B. (2003). Racism, ethnicity and criminology. Developing minority perspectives. *British Journal of Criminology, 43*(2), 269–290.Plotkin, H. C. (1994). *Darwin machines and the nature of knowledge.* Cambridge, MA: Harvard University Press.

Quillian, L., Pager, D., Hexel, O., & Midtbøen, A. H. (2017). Meta-analysis of field experiments shows no change in racial discrimination in hiring over time. *Proceedings of the National Academy of Sciences, 114*(41), 10870–10875.

Rainwater, L. (1970). The problem of lower class culture. *Journal of Social Issues, 26*(2), 133–148.

Reardon, S. F., & Bischoff, K. (2011). Income inequality and income segregation. *American Journal of Sociology, 116*(4), 1092–1153.

Reiman, J. (1979). *The rich get richer and the poor get prison.* New York, NY: Wiley.

Ridley, S., Bayton, J. A., & Outtz, J. H. (1989). *Taxi service in the district of Columbia: Is it influenced by Patron's race and destination?* Washington, DC: Lawyer's Committee for Civil Rights Under the Law.

Roscigno, V. J. (2007). *The face of discrimination: How race and gender impact work and home lives.* Lanham, MD: Rowman & Littlefield.

Rosenblatt, P., Edin, K., & Zhu, Q. (2016). I do me: Young black men and the struggle to resist the streets. In O. Patterson & E. Fosse (Eds.), *The cultural matrix: Understanding black youth* (pp. 229–251). Cambridge, MA: Harvard University Press.

Rugh, J. S., & Massey, D. S. (2010). Racial segregation and the American foreclosure crisis. *American Sociological Review, 75*(5), 629–651.

Russell, K. K. (1992). Development of a black criminology and the role of the black criminologist. *Justice Quarterly, 9,* 667–684.

Russell-Brown, K. (2009). *The color of crime* (2nd ed.). New York, NY: New York University Press.

Sampson, R. J. (1987). Urban black violence: The effect of male joblessness and family disruption. *American Journal of Sociology, 93*(2), 348–382.

Sampson, R. J. (2012). *Great American city: Chicago and the enduring neighborhood effect.* Chicago, IL: University of Chicago Press.

Sampson, R. J. (2016). Continuity and change in neighborhood culture: Toward a structurally embedded theory of social altruism and moral cynicism. In O. Patterson & E. Fosse (Eds.), *The cultural matrix: Understanding black youth* (pp. 201–228). Cambridge, MA: Harvard University Press.

Sampson, R. J., & Bean, L. (2006). Cultural mechanisms and killing fields: A revised theory of community-level racial inequality. In R. Peterson, L. Krivo, & J. Hagan (Eds.), *The many colors of crime: Inequalities of race, ethnicity and crime in America* (pp. 8–36). New York, NY: New York University Press.

Sampson, R. J., & Laub, J. H. (1995). *Crime in the making: Pathways and turning points through life*. Cambridge, MA: Harvard University Press.

Sampson, R. J., & Wilson, W. J. (1995). Toward a theory of race, crime, and urban inequality. In J. Hagan & R. Peterson (Eds.), *Crime and inequality* (pp. 37–54). Stanford, CA: Stanford University Press.

Schulman, K. A., Berlin, J. A., Harless, W., Kerner, J. F., Sistrunk, S., Gersh, B. J., . . . Eisenberg, J. M. (1999). The effect of race and sex on physicians' recommendations for cardiac catheterization. *New England Journal of Medicine*, *340*(8), 618–626.

Sellers, R. M., Copeland-Linder, N., Martin, P. P., & Lewis, R. H. (2006). Racial identity matters: The relationship between racial discrimination and psychological functioning in African American adolescents. *Journal of Research on Adolescence*, *16*(2), 187–216.

Sellers, R. M., Caldwell, C. H., Schmeelk-Cone, K. H., & Zimmerman, M. A. (2003). Racial identity, racial discrimination, perceived stress, and psychological distress among African American young adults. *Journal of Health and Social Behavior*, 302–317.Sharkey, P. (2013). *Stuck in place: Urban neighborhoods and the end of progress toward racial equality*. Chicago, IL: University of Chicago Press.

Sharkey, P. S., & Sampson, R. J. (2015). Violence, cognition, and neighborhood inequality in America. In *Social neuroscience: Brain, mind, and society* (pp. 320–329). Cambridge, MA: Harvard University Press.

Sharkey, P. T., Tirado-Strayer, N., Papachristos, A. V., & Raver, C. C. (2012). The effect of local violence on children's attention and impulse control. *American Journal of Public Health*, *102*(12), 2287–2293.

Shonkoff, J. P., Garner, A. S., Siegel, B. S., Dobbins, M. I., Earls, M. F., McGuinn, L., . . . Committee on Early Childhood, Adoption, and Dependent Care. (2012). The lifelong effects of early childhood adversity and toxic stress. *Pediatrics*, *129*(1), e232–e246.

Simons, R. L., & Burt, C. H. (2011). Learning to be bad: Adverse social conditions, social schemas, and crime. *Criminology*, *49*(2), 553–598.

Simons, R. L., Burt, C. H., Barr, A. B., Lei, M. K., & Stewart, E. (2014). Incorporating routine activities, activity spaces, and situational definitions into the social schematic theory of crime. *Criminology*, *52*(4), 655–687.

Simons, R. L., Chen, Y. F., Stewart, E. A., & Brody, G. H. (2003). Incidents of discrimination and risk for delinquency: A longitudinal test of strain theory with an African American sample. *Justice Quarterly*, *20*(4), 827–854.

Simons, R. L., Simons, L. G., Burt, C. H., Drummund, H., Stewart, E., Brody, G. H., . . . Cutrona, C. (2006). Supportive parenting moderates the effect of discrimination upon anger, hostile view of relationships, and violence among African American boys. *Journal of Health and Social Behavior*, *47*(4), 373–389.

Simpson, J. A., & Belsky, J. (2008). Attachment theory within a modern evolutionary framework. In J. Cassidy & P. R. Shaver (Eds.), *Handbook of attachment: Theory, research, and clinical applications* (Vol. 2, pp. 131–157). New York: Guilford Press.

Squires, G. D. (2003). Racial profiling, insurance style: Insurance redlining and the uneven development of metropolitan areas. *Journal of Urban Affairs, 25*(4), 391–410.

Stevenson, H. C. (Ed.). (2003). *Playing with anger: Teaching coping skills to African American boys through athletics and culture.* Westport, CT: Praeger.

Stevenson Jr, H. C. (1995). Relationship of adolescent perceptions of racial socialization to racial identity. *Journal of Black Psychology, 21*(1), 49–70.

Stevenson, H. C., Reed, J., Bodison, P., & Bishop, A. (1997). Racism stress management: Racial socialization beliefs and the experience of depression and anger in African American youth. *Youth and Society, 29,* 197–222.

Stewart, E. A., & Simons, R. L. (2006). Structure and culture in African American adolescent violence: A partial test of the "code of the street" thesis. *Justice Quarterly, 23*(1), 1–33.Stuart, F. (2016). *Down, out, and under arrest: Policing and everyday life in Skid Row.* Chicago, IL: University of Chicago Press.

Swidler, A. (1986). Culture in action: Symbols and strategies. *American Sociological Review,* 273–286.

Thompson, V. L. S. (1994). Socialization to race and its relationship to racial identification among African Americans. *Journal of Black Psychology, 20*(2), 175–188.

Thornton, M. C., Chatters, L. M., Taylor, R. J., & Allen, W. R. (1990). Sociodemographic and environmental correlates of racial socialization by Black parents. *Child Development, 61*(2), 401–409.

Unnever, J. D. (2014). A theory of African American offending: A test of core propositions. *Race and Justice, 4*(2), 98–123.

Unnever, J. D., Cullen, F. T., & Barnes, J. C. (2016). Racial discrimination, weakened school bonds, and problematic behaviors: Testing a theory of African American offending. *Journal of Research in Crime and Delinquency, 53*(2), 139–164.

Unnever, J. D., Cullen, F. T., & Barnes, J. C. (2017). Racial discrimination and pathways to delinquency: Testing a theory of African American offending. *Race and Justice, 7*(4), 350–373.

Unnever, J. D., Cullen, F. T., Mathers, S. A., McClure, T. E., & Allison, M. C. (2009). Racial discrimination and Hirschi's criminological classic: A chapter in the sociology of knowledge. *Justice Quarterly, 26*(3), 377–409.

Unnever, J. D., & Gabbidon, S. L. (2011). *A theory of African American offending: Race, racism, and crime.* New York, NY: Taylor & Francis.

Webster, Y. (1992). *The racialization of America.* New York, NY: St. Martin's.

West-Eberhard, M. J. (2003). *Developmental plasticity and evolution.* Oxford: Oxford University Press.

Wilson, W. J. (1987). *The truly disadvantaged: The inner city, the underclass, and public policy.* Chicago: University of Chicago.

Wilson, W. J. (1996). When work disappears. *Political Science Quarterly, 111*(4), 567–595.

Wilson, W. J. (2006). Social theory and the concept 'underclass.' In D. B. Grusky, & R. Kanbur (Eds.), *Poverty and Inequality* (pp. 103–116). Stanford, CA: Stanford University Press.

Wilson, W. J. (2009). *More than just race: Being black and poor in the inner city (issues of our time).* New York, NY: W. W. Norton.

Wilson, W. J. (2016). Black youths, joblessnessness, and the other side of "Black Lives Matter". *Ethnic and Racial Studies, 39*(8): 1450–1457.

Wilson, M., & Daly, M. (1997). Life expectancy, economic inequality, homicide, and reproductive timing in Chicago neighbourhoods. *BMJ: British Medical Journal, 314*(7089), 1271–1274.

Wilson, W. J., & Katz, H. (2018). Reassessing "toward a theory of race, crime, and urban inequality": Enduring and new challenges in 21st century America. *Du Bois Review: Social Science Research on Race, 15*(1), 13–24.

Winkler, E. N. (2010). "I learn being black from everywhere I go": Color blindness, travel, and the formation of racial attitudes among African American adolescents. *Sociological Studies of Children and Youth, 13*, 423–453.

Wissoker, D. A., Zimmermann, W., & Galster, G. C. (1998). *Testing for discrimination in home insurance.* Washington, DC: Urban Institute.

Wolfgang, M. E., & Ferracuti, F. (1967). *The subculture of violence: Towards an integrated theory in criminology.* London, UK: Tavistock Publications.

Wong, C. A., Eccles, J. S., & Sameroff, A. (2003). The influence of ethnic discrimination and ethnic identification on African American adolescents' school and socioemotional adjustment. *Journal of Personality, 71*(6), 1197–1232.

Yinger, J. (1995). *Closed doors, opportunities lost: The continuing costs of housing discrimination.* New York, NY: Russell Sage Foundation.

Young, A. A. (2006). *The minds of marginalized black men: Making sense of mobility, opportunity, and future life chances.* Princeton, NJ: Princeton University Press.

Young, E. S., Griskevicius, V., Simpson, J. A., Waters, T. E., & Mittal, C. (2018). Can an unpredictable childhood environment enhance working memory? Testing the sensitized-specialization hypothesis. *Journal of Personality and Social Psychology, 114*(6), 891–908.

10

Forgotten Offenders: Race, White-Collar Crime, and the Black Church

Michael L. Benson and Jay P. Kennedy

Race and White-Collar Crime

If one Googles the term "white-collar offender" and asks for images, the resulting screen is packed with pictures of middle-aged White men. Scroll down and the occasional face of color appears but only at a rate of about 1 per 25 images. As far as the internet is concerned, it would appear that white-collar crime is committed almost exclusively by White men. One would get the same impression from the early classic works on white-collar crime (Sutherland, 1940, 1949; Clinard, 1946, 1952; Geis, 1977). Absolutely no mention of race can be found in any of these works, indeed in any of the early works on white-collar crime. But things changed briefly in the 1980s when Hirschi and Gottfredson (1987) published their controversial article on the causes of white-collar crime. In that article and a follow-up piece (Hirschi & Gottfredson, 1989), they argued that official statistics from the FBI's Uniform Crime Reports (UCR) indicated that Blacks are overrepresented in white-collar crime, just as they are in many forms of street crime. They based this view on the distribution of arrests for embezzlement and fraud by race, which in the early 1980s showed higher arrest rates among Blacks than Whites even after controlling for access to white-collar job opportunities. The overrepresentation of Blacks in the UCR

253

data continues to the present time. In 2016, Blacks accounted for 30.5% of persons arrested for fraud as well as 35.8% of persons arrested for embezzlement (U.S. Federal Bureau of Investigation, 2016). Given that Blacks make up about 13% of the U.S. population, they would appear to be overrepresented in these forms of white-collar crime.

The ideas on race and white-collar crime advanced by Hirschi and Gottfredson were quickly contested by Steffensmeier (1989) and others (Wheeler, Weisburd, Waring, & Bode, 1988, 1991; Benson & Moore, 1992; Reed & Yeager, 1996; Yeager & Reed, 1998). The critics argued that the crimes investigated by Hirschi and Gottfredson were not real white-collar crimes because most of them are not occupationally related. Hirschi and Gottfredson were also accused of ignoring the high-level white-collar crimes that do not appear in the UCR, such as antitrust and securities violations, which in that time period were committed overwhelmingly by White males (Weisburd, Wheeler, Waring, & Bode, 1991). This bimodal distribution is where the contemporary understanding of the relationship between race and white-collar crime now stands. Blacks appear to constitute a significant percentage of those who commit nonoccupational white-collar crimes (e.g., check fraud and identity theft), while Whites are overrepresented among occupationally related, complex, and high-level offenses (e.g., antitrust and securities offenses) (Weisburd et al., 1991; Shover & Hochstetler, 2006; Friedrichs, 1996, 2007). The main reason put forth to explain the underrepresentation of Blacks in mid- to high-level white-collar crimes is their lack of access to the types of occupational positions that are needed to commit these more complex occupationally based crimes (Benson & Simpson, 2015; Klenowski & Dodson, 2016).

However, since the 1980s when most of the empirical work on race and white-collar crime was conducted, access to educational and occupational opportunities for Blacks has improved. This has led to greater numbers of Blacks in occupations where opportunities for white-collar crime are assumed to be available (U.S. Equal Employment Opportunity Commission, 2015). Hence, it is important to ascertain whether their patterns of involvement in white-collar crime have changed as well. It may be the case that at certain organizational levels (higher administrative and management ranks, such as director-level positions and above), white-collar crime by Whites is more prevalent because Whites are overrepresented in such positions, while at other organizational levels (line-level through mid-level management), there are no race-based differences in opportunities to offend and hence no race-based differences in rates of offending. If observed, this pattern of results would support the racial invariance hypothesis. If, on the other hand, Blacks are over-represented in particular types of white-collar crimes, this may support the racial exceptionalism hypothesis.

In this chapter, we investigate the racial invariance and exceptionalism hypotheses by using official data from the U.S. Sentencing Commission (USSC) to determine whether the involvement of Blacks in white-collar crime has changed since the 1980s. Further, because almost nothing is known about the crimes committed by Black white-collar offenders, we present a more qualitative analysis of a form of white-collar crime that is intimately linked to the Black historical experience in the United States, that is fraud by pastors in Black Churches. Our analysis suggests that the racial exceptionalism thesis may need to be modified to be applied to white-collar crime. Before proceeding to our data analysis, however, we first consider the relevance of the racial invariance and racial exception-alism hypotheses in regard to Black involvement in white-collar crime. Then we briefly review what little historical data there are on race and white-collar crime, followed by our own data and analysis.

White-Collar Crime: Racial Invariance or Racial Exceptionalism?

The racial invariance thesis holds that an individual's race has noth-ing to do with that person's likelihood of offending. In theoretical terms, this means that race in and of itself is not a cause of crime. Rather, the causes of crime involve factors that are either personal (e.g., neu-ropsychological deficits or an abusive childhood), social (e.g., blocked opportunities or criminal peers), or structural (e.g., residence in a dis-advantaged neighborhood) in nature or some combination of all three. Race is involved in crime causation only to the extent that it influences exposure to these factors. Statistically, the invariance thesis implies that if Blacks and Whites are placed in the same structural and social con-ditions, their levels of offending will be equal. In contrast, the racial exceptionalism thesis holds the unique history of slavery, subjugation, and ongoing discrimination experienced by Blacks in America leads to deeply felt feelings of anger and hostility toward the White authoritarian power structure. As a result, Blacks are less likely to develop, or have a strong investment in, attitudes, beliefs, and behaviors espoused by tra-ditional American society and may develop alternative subgroup norms. Although the personal, social, and structural causes of crime obviously have some influence on Black offending, they do not, according to the exceptionalism view, completely account for it.

The racial invariance and racial exceptionalism hypotheses have been explicated and debated at some length in regard to ordinary street crime (Unnever & Owusu-Bempah, this volume; Sampson, this volume; Wilson & Katz, 2018), but as far as we know, no attention has been paid to the validity of either of these hypotheses in regard to white-collar crime. Indeed, Blacks who commit white-collar crimes have been entirely overlooked in criminology. They are forgotten offenders. If the racial invariance thesis is true, then we would expect that controlling for access to white-collar crime opportunities, Blacks and Whites would offend at similar rates. It is not exactly clear, however, what predictions should be drawn regarding racial exceptionalism and white-collar crime. One possibility is that holding opportunity constant, Blacks offend at a higher rate than Whites because of their anger over racism in American society. White-collar crime would be a way of striking back at the White establishment (Unnever & Owusu-Bempah, this volume). However, it is also possible that holding opportunity constant, Blacks would offend less than Whites. This could happen, because Blacks who achieve enough occupational success to have access to a white-collar crime opportunity may be especially chary of doing anything that would jeopardize that achievement, even though they may also experience discrimination in the world of corporate America (Davis & Watson, 1985). In other words, Blacks who have white-collar jobs may have particularly strong stakes in conformity and a strong fear of falling from grace. However, Whites who hold high-level occupational positions may feel that their chances of being caught and punished for a white-collar crime are very low because of the status shield that Whiteness provides and because of historically low rates of prosecution for white-collar-type crimes. Hence, they may have a very rational lack of fear when it comes to committing white-collar crime (Harris & Shaw, 2000). At this point, with no empirical data available, it is not possible to weigh the likelihood of these different potentialities, but the data that we introduce may help to begin to shed some light on them.

Historical Data on Race and White-Collar Crime

In the early 1980s, the National Institute of Justice (NIJ) funded two studies of sentencing in Federal District Courts. One was conducted at Yale University and was directed by Stanton Wheeler. The other was undertaken by Brian Forst and William Rhodes. In both studies, the researchers collected data on individuals convicted of a selection of white-collar-type crimes in certain federal district courts in the mid-1970s. Although neither of these projects was designed to look closely at the relationship between race and white-collar crime, both included race and ethnicity as variables, and below we reproduce some previously published results based on data from these studies (Wheeler et al., 1988; Benson & Kerley, 2000). Unfortunately, race is treated in a very crude fashion in both studies, and Blacks are not singled out as a specific racial group. Rather, all non-Whites (Blacks, Asians, American Indians, and Hispanics) are lumped together and compared to Whites as a group, but the non-Whites were predominantly Black (Weisburd et al., 1991, pp. 48–49).

Table 10.1 is based on the Yale study and shows that as a group, persons convicted of white-collar crimes are much more likely to be White than those convicted of common crimes. Over 80% of the white-collar criminals are White compared to only about a third of the common criminals. The white-collar criminals included individuals convicted of antitrust offenses, securities fraud, income tax violations, bribery, credit and lending fraud, false claims, mail fraud, and bank embezzlement, while offenses that were nonviolent property crimes, such as postal theft and forgery, were used to identify common criminals. Given that approximately 20% of the white-collar criminals were non-White, it is possible that Blacks are slightly overrepresented here, assuming that they constituted approximately 12% of the U.S. population in the 1970s. But since the non-White category includes other races and ethnicities, we cannot say for sure one way or the other.

Table 10.1

Percent White and Non-White of White-Collar and Common Criminals in the Yale Study

	White-Collar*	Common**
White	81.7%	34.3%
Non-White	19.3%	65.7%

* White-collar criminals includes persons convicted of antitrust offenses, securities fraud, income tax violations, bribery, credit and lending fraud, false claims, mail fraud, and bank embezzlement.
** Common criminals includes persons convicted of nonviolent property crimes such as postal theft or forgery.
(Adapted from Tables III and IV in Wheeler et al., 1988)

A different picture emerges, however, when the individual offenses that make up the white-collar crime category are examined. Table 10.2 shows the percentage White by statutory offense for both the Yale and the Forst and Rhodes studies, and for the sake of comparison with data presented below, Table 10.2 also shows the percentage non-White in parentheses. The offenses examined in the two studies overlap but are not identical. The Forst and Rhodes study did not look at antitrust, securities, or credit and lending offenses. Instead, it included postal embezzlement, which the Yale study did not. As Table 10.2 shows, the percentage White for the offenses that are common to both studies are quite similar, but the percentage of White offenders varies dramatically across the statutory offense categories. While a substantial percentage of those convicted of false claims were non-White, it would not be an exaggeration to say that in the 1970s, the chance of a non-White person being convicted of an antitrust or securities offense was virtually zero. Over 99% of the offenders in these categories were White. In addition, close to 90% of the income tax convictions involved Whites. Hence, it seems safe to assume that Blacks were significantly underrepresented in these offense categories, but they may have been overrepresented in the other offense categories where the percentage White ranges

Table 10.2

Percent White of White-Collar Offenders by Statutory Offense in the Yale* and Forst & Rhodes** Studies

	Yale	(%NW)	Forst & Rhodes	(%NW)
Antitrust	99.1	(0.9)	—	
Securities Fraud	99.6	(0.6)	—	
Income Tax	87.1	(12.9)	89.3	(10.7)
Bribery	83.3	(16.7)	77.5	(22.5)
Credit and Lending Fraud	71.5	(28.5)	—	
False Claims	61.8	(38.2)	72.8	(27.2)
Mail Fraud	76.8	(23.2)	78.7	(21.3)
Bank Embezzlement	74.1	(25.9)	75.5	(24.5)
Postal Embezzlement	—		65.0	(35.0)

* Adapted from Table VII in Wheeler et al. (1988).
** Adapted from Table 1 Benson and Kerley (2000).

from 61.8% for false claims to 83.3% for bribery in the Yale study. However, we cannot be sure what proportion of the non-Whites were Black as opposed to other racial or ethnic groups. Taken together, the results presented in Tables 10.1 and 10.2 suggest that the relationship between race and white-collar crime is not straightforward and that the common stereotype of the white-collar offender as a White person is not accurate. Given that in the 1970s, Whites accounted for approximately 87% of the U.S. population, the results presented above suggest that for the offenses of bribery, credit and lending fraud, false claims, mail fraud, bank embezzlement, and postal embezzlement, Whites are underrepresented and non-Whites overrepresented. But for antitrust and securities offenses, which are the most serious, harmful, and lucrative white-collar offenses (Weisburd et al., 1991), non-Whites are dramatically underrepresented.

Race and Contemporary White-Collar Offenders

Four decades have passed since the Yale study and the Forst and Rhodes study were conducted, and during that time, America has changed. Most importantly for our purposes, Blacks have made significant advances in obtaining white-collar jobs. For example, according to a 2015 report from the U.S. Equal Employment Opportunity Commission, in 1966, Blacks accounted for less than 1% of all executive and mid-level officials and managers in the American workforce, but by 2013, this number had increased to 6.77%. During this same period, the participation rate for Black professionals increased from 1.32% to 7.6%. Likewise, the participation rate for Black technicians grew from 4.07% to 13.25%, and for office and clerical workers, the rate increased from 3.53% to 15.76%. Admittedly, Blacks are still underrepresented in managerial and professional occupations, but they have nevertheless made advances in obtaining white-collar-type jobs. Thus, it is reasonable to question whether their involvement in white-collar-type crimes, which are often dependent on one's occupational position, has also changed. In short, do the racial patterns in white-collar offending found in the 1970s still hold?

Data from the U.S. Sentencing Commission (USSC) can be used to begin to answer this question. Since 2002, the USSC has made available on an annual basis detailed information on every person convicted of a federal crime, including the race and ethnicity of convicted persons as well as the exact statutory offense(s) for which they were convicted.

Table 10.3

Percent Black of White-Collar Offenders Nationwide in 2002 and 2015

	2002	2015
Black	**23.8%**	**28.9%**

For the years 2002–2015, we identified all of the individuals convicted of the statutory offenses used in the Yale study. Table 10.3 presents the percentage Black involvement in the eight statutory offenses combined in 2002 and 2015 nationwide.

It is immediately apparent from Table 10.3 that Black involvement in white-collar crime has increased since the 1970s. Back then, all non-Whites made up only 19.7% of the white-collar offenders in the seven districts included in the Yale study, but in 2002, Blacks alone accounted for 23.8% of convictions nationwide for these same offenses, and by 2015, that proportion had increased to 28.9%. As shown in Figure 10.1, the increase in the convictions of Blacks for these offenses has fluctuated from year to year between 2002 and 2015, but overall, the trend appears to be moving steadily upward.

The increase in white-collar offending by Blacks, however, has not occurred evenly across all offense categories, and for one category, antitrust, there has been no increase at all. Zero Blacks were convicted of antitrust offenses in either 2002 or 2015 (see Table 10.4), and though it is not shown in the table, the same is true for all the years in between. Blacks did increase their presence in securities fraud and bribery quite dramatically, but their involvement in the other four types of white-collar offenses appears not to have increased quite so much. For example, in the Yale study of the 1970s, non-Whites accounted for 28.5% of credit and lending fraud and 38.2% of false claims offenses. In 2015, Blacks by themselves made up 21.9% and 27.3%, respectively, of the same offenses. Assuming that at least some of the non-Whites in the Yale study are not Black but either Hispanics, Asians, or members of other groups, then it would appear that Black involvement in these particular white-collar offenses has remained about the same.[1]

Taken together, the results in Tables 10.2, 10.3, and 10.4 indicate that the involvement of Blacks in certain selected white-collar offenses has increased for some offenses over the course of the last four decades, but Blacks are still underrepresented in the most serious forms of white-collar crime, such as antitrust and securities offenses. We suspect that this

Figure 10.1

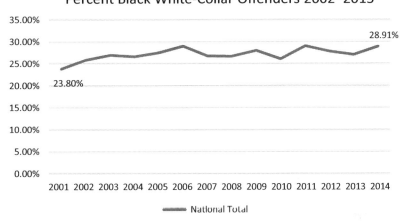

Percent Black White-Collar Offenders 2002–2015

Table 10.4

Percent Black of White-Collar Offenders Nationwide in 2002 and 2015 by Statutory Offense

Offense	2002	2015
Antitrust	0.0%	0.0%
Securities Fraud	8.2	6.9
Income Tax	7.0	12.0
Bribery	16.2	33.0
Credit and Lending Fraud	21.9	23.3
False Claims	27.3	32.1
Mail Fraud	24.0	27.2
Bank Embezzlement	22.7	6.9

change is due primarily to the improvement in access to white-collar-type jobs that has occurred for Blacks over the same time period. The significance of these findings for the racial invariance and racial exceptionalism hypotheses is not obvious. Given their proportion in the general population, Blacks do appear to be overrepresented in certain white-collar crimes, including credit and lending fraud, false claims, and mail fraud. This may support the racial exceptionalism hypothesis, but we cannot be sure because the USSC data tells us nothing about the structural positions occupied by the Blacks who commit these offenses and nothing about their exposure to other criminogenic conditions. Hence, we turn now to a different approach to examining the invariance and exceptionalism hypotheses. Here, we focus on a particular form of white-collar crime that is intimately linked to the Black historical experience.

White-Collar Crime in the Black Church

Proverbs 22:16: One who oppresses the poor to increase his wealth and one who gives gifts to the rich—both come to poverty.

As we noted above, according to the racial invariance hypothesis, we would expect to find similarities in white-collar offending rates among Blacks and Whites in situations where Blacks occupy white-collar-type positions where they are not constantly confronted with discrimination or obstacles to career mobility. We would also expect to find similar types of offending should Blacks and Whites have equal access to positions that allow opportunities to engage in similar types of white-collar crime. Yet as the proponents of the racial exceptionalism thesis argue, finding such a situation is extremely difficult if not impossible in America. This reality creates significant challenges to investigating white-collar crimes from the perspective of race. The socioeconomic struggles faced by minorities, particularly Blacks, extend throughout the history of this country and are still reflected in very real barriers to social and economic achievement. The white-collar crimes that are typically examined within the criminological literature focus upon acts committed by individuals in lofty corporate positions or other positions of power and authority, where, as the EEOC data indicate, minorities are underrepresented.

In order to compare white-collar offending among Blacks and Whites, one needs to find a social context where the weight of institutional racism and concentrated disadvantage is less pronounced. This requires identifying white-collar crimes committed by Blacks within organizations founded, controlled, or led by Blacks. It is also important that these situations center on abuses of power or position and where potential victims are likely to view the offender as a respectable and legitimate authority figure. One such place exists in American society: the Black Church.

In her study of the Black Church and African-American empowerment, Calhoun-Brown (1999) states that "primarily because of racism and discrimination in America, black churches and denominations were established separately from their white counterparts." The Black church has long been a source of religious, social, and emotional support for Blacks in America, and research has demonstrated the strong connections between Black Churches, community advancement, and racial progress for Blacks (Taylor, Thornton, & Chatters, 1987). Today, religion remains highly segregated, with particular denominations formed for the purpose of serving Blacks and the Black community (Sherkat, 2002). For many in the Black community, the church is an important source of social support, forming the hub of essential social networks that come to form a "quasi-family in terms of their norms related to expectations, obligations, and reciprocity" (Taylor, Lincoln, & Chatters, 2005). Furthermore, Black Churches have traditionally been places of status equalization, where upper-, middle-, and lower-class Blacks come together on equal footing, and a place where one's background does not inhibit one's ability to seek out and obtain leadership positions (Brown & Brown, 2003; Frazier, 1963).

At the head of the Black Church stands the senior pastor, or some similar leadership position. The pastors of Black Churches have long been a strong tower of faith to their congregations, and many have undertaken the roles of counselor, financial advisor, and social activist, among others. The significant influence of a Black pastor's words to his or her congregation have been channeled to address serious issues within the Black community, including the reluctance of many Blacks to seek out mental health services (Allen, Davey, & Davey, 2010). Largely due to the charisma and determination of the clergy, Black Churches seek to be independent and to be representative of the highest social ideals, including fiscal responsibility, dedication and service to the community, and inclusivity of the poor along with the rich (Billingsley & Caldwell, 1991). Black pastors are often seen as "change agents who facilitate the process of change and motivate or inspire members of their congregations to perform beyond expectations" (Langley & Kahnweiler, 2003). Unfortunately, the immense power, respect, and authority given to Black pastors has been at times corrupted and turned into a vehicle through which pastors steal from or extort their members for their personal pecuniary gain.

The relationships among spiritual and material success enjoyed by some Black pastors have been highlighted in the reality TV show

Preachers of L.A., which perpetuates the stereotype that success in the pulpit leads to wealth. In particular, the show reinforces the belief held by many that Black pastors often use their positions for financial self-enrichment (BET, 2013; Cottman, 2013; Mattera, 2013). Black pastors have been accused of taking advantage of low-income members, under the guise of tithing to the church, to support lavish lifestyles and multimillion-dollar incomes (Drayton, 2016; Shaw, 2014). According to the *Atlanta Black Star* (2014), several Black pastors had a net worth that was at least 200 times greater than the average household income of the communities served by those pastors. This rivals the pay disparities that exist between the top 350 CEOs for for-profit firms and the typical worker's pay in those firms (Donnelly, 2017). The Black pastors chronicled by the *Atlanta Black Star* are well-known pastors, who often serve as exemplars for pastoral success.

Black pastors come from a variety of socioeconomic and educational backgrounds, and they may have had no formal training or vetting prior to taking up their first ministerial role. It is their works within the church and the community, and the quality of the interactions they have with church members that define them. Because pastors handle a range of social and personal issues for their members, they come to be seen as trusted sources of knowledge, information, and wisdom whose advice is earnestly solicited and heeded (Allen et al., 2010). Some Black pastors have come to be the administrative and spiritual heads of "multibillion dollar enterprises" (Sherkat, 2002) that deliver the word of God to followers, service community and social needs, provide programing for youth, the poor, and the elderly, and lead political and social activism within the community.

It is within the context of the Black Church, and in the position of the church pastor, that white-collar crimes committed by Blacks can most visibly be seen. This context strips away the social structural, historical, and racial barriers that inhibit Blacks and other minorities from occupying high-level organizational positions in which opportunities for white-collar crime are prevalent. Within the Black Church, there is a naturally occurring condition where issues related to race and marginalization do not create disparities in access to opportunities to abuse power, trust, and position.

Case Identification

To investigate white-collar crimes committed by Black pastors, we searched the Internet to identify cases covered by local news media.

Because of the high-profile nature of church clergy, as well as their notoriety and position of respectability within the community, crimes committed by pastors tend to be well covered by the media. And nowadays television and print media utilize online platforms with regularity. Hence, we searched for cases on embezzlement and fraud within churches, as perpetrated by church clergy, and where congregants were identified as victims. The main focus of our study is the Black pastor who through their position and influence has victimized their congregation, and in so doing has engaged in white-collar offenses. However, because we are interested in exploring issues of race in white-collar offending, we compare church-based white-collar crimes committed by Black clergy to those committed by White clergy.

A convenience sampling approach was taken for case selection. Using Google, a search was conducted using the terms "embezzlement," "church," and "pastor." From the search results, we selected a total of 40 cases, all of which involved adjudicated offenders; 20 cases involved Black pastors and 20 involved White pastors. We reviewed 18 pages of search results. However, in many cases we found multiple results for a single incident. Where this occurred, case information from all pertinent results was analyzed as one incident.

It is worth noting that it was substantially easier to find stories of Black pastors engaging in white-collar crimes through their positions than it was to find White pastors doing the same. While we were able to find 20 White pastors who had committed white-collar crimes, it did appear that Blacks were more prevalent in our search results, as the initial search results were almost exclusively comprised of Black pastors. Unique cases involving Black pastors were more common on every page of the search results until the 11th page, making up 68% of results from the first 5 pages and 73% of results for the first 10 pages. The 20 cases involving Black pastors were identified by the 8th page of search results, while it took an additional 10 pages of search results to identify the 20 White pastors.

Cases were selected in the order in which they appeared in the search listing, and there is nothing to suggest that these cases would be significantly different from other cases found later in the search. More importantly, there is nothing to suggest that the instances of white-collar crime committed by Black pastors that were selected for inclusion would be substantially different, based only on the ordering of results, from those committed by White pastors.

The race of the offender was determined by examining a photo of the individual, which was typically provided in the news stories along with the reported case information. However, in several cases, no picture of the offender was provided in the news reports. In these instances, secondary searches were made using key words unique to that case in order to locate a picture of the individual. The case was only included if a picture could be found and positive verification could be made that the individual in the picture was the individual involved in the case; if no picture could be verified, the case was not included.

Case information was downloaded from the Internet and converted to a Word document for coding and analysis. Coding involved reading each case and cataloguing a range of variables, including the following:

- dollar-value loss associated with the scheme
- type of scheme perpetrated
- whether the pastor acted alone or with conspirators
- offender's race
- age and gender of the offender(s)
- specific charges brought against the offender(s)

Analyses involved a series of descriptive assessments of case features, comparisons of the cases by race, and qualitative content analyses of each case description.

Race, Opportunity, and Pastoral White-Collar Crimes

The pastoral crimes we investigated were all covered by local news outlets, and in most cases, only state charges were filed. In total, the 40 sampled offenders were charged with 54 crimes. The most common charge brought against the offenders was embezzlement (42.5% of cases), and the next two most common charges were theft/looting/stealing (32.5% of cases) and fraud (27.5% of cases). Much less common were charges of money laundering (10% of cases), tax evasion and securities violations (5% of cases, respectively), and filing a false tax return and misapplication of fiduciary property (2.5% of cases, respectively).

All of the pastors in our investigation were male, which is not necessarily a novel finding. Several major religious denominations still do not ordain women to be clergy, and according to research by Masci (2014), only 11% of churches and synagogues in the U.S. were led by female clergy. Clearly, opportunities for pastoral-related white-collar crimes are more prevalent for males than for females. Additionally, even when females do head a congregation, their opportunities to steal substantial amounts are often limited because female clergy tend to serve small churches in rural communities that have fewer financial and social resources (McDuff, 2001). This may be part of the reason that female clergy earn substantially lower salaries than their male counterparts (Chaves, Anderson, & Schleifer, 2013). Alternatively, it may simply be that case that the gender-based wage disparities found throughout American society are also prevalent within the church.

The pastors ranged in age from 30 to 75 years old with an average age of 53; there was no significant difference in the average age of Black relative to White offenders. This fits the demographic profile of white-collar offenders, who are typically middle-aged or older, and reflects the reality that teens and individuals in their 20s typically do not have access to occupational positions that afford opportunities for white-collar crime. While individuals younger than 30 can and oftentimes do engage in white-collar crimes, and individuals younger than 30 some-times are pastors, the majority of white-collar offenders and the major-ity of pastors tend to be middle-aged or older. Reported losses ranged between a low of $5,567 to a high of $11,000,000, with the average scheme netting an offender around $1,154,000; the median loss from the schemes we examined was $175,000. While crimes committed by Black pastors had higher average losses, it was not significantly higher than crimes committed by White offenders.

In exactly 75% of the schemes we investigated, the pastor acted alone. Schemes perpetrated by Black pastors were not more likely to be solitary crimes than those committed by White pastors. The content analysis of activities involved in the schemes led to one of the more pro-vocative findings of the investigation. The scheme activities as reported by the media were analyzed and coded for key words and phrases that described the essence of the offender's activities. These codes were then grouped into similar categories, which reflected one of three distinct types of white-collar crime: embezzlement, confidence scheme, or iden-tity theft scheme. A substantial majority of the schemes (82.5%) were categorized as embezzlement; six (15.0 %) were confidence schemes, and one scheme (2.5%) involved identity theft.

The identity-theft scheme involved a pastor and several cocon-spirators stealing credit card numbers from congregation members through a credit card swiping scheme. The individuals then used the stolen credit cards to purchase items and conduct fraudulent transac-tions to gain access to cash. A review of the several embezzlement schemes showed no discernable race-based differences in the ways in which schemes were conducted. Irrespective of their race, pastors used their positions either to divert funds directly from church coffers or to intercept funds intended for the church. These funds were then used to pay for the pastor's personal expenses, to support lavish lifestyles, purchase and maintain property, and in some cases to support extramarital affairs. Table 10.5 displays examples of the embezzlement schemes we examined.

Table 10.5

Narrative Descriptions of Pastoral Embezzlement Schemes

During the investigation it was found that multiple checks written to and by the church were deposited into accounts held by the defendant. Some congregants noticed discrepancies in the annual tithing statements they received from the church, which reflected a difference between what they had given the church and what the church was reporting in its tax statement.

The longtime pastor of a Lutheran church was convicted of pocketing donations from parishioners totaling about $70,000. Some of that money went into the pastor's personal retirement account.

A Chicago pastor was charged with spending about $100,000 intended for his church to purchase lavish dinners, jewelry for his wife, and everyday expenses. While the investigation was ongoing, the pastor transferred to a new church. After parishioners at his new church found out about the embezzlement, nearly 40 families left the parish, and stewardship dropped $250,000. It was also discovered that he diverted money from a trust several parishioners had left for the construction of a cultural center.

A church pastor used the church's ATM card to steal tens of thousands of dollars from the churches savings account. The pastor admitted to stealing the funds to support an extramarital affair with a 20-year-old woman he met online. In a statement, church members said they are saddened by the actions of their former pastor. They believe the situation is between the pastor, God, and the judicial process.

The pastor received offerings in the mail from church members who were unable to attend service. He then deposited the money into a secret account, unknown to other church members or church leaders. He used that account to withdraw cash and write checks payable to himself that were deposited into his personal bank account. He diverted checks of more than $250,000 in tithes and offerings over the course of a decade and funneled the cash into his personal banking account, and he spent the money at retailers including Victoria's Secret.

Pastor solicited donations to his church community center, then diverted nearly $1 million to his personal bank accounts. Used these funds to support his lavish lifestyle, including the purchase of a luxury home, a Rolex watch, and a monogramed full-length mink coat. He also withdrew large sums of money from the church bank accounts, which he used to remodel his home, pay for extravagant dinners, and take vacations to luxury resorts and casinos.

It seems clear that churches provide motivated pastors an easy way to obtain the funds needed to live a lavish lifestyle by supplementing their income with the tithes and offerings of the congregation. The trust and responsibility given to pastors reflects their position as a steward of God to the world and places them beyond the typical scrutiny given to other people who have fiduciary responsibilities to a group or organization. Furthermore, the pastor's position as spiritual leader of the church reflects the perspective that the pastor serves God through his or her service to the church and its congregation. Theft or embezzlement from the church would be a theft from and abuse of God, an offense that reaches beyond secular law and physical punishment. It seems the ethereal influence of religion may be for many churches a substitute for formal financial controls and oversight, particularly within Black Churches, many of which have never had a financial audit (LifeWay, 2016).

While embezzlement was the predominant method by which pastors stole from their congregations and others, the most nefarious type of scheme was the confidence scheme. On average, confidence schemes led to losses of just over $3,655,000, while embezzlement schemes had an average loss of $718,000. Central to any successful confidence scheme is the ability of the schemer to develop a trust relationship with the victim, and some of the best schemes involve some level of emotional investment on the part of the victim. When a pastor initiates a confidence scheme, he or she abuses congregants' religious faith, as well as the trust they have placed in the position that is supposed to serve the people as a vehicle through which God's will is accomplished.

Given the availability of criminal opportunities for both Black and White pastors that come with a leveraging of the Bible and religious rhetoric, we expected to find that these schemes were committed by Black and White pastors with equal regularity. This was not the case, as five of the six confidence schemes included in our analysis were committed by Black pastors. The opportunity to engage in a confidence scheme is not race based, as these crimes rely upon abuses of trust. The significant amounts of trust and respect afforded to pastors by their congregants also appear to be racially invariant. Yet finding that Black pastors engaged in the majority of confidence schemes in our sample may point to important race-based differences in opportunities for particular forms of white-collar crime.

The social and historical context within which the Black Church developed has afforded Black pastors a premium position from which to engage in various types of white-collar crime, and it has brought ample targets to motivated pastors (Ellison & Taylor, 1996). We found that five Black pastors, but only one White pastor, used their position and authority to convince congregants to invest money in confidence schemes. The pastors used Biblical scripture and references to God's favor to reinforce the legitimacy of their claims and as a way to give credibility to their activities.

For example, in one confidence scheme, a pastor and several coconspirators convinced congregants to invest in their microfinance business, which was allegedly established to help poor people in developing countries. The group promised guaranteed rates of return but instead conducted risky trading on the foreign-exchange currency markets and used invested funds to purchase a $1.75 million residence and to pay for other personal expenses. When investors questioned the group about when they would receive financial returns, the defendants blamed delays on the 2008 financial crisis. One congregant recalled the following exchange he had with the pastor: "I asked him like, 'Hey, that's a nice car.'" "He said, 'Yeah, $100,000 car. If you save up your money, God's going to bless you.' Come to find out now, it was actually part of our money."

In another scheme, the pastor of a church falsely represented himself as a financial advisor, working to invest congregants' funds in retirement and investment accounts. However, an investigation determined that he never made any investments but rather deposited over $1 million into his own accounts and used them for his own personal benefit. The pastor used his position within the church to find his clients and often quoted to them a passage from the Book of Acts, which says "The blessing is in your giving." One investor claimed they gave the pastor nearly $100,000, yet the pastor eventually stopped returning their phone calls and emails and even stopped attending his own church.

In an even more egregious use of religion to support pastoral white-collar crimes, the pastor of a church in a highly depressed urban area exploited retirees and laid-off workers by getting them to invest in his personal real-estate business. In reality, the business was in financial ruin, and none of the invested funds were put into the real-estate operation. The pastor and a coconspirator often facilitated what they called "Blessed Life Conferences" at churches across the country as a way to enlist new clients. These conferences relied upon a heavy use of Biblical rhetoric to woo potential clients. The pastor also frequently stated that because he was a man who would "pray for your children," he was more trustworthy than a financial advisor or banker. In total, the pastor and his associate stole nearly $6.7 million from investors across the country, who were promised high rates of return on their investments. The pair also advertised their scheme on a local religious radio station and encouraged laid-off workers who had recently received severance packages to consult them as a way to increase their financial returns.

Concluding Thoughts

Except for a brief flurry of interest in the 1980s when Hirschi and Gottfredson (1987) published their controversial articles on the causes of white-collar crime, race as it relates to white-collar crime has been virtually ignored by criminologists with only a few exceptions (Friedrichs, 1996; Benson & Simpson, 2015). Given the stereotype of the white-collar offender, this oversight is perhaps not particularly surprising, but it is unfortunate. The disadvantageous structural and social conditions under which so many Blacks live have long been cited as reasons for their overrepresentation in many forms of street crime, especially when such conditions worsen (Wilson, 1987; Sampson & Wilson, 1995). But this focus on Black disadvantage, while certainly understandable and warranted, means that criminologists have not paid attention to potential improvements in the Black experience and what they might mean for Black involvement in crime, especially white-collar crime. Further, the exclusive focus on street crime has led criminologists to overlook the potential criminogenic elements of the one institution in America where Blacks dominate in leadership roles—the Black Church.

National Trends in Race and White-Collar Crime

Black involvement in some but not all white-collar crimes has increased over the course of the past four decades. In the first decades of the 21st century, no Blacks were convicted of federal antitrust violations. There are at least three possible explanations for this result. First, Blacks may simply not yet have access to the executive-level leadership positions that are typically held by those who commit antitrust violations, at least not in the industries where such violations have occurred recently. Second, Blacks could have access to leadership positions in those industries, but, as with women, they could still be excluded from the informal criminal networks that orchestrate these offenses (Steffensmeier, Schwartz, & Roche, 2013; Benson & Gottshalk, 2015). Third, even if they do have access to opportunities to commit antitrust offenses,

Blacks may be more reluctant than Whites to get involved because of a greater fear that they would lose all that they have struggled so hard to achieve. Similar factors may be involved in the underrepresentation of Blacks in securities fraud. We leave it to future researchers to explore these possibilities and turn now to those offenses where Black involvement has increased.

Since the 1970s, Black involvement in bribery, credit and lending fraud, false claims, and mail fraud appears to have increased, and in 2015, Blacks were overrepresented in all of these offenses given their proportion of the general population. We suspect that at least some of this increase is due to the greater access that Blacks now have to white-collar-type jobs. But we do not want to overemphasize this possibility, because these particular white-collar crimes are not always based in legitimate occupations. For example, both mail fraud and lending and credit fraud can be committed as part of con games or scams set up by people who do not work for legitimate businesses, such as certain telemarketing schemes and charity frauds. From the raw numbers presented here, it is not clear whether this pattern of results supports either the racial invariance or racial exceptionalism hypotheses. Even though Black access to white-collar jobs has improved, America still remains a nation of two societies—White and Black. Unemployment and economic disadvantage are still much worse among Blacks than Whites (U.S. Bureau of Labor Statistics, 2018; Pew Research Center, 2016), and White racism certainly plays some role in this disparity. Although it might require some tweaking of the exceptionalism hypothesis, it would not be entirely unreasonable for supporters of the hypothesis to argue that the overrepresentation of Blacks in these particular white-collar crimes is rooted in their unique historical experience. For example, even though Black access to white-collar jobs has improved, they are still relatively deprived compared to Whites, and their historically based and seemingly inevitable relative deprivation compared to Whites could drive their seemingly high rates of white-collar offending. White-collar crime scholars have argued that white-collar crime should be expected to flourish in the modern age because more people have access to the skills and tools of white-collar crime—telephones, computers, fax machines, college degrees, and office jobs—(Benson & Simpson, 2015; Shover & Hochstetler, 2006; Weisburd et al., 1991). Throughout the 20th century, as Blacks along with Whites have moved away from farming and manual labor occupations toward office work, they were exposed to the same opportunities to commit white-collar crimes as Whites, and they adapted to this new landscape of opportunity by adopting new forms of crime. But in this new landscape, they carried with them all of the historical baggage of the Black experience in America.

At this point in time, we can only speculate on why Black involvement in particular forms of white-collar crime has increased, but we suggest that this trend represents an important potential avenue of research for a Black Criminology. For too long, the study of race and crime has focused exclusively on the truly disadvantaged and their involvement in common forms of street crime. The criminology of middle-class Blacks has been largely ignored. We suggest it is high time to investigate how the criminological activity of this segment of the Black population has evolved and been shaped by their ongoing social and economic experiences in America.

Pastoral Crime in Black Churches

The racial exceptionalism hypothesis focuses primarily on how the Black historical experience in America exacerbates offending by Blacks, but this same history can also shape the nature of Black victimization. Just as White racism pushed Blacks into racially segregated neighborhoods and communities, where intrarace crime flourished, it also pushed them into racially segregated places of worship. The residential segregation of Blacks was mirrored by their spiritual segregation in Black Churches, and in these churches, Black pastors have long ruled supreme, providing guidance and counseling to their ministries in virtually all areas of life. However, the enormous moral authority that Black pastors have in the Black community is a double-edged sword. On the one hand, pastors can represent a beacon of hope, stability, and understanding to their followers as leaders who can be trusted to always put the interests of the people above their own interests. On the other hand, however, as figures in whom such enormous trust is placed, Black pastors are also uniquely situated to abuse trust. And they have many opportunities to do so, precisely because Blacks are markedly more religious than Whites (Pew Research Center, 2009).

Due to the power and authority held by Black pastors, and because the Black Church evolved as a parallel institution to the White church, our investigation appears to highlight the force and importance of both racial exceptionalism and the racial invariance hypotheses. In terms of racial invariance, we found that Black and White pastors engage in similar types of offending, yet they likely engage in these crimes at different rates. The development, structure, and history of the church in America afford Black and White pastors ample opportunities to commit white-collar crimes, yet they also affect the frequency with which certain crimes are committed. Finding that embezzlement was the most common type of white-collar crime committed by all pastors is a reflection of the way in which the church structure and the position of pastor influence opportunities for crime.

Regarding racial exceptionalism, it is unlikely that the unique history of slavery and structural disadvantage faced by Blacks in America has led pastors to engage in white-collar crimes as a way to resist White authoritarian hierarchy. Rather, the development and perseverance of the Black Church, a social and religious institution founded and maintained to support Black culture and to redress racial inequalities, is the embodiment of Blacks' resistance to White religious authoritarianism. During slavery, Christianity was forced upon African slaves by White slave owners to the detriment of the Africans' indigenous Pagan beliefs. The development of prominent, successful, and powerful Black Churches means that Blacks no longer needed to rely upon Whites to find God and practice religion. Blacks were able to form and rely upon their own religious and authoritarian structures.

However, it is within the church that Black congregations likely have the greatest potential to become victims of criminally motivated Black pastors. These offenders hold juxtaposing roles: first as the figurehead of an important religious, cultural, and social institution within the community, and second, as the perpetrator of white-collar schemes designed for self-enrichment. As such, slavery, religion, and the troubled racial history of America may be related to Black pastoral crime in an important way that supports novel conceptualizations of the racial exceptionalism hypothesis. Namely, by resisting the White religious authority that underscores America's history of segregation and racial exclusion through the development of legitimate social institutions (i.e., the Black Church), otherwise disenfranchised Blacks have an opportunity to obtain high social status and respected positions of authority. It is through the legitimate organizations that stand in opposition to America's history of racial intolerance that opportunities for pastoral white-collar crimes committed by Blacks against Blacks can be found.

It is a sad irony that the institutions that afford Blacks opportunities for support and advancement which have been systematically denied to them elsewhere in America also expose them to potential victimization. The Black Church may exist to support the religious, economic, and social growth of Blacks in America, yet as our investigation shows, these altruistic goals do not negate the substantial influence and deviant pull of greed. It must also be remembered that the racially segregated nature of churches in America means that the victims and offenders involved in pastoral white-collar crimes likely share the same racial categorization. White churches are most likely to be victimized by White pastors, and Black Churches are most likely to be victimized by Black pastors.

As mentioned earlier, it was not difficult to find instances of Black and White pastors committing white-collar crimes targeting their churches and their congregations. Yet the offenses of Black pastors were more prominent in early search results. It may be the case that the search algorithms employed by the search engine used to identify cases were influenced by prior browsing history. Searching for information relative to the topic of race and white-collar crime may have primed the search engine to populate results for Black pastors ahead of those related to White pastors. It may also be the case that the highly respected status of Black pastors and the paucity of other Black white-collar offenders causes Black pastors to receive greater media attention than White pastors. In short, similar to other crimes, the crimes of Black pastors may simply be covered more widely and in greater depth than those of White pastors (Welch, 2007).

Regardless of the reasons why Black pastors appeared more frequently in early search results relative to White pastors, the search results clearly show that pastors of all races have ample opportunities to commit white-collar crimes. At the same time, it must be reiterated that race influences opportunities for white-collar offending through its effect on structural barriers to high-level positions, which are removed within the context of religion.

Black Churches place an incredible amount of trust, responsibility, and authority in the hands of their pastors, and they afford a large amount of respect to these individuals and their positions. Furthermore, Blacks generally see the church as central to the social and economic well-being of the community (Holloman, Gasman, & Anderson-Thompkins, 2003), with pastors taking the lead in championing important social causes. Despite the fact that these pastors may have no formal training or education, they serve their congregations as marriage and personal counselors, advise them on important life decisions, help to shape the political agenda of the community, and oftentimes give advice to congregants on financial matters. Because the church in America is so racially segregated and Black pastors victimize Black congregants, the financial, social, and personal impacts of pastoral white-collar crimes will concentrate within an already disadvantaged population.

In conclusion, we urge other scholars to turn their attention to the issue of white-collar crime committed by Blacks. Although racism still plagues America, at least some segments of the Black community have made economic and occupational gains, and it is important to consider how this change in their social positions may influence their involvement in crime. While economic and occupational advances may reduce their involvement in street crime, it may at the same time increase their involvement in white-collar crime as they are exposed to more white-collar crime opportunities along with racism in the workplace. Evidence suggests that something is going on, as Blacks have increased their levels of participation in several common forms of white-collar crime, excluding only antitrust offenses, and they are disproportionately represented in some forms. These developments raise intriguing questions for the racial invariance and racial exceptionalism hypotheses. In addition, it is important to recognize that just as racism created segregated communities where Blacks are victimized by other Blacks at high rates, racism also led to the formation of social institutions within the Black community, most notably the Black Church, that paradoxically create opportunities for Black white-collar offenders.

Note

1. The dramatic decline in Black involvement in bank embezzlement is a puzzle that we do not attempt to solve here. For reasons that are not known to us, there has been a substantial decrease in federal convictions for bank embezzlement over the past decade and a half. They dropped from 375 in 2002 to 58 in 2015.

References

Allen, A. J., Davey, M. P., & Davey, A. (2010). Being example to the flock: The role of church leaders and African American families seeking mental health care services. *Contemporary Family Therapy, 32*(2), 117–134.

Atlanta Black Star. (2014, June). 8 Black Pastors whose net worth is 200 times greater than folk in their local communities. Retrieved from http://atlantablack star.com/2014/06/26/8-black-pastors-whose-net-worth-is-200-times-greater-than-folks-in-their-local-community/

Benson, M. L., & Gottshalk, P. (2015). Gender and white-collar crime in Norway: An empirical study of media reports. *International Journal of Law, Crime and Justice, 43*(4), 535–552.

Benson, M. L., & Kerley, K. R. (2000). Life course theory and white-collar crime. In H. N. Pontell & D. Shichor (Eds.), *Contemporary issues in crime and criminal justice: Essays in honor of Gilbert Geis* (pp. 121–136). Saddle River, NJ: Prentice Hall.

Benson, M. L., & Moore, E. (1992). Are white-collar and common offenders the same: An empirical and theoretical critique of a recently proposed general theory of crime. *Journal of Research in Crime and Delinquency, 29*(3), 251–272.

Benson, M. L., & Simpson, S. S. (2015). *Understanding white-collar crime: An opportunity perspective* (2nd ed.). New York, NY: Routledge.

BET. (2013, October). *Black Pastors denounce the reality show the preachers of LA*. Retrieved from www.bet.com/news/national/2013/10/17/black-pastors-denounce-the-reality-show-the-preachers-of-la.html

Billingsley, A., & Caldwell, C. H. (1991). The church, the family, and the school in the African American community. *The Journal of Negro Education, 60*(3), 427–440.

Brown, R. K., & Brown, R. E. (2003). Faith and works: Church-based social capital resources and African American political activism. *Social Forces, 82*(2), 617–641.

Calhoun-Brown, A. (1999). The image of God: Black theology and racial empowerment in the African American community. *Review of Religious Research, 40*(3), 197–212.

Chaves, M., Anderson, S., & Schleifer, C. (2013). *The triangle clergy compensation study: Preliminary results and interpretations*. Unpublished manuscript. Duke University.

Clinard, M. (1946). Criminological theories of violations of wartime regulations. *American Sociological Review, 11*, 258–270.

Clinard, M. (1952). *The black market: A study of white-collar crime*. New York, NY: Rinehart and Company.

Cottman, M. H. (2013, May). *Black Pastors to star in reality TV show*. Retrieved from www.theroot.com/black-pastors-to-star-in-reality-tv-show-1790896525

Steffensmeier, D. J., Schwartz, J., & Roche, M. (2013). Gender and twenty-first century corporate crime: Female involvement and gender gap in Enron-Era Corporate Frauds. *American Sociological Review, 78*(3): 448–476.

Davis, G., & Watson, G. (1985). *Black life in corporate America: Swimming in the mainstream*. South Shore, MA: Anchor Books.

Donnelly, G. (2017, July). *Top CEOs make more in two days than an average employee does in one year*. Retrieved from http://fortune.com/2017/07/20/ceo-pay-ratio-2016/

Drayton, T. (2016, July). *Black women: Stop making these Pastors Rich, please!* Retrieved from http://clutchmagonline.com/2016/07/black-women-stop-making-these-pastors-rich-please/

Ellison, C. G., & Taylor, R. J. (1996). Turning to prayer: Social and situational antecedents of religious coping among African Americans. *Review of Religious Research, 38*(2), 111–131.

Frazier, E. F. (1963). *The Negro Church in America*. New York, NY: Schocken.

Friedrichs, D. O. (1996). White-collar crime and the class-race-gender construct. In M. D. Schwartz & D. Milovanovic (Eds.), *Race, gender, and class in criminology: The intersection* (pp. 141–158). New York, NY: Garland Publishing, Inc.

Friedrichs, D. O. (2007). *Trusted criminals : White collar crime in contemporary society* (3rd ed.). Belmont, CA: Thomson Wadsworth.

Geis, G. (1977). The heavy electrical equipment antitrust cases of 1961. In G. Geis & R. F. Meier (Eds.), *White-collar crime: Offenses in business, politics, and the professions* (Revised ed., pp. 117–132). New York, NY: Free Press.

Harris, A. R., & Shaw, J. A. W. (2000). Looking for patterns: Race, class, and crime. In J. F. Sheley (Ed.), *Criminology: A contemporary handbook* (3rd ed., pp. 129–164). Belmont, CA: Thompson Wadsworth.

Hirschi, T., & Gottfredson, M. (1987). Causes of white-collar crime. *Criminology, 25*(4), 949–974.

Hirschi, T., & Gottfredson, M. (1989). The significance of white-collar crime for a general theory of crime. *Criminology, 27*(2), 359–371.

Holloman, D. B., Gasman, M., & Anderson-Thompkins, S. (2003). Motivations for philanthropic giving in the African American church: Implications for Black college fundraising. *Journal of Research on Christian Education, 12*(2), 137–169.

Klenowski, P. M., & Dodson, K. D. (2016). Who commits white-collar crime, and what do we know about them. In S. R. Van Slyke, M. L. Benson, & F. T. Cullen (Eds.), *The Oxford handbook of white-collar crime* (pp. 101–126). New York, NY: Oxford University Press.

Langley, W. M., & Kahnweiler, W. M. (2003). The role of pastoral leadership in the socio-politically active African American church. *Organization Development Journal, 21*(2), 43–51.

LifeWay. (2016). Pastor views on Church finances: Survey of protestant Pastors. Retrieved from http://lifewayresearch.com/2017/08/03/1-in-10-churches-have-had-funds-stolen/

Masci, D. (2014, September 9). The divide over ordaining women. *Pew Research Center*. Retrieved from www.pewresearch.org/fact-tank/2014/09/09/the-divide-over-ordaining-women/

Mattera, J. (2013, October). *7 Negative stereotypes 'preachers of LA' promotes*. Retrieved from www.charismanews.com/opinion/41430-7-negative-stereotypes-preachers-of-la-promotes

McDuff, E. M. (2001). The gender paradox in work satisfaction and the protestant clergy. *Sociology of Religion, 62*(1), 1–21.

Pew Research Center. (2009). *A religious portrait of African Americans*. Washington, DC: Pew Research Center. Retrieved January 16, 2018, from www.pewforum.org/2009/01/30/a-religious-portrait-of-african-americans/

Pew Research Center. (2016). *Demographic trends and economic well-being*. Washington, DC: Pew Research Center. Retrieved January 16, 2018, from www.pewsocialtrends.org/2016/06/27/1-demographic-trends-and-economic-well-being/

Reed, G. E., & Yeager, P. C. (1996). Organizational offending and neoclassical criminology: Challenging the reach of a general theory of crime. *Criminology, 34*(3), 357–382.

Sampson, R. J., & Wilson, W. J. (1995). Toward a theory of race, crime and urban inequality. In J. Hagan & R. Peterson (Eds.), *Crime and inequality* (pp. 37–54). Stanford, CA: Stanford University Press.

Shaw, A. R. (2014, July). *Black Pastors blasted for earning millions while preaching to low-income communities*. Retrieved from https://rollingout.com/2014/07/02/black-pastors-blasted-earning-millions-preaching-low-income-communities/

Sherkat, D. E. (2002). African-American religious affiliation in the late 20th century: Cohort variations and pattern switching, 1973–1998. *Journal for the Scientific Study of Religion, 41*(3), 485–493.

Shover, N., & Hochstetler, A. (2006). *Choosing white-collar crime*. New York, NY: Cambridge University Press.

Steffensmeier, D. J. (1989). On the causes of "white-collar" crime: An assessment of Hirschi and Gottfredson's claims. *Criminology, 27*(2), 345–358.

Sutherland, E. H. (1940). White-collar criminality. *American Sociological Review*, *5*, 1–12.

Sutherland, E. H. (1949). *White collar crime*. New York, NY: Dryden Press.

Taylor, R. J., Lincoln, K. D., & Chatters, L. M. (2005). Supportive relationships with church members among African Americans. *Family Relations*, *54*(4), 501–511.

Taylor, R. J., Thornton, M. C., & Chatters, L. M. (1987). Black Americans' perceptions of the sociohistorical role of the church. *Journal of Black Studies*, *18*(2), 123–138.

U.S. Bureau of Labor Force Statistics. (2015). *Labor force statistics for the current population survey*. Washington, DC: U.S. Bureau of Labor Statistics. Retrieved January 16, 2018, from www.bls.gov/web/empsit/cpsee_e16.htm

U.S. Equal Employment Opportunity Commission. (2015). *American experiences versus American expectations*. Washington, DC: U.S. Equal Employment Opportunity Commission. Retrieved January 5, 2018, from www.eeoc.gov/eeoc/statistics/reports/american_experiences/

U.S. Federal Bureau of Investigation. (2016). *Crime in the United States*. Washington, DC: U.S. Government Printing Office. Retrieved January 5, 2018, from https://ucr.fbi.gov/crime-in-the-u.s/2016/crime-in-the-u.s.-2016/topic-pages/tables/table-21

Unnever, J. D. (this volume). Assessing the racial invariance thesis. In J. D. Unnever, S. L. Gabbidon, & C. Chouhy (Eds.), *Building a Black criminology: Race, theory, and crime* (*Advance in criminological theory*, Vol. 24, pp. 77–100). New York, NY: Routledge.

Unnever, J. D., & Owusu-Bempah, A. (this volume). A Black criminology matters. In J. D. Unnever, S. L. Gabbidon, & C. Chouhy (Eds.), *Building a Black criminology: Race, theory, and crime* (*Advance in criminological theory*, Vol. 24, pp. 3–28). New York, NY: Routledge.

Weisburd, D., Wheeler, S., Waring, E., & Bode, N. (1991). *Crimes of the middle classes: White-collar offenders in the federal courts*. New Haven, CT: Yale University Press.

Welch, K. (2007). Black criminal stereotypes and racial profiling. *Journal of Contemporary Criminal Justice*, *23*(3), 276–288.

Wheeler, S., Weisburd, D., Waring, E., & Bode, N. (1988). White collar crime and criminals. *American Criminal Law Review*, *25*, 331–357.

Wilson, W. J. (1987). *The truly disadvantaged*. Chicago, IL: University of Chicago Press.

Wilson, W. J., & Katz, H. (2018). Reassessing "Toward a theory of race, crime and urban inequality": Enduring and new challenges in 21st century America. *Du Bois Review: Social Science Research on Race*, *15*(1), 13–34.

Yeager, P. C., & Reed, G. E. (1998). Of corporate persons and straw men: A reply to Herbert, Green and Larragoite. *Criminology*, *36*(4), 885–897.

Part III

Social Control

11

Racial Threat and Social Control: A Review and Conceptual Framework for Advancing Racial Threat Theory

Ben Feldmeyer and Joshua C. Cochran

Research has consistently shown that the more invasive, intensive, and punitive emphases of the criminal justice system have most often fallen on men and women of color, while Whites and those with greater social, financial, and political capital tend to receive more favorable treatment. As such, it is not surprising that scholars have called for development of a Black Criminology (Russell, 1992; Unnever & Gabbidon, 2011) and described elements of the U.S. criminal justice system as a 21st-century racial caste system, a "New Jim Crow," and a system of "malign neglect" toward minorities (Alexander, 2010; Cole, 1999; Tonry, 1995).

Scholars have offered a variety of explanations for such racial inequalities (Mears, Cochran, & Lindsey, 2016). Yet few of these arguments have been as provocative or received as much empirical attention as Blalock's (1967) "racial threat" theory (and related group threat positions; see Blumer, 1958; Bobo & Hutchings, 1996; Liska, 1992).[1] According to racial threat positions, inequalities in the criminal justice system are neither accidental nor unintentional. Instead, the criminal justice system is seen as a tool used by Whites and those in power to maintain their positions of dominance and control minority populations that pose potential threats. Thus, as minority groups increase in size and begin to vie for economic and political power, Whites may

283

be increasingly likely to apply more imposing social controls to maintain the status quo. In other words, racial threat theory contends that the White majority is in the driver's seat of the U.S. government, law, economy, and criminal justice system and uses these systems to avoid having to "give up the keys," so to speak, to other groups.

As we review in the following sections, scholars have produced close to 100 empirical analyses testing racial threat effects across a wide range of criminal justice outcomes. Using racial composition as a proxy for racial threat (e.g., percentage Black), research suggests that larger minority populations are linked to increases in size of police force, police expenditures, fear of crime, public support for punitiveness, offender voting restrictions, and racial disparities in arrests, convictions, incarceration, sentence length, and death penalty decisions (e.g., see Behrens, Uggen, & Manza, 2003; Chiricos, McEntire, & Gertz, 2001; Dollar, 2014; Feldmeyer & Ulmer, 2011; Jacobs & Carmichael, 2004; King & Wheelock, 2007; Ousey & Lee, 2008). In sum, there is no shortage of research illustrating that social control of minorities is amplified in places with large or growing Black (and sometimes Latino and immigrant) populations.

However, racial threat theory and our understanding of the precise interworking of population composition, threat, and social control is far from settled. The empirical evidence on racial threat theory has, in fact, been mixed. In addition, there are also considerable theoretical ambiguities about racial threat that have yet to be resolved. This "theoretical fog," as we refer to it, is one caused by inconsistencies in how threat is operationalized and tested and, by extension, ambiguity about how, when, where, and to whom racial threat is applied. For example, should racial threat be measured as a single overarching form of threat (e.g., percentage Black) or one that has different dimensions (e.g., political, economic, cultural, and criminal threats)? Does racial threat operate at a state, county, or neighborhood level, or perhaps at an even more local level (e.g., based on racial composition of defendants in a courtroom)? In addition, do racial threat effects emerge across all types of social controls, or are they more likely to manifest in some settings, conditions, and arms of the criminal justice system than others?

In light of the questions surrounding racial threat, our goal in this chapter is twofold. First, we provide an overview of the state of racial threat theory and literature as it relates to criminology and criminal justice research. Second, using this synthesis and "state of the theory" as a backdrop, we identify key gaps in research and, accordingly, develop a conceptual framework for systematically advancing future research in ways that may begin to "lift the fog" that has encompassed empirical scholarship on racial threat.

Racial Threat Theory

Fifty years ago, Huber M. Blalock (1967) introduced racial threat theory with the publication of his seminal book, *Toward a Theory of Minority-Group Relations*. As Blalock explains, there had been no shortage of social science research on discrimination, race, and power structures. However, prior work had largely been descriptive, documenting the existence of racial discrimination across a variety of institutions and social settings (e.g., examinations of "the Negro" in the church, labor, medicine, business, etc.) but offering few systematic frameworks that could account for variation in discrimination. As he puts it, research on discrimination had highlighted a "bewildering number of facts and an absence of explicit theoretical generalizations or even tentative propositions" (Blalock, 1967, p. 35). Thus, Blalock set out to fill this gap in research by (1) describing the macro-level patterns of discrimination toward minorities found in the United States and (2) developing a testable theoretical framework that could account for these patterns of racial discrimination and for race relations more broadly.

Blalock's theory of minority-group relations offers dozens of hypotheses on the patterns and sources of discrimination, but criminologists and social scientists have largely reduced his theory to one core idea: *As the percentage minority in the population increases, they will be viewed as a greater threat to the White majority and will be subject to increased discrimination and social control*. This single "racial threat" hypothesis, for which he is largely remembered, accounts for only a small share of Blalock's (1967) seminal book. Blalock provides 97 specific theoretical propositions outlining the conditions shaping group discrimination. Less than a quarter of these propositions have anything to do with minority percentage, and it is not until the final substantive chapter of the book (Chapter 5) that he explicitly argues that minority percentage might drive prejudice and group discrimination. In fact, his 78th hypothesis is the first point at which Blalock introduces the concept of "minority percentage" and discrimination.

At that point, Blalock (1967, p. 143) presents what he calls "one of the most frequent 'common sense' generalizations made in the field of minority-group relations"—specifically, that discrimination increases with the relative size of minority groups. However, he then illustrates that this "commonsense" hypothesis is much more nuanced and complex than it would seem on the surface. He explains that discrimination is generally low when a minority group is small. In small numbers, they pose little threat to the majority and do not garner serious attention or concern. As the minority percentage increases, discrimination toward a group grows. Furthermore, he argues that it grows in a curvilinear pattern and that the direction of the curve depends upon the type of threat posed by the growing minority. Specifically, he outlines two types of threat that increase in different ways with growth in the minority population: (1) economic competition and (2) power threat.

Blalock's (1967, p. 147) *economic competition* position suggests that "economic discrimination" toward minority groups increases as their share of the population grows but that the slope of this effect tapers off at higher levels of percent minority (an inverted U shape). When their numbers are small, he suggests that minority groups do not truly compete for economic resources with the majority in any way that would generate threat or a notable response. In contrast, he argues that competition is at its highest when groups are relatively equal in size and are equally competitive for jobs and economic opportunities. Yet Blalock also argues that there is a threshold effect in which further increases in minority composition carry less additional weight for economic threat. For example, he suggests that an increase in percentage Black from 10% to 20% generates greater competition, threat, and discrimination than an increase from 50% to 60% Black, at which point economic discrimination may be near its peak.

Blalock's second position on *power threat* also suggests a curvilinear relationship between minority percentage and discrimination, but in cases of power threat, discrimination increases exponentially as the minority share rises (a curve upward with increasing slope). Why the different "threat curve" for power threat compared to economic competition? Blalock (1967, p. 154) argues that it reflects an effort to maintain the same balance of power or "power equilibrium" between the majority and minority groups. When minority populations are near zero, the majority holds nearly all of the political advantage and influence, and little discrimination is required to maintain the balance of power. Blalock (1967, p. 160) argues that in such instances, Whites may simply rely on "gentleman's agreements" and "gate-keepers of discrimination" (e.g., employers, realtors, bankers) to control a minority group through uncoordinated individual acts of discrimination. However, as a minority group grows, it takes increasing levels of mobilization, resources, and discrimination for the majority to maintain the same degree of control and power over them. In other words, those in power will find it increasingly difficult and requiring exponentially greater resources to maintain the power gap they enjoyed when the minority consisted of only a handful of people. According to Blalock (1967), it is at this point that Whites may begin coordinated group efforts of discrimination, such as voter restriction or Jim Crow laws on segregation.

It is easy to see why these discussions of minority percentage and discrimination became the centerpiece of Blalock's (1967) work and have attracted so much scholarly attention over the last 50 years. His points on minority population composition and threat are intuitive and filled with illustrative examples. They also lend themselves to measurement and testing by focusing on minority percentage measures that are available in U.S. census data. At the same time, however, Blalock offers few predictions about the specific methods and forms of control that the White majority might use. More importantly for criminology, Blalock says almost nothing about the criminal justice system or formal social controls (including the police, courts, and laws) and how they might be used in response to growing minority populations. How then did racial threat theory become such a centerpiece in criminological research?

Linking Racial Threat to Social Control

Blalock receives and deserves much credit, but the racial threat perspective developed slowly and organically through the work of numerous scholars. Notably, Herbert Blumer (1958) wrote on the subject nearly a decade before publication of Blalock's (1967) seminal book. Blumer suggests that racial prejudice is a macro-level group position rather than simply the sum of individual attitudes. Blumer claims that racial prejudice and discrimination are collective processes shaped by larger group relations and social positions. Specifically, he describes four dominant group "feelings" (Blumer, 1958, p. 4), which include

(1) a feeling of superiority, (2) a feeling that the subordinate race is intrinsically different and alien, (3) a feeling of proprietary claim to certain areas of privilege and advantage, and (4) a fear and suspicion that the subordinate race harbors designs on the prerogatives of the dominant race (see also Bobo & Hutchings, 1996).

In short, Blumer suggests that group position, competition, and the potential threat posed by other racial groups is the engine behind racial prejudice among the majority, an idea which closely parallels Blalock's hypothesis and helped form the foundation of racial threat theory as it is known in the contemporary literature.

Many other hands also had a role in refining and extending the concept of racial threat and showing how it applies to criminological research. Richard Quinney (1977, p. 107) helped draw connections between racial threat theory and criminology by arguing that the criminal justice system is a "euphemism for controlling the class struggle and administering legal repression" of groups that pose a threat to those in positions of privilege. Austin Turk (1969) and Robert Blauner (1972) offered substantial advances to racial threat positions by explicitly linking them to formal mechanisms of social control within the criminal justice system. They argue that law formation and law enforcement are two of the primary tools used to control culturally dissimilar minority groups that pose a threat to the existing social order. Finally, Allen Liska and colleagues' (1992; Liska, Lawrence, & Benson, 1981; Liska, Chamlin, & Reed, 1985) "social threat and social control" perspective extended these arguments and provided even closer links between the idea of group threat and the social controls commonly studied in criminology. Liska (1992) argues that in addition to posing a social and political threat, minority groups are often viewed as criminal threats that elicit more severe applications of law and law enforcement.

Taken together, these positions built on the core principles first posed by Blalock (1967) and Blumer (1958) to collectively form racial threat theory as it is known throughout contemporary criminology, suggesting that (1) larger shares of minorities generate perceptions of threat among the majority and (2) the criminal justice system offers some of the most suitable tools available to the majority for exerting control over "threatening" minority groups.

Empirical Tests of Racial Threat Theory

In this section, we review the empirical literature examining racial threat's impact on social controls within the criminal justice system. As we describe below, early tests of racial threat positions, appearing in the 1970s and 1980s, focused first on the relationships between racial context and law enforcement (size of police force, police expenditures, arrests). This literature then quickly expanded to focus on a variety of

criminal justice sanctions and responses, including sentencing decisions, public support for punitiveness, fear of crime, voting rights of
convicted offenders, and application of the death penalty, among others.
For the purposes of our review, this literature can be organized into four
main areas of study: (1) *law enforcement*, (2) *sentencing and courts*, (3)
perceptions of threat, and (4) *laws and policies*. Our goal here is not to
provide an exhaustive examination of every study that has tested racial
threat or included percentage Black as a predictor of criminal justice
sanctions. Such a review would fill a book rather than a single chapter.
Instead, our goal is to provide a conceptual summary of the literature—
to "take stock" of racial threat theory as it has been tested in criminology
and criminal justice.

Racial Threat and Law Enforcement

In the decades immediately following Blalock (1967) and Blumer's
(1958) original work, treatments of racial threat were largely theoretical with few empirical tests. However, this changed rapidly in the late
1970s and 1980s, when scholars like Jackson and Carroll (1981), Liska
and Chamlin (1984; also see Chamlin, 1989; Liska, 1987, 1992; Liska
et al., 1981, 1985), Huff and Stahura (1980), Jacobs (1979), and Greenberg, Kessler, and Loftin (1985) produced a flood of empirical studies
examining the effects of racial context on policing.

The analyses in this line of research have focused on the effects of
racial composition on (1) *police force size and expenditures* and (2) *use
of arrests*. Drawing from the early theoretical arguments provided by
Blalock (1967), Blumer (1958), and Turk (1969; see also Blauner, 1972;
Quinney, 1977), the expectation was that police force size, expenditures,
and use of arrests were not simply a response to the level of crime in an
area. Rather, they may also be a response to the potential threat posed by
large or growing minority groups.

Law Enforcement Size and Expenditures.   Research examining racial
threat effects on police force size and expenditures offers (mostly) *consistent support for racial threat theory*. Early works indicate that the
percentage Black or the percentage non-White population is associated
with more law enforcement officers per capita and greater police spending, net of crime rates and social-demographic characteristics of places
(Chamlin, 1989; Huff & Stahura, 1980; Jackson, 1986; Jackson & Carroll, 1981; Jacobs, 1979; Liska et al., 1981). Likewise, more recent

analyses reveal similar associations (Brandl, Chamlin, & Frank, 1995; D'Alessio, Eitle, & Stolzenberg, 2005; Jacobs & Helms, 1997, 1999; Kent & Jacobs, 2004; Stults & Baumer, 2007).

There are, though, important complexities. For example, the effects of racial threat are generally stronger in Southern areas (Greenberg et al., 1985; Liska et al., 1981; but see Jackson & Carroll, 1981) and when using time-lagged measures rather than static measures of percentage minority (Chamlin, 1989; Greenberg et al., 1985; Liska et al., 1981). Research also suggests that racial segregation conditions threat effects (Chamlin, 1989; Chamlin & Liska, 1992; Kent & Jacobs, 2005; Liska et al., 1981; Stults & Baumer, 2007; see also Kent & Carmichael, 2014). However, results conflict as to whether more or less segregation amplifies effects of racial threat.

Use of Arrests.   The literature centered on police use of arrests offers *relatively little support for racial threat arguments*, especially compared with the literature on police force size. An early analysis by Liska et al. (1985) found that percentage non-White population leads to greater certainty of arrests for Index offenses. Since then, analyses of arrests have produced a mix of null effects or findings that contradict racial threat arguments. Multiple studies find that the size of the minority population is actually linked to lower (rather than higher) arrest rates for non-White and Black populations (Liska & Chamlin, 1984; Parker, Stults, & Rice, 2005; Stolzenberg, D'Alessio, & Eitle, 2004; Stucky, 2012). For example, research by Eitle, D'Alessio, & Stolzenberg (2002) indicates that levels of Black-on-White crime (which they use as a proxy for minority "criminal threat") are linked to increased Black–White arrest ratios, but they find no effects of Black political or economic threat on Black arrests (see also Ousey & Lee, 2008). Despite limited exceptions (see Kane, Gustafson, & Bruell, 2013; Liska et al., 1985), research provides little consistent evidence that racial composition or racial threat shape arrest patterns across U.S. locales.[2]

Racial Threat and Sentencing

Examinations of racial threat in sentencing are relatively young compared to the law enforcement studies described above. What is now a burgeoning body of racial threat and sentencing studies began largely after year 2000. Since then, court sanctioning practices have arguably become the most commonly studied area in the racial threat literature.

The sentencing literature offers a *complicated and mixed body of evidence for racial threat positions*. Studies that support the theory show that the percentage of Blacks in the population is linked to a variety of disadvantageous and more punitive court outcomes. These include disproportionate rates of imprisonment for racial and ethnic minorities (Bridges & Crutchfield, 1988; Jacobs & Carmichael, 2001), increased likelihood of incarceration for minorities (Myers & Talarico, 1987; Weidner, Frase, & Schultz, 2005), larger racial and ethnic disparities in prison sentence lengths (Ulmer & Johnson, 2004), and increased likelihoods of disadvantageous departures from state sentencing guidelines for minorities (Johnson, 2005). Studies also suggest that judges are less likely to withhold adjudication for Black defendants as Black population size and disadvantage increase (Bontrager, Bales, & Chiricos, 2005). Research examining federal sentencing also indicates judges are less likely to give minority defendants downward (lenient) sentencing departures in places with large Black and Latino populations (Johnson, Ulmer, & Kramer, 2008) and tend to give noncitizens harsher sentences in districts with growing noncitizen populations (Light, Massoglia, & King, 2014).

However, the literature identifies important nuances and inconsistencies among these findings. For example, Ulmer and Johnson (2004) find that county-level Black and Latino populations are positively related to racial disparities in state court sentence lengths but not to racial/ethnic differences in incarceration decisions. Other studies raise questions about the extent to which racial threat effects are diffuse or targeted—that is, whether a large or growing minority population increases punitiveness for all defendants (diffuse effects) or only for minority defendants (targeted effects; see Zane, 2017). Ulmer and Bradley (2006) find that a larger Black population increases the "trial penalty" generally, for all defendants, not just those who are Black. In contrast, Caravelis, Chiricos, and Bales (2011, 2013) report that dynamic measures of threat (e.g., increases in percentage Black) contribute to increased application of "habitual" offender designations for minority but not White defendants.

Studies also underscore the need to differentiate between racial and ethnic threat. Empirical analyses by Feldmeyer and Ulmer (2011) and Feldmeyer, Warren, Siennick, and Neptune (2015), respectively, find evidence of racial threat effects on federal and state court (Florida) sentencing for Black defendants. However, in both studies, larger shares of Latino and immigrant populations actually contribute to more lenient sentencing outcomes for both Latino and Black defendants. Wang and

Mears (2010a, 2010b) report similar findings, noting that racial threat (measured as percent Black and change in percent Black) increases the risk of incarceration for Black defendants in state courts but that Latino population composition has little impact on Latino incarceration (see also Wang & Mears, 2015).

In addition, other studies report that the percentage of minority residents in the population has no effect on racial differences in state sentencing (Britt, 2000; Weidner & Frase, 2003), federal drugs sentencing (Kautt, 2002), or juvenile court outcomes (Davis & Sorensen, 2013; Leiber, Peck, & Rodriguez, 2016; Thomas, Moak, & Walker, 2013; Zane, 2017). Taken together, sentencing research has shown some support for racial threat positions but has also offered many analyses that provide either mixed or contradictory findings to group threat hypotheses.

Perceptions of Racial Threat

Public opinion research has resulted in a more consistent set of findings than the policing and sentencing literatures, offering *strong and consistent support for racial threat theory*. Broader sociological research shows that large or growing minority populations lead to increased levels of prejudice and perceptions of threat toward minority groups (e.g., see Giles & Evans, 1985, 1986; Pettigrew, 1959; Quillian, 1995, 1996; Taylor, 1998).[3] Within criminology specifically, studies of perceptions and threat have focused on (1) fear of crime associated with minorities and perceptions of minority "criminal threat" and (2) support for punitiveness. Although this criminological body of scholarship is in its nascent stages, findings generally align with the broader sociological research described above.

Fear of Crime and Minority Criminal Threat.   Studies consistently show that size and growth of the Black population (either real or perceived) and greater interracial contact are linked to increased fear of crime and perceptions of minority criminality (Chiricos et al., 1997, 2001; Covington & Taylor, 1991; Liska, Lawrence, & Sanchirico, 1982; Mears & Stewart, 2010; Mears, Mancini, & Stewart, 2009; Mears, Pickett, Golden, Chiricos, & Gertz, 2013; Moeller, 1989; Pickett, Chiricos, Golden, & Gertz, 2012; Quillian & Pager, 2001; Skogan, 1995; Taylor & Covington, 1993). Contact with minorities more generally is linked to increases in Whites' perceptions of criminality associated with all race/ethnic groups, and contact specifically with Latinos may adversely affect Whites' perceptions of Latinos (Chiricos et al., 2001; Eitle & Taylor, 2008; Mears et al., 2013; Wang, 2012; see, however, Drakulich, 2009).

Here, again, contextual characteristics matter. There are some indications that these effects may be limited to places with particularly large minority populations (see Chiricos et al., 2001; Eitle & Taylor, 2008). But in sum, findings largely indicate that racial composition serves as "a kind of shorthand equation between blackness and crime" (or perhaps between Latinos, immigrants, and crime) that generates increased perceptions of victimization risk, fear, and stereotypes of minority criminal threat among White populations (Chiricos et al., 2001, p. 335).

Support for Punitiveness.   Researchers have sought to disentangle how population composition and threat might link to more, or tougher, social controls by examining linkages between minority population size and citizen support for punitiveness, both generally and targeted toward minorities. Like above, these studies generally provide *strong and consistent support for racial threat theory* by finding that the public supports more punitive criminal justice sanctions in places with relatively large or growing minority populations, net of crime rates and other social-ecological conditions. For example, research by King and Wheelock (2007) finds that growth in Black populations is linked to increased public support for more punitive criminal justice sanctions. These views are more pronounced among Whites and occur in response to beliefs that African Americans pose an economic threat. Ousey and Unnever (2012, p. 589) report similar findings in an analysis of 27 European countries. They find that greater prevalence of minority ethnic groups (measured as "ethnic fractionization") is linked to increased "out-group animus," which in turn contributes to public support for more severe criminal justice sanctions (see also studies on capital punishment by Baumer, Messner, & Rosenfeld, 2003; Phillips, 1986).

There is also growing evidence that threat effects on public support for punitiveness extend to Latinos and immigrants and may reflect emerging forms of "ethnic/immigrant threat." For example, research indicates that measures of Latino threat are associated with increased public support for punitive crime control policies (Stewart, Martinez, Baumer, & Gertz, 2015; Welch, Payne, Chiricos, & Gertz, 2011) and with support for judges' use of offender ethnicity in sentencing (Johnson, Stewart, Pickett, & Gertz, 2011). Research also shows that exposure to immigrant populations and beliefs that immigrants pose cultural and economic threats are associated with increased support for border controls (Chiricos, Stupi, Stults, & Gertz, 2014).

Punitive Laws and Policies

There is a relatively smaller body of research examining the relationships between racial/ethnic composition and more punitive criminal justice policies. Studies that do exist have focused primarily on (1) use of the death penalty and (2) felon disenfranchisement laws.

In regards to the death penalty, research offers somewhat *mixed findings concerning racial threat effects on use of capital punishment.* Baumer and colleagues (2003) find that minority population size is positively associated with greater public support for the death penalty. However, estimates of racial threat effects on actual implementation of death sentences are less conclusive. Early work by Phillips (1986) shows that, in direct opposition to racial threat arguments, racial disparities in executions are at their smallest in counties with the largest shares of Black residents. A series of more recent empirical analyses by Jacobs, Carmichael, and colleagues (2002, 2004, 2005) offer contrary findings. Specifically, Jacobs and Carmichael (2002, 2004) find that states with relatively large African American populations (above the median) are more likely to both adopt and use the death penalty at least once. This effect also appears to be more pronounced in states with greater histories of lynching, suggesting that state violence may have replaced lynching as a form of lethal control over Black populations (Jacobs, Carmichael, & Kent, 2005). However, they also find that racial composition does not predict the number of death sentences above 1, and Latino composition has no significant effects on death penalty adoption or use in their analyses.

Research also shows that *racial composition has strong effects on the application of felon disenfranchisement laws.* This body of research is small and is limited to several pioneering studies conducted by Behrens, Uggen, and Manza (2003; Manza & Uggen, 2006; Uggen & Manza, 2002). As they note, laws concerning voting rights (and other restrictions) for felony offenders have varied widely over time and across state lines, ranging from nearly no restriction of voting rights to permanent loss of voting privileges resulting from a felony conviction. On the surface, these restrictions are described as racially neutral "tough on crime" measures, aimed at increasing punishment for offenders who choose to commit serious crimes. However, Behrens et al. (2003) and

Manza and Uggen (2006) illustrate that these laws are not distributed in racially neutral ways. In line with racial threat positions, they show that the racial composition of state populations, and especially state prison populations, shapes how states handle felon disenfranchisement. States with larger shares of minorities in prison are more likely to pass voting restriction laws, and less likely to repeal them, over time. Moreover, they illustrate that these policies have had profound consequences, perhaps changing the outcomes of several close U.S. senate and presidential elections (Uggen & Manza, 2002).

New Directions for Advancing Racial Threat
Theory and Research

Taken together, attention to racial threat and its impacts on social control has undergone interesting growth and exploration. Yet the review above also highlights that a diverse range of inconsistencies and looming questions remain in the literature. Indeed, 50 years after publication of Blalock (1967) and Blumer's (1958) original theories, racial threat theory has seen far less conceptual evolution than that experienced by many other criminological theories during this same time period. Consider, for example, social disorganization theory. It underwent decades of revisions as scholars debated the role of culture, the systemic model of social disorganization, and the importance of collective efficacy (see Cullen, Wilcox, Sampson, & Dooley, 2015; Wilcox, Cullen, & Feldmeyer, 2018). By contrast, racial threat research continues to use the same measures of racial and ethnic context (e.g., percentage Black) first proposed by Blalock (1967) as proxy measures of threat and has seen few systematic efforts to advance how threat is conceptualized, measured, or tested.

Why is this the case? Although racial threat has received substantial empirical attention (we identified nearly 100 criminology-related studies), this literature has seen many inconsistencies in how it examines threat. These inconsistencies, combined with the sheer size of this literature, have made it unwieldy for gaining a comprehensive picture of where racial threat research stands and how it should move forward. There is no clear consensus, for example, about the most appropriate way to operationalize perceptions of threat (e.g., measures of percentage minority versus measures of perceptions of threat) or the unit of analysis at which it operates (neighborhood, city, county, or state). Few studies have examined different forms of racial threat (economic, political, and criminal threats) or the conditions that might moderate threat effects on social control. We have only a limited understanding of the mechanisms through which racial context might work to influence individuals' perceptions of threat. And there is, by extension, no clear direction for how the literature might proceed to sort out such questions.

Taken together, we argue that the current situation in the threat literature has led to what can best be described as a "theoretical fog" surrounding racial threat research. The "fog" is one that has created challenges for understanding key gaps in the empirical racial threat literature and identifying new and better ways to systematically test racial threat's effects. Our goal, then, in the remaining pages is to identify areas of racial threat research that remain unclear and offer suggestions for advancing this literature in concrete ways that may begin to lift this fog.

Specifically, we offer a series of targeted recommendations to help sharpen racial threat theory both conceptually and methodologically. We have organized these recommendations under three key dimensions that highlight critical debates and points of ambiguity requiring researchers' attention to move the literature forward—namely, (1) measuring threat, (2) identifying the causes and types of threat, and (3) understanding causal mechanisms linking threat to social control. These dimensions are interlinked, and the set of recommendations under each overlap and inform one another. But we also view these as distinct dimensions, each of which is deserving of dedicated research attention.

Dimension 1: Measuring Threat

Dating back to Blalock's (1967) original work, research assessing the effects of racial threat has relied on measures of racial composition (percentage Black) within a county, city, or state as a proxy for "threat." This practice remains the standard for testing racial threat. To illustrate, we compiled a list of racial threat studies (or related ethnic or social threat) published over the past 10 years in four leading criminology journals (*Criminology, Journal of Research in Crime and Delinquency, Justice Quarterly*, and *Journal of Quantitative Criminology*). A list of these studies along with a description of their measurement of threat appears in Table 11.1. The table reveals that 23 of the 33 studies (about 70%) operationalized threat using *indirect measures* of minority population composition, such as percentage Black or growth in Black or Latino populations. Only 8 studies (about 24%) *directly* measured perceptions of "threat."

Table 11.1

Operationalization of Threat in Select Criminology Journals, 2008–2017

Article	Outcome of interest	Racial/ethnic composition as threat?	Unit of Analysis (Threat)
Ousey & Lee, 2008	Arrest rates	No	Census tract
Johnson et al., 2008	Downward sentencing departures	Yes	Federal district
Eitle & Monahan, 2009	Arrest rates	Yes	City
Johnson & Kuhns, 2009	Support for police use of force	No	Individual
Keen & Jacobs, 2009	Ratio of African American to White prison admissions	Yes	State
Stewart et al., 2009	Perceived racial discrimination by police	Yes	Neighborhood
Lin, Grattet, & Petersilia, 2010	Parole revocation decision	Yes	County
Unnever & Cullen, 2010	Support for capital punishment	No	Individual
Payne & Welch, 2010	Disciplinary response	Yes	School
Wang & Mears, 2010[a]	Incarceration decision	Yes	County
Wang & Mears, 2010[b]	Sentencing decision	Yes	County
Feldmeyer & Ulmer, 2011	Sentence length	Yes	District
Johnson et al., 2011	Support for use of ethnicity in punishment	Yes	Individual, county
Lum, 2011	Police pathway decisions	Yes	Census block group
Smith & Sturgis, 2011	Fear of crime	No	Neighborhood
Stemen & Rengifo, 2011	Use of structured sentencing, incarceration rates	Yes	State

(*Continued*)

Table 11.1 (Continued)

Article	Outcome of interest	Racial/ethnic composition as threat?	Unit of Analysis (Threat)
Unnever, Gabbidon, & Higgins, 2011	Perception of criminal injustice	No	Individual
Heimer, Johnson, Lang, Rengifo, & Stemen, 2012	Imprisonment rates	Yes	State
Ousey & Unnever, 2012	Punitive attitudes toward criminals	No	Country, individual
Unnever & Cullen, 2012	Support for the death penalty	No	Individual
Stucky, 2012	Violent crime arrest rate	Yes	City
Wang, 2012	Perceived criminal threat of undocumented immigrants	Yes	Zip code, individual
Caravelis et al., 2013	Career offender designation	Yes	County
Kane et al., 2013	Misdemeanor arrests	Yes	Census tract
Mears et al., 2013	Perceived Black criminality & victimization likelihood	No	Individual
Ramirez, 2013	Punitive sentiment	Yes	Individual, national, school
Chen, 2014	Administration of Three Strikes Law	Yes	County
Campbell, Vogel, & Williams, 2015	Incarceration rate	Yes	State
Feldmeyer et al., 2015	Court sentencing decisions	Yes	County
Pickett, 2016	Support for expanded police powers	No	Individual
Stupi, Chiricos, & Gertz, 2016	Border control and internal control policy support	No	Individual

Article	Outcome of interest	Racial/ethnic composition as threat?	Unit of Analysis (Threat)
Hughes, Warren, Stewart, Tomaskovic-Devey, & Mears, 2017	Out-of-school suspensions	Yes	School
Levchak, 2017	Police stop outcomes	Yes	Precinct

Note: Results from a systematic literature review of all studies published in the following journals between 2008 and 2017: Criminology, Journal of Research in Crime and Delinquency, Justice Quarterly, and Journal of Quantitative Criminology.

Measuring threat using racial context may be problematic for at least two reasons. First, such indirect measures simply may not be measuring threat at all. Blalock (1967, p. 144) suggested, for example, that census measures of racial composition are blunt instruments and are "often inadequate for obtaining reasonably direct measures of discriminatory behavior" or threat. As he further acknowledged, threat has to be "taken as an unmeasured intervening variable" when using measures of racial composition, which is less than ideal (Blalock, 1967, p. 144).

Second, there is no consensus about the proper unit of analysis for assessing racial composition and racial threat effects on social controls. Empirical studies cover the gamut of possibilities, including neighborhoods, counties, states, and national examinations. Which is most appropriate? Ideally, the literature would provide guidance on both the level at which racial composition and/or threat might operate and whether this level varies for different actors or components of social control. Based on these issues, we offer two recommendations.

Recommendation 1.1. Systematically Evaluate Internal Validity, or the Degree to Which Minority Population Composition Measures Perceptions of "threat". There is, as we illustrated above, a sizable literature suggesting that large or growing minority populations generate greater prejudices, support for punitiveness, and fear of crime (see King & Wheelock, 2007; Mears et al., 2013; Taylor, 1998). However, what is less clear is whether this is specifically because larger minority groups generate a sense of "threat" among the White majority or if some other phenomenon explains the association. Furthermore, do measures of racial/ethnic composition generate threat, punitiveness, and discrimination in the same way for different people? Public perception and the White population's sense of minority threat may be shaped by the size of the minority population, but are criminal justice actors, such as judges and police officers, equally swayed by the presence of more minorities? In order to address this, research is needed that *directly measures threat* and identifies whether it *mediates* the relationships between racial composition and social controls.

We highlight three noteworthy studies that have begun this work. For example, Stults and Baumer (2007) offer a useful example of how future studies might address this issue. The authors use geocoded General Social Survey (GSS) data to examine the extent to which self-reported measures of threat (economic and political) explain the effect of percentage Black on police force size. The study finds that direct, self-report measures of threat explain roughly one-third of the association between percentage Black and police force size. Similarly, research by Ousey and Unnever (2012) finds that greater racial/ethnic diversity in European nations contributes to greater perceptions of threat and intolerance toward minorities, which, in turn, leads to more support for punitiveness. Last, research by Pickett et al. (2012) directly measures perceptions of minority criminal threat (racial typification of crime) and examines whether it mediates the relationship between racial composition of neighborhoods and fear of victimization.

These studies aside, extant research provides little insight into what is the core assumption in studies that utilize racial context to measure threat—that large or growing minority populations actually generate increased fear and threat, which in turn leads to more severe punishments for these groups. As Ousey and Unnever (2012, p. 566) note, "although we know that punitiveness often is more severe in places with larger ethnic minority populations, we have only a rudimentary grasp of *why* this is the case" (emphasis in original). This is particularly true for studies involving judges, police officers, and other criminal justice actors. If arrests or sentence lengths for minorities are worse in places with larger minority populations, is this because police officers and judges view them as a growing threat? Is it because the public feels threatened and exerts pressure on criminal justice actors? Or is it due to other unmeasured variables that are related to both minority composition and punitiveness?

Going forward, if studies that compare proxy measures of threat to actual, perceptual measures of threat continue to find strong associations, it would increase confidence in findings in the literature to date. If, however, an accumulation of assessments finds that the two do not track relatively closely to one another, it would raise questions about the degree to which "threat" is driving the links between racial composition and social control outcomes.

Recommendation 1.2. Assess the Influence of Unit of Analysis in Tests of Racial Threat.   Consideration of racial context as a measure of threat leads to a second, key pragmatic concern—determining the proper unit of analysis. Prior research has often made such determinations out of convenience. If, say, sentencing data are grouped within judicial districts or counties, studies will typically use racial compositional measures aggregated to the judicial district or county (e.g., Feldmeyer & Ulmer, 2011; Light et al., 2014; Wang & Mears, 2010a, 2010b). Likewise, analyses using citywide policing data have relied on city-level measures of percentage minority to measure threat (Liska & Chamlin, 1984; Liska et al., 1985; Ousey & Lee, 2008).

How, though, should scholars proceed? Does the racial composition of a state or region generate threat and punitiveness for minorities, or is racial threat driven by more local contexts? Unfortunately, the original theorists provide little guidance, and there is likely no singular solution. We suggest instead that scholars revisit theoretical hypotheses and subject those hypotheses to empirical scrutiny for each area of study (e.g., sentencing, policing, felon disenfranchisement). That is, scholars should construct specific theoretical arguments about how exactly variation in population composition should track with variation in individuals' and groups' perceptions of minority group threat. It seems unlikely that percentage minority generates threat in the same way across all units of analysis. Thus, it may be the case that some units of analysis are more appropriate for some questions. For example, state-level measures of threat may indeed impact state-level processes, such as support for or passage of a state law to disenfranchise felons (Behrens et al., 2003; Manza & Uggen, 2006). But do state minority populations track well with the types of threat perceptions that might affect a judge's decision making in a rural court? Perhaps, but it seems less likely. Instead, a judge's perceptions that minorities are dangerous or threatening may be strongly affected by the population composition of the defendants coming in and out of the courtroom—i.e., a more local level—than by the larger statewide racial context (e.g., Steffensmeier, Ulmer, & Kramer, 1998).

As racial threat research moves forward, it will be important for scholars to consider how different units of analysis may impact racial threat effects and whether local or regional racial contexts are likely to shape different forms of social control.

Dimension 2: Identifying the Causes and Types of Threat

Dimension 2 is inextricably related to dimension 1 but constitutes a distinct set of research challenges (and, as it goes, recommendations). Inspection of the racial threat literature reveals that scholars' primary focus has been on identifying the presence of threat effects (e.g., identifying percentage Black effects on social controls) with less attention to differentiating between the sources or types of threat. Perhaps, then, we have been too hasty. There is a dearth of empirical research that has worked to understand the process or development of threat and the different types of threat that may exist.

Recommendation 2.1. Systematically Examine Different Types of Racial Threat Effects.   Blalock (1967) originally suggested that racial threat came in (at least) two different forms—economic and political. Since then, scholars have also argued that criminal threat (and cultural threats) associated with minority groups may influence the application of social controls (Eitle, D'Alessio, & Stolzenberg, 2002; Johnson et al., 2011; Liska, 1992). However, studies do not typically differentiate between these or other sources/types of threat.

This is concerning for three reasons. First, criminal justice actors and the public may be impacted by one but not other forms of threat. Criminal threat (but not political threat) associated with a racial/ethnic group might shape how a judge responds to minorities in the courtroom or how a police officer reacts in traffic stops. Likewise, political threats might uniquely shape the actions of legislators and public perceptions, even if economic threats do not. Second, the standard racial composition measures used in prior research may capture one or two forms of racial threat but are not likely to capture all forms of threat simultaneously. As a result, when we observe relationships between, say, percentage Black and increased court punitiveness, it is unclear whether they are being driven by political, economic, criminal, cultural, or other threats. Third,

Blalock (1967) argued that different threats operated in different ways, and even hypothesized differences in the functional form of each type of threat. However, such possibilities have, with few exceptions (see below), been largely ignored.

Eitle et al. (2002) offer one of the few studies to separately examine political, economic, and criminal forms of racial threat. They report that criminal threat (measured as interracial violence) is a strong predictor of Black arrest rates, but they find no significant effects for measures of Black political or economic threat. Similarly, Johnson et al. (2011) find that measures of criminal and economic threat, but not political threat, are linked to greater public support for judicial use of ethnicity in sentencing decisions. However, more work along the lines of these studies is needed to help identify the ways in which different types of threat matter, or not, for different forms of social control.

Recommendation 2.2. Systematically Examine the "Contact Hypothesis" and the Role of Experiences—Both Personal and Vicarious—on Perceptions of Threat.   Scholarship is needed that examines how personal experiences impact group threat. A large body of literature exists across academic fields focused on understanding the development of racial and ethnic biases (e.g., Bobo, 1999; Sears & Henry, 2003). More work along this line is needed that identifies the experiences that contribute to citizens' perceptions that minority groups are threatening or dangerous. For example, experiences with interracial victimization or vicarious experiences via family and friends may contribute to perceptions of criminal threat toward members of other race/ethnic groups. Similarly, personal experiences of joblessness or exposure to patterns of economic hardship could create more fertile environments for economic threat aimed at minority groups. Yet we currently know little about how such experiences impact racial threat.

Relatedly, racial threat research has given surprisingly little attention to the "contact hypothesis," which argues that interactions between the White majority and out-group members lead to greater racial tolerance and help to dispel adverse stereotypes held by Whites about minorities (e.g., Allport, 1954; Mears et al., 2013; Pettigrew & Tropp, 2006). Notably, this position is contradictory to the racial threat hypothesis, which suggests that increasing minority population size (which, in theory, should increase interracial contact) increases threat and conflict. Few studies have sought to resolve these competing claims (see, however, Semyonov, Raijman, Tov, & Schmidt, 2004). In fact, most racial threat studies provide only a cursory discussion of the contact hypothesis, if it is mentioned at all, and this typically occurs only when study results contradict racial threat claims (e.g., see Feldmeyer & Ulmer, 2011; Feldmeyer et al., 2015). Thus, efforts to more closely disentangle the experiences that contribute to racial threat should include renewed attention to understanding the role of intergroup contact.

Recommendation 2.3. Examine the Stability of Perceptions of Threat. The threat literature implicitly relies on the assumption that individuals' perceptions of threat are malleable. Allegedly, they change as minority populations grow. They change as immigrants enter the country. They may change when, say, people watch the news or as a result of direct experience with outgroup members. These and a host of related arguments are implied across studies of racial threat. However, research in sociology and psychology indicates that perceptions are sticky and somewhat stable over time (e.g., Henry & Sears, 2009; Miller & Sears, 1986). Which is true? Or, if both are true, under what circumstances can variables, like changing population composition, impact the perceptions of individuals and groups, and under what circumstances should we anticipate change in threat perceptions? Or is it that perceptions of threat change little, but they manifest differently under different circumstances?

Recommendation 2.4. Examine the Role of Media Consumption on Citizens' Perceptions of Threat. Among the experiences that may affect threat perceptions, the role of media and individuals' patterns of media consumption deserve special attention (Bjornstrom, Kaufman, Peterson, & Slater, 2010; Entman & Rojecki, 2000). With the advent of the Internet, media and news consumption has evolved in myriad ways. Media exposure may act as a primary contributor to individual's perceptions of threat, yet scholars have paid only limited attention to how the media shapes racial threat and how changing patterns in media consumption might work to diminish or exacerbate threat perceptions. A range of competing theoretical hypotheses might be developed and should be subjected to empirical scrutiny. For example, it is plausible that easier access to news and information online works to better dispel false and harmful stereotypes that might contribute to levels of minority threat. At the same time, sensational coverage of high-profile crimes and ample access to media that fits a given perspective—ideological echo chambers—may work to exacerbate or further entrench people's biases and perceptions.

Dimension 3: Understanding the Causal Mechanisms Linking Threat to Social Control

Our final critique of the literature and set of recommendations can be summarized as follows: The current literature has not offered explicit causal models explaining racial threat effects across different stages of the criminal justice system. That is, we currently know little about the precise theoretical mechanisms that can explain (1) *why* minority composition might increase threat and punitiveness for minorities across each type of social control, (2) *where* these effects are most likely to be seen within the criminal justice system (e.g., policing, courts, legislation), and (3) *who* is impacted by the effects of racial threat (increases in punitiveness for everyone or only for select minority groups).

Here we develop recommendations for research that seeks to more precisely assess how exactly racial threat and outgroup size lead to changes or disadvantages in the criminal justice system. A similar theme emerges across each recommendation. There is a need to develop explicit hypotheses about how threat works and to develop criteria to assess when those hypotheses are supported, or not.

Recommendation 3.1. Theorize and Test the Precise Causal Mechanisms Explaining Why Racial Threat Contributes to Each Social Control Outcome. The most common theoretical model used in prior research is the most ambiguous one—growing minority groups create a general sense of "threat" among the majority that results in greater social controls across a variety of decision points in the criminal justice system. However, this theorizing is nebulous, and scholars should work to provide more explicit theoretical propositions for each social control outcome.

How so? It should, we think, start with revisiting the fundamental theoretical linkages between threat and the actions of key decision makers. How do we anticipate that increasing minority population percentage would shape perceptions of group threat and, in turn, manifest in the everyday decisions of police administrators, judges, prosecutors, or lawmakers? Is it, for example, that judges are, like any other citizens, impacted by the growing minority population and inclined to perceive the minority groups as a threat that must be controlled with harsh sentences? Even then, and even in the face of evidence of racial disproportionalities in judicial decision making, how can researchers be sure that the cause stems from perceived threat and not other sources of implicit or explicit biases that judges may hold? Similarly, what types of racial contexts and circumstances would we expect to generate "threat" among police officers, and will these threats necessarily lead to greater enforcement among law enforcement officers? It is likely that the mechanisms and ways in which racial context shape threat and social controls are different for judges, police officers, lawmakers, and the general public. Thus, there is a need to develop theoretical frameworks that outline these mechanisms *as they apply specifically to different areas of study within criminology* (e.g., sentencing, policing, etc.).

Recommendation 3.2. Differentiate Where Racial Threat Effects Are Most Likely Across Different Stages of the Criminal Justice System. A trend in prior racial threat research is the implicit assumption that threat operates in some form across nearly all stages and decision points within the criminal justice system. This assumption, however, has not been explored systematically and is seemingly untenable. The criminal justice system includes many decision points, but when would we expect racial and ethnic threat (and not just an individual's race/ethnicity) to matter?

There are, for example, a range of decision points that are constrained in ways that might limit the ability of racial context and racial threat to impact decision making. Prior sentencing studies underscore the importance of differentiating between more and less serious offenses when examining disparities in sentencing outcomes. This is based on the simple logic that for the most egregious offenses, such as murder, there is less room for court actors' biases to create sentencing disparities (see Spohn, 2000; Ulmer, 2012).[4] There are also reasons to anticipate that certain criminal justice actors may be less likely to perceive heightened threats of minority groups. Recent research on disparities in the use of solitary confinement in prisons finds, for example, non–statistically significant impacts of race on prison officials' decisions to transfer inmates to disciplinary confinement as a result of in-prison infractions (e.g., Cochran, Toman, Mears, & Bales, 2017). Cochran and colleagues (2017) suggest one possibility is that prison officers may not perceive threat in the same way others, like judges or prosecutors, do due to the nature of working in a state prison—a setting that, in many states, is majority Black and where all inmates have felony criminal records.

Thus, there are some situations and decision points where far less room exists for contextual factors, like the percentage of Black residents, to have an impact on punishment. Other decisions within the criminal justice system are subject to far greater discretion (prosecutors' decisions, formation of laws) and may be much more vulnerable to the influence of racial context and racial threat. Studies that systematically evaluate differences in the capacity and strength of racial threat effects across such decision points would help illuminate the scope of racial threat and highlight the decision points in which it may have stronger effects on punishment.

Recommendation 3.3. Differentiate Between Diffuse Versus Targeted Impacts of Threat (i.e., Identify "Who" Is Impacted by Threat).   There is little consensus about whether threat operates in a way that is "diffuse," such that it increases punitive outcomes for *all individuals* in the criminal justice system, or in a way that is "targeted," such that it *only impacts specific groups* (e.g., minority suspects or defendants; see Zane, 2017, p. 4). As the minority population increases and group threat rises, does this lead to a broad net widening of criminal justice sanctions with sweeping increases in social controls (diffuse threats)? Or alternatively, does threat only result in more targeted punishment aimed at Blacks, Latinos, and the minority groups that are the source of these threats?

On the one hand, studies exist that adopt or assess the "diffuse" perspective. For example, racial threat analyses focusing on public attitudes and perceptions have largely examined racial composition effects on overall fear of crime, public support for the death penalty, and desires for greater criminal justice sanctions generally (Baumer et al., 2003; Chiricos et al., 2001; Ousey & Unnever, 2012). Similarly, racial threat tests of policing have often examined associations between racial composition and larger police forces, expenditures, and greater certainty of arrests overall (rather than targeted enforcements aimed at minorities) (Jackson & Carroll, 1981; Kane et al., 2013; Kent & Jacobs, 2004; Liska et al., 1981, 1985; Stolzenberg et al., 2004).

On the other hand, other studies operate under the assumption that threat effects are specific or "targeted" to minority groups. Sentencing studies, for example, have commonly used cross-level interactions to assess whether Black (or Latino) defendants receive harsher outcomes in areas with higher percentages of Black (or Latino) residents (Caravelis et al., 2011, 2013; Feldmeyer & Ulmer, 2011; Feldmeyer et al., 2015; Light et al., 2014; Ulmer & Bradley, 2006; Ulmer & Johnson, 2004;

Wang & Mears, 2015; Zane, 2017). Likewise, policing studies and public opinion analyses have focused on the impact of racial composition on minority arrests and fear of minority crime (or support for punitiveness toward racial/ethnic minorities) (e.g., see Eitle et al., 2002; Johnson et al., 2011; Mears et al., 2013; Ousey & Lee, 2008; Parker et al., 2005; Pickett et al., 2012; Stewart et al., 2015; Stolzenberg et al., 2004).

We are left, though, with no clear theoretical or empirical consensus about whether racial composition and racial threat are supposed to generate targeted punitiveness toward the minorities that are perceived as threatening or a more global capacity for social control. Alternatively, the precise nature of the effects may be conditioned by circumstances or contexts. Future research that separates each of these forms of threat and systematically examines their influences is needed to gain greater clarity on this issue (see, e.g., Zane, 2017).

Conclusion

As illustrated in our review above, racial threat theory has enjoyed widespread attention within criminology since its inception 50 years ago. The theory offers a meaningful framework for understanding how minority composition translates into perceptions of fear, stereotypes, and ultimately disproportionate punitiveness within the criminal justice system. In addition, empirical research offers many signs of support for this perspective, indicating that racial context has profound implications on social control. Yet an honest survey of the literature also reveals that the theory does not have universal support and has seen an array of mixed and contradictory evidence. Perhaps more concerning, racial threat theory continues to be clouded by ambiguities about the measurement, mechanisms, and nature of racial threat that may be at work in the criminal justice system. Thus, after 50 years of empirical testing, we have as many questions as we do answers about how, when, where, why, and to whom racial threat applies.

Going forward, it is our hope that researchers will address the unanswered questions and issues raised here in order to advance racial threat theory and gain a more nuanced understanding of racial threat effects on social controls. We urge researchers to apply the same intense scrutiny, careful revisions, and fine tuning to racial threat theory that have been applied to other theoretical traditions within criminology (e.g., social disorganization as it progressed from Shaw and McKay's original model to the network-based systemic and collective efficacy models). To do so, research must begin to move beyond the standard analyses of racial threat that have dominated the literature, where the focus has been on identifying whether percentage minority affects different social controls. Instead, scholars must dedicate focused efforts on unpacking the mechanisms at work in racial threat effects and identifying the theoretical models, measures, and units of analyses that are most appropriate for each type of social control. Such efforts will go a long way toward helping clear the fog that clouds our understanding of racial threat and its unique effects on social control of minorities. Moreover, this work is more than academic. Advancement of the racial threat literature has clear implications for theory, research, and policy, especially that which seeks to understand and reduce racial and ethnic inequalities in the application of criminal justice.

Notes

1. Research has referred to racial threat as a theory, hypothesis, position, perspective, and framework, and at times referred to it as the minority group threat theory or position. Thus, we use these terms interchangeably to describe this body of literature and the related theoretical positions.
2. A limited body of research suggests, too, that minority population size is positively associated with police officers' decisions to use force (see, e.g., Jacobs & O'Brien, 1998; Liska & Yu, 1992).
3. Quillian (1995, 1996; see also 2006) provides several foundational tests of racial threat and prejudice, which offer strong and consistent evidence that minority population composition is a key source of racial prejudice. Building on Blumer's (1958) group position theory, Quillian (1995) finds that the size of "subordinate groups" and economic conditions of nations explains the majority of racial prejudice levels across 12 European nations. Similarly, Quillian (1996) notes that percentage Black population and per-capita income combine to explain one-third of the decline in racial prejudice that occurred during the 1970s and 1980s and about one-half of the differences in racial prejudice between the South and North during this period (see also Taylor, 1998; and studies from European contexts: Hjerm & Nagayoshi, 2011; Hood & Morris, 1998; McLaren, 2003).
4. There is, however, contradictory evidence showing that minorities consistently receive more punitive outcomes in capital court cases (see Walker, Spohn, & DeLone, 2006).

References

Alexander, M. (2010). *The new Jim Crow*. New York, NY: The New Press.
Allport, G. W. (1954). *The nature of prejudice*. Cambridge, MA: Addison-Wesley.
Baumer, E., Messner, S., & Rosenfeld, R. (2003). Explaining spatial variation in support for capital punishment: A multilevel analysis. *American Journal of Sociology, 108*(4), 844–875.

Behrens, A., Uggen, C., & Manza, J. (2003). Ballot manipulation and the "menace of negro domination": Racial threat and felon disenfranchisement in the United States, 1850–2002. *American Journal of Sociology, 109*(3), 559–605.

Bjornstrom, E. E., Kaufman, R. L., Peterson, R. D., & Slater, M. D. (2010). Race and ethnic representations of lawbreakers and victims in crime news: A national study of television coverage. *Social Problems, 57*(2), 269–293.

Blalock, H. M., Jr. (1967). *Toward a theory of minority-group relations.* New York, NY: Wiley.

Blauner, B. (1972). *Racial oppression in America.* New York, NY: Harper & Row.

Blumer, H. (1958). Race prejudice as a sense of group position. *Sociological Perspectives, 1*(1), 3–7.

Bobo, L. D. (1999). Prejudice as group position: Microfoundations of a sociological approach to racism and race relations. *Journal of Social Issues, 55*, 445–472.

Bobo, L. D., & Hutchings, V. L. (1996). Perceptions of racial group competition: Extending Blumer's theory of group position to a multiracial social context. *American Sociological Review, 61*(6), 951–972.

Bontrager, S., Bales, W., & Chiricos, T. (2005). Race, ethnicity, threat and the labeling of convicted felons. *Criminology, 43*(3), 589–622.

Brandl, S. G., Chamlin, M. B., & Frank, J. (1995). Aggregation bias and the capacity for formal crime control: The determinants of total and disaggregated police force size in Milwaukee, 1934–1987. *Justice Quarterly, 12*(3), 543–562.

Bridges, G. S., & Crutchfield, R. D. (1988). Law, social standing and racial disparities in imprisonment. *Social Forces, 66*(3), 699–724.

Britt, C. L. (2000). Social context and racial disparities in punishment decisions. *Justice Quarterly, 17*(4), 707–732.

Campbell, M. C., Vogel, M., & Williams, J. (2015). Historical contingencies and the evolving importance of race, violent crime, and region in explaining mass incarceration in the United States. *Criminology, 53*(2), 180–203.

Caravelis, C., Chiricos, T., & Bales, W. (2011). Static and dynamic indicators of minority threat in sentencing outcomes: A multi-level analysis. *Journal of Quantitative Criminology, 27*(4), 405–425.

Caravelis, C., Chiricos, T., & Bales, W. (2013). Race, ethnicity, threat, and the designation of career offenders. *Justice Quarterly, 30*(5), 869–894.

Chamlin, M. B. (1989). A macro social analysis of change in police force size, 1972–1982—controlling for static and dynamic influences. *Sociological Quarterly, 30*(4), 615–624.

Chamlin, M. B., & Liska, A. E. (1992). Social structure and crime control revisited: The declining significance of intergroup threat. *Social Threat and Social Control, 103–112.*

Chen, E. Y. (2014). In the furtherance of justice, injustice, or both? A multilevel analysis of courtroom context and the implementation of three strikes. *Justice Quarterly, 31*(2), 257–286.

Chiricos, T., Hogan, M., & Gertz, M. (1997). Racial composition of neighborhood and fear of crime. *Criminology, 35*(1), 107–128.

Chiricos, T., McEntire, R., & Gertz, M. (2001). Perceived racial and ethnic composition of neighborhood and perceived risk of crime. *Social Problems, 48*(3), 322–340.

Chiricos, T., Stupi, E., Stults, B., & Gertz, M. (2014). Undocumented immigrant threat and support for social controls. *Social Problems, 61*(4), 673–692.

Cochran, J. C., Toman, E. L., Mears, D. P., & Bales, W. D. (2017). Solitary confinement as punishment: Examining in-prison sanctioning disparities. *Justice Quarterly*, 1–31.

Cole, D. (1999). *No equal justice: Race and class in the American criminal justice system.* New York, NY: The New Press.

Covington, J., & Taylor, R. B. (1991). Fear of crime in urban residential neighborhoods: Implications of between- and within-neighborhood sources for current models. *The Sociological Quarterly, 32*(2), 231–249.

Cullen, F. T., Wilcox, P., Sampson, R. J., & Dooley, B. D. (2015). *Challenging criminological theory: The legacy of Ruth Rosner Kornhauser.* New Brunswick, NJ: Transaction.

D'Alessio, S. J., Eitle, D., & Stolzenberg, L. (2005). The impact of serious crime, racial threat, and economic inequality on private police size. *Social Science Research, 34*(2), 267–282.

Davis, J., & Sorensen, J. R. (2013). Disproportionate juvenile minority confinement: A state-level assessment of racial threat. *Youth Violence and Juvenile Justice, 11*(4), 296–312.

Dollar, C. B. (2014). Racial threat theory: Assessing the evidence, requesting redesign. *Journal of Criminology, 2014,* 1–7.

Drakulich, K. M. (2009). But is it racial profiling? Policing, pretext stops, and the color of suspicion. *Contemporary Sociology: A Journal of Reviews, 38*(1), 38–39.

Eitle, D., D'Alessio, S. J., & Stolzenberg, L. (2002). Racial threat and social control: A test of the political, economic, and threat of black crime hypotheses. *Social Forces, 81*(2), 557–576.

Eitle, D., & Monahan, S. (2009). Revisiting racial threat thesis: The role of police organizational characteristics in predicting race-specific drug arrest rates. *Justice Quarterly, 26*(3), 528–561.

Eitle, D., & Taylor, J. (2008). Are Hispanics the new "Threat"? Minority group threat and fear of crime in Miami-Dade county. *Social Science Research, 37*(4), 1102–1115.

Entman, R. M., & Rojecki, A. (2000). *The black image in the white mind: Media and race in America.* Chicago, IL: University of Chicago Press.

Feldmeyer, B., & Ulmer, J. T. (2011). Racial/ethnic threat and federal sentencing. *Journal of Research in Crime and Delinquency, 48*(2), 238–270.

Feldmeyer, B., Warren, P. Y., Siennick, S. E., & Neptune, M. (2015). Racial, ethnic, and immigrant threat: Is there a new criminal threat on state sentencing? *Journal of Research in Crime and Delinquency, 52*(1), 62–92.

Giles, M. W., & Evans, A. S. (1985). External threat, perceived threat, and group identity. *Social Science Quarterly, 66*(1), 50–66.

Giles, M. W., & Evans, A. S. (1986). The power approach to intergroup hostility. *The Journal of Conflict Resolution, 30*(3), 469–486.

Greenberg, D. F., Kessler, R. C., & Loftin, C. (1985). Social inequality and crime control. *The Journal of Criminal Law and Criminology, 76*(3), 684–704.

Heimer, K., Johnson, K. R., Lang, J. B., Rengifo, A. F., & Stemen, D. (2012). Poverty, African-American presence, and social welfare. *Journal of Quantitative Criminology, 28*(2), 219–244.

Henry, P. J., & Sears, D. O. (2009). The crystallization of contemporary racial prejudice across the lifespan. *Political Psychology, 30,* 569–590.

Hjerm, M., & Nagayoshi, K. (2011). The composition of the minority population as a threat: Can real economic and cultural threats explain xenophobia? *International Sociology, 26*(6), 815–843.

Hood, M. V., & Morris, I. L. (1998). Give us your tired, your poor, . . . but make sure they have a green card: The effects of documented and undocumented migrant context on Anglo opinion toward immigration. *Political Behavior, 20*(1), 1–15.

Huff, C. R., & Stahura, J. M. (1980). Police employment and suburban crime. *Criminology, 17*(4), 461–470.

Hughes, C., Warren, P. Y., Stewart, E. A., Tomaskovic-Devey, D., & Mears, D. P. (2017). Racial threat, intergroup contact, and school punishment. *Journal of Research in Crime and Delinquency, 54*(5), 583–616.

Jackson, P. I. (1986). Black visibility, city size, and social control. *The Sociological Quarterly, 27*(2), 185–203.

Jackson, P. I., & Carroll, L. (1981). Race and the war on crime: The sociopolitical determinants of municipal police expenditures in 90 non-southern U.S. cities. *American Sociological Review, 46*(3), 290–305.

Jacobs, D. (1979). Inequality and police strength: Conflict theory and coercive control in metropolitan areas. *American Sociological Review, 44*, 913–925.

Jacobs, D., Carmichael, J., & Kent, S. L. (2005). Vigilantism, current racial threat, and death sentences. *American Sociological Review, 70*(4), 656–677.

Jacobs, D., & Carmichael, J. T. (2001). The politics of punishment across time and space: A pooled time-series analysis of imprisonment rates. *Social Forces, 80*(1), 61–89.

Jacobs, D., & Carmichael, J. T. (2002). The political sociology of the death penalty: A pooled time-series analysis. *American Sociological Review, 67*(1), 109–131.

Jacobs, D., & Carmichael, J. T. (2004). Ideology, social threat, and the death sentence: Capital sentences across time and space. *Social Forces, 83*(1), 249–278.

Jacobs, D., & Helms, R. E. (1997). Testing coercive explanations for order: The determinants of law enforcement strength over time. *Social Forces, 75*, 1361–1392.

Jacobs, D., & Helms, R. E. (1999). Collective outbursts, politics, and punitive resources: Toward a political sociology of spending on social control. *Social Forces, 77*(4), 1497–1523.

Jacobs, D., & O'Brien, R. M. (1998). The determinants of deadly force: A structural analysis of police violence. *American Journal of Sociology, 103*(4), 837–862.

Johnson, B. D. (2005). Contextual disparities in guidelines departures: Courtroom social contexts, guidelines compliance, and extralegal disparities in criminal sentencing. *Criminology, 43*(3), 761–796.

Johnson, B. D., Stewart, E. A., Pickett, J., & Gertz, M. (2011). Ethnic threat and social control: Examining public support for judicial use of ethnicity in punishment. *Criminology, 49*(2), 401–441.

Johnson, B. D., Ulmer, J. T., & Kramer, J. H. (2008). The social context of guidelines circumvention: The case of federal district courts. *Criminology, 46*(3), 737–783.

Johnson, D., & Kuhns, J. B. (2009). Striking out: Race and support for police use of force. *Justice Quarterly, 26*(3), 529–623.

Kane, R. J., Gustafson, J., & Bruell, C. (2013). Racial encroachment and the formal control of space: Minority group-threat and misdemeanor arrests in urban communities. *Justice Quarterly, 30*(6), 957–982.

Kautt, P. M. (2002). Location, location, location: Interdistrict and intercircuit variation in sentencing outcomes for federal drug-trafficking offenses. *Justice Quarterly, 19*(4), 633–669.

Keen, B., & Jacobs, D. (2009). Racial threat, partisan politics, and racial disparities in prison admissions: A panel analysis. *Criminology, 47*(1), 209–238.

Kent, S. L., & Carmichael, J. T. (2014). Racial residential segregation and social control: A panel study of the variation in police strength across U.S. cities, 1980–2010. *American Journal of Criminal Justice, 39*(2), 228–249.

Kent, S. L., & Jacobs, D. (2004). Social divisions and coercive control in advanced societies: Law enforcement strength in eleven nations from 1975 to 1994. *Social Problems, 51*(3), 343–361.

Kent, S. L., & Jacobs, D. (2005). Minority threat and police strength from 1980 to 2000: A fixed-effects analysis of nonlinear and interactive effects in large U.S. cities. *Criminology, 43*(3), 731–760.

King, R. D., & Wheelock, D. (2007). Group threat and social control: Race, perceptions of minorities and the desire to punish. *Social Forces, 85*(3), 1255–1280.

Leiber, M. J., Peck, J. H., & Rodriguez, N. (2016). Minority threat and juvenile court outcomes. *Crime & Delinquency, 62*(1), 54–80.

Levchak, P. J. (2017). Do precinct characteristics influence stop-and-frisks in New York City? A multi-level analysis of post-stop outcomes. *Justice Quarterly, 34*(3), 377–406.

Light, M. T., Massoglia, M., & King, R. D. (2014). Citizenship and punishment: The salience of national membership in U.S. criminal courts. *American Sociological Review, 79*(5), 825–847.

Lin, J., Grattet, R., & Petersilia, J. (2010). "Back-end sentencing" and reimprisonment: Individual, contextual, and community predictors of parole sanctioning decisions. *Criminology, 48*(3), 759–795.

Liska, A. E. (1987). A critical examination of macro perspectives on crime control. *Annual Review of Sociology, 13*(1), 67–88.

Liska, A. E. (1992). *Social threat and social control*. Albany, NY: State University of New York Press.

Liska, A. E., & Chamlin, M. (1984). Social structure and crime control among macrosocial units. *American Journal of Sociology, 90*(2), 383–395.

Liska, A. E., Chamlin, M., & Reed, M. (1985). Testing the economic production and conflict models of crime control. *Social Forces, 64*(1), 119–138.

Liska, A. E., Lawrence, J., & Benson, M. (1981). Perspectives on the legal order: The capacity for social control. *American Journal of Sociology, 87*(2), 413–426.

Liska, A. E., Lawrence, J. J., & Sanchirico, A. (1982). Fear of crime as a social fact. *Social Forces, 60*(3), 760–770.

Liska, A. E., & Yu, J. (1992). Specifying and testing the threat hypothesis. In A. Liska (ed.), *Social threat and social control* (pp. 53–68). Albany: State University of New York Press.

Lum, C. (2011). The influence of places on police decisions pathways: From call for service to arrest. *Justice Quarterly, 28*(4), 631–665.

Manza, J., & Uggen, C. (2006). *Locked out: Felon disenfranchisement and American democracy*. New York, NY: Oxford University Press.

McLaren, L. M. (2003). Anti-immigrant prejudice in Europe: Contact, threat perception, and preferences for the exclusion of migrants. *Social Forces, 81*(3), 909–936.

Mears, D. P., Cochran, J. C., & Lindsey, A. M. (2016). Offending and racial and ethnic disparities in criminal justice: A conceptual framework for guiding theory and research and informing policy. *Journal of Contemporary Criminal Justice, 32*, 78–103.

Mears, D. P., Mancini, C., & Stewart, E. A. (2009). Whites' concern about crime: The effects of interracial contact. *Journal of Research in Crime and Delinquency, 46*(4), 524–552.

Mears, D. P., Pickett, J., Golden, K., Chiricos, T., & Gertz, M. (2013). The effect of interracial contact on whites' perceptions of victimization risk and black criminality. *Journal of Research in Crime and Delinquency, 50*(2), 272–299.

Mears, D. P., & Stewart, E. A. (2010). Interracial contact and fear of crime. *Journal of Criminal Justice*, *38*(1), 34–41.

Miller, S. D., & Sears, D. O. (1986). Stability and change in social tolerance: A test of the persistence hypothesis. *American Journal of Political Science*, *30*, 214–236.

Moeller, G. (1989). Fear of criminal victimization—The effect of neighborhood racial composition. *Sociological Inquiry*, *59*(2), 208–221.

Myers, M. A., & Talarico, S. M. (1987). *The social contexts of criminal sentencing.* New York, NY: Springer.

Ousey, G. C., & Lee, M. R. (2008). Racial disparity in formal social control: An investigation of alternative explanations of arrest rate inequality. *Journal of Research in Crime and Delinquency*, *45*(3), 322–355.

Ousey, G. C., & Unnever, J. D. (2012). Racial—ethnic threat, out-group intolerance, and support for punishing criminals: A cross-national study. *Criminology*, *50*(3), 565–603.

Parker, K. F., Stults, B. J., & Rice, S. K. (2005). Racial threat, concentrated disadvantage and social control: Considering the macro-level sources of variation in arrests. *Criminology*, *43*(4), 1111–1134.

Payne, A. A., & Welch, K. (2010). Modeling the effects of racial threat on punitive and restorative school discipline practices. *Criminology*, *48*(4), 1019–1062.

Pettigrew, T. F. (1959). Regional differences in anti-negro prejudice. *The Journal of Abnormal and Social Psychology*, *59*(1), 28–36.

Pettigrew, T. F., & Tropp, L. R. (2006). A meta-analytic test of intergroup contact theory. *Journal of Personality and Social Psychology*, *90*(5), 751–783.

Phillips, C. D. (1986). Social structure and social control: Modeling the discriminatory execution of blacks in Georgia and North Carolina, 1925–35. *Social Forces*, *65*(2), 458–475.

Pickett, J. T. (2016). On the social foundations for crimmigration: Latino threat and support for expanded police powers. *Journal of Quantitative Criminology*, *32*(1), 103–132.

Pickett, J. T., Chiricos, T., Golden, K. M., & Gertz, M. (2012). Reconsidering the relationship between perceived neighborhood racial composition and whites' perceptions of victimization risk: Do racial stereotypes matter? *Criminology*, *50*(1), 145–186.

Quillian, L. (1995). Prejudice as a response to perceived group threat: Population composition and anti-immigrant and racial prejudice in Europe. *American Sociological Review*, *60*(4), 586–611.

Quillian, L. (1996). Group threat and regional change in attitudes toward African-Americans. *American Journal of Sociology*, *102*(3), 816–860.

Quillian, L. (2006). New approaches to understanding racial prejudice and discrimination. *Annual Review of Sociology*, *32*(1), 299–328.

Quillian, L., & Pager, D. (2001). Black neighbors, higher crime? The role of racial stereotypes in evaluations of neighborhood crime. *American Journal of Sociology*, *107*(3), 717–767.

Quinney, R. (1977). *Class, state, and crime: On the theory and practice of criminal justice.* New York, NY: David McKay Company Inc.

Ramirez, M. D. (2013). Punitive sentiment. *Criminology*, *51*(2), 329–364.

Russell, K. K. (1992). Development of a black criminology and the role of the black criminologist. *Justice Quarterly*, *9*(4), 667–683.

Sears, D. O., & Henry, P. J. (2003). The origins of symbolic racism. *Journal of Personality and Social Psychology*, *85*, 259–275.

Semyonov, M., Raijman, R., Tov, A. Y., & Schmidt, P. (2004). Population size, per-ceived threat, and exclusion: A multiple-indicators analysis of attitudes toward foreigners in Germany. *Social Science Research, 33*, 681–701.

Skogan, W. G. (1995). Crime and the racial fears of white Americans. *The Annals of the American Academy of Political and Social Science, 539*(1), 59–71.

Smith, I. B., & Sturgis, P. (2011). Do neighborhoods generate fear of crime? An empirical testing using the British Crime Survey. *Criminology, 49*(2), 331–369.

Spohn, C. (2000). *Thirty years of sentencing reform: The quest for a racially neutral sentencing process*. Washington, DC: National Institute of Justice.

Steffensmeier, D., Ulmer, J., & Kramer, J. (1998). The interaction of race, gender, and age in criminal sentencing: The punishment cost of being young, black, and male. *Criminology, 36*(4), 763–798.

Stemen, D., & Rengifo, A. F. (2011). Policies and imprisonment: The impact of structured sentencing and determinate sentencing on state incarceration rates. *Justice Quarterly, 28*(1), 174–201.

Stewart, E. A., Martinez, R., Baumer, E. P., & Gertz, M. (2015). The social context of Latino threat and punitive Latino sentiment. *Social Problems, 62*(1), 68–92.

Stewart, E. A., Baumer, E. P., Brunson, R. K., & Simons, R. L. (2009). Neighbor-hood racial context and perception of police-based racial discrimination among Black youth. *Criminology, 47*(3), 847–887.

Stolzenberg, L., D'Alessio, S. J., & Eitle, D. (2004). A multilevel test of racial threat theory. *Criminology, 42*(3), 673–698.

Stucky, T. D. (2012). The conditional effects of race and politics on social control: Black violent crime arrests in large cities, 1970 to 1990. *Journal of Research in Crime and Delinquency, 49*(1), 3–30.

Stults, B., & Baumer, E. (2007). Racial context and police force size: Evaluating the empirical validity of the minority threat perspective. *American Journal of Sociology, 113*(2), 507–546.

Stupi, E. K., Chiricos, T., & Gertz, M. (2016). Perceived criminal threat from undoc-umented immigrants: Antecedents and consequences for policy preferences. *Justice Quarterly, 33*(2), 239–266.

Taylor, M. C. (1998). How white attitudes vary with the racial composition of local populations: Numbers count. *American Sociological Review, 63*(4), 512–535.

Taylor, R. B., & Covington, J. (1993). Community structural change and fear of crime. *Social Problems, 40*(3), 374–397.

Thomas, S. A., Moak, S. C., & Walker, J. T. (2013). The contingent effect of race in juvenile court detention decisions: The role of racial and symbolic threat. *Race and Justice, 3*(3), 239–265.

Tonry, M. H. (1995). *Malign neglect*. New York, NY: Oxford University Press.

Turk, A. T. (1969). *Criminality and legal order*. Chicago, IL: Rand McNally.

Uggen, C., & Manza, J. (2002). Democratic contraction? Political consequences of felon disenfranchisement in the United States. *American Sociological Review, 67*(6), 777–803.

Ulmer, J. T. (2012). Recent developments and new directions in sentencing research. *Justice Quarterly, 29*(1), 1–40.

Ulmer, J. T., & Bradley, M. S. (2006). Variation in trial penalties among serious violent offenses. *Criminology, 44*(3), 631–670.

Ulmer, J. T., & Johnson, B. (2004). Sentencing in context: A multilevel analysis. *Criminology, 42*(1), 137–178.

Unnever, J. D., & Cullen, F. T. (2010). Racial-ethnic intolerance and support for capital punishment: A cross-national comparison. *Criminology, 48*(3), 831–846.

Unnever, J. D., & Cullen, F. T. (2012). White perceptions of whether African-Americans are prone to violence and support for the death penalty. *Journal of Research in Crime and Delinquency, 49*(4), 519–544.

Unnever, J. D., & Gabbidon, S. L. (2011). *A theory of African American offending: Race, racism, and crime.* New York, NY: Routledge.

Unnever, J. D., Gabbidon, S. L., & Higgins, G. E. (2011). The election of Barack Obama and perceptions of criminal injustice. *Justice Quarterly, 28*(1), 23–45.

Walker, S., Spohn, C., & DeLone, M. (2006). *The color of justice: Race, ethnicity, and crime in America* (4th ed.). Belmont, CA: Thompson Wadsworth.

Wang, X. (2012). Undocumented immigrants as perceived criminal threat: A test of the minority threat perspective. *Criminology, 50*(3), 743–776.

Wang, X., & Mears, D. P. (2010a). A multilevel test of minority threat effects on sentencing. *Journal of Quantitative Criminology, 26*(2), 191–215.

Wang, X., & Mears, D. P. (2010b). Examining the direct and interactive effects of changes in racial and ethnic threat on sentencing decisions. *Journal of Research in Crime and Delinquency, 47*(4), 522–557.

Wang, X., & Mears, D. P. (2015). Sentencing and state-level racial and ethnic contexts. *Law & Society Review, 49*(4), 883–915.

Weidner, R. R., & Frase, R. S. (2003). Legal and extralegal determinants of inter-county differences in prison use. *Criminal Justice Policy Review, 14*(3), 377–400.

Weidner, R. R., Frase, R. S., & Schultz, J. S. (2005). The impact of contextual factors on the decision to imprison in large urban jurisdictions: A multilevel analysis. *Crime & Delinquency, 51*(3), 400–424.

Welch, K., Payne, A. A., Chiricos, T., & Gertz, M. (2011). The typification of Hispanics as criminals and support for punitive crime control policies. *Social Science Research, 40*(3), 822–840.

Wilcox, P., Cullen, F. T., & Feldmeyer, B. (2018). *Communities and crime: An enduring American challenge.* Philadelphia, PA: Temple University Press.

Zane, S. N. (2017). Exploring the minority threat hypothesis for juveniles in criminal court: Static versus dynamic threat and diffuse versus targeted effects. *Youth Violence and Juvenile Justice,* advance online publication. doi:10.1177/1541 204017730388.

12

Race and the Procedural Justice Model of Policing

Hannah D. McManus, Jillian G. Shafer,
and Amanda K. Graham

In the United States, police–minority relations are in crisis. A series of high-profile incidents involving the deaths of Black citizens at the hands of police officers have brought forth troubling questions regarding the quality and nature of policing in the minority communities of America (Sparrow, 2016). A growing chorus of voices has expressed concerns of police bias, abuse of force, and use of overly aggressive tactics in the inner-city communities with the greatest need of police protection (Engel & Eck, 2015). Confronted with nationwide protests and demands for change, police executives, researchers, and policymakers alike have turned to the wisdom of the procedural justice model of policing— touting this model as the key to restoring public confidence and trust in the police.

In many ways, the procedural justice model of policing is presented as a general model—the ultimate cure for poor police–community relations. And while, ideally, this cure would work equally for police agencies across different community contexts, the history of polic- ing research suggests limited instances of such generalizable success. Furthermore, the substantial amount of literature outlining differences in experiences with and perceptions of police according to race (see, e.g., Hagan, Shedd, & Payne, 2005; National Research Council, 2004; Weitzer & Tuch, 2004, 2006) suggests that a race-specific approach to the study of procedural justice and its impact on police–community relations is imperative. Specifically, the history of racial discrimination in America, the frequency and nature of police contact with minority citizens, and the legal socialization of Black Americans are likely to impact the effects of the procedural justice model of policing in these communities. The intersection of race and procedural justice warrants greater attention—applying a Black Criminological approach is the perfect opportunity.

In this vein, this current chapter will explore the procedural justice model of policing, as developed by Tom R. Tyler and colleagues, and discuss the contemporary crisis in American policing that has brought this model to the forefront of police reform efforts. It will then consider the application and effectiveness of procedural justice in minority communities, using evidence of the impact of the procedural justice model and the nature of public perceptions of police to inform this discussion. This chapter will conclude with the presentation of a Black Criminology model of procedural justice, highlighting the components of the model and its implications for the future of inner-city policing.

The Procedural Justice Model

In the 1970s, researchers studying the psychology of justice began to explore the impact of procedural fairness on individuals' satisfaction with the criminal justice system. Driven by Thibaut and Walker's (1975) investigation of a person's willingness to accept court decisions, this body of work suggests that individuals' evaluations of the justice system are affected not just by the outcomes of their specific encounters with the system but by the *fairness of the process used* to arrive at those outcomes (Thibaut & Walker, 1975; Tyler, 1987). For example, even in the face of a negative outcome (e.g., guilty verdict), it has been found that individuals are more likely to report their satisfaction with both the outcome and the decision maker when they perceive the decision-making process as fair (Thibaut & Walker, 1975; Tyler, 1988). Finding this to be true across many different contexts, researchers began to advertise procedural justice as one way authorities can build and maintain satisfaction and support from the people they interact with (see, e.g., Folger & Greenberg, 1985; Greenberg & Tyler, 1987; Lind & Tyler, 1988; Tyler, 1987; Tyler & Caine, 1981; Tyler & Folger, 1980; Walker & Lind, 1984).

Tom R. Tyler can be credited with the expansion of this procedural justice model and the application of its social-psychological framework to policing (Reisig, Bratton, & Gertz, 2007; see, e.g., Tyler & Folger, 1980; Tyler, 1988, 1990). Specifically, over the course of his work, Tyler has suggested that the procedural justice model can apply to citizens' assessments of police legitimacy. Legitimacy refers to "a property of an authority that leads people to feel that the authority or institution is entitled to be deferred to and obeyed" (Sunshine & Tyler, 2003, p. 514). This involves an individual's internalized sense of trust in and commitment to the law and its actors. Using the procedural justice framework, police legitimacy is viewed as a product of *how* the police act and make decisions when exercising their authority. Specifically, Tyler highlights the direct relationship between the fairness of police treatment in police–citizen encounters and how citizens perceive both the encounter and the police (Mazerolle, Antrobus, Bennett, & Tyler, 2013a; Sunshine & Tyler, 2003; Tyler, 1990, 2003; Tyler & Fagan, 2008). Therefore, the procedural justice model of policing focuses primarily on citizens' experiences in their interactions with police. This model encourages police officers to view each encounter with a citizen as an opportunity to enhance police legitimacy through the quality and fairness of the interaction (Schulhofer, Tyler, & Huq, 2011).

Elements of Procedural Justice

In 1988, Tyler outlined six potential criteria related to individuals' judgments of fairness: control/representation, consistency, impartiality, decision accuracy, correctability, and ethicality (see Tyler, 1988, 1990 Part Four for full description). However, following initial tests of these criteria (Tyler, 1988, 1990), Tyler reduced these down to four key elements of procedural justice: participation, neutrality, respect, and trustworthiness. The first key element, participation, suggests that in police–citizen encounters, an individual is more likely to perceive the police as fair if they are provided the opportunity to participate (e.g., tell their side of the story) in the process of the encounter. The second key element, neutrality, proposes that evidence of objectivity in the officer's decision making enhances the individual's perception of fairness. Respect refers to the quality of interpersonal treatment within the encounter. Specifically, in police–citizen encounters, people value being treated with politeness and having their rights acknowledged. Finally, trustworthiness indicates that individuals are more likely to perceive their encounters with the police as fair if the officer appears to care about their well-being and considers their needs and concerns (Meares &

Tyler, 2017; Tyler, 1988, 1990, 2004, 2005; Tyler & Huo, 2002). Studies assessing these elements typically find that they are highly correlated and that all four elements are strongly associated with evaluations
of justice in decision making and treatment (e.g., Tyler, 1990; Tyler &
Fagan, 2008; Worden & McLean, 2014). As such, these elements are
viewed to provide an important prescriptive model for police legitimacy, describing a method by which officers can use their authority
in fair and just ways through the "quality of treatment" and "quality
of decision-making process" (Mazerolle, Bennett, Davis, Sargeant, &
Manning, 2013; Reisig et al., 2007; Meares & Tyler, 2017; Schulhofer
et al., 2011; Sunshine & Tyler, 2003).

Proponents of the procedural justice model suggest that enhancing
public perceptions of police legitimacy through the fairness of treatment and decision-making processes in police–citizen encounters can
have important implications for (1) police effectiveness and (2) police–
community relations (Sunshine & Tyler, 2003; Tyler & Huo, 2002). For
example, some argue that a procedural justice–based approach allows
the police to effectively control crime by increasing individuals' willingness to comply with and assist police (Sunshine & Tyler, 2003; Tyler,
1990, 2001; Tyler & Huo, 2002). Specifically, procedurally just encounters with police are likely to enhance perceptions of police legitimacy—
encouraging feelings of trust in and responsibility to the law. In turn,
these perceptions encourage lawful behavior and cooperation with
police (Sunshine & Tyler, 2003; Tyler & Huo, 2002; Mazerolle, Bennett,
et al., 2013). With a renewed sense of respect and trust in the law and
police, citizens feel a sense of duty to co-produce public safety, making
the police more effective in preventing and controlling crime.

In addition to enhancing police effectiveness, a primary assumption
of the procedural justice model is that police use of procedural justice
in their interactions with citizens will positively impact police–community relations (Tyler, Goff, & MacCoun, 2015). Community residents'
perceptions of police fairness are identified as contributors to global
attitudes (e.g., satisfaction, confidence, trust) toward police (Eck &
Rosenbaum, 1994; Tyler, 1990, 2001; Tyler & Huo, 2002). In turn, these
attitudes may influence the nature of the relationship between the police
and the communities they serve. Ideally, the positive experiences and
satisfaction generated from procedurally just encounters with the police
will accumulate over time—improving collective community opinions
and motivating solidarity between the police and the community they
serve (Sunshine & Tyler, 2003; Tyler, Goff, & MacCoun, 2015). These

potential implications of the procedural justice model of policing have proven particularly important as police have undergone a period of change and innovation in the past three decades. The following section describes the emergence of the proactive policing movement in the United States and discusses the collateral consequences of this movement that would ultimately bring the procedural justice model to the forefront of police reform efforts.

The Rise of Proactive Policing in the Inner Cities in Crisis

The proactive policing movement in the United States emerged in the 1980s and 1990s in response to a crisis of public confidence in police. Beginning in the 1960s, police were faced with the convergence of several political, legal, and social controversies that swept over American society (National Academies of Sciences, 2018). Race riots and war protests in the 1960s escalated social unrest and increased conflict in police interactions with both young and minority populations (National Advisory Commission on Civil Disorders, 1968). Simultaneously, high levels of violent and drug-related crime that rose continuously from the 1960s to the early 1990s, particularly in the urban centers of America, generated widespread fear of crime among American citizens. Furthermore, major research findings exploring the impact of traditional, reactive policing strategies, such as random preventive patrol, rapid response to calls for service, and follow-up investigations (i.e., the standard model of policing; see Weisburd & Eck, 2004), motivated strong skepticism regarding police ability to effectively prevent and control crime (e.g., Greenwood, Chaiken, & Petersilia, 1977; Kelling, Pate, Dieckman, & Brown, 1974; President's Commission on Law Enforcement and Administration of Justice, 1967; Spelman & Brown, 1981). Indeed, by the end of the 20th century, many scholars began to express their doubts that police could have a meaningful impact on crime at all (e.g., Bayley, 1990; Gottfredson & Hirschi, 1990).

Faced with this crisis, police, policy makers, and scholars began to rethink the fundamental mission and core tactics of American policing, exploring new ways the police may address crime and improve police–community relationships. The result of these concerted efforts was the development of numerous innovative strategies in the 1980s and 1990s that take a proactive approach to policing (National Research Council, 2004; Weisburd & Braga, 2006). The proactive policing model encourages police to use strategic approaches in preventing and controlling problems of crime and disorder. The strategies, such as problem-oriented policing, broken windows policing, and hot spots policing (among others), are characterized by the mobilization of resources through police initiative and a focus on targeting the underlying causes of crime and disorder (National Academies of Sciences, 2018). Offering new opportunities for police to address crime effectively, the proactive policing movement quickly spread across the "landscape of American policing" (National Academies of Sciences, 2018).

These proactive policing approaches were used heavily in inner-city areas across the United States that had been plagued with high rates of crime for decades. The simultaneous reduction in crime and disorder, particularly in larger American cities (e.g., New York City), in this new, proactive era of policing was remarkable (Fagan, Zimring, & Kim, 1998; Zimring, 2007). In 1993, the high levels of crime that had been sustained for almost three decades began to decrease in almost all categories nationwide. Entering the 21st century, most serious crime rates had decreased by 35% (Zimring, 2007). While debates concerning how much of this crime reduction was caused by the shift of policing to more proactive strategies remain, research suggests that police deserve some credit for the decrease in crime (Eck & Maguire, 2000; Engel & Eck, 2015; Zimring, 2007).

While police reformers might have envisioned that improving police effectiveness in preventing and controlling crime would also enhance public confidence and trust in police, research suggests that public perceptions have experienced only marginal improvements in recent decades (Meares & Tyler, 2017; Tyler, Jackson, & Mentovich, 2015). Instead, many citizens, particularly Black Americans, have expressed dissatisfaction with the nature of police practices in the United States (Engel & Eck, 2015; Meares & Tyler, 2017). This dissatisfaction can be viewed as a product of the heavy use of aggressive enforcement tactics, such as pretext stops, stop, question, and frisk, and order maintenance or zero-tolerance policing, that emerged alongside other proactive policing strategies. Critics of aggressive enforcement have noted that minorities, particularly poor Black Americans, are often the most affected by police strategies targeting violence and disorder in inner cities (Engel, Smith, & Cullen, 2012; Gelman, Fagan, & Kiss, 2007; Rosenbaum, 2006; Taylor, 2006; Weitzer, 2000). Use of these tactics often translates into more frequent, and often more intrusive, police-initiated contacts with Black citizens (Butler, 2017; Hayes, 2017; Johnson, Wilson, Maguire, & Lowrey-Kinberg, 2017; National Academies of Sciences, 2018; Tyler, Jackson, & Mentovich, 2015). A substantial amount of research supports this observation (Johnson et al., 2017; Smith, Rojek, Petrocelli, & Withrow, 2017). Specifically, studies have found racial disparities across a wide array of policing outcomes, including pedestrian stops (see, e.g., Fagan, Geller, Davies, & West, 2010; Gelman et al., 2007), vehicle stops (see, e.g., Alpert, Dunham, & Smith, 2007; Epp, Maynard-Moody, & Haider-Markel, 2014), discretionary searches (see, e.g., Engel & Johnson, 2006), arrests (see, e.g., Kochel, Wilson, & Mastrofski, 2011), and use of force (see, e.g., Paoline, Gau, & Terrill, 2016). These disparities have brought the legality of several proactive policing strategies into question (e.g., *Floyd v. City of New York*, 2013), with some critics characterizing aggressive enforcement in inner-city communities as a form of "psychological warfare" perpetuating the second-class status of Black citizens in the United States (Butler, 2017; Forman, 2017; Hayes, 2017). Collectively, these tactics have succeeded in alienating many police agencies from the inner-city communities they serve.

Public confidence and trust in police have been further shaken by the recent series of highly publicized incidents involving the deaths of unarmed Black American men at the hands of police officers (Nix, Campbell, Byers, & Alpert, 2017; Sparrow, 2016; Weitzer, 2015). For many, the quick succession of these incidents provides evidence of a much larger national problem (Sherman, 2018; Zimring, 2017). Perceptions of a pattern of racial discrimination and excessive use of force by police spurred the creation of a national movement, the Black Lives Matter (BLM) movement. The Black Lives Matter movement asserts that the systemic nature of racial bias and pervasive character of police authority in the United States has dangerous consequences for Black Americans (Garza, 2014). While the creators of this movement observe that racial biases are inherent in everyone, the efforts of this movement have largely been directed at the police, as they are the most visible—symbolically and literally—arms of a systematically biased society. The social activists and protests associated with this movement have increased speculation that effectiveness in reducing crime and disorder should not be the only metric for the evaluation of police practice (Engel & Eck, 2015; National Academies of Sciences, 2018). Instead, to improve police relations with minority communities, the quality and equity of police services must also be primary considerations.

Effectiveness of Procedural Justice in Policing

As conflict grew between activists, minority communities, the police, and their supporters, President Obama commissioned the Task Force on

21st Century Policing. In 2014, a panel of experts, including a range of policing scholars, practitioners, and civil rights activists, traveled across the country, observing spoken and written testimony from over 200 subject matter experts. Subjects ranged from police use of force and tactical police strategies to police legitimacy and community relations. The experts arranged their efforts into a final report outlining six pillars of policing, each dealing with the effectiveness, efficiency, and/or equity of the police. Of the six pillars presented in the *President's Task Force on 21st Century Policing Final Report* (2015)[1], three directly cite procedural justice, and all mention improving relations between communities (and community members) and the police. It is clear the authors believed police should move to a procedural justice model of policing to improve citizen trust and legitimacy (Pillar 1: Trust and Legitimacy), enhance the techniques of deescalation and conflict resolution (Pillar 5: Training and Education), and improve overall community relations and coproduction of safety (Pillar 4: Community Policing and Crime Reduction). The *Task Force* mimicked the sentiments described by most police institutions and associations in the past 5 years, including the International Association of Chiefs of Police (IACP), the National Fraternal Order of Police (FOP), and Police Executive Research Forum (PERF) among other regional and local organizations.

Assessing the Evidence

Figure 12.1 displays Tyler's formulation of the procedural justice model of policing. Working backward, this model suggests citizens obey the law and/or requests by police because they understand police authority serves a purpose. Citizens trust police officers and are confident that officers will use their authority as a tool to keep them safe, and thus understand it may be used against them to keep others safe. This trust and confidence in police provides the base for police legitimacy. Citizens formulate these general feelings of the police by accumulating experiences or encounters with the police. When officers allow citizens to participate, are neutral in their decision making, are respectful within the interaction, and appear trustworthy (i.e., when officers exhibit procedurally just behaviors and decision making), these encounters are more likely to be viewed as positive. In sum, the procedural justice model of policing suggests that citizens' experiences in their encounters with police, particularly whether they perceive those individual encounters as procedurally just, have important implications for (1) their satisfaction

Figure 12.1
Tyler's Procedural Justice Model of Policing

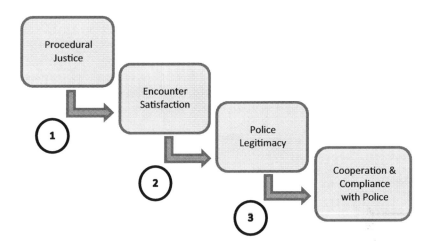

with the encounter, (2) their general perceptions of police, including police legitimacy, and (3) their willingness to cooperate with the police.

Researchers have invested substantial time and effort to test the relationships outlined in this causal model of procedural justice—though, notably, no single study has tested the entire model (National Academies of Sciences, 2018). A review of these research efforts demonstrates considerable variation across studies in the implementation, measurement, and evaluation of procedural justice.[2] However, there appears to be consistent evidence of the relationships proposed by the model (Donner, Maskaly, Fridell, & Jennings, 2015; Mazerolle, Bennett, Davis, Sargeant, & Manning, 2013). Some of the most compelling evidence regarding the impact of procedural justice stems from experimental studies that explore the effects of fair and impartial policing on citizens' perceptions of police and cooperative/compliant behavior (e.g., Lowrey, Maguire, & Bennett, 2016; MacQueen & Bradford, 2015; Mazerolle, Antrobus, Bennett, & Tyler, 2013; Mazerolle, Bennett, Antrobus, & Eggins, 2012; Sahin, 2014). In one such study, referred to as the Queensland Community Engagement Trial, Mazerolle and colleagues (2012) implemented a randomized controlled trial delivering experimental treatment of procedural justice during traffic stops for drunk driving. Randomly selected officers were trained to incorporate a procedural justice script in their short encounters with drivers during random breath testing (RBT). Citizen perceptions of those officers were compared with perceptions of officers that were not trained to use this script. To provide insight on their experience, each driver was given a survey to complete later and return to the researchers. Though suffering from low survey response rates (approximately 13% of stopped individuals responded), findings from this study suggest that the incorporation of procedural justice in traffic stops can enhance citizen perceptions of the fairness of the encounter, satisfaction with police, and compliance with police (Mazerolle et al., 2012).

The positive findings reported from the Queensland Community Engagement Trial are supported by larger reviews of procedural justice research. For example, in their systematic review of 28 studies analyzing procedural justice within the context of police–citizen encounters, Donner and colleagues (2015) concluded that individuals' perceptions of procedural justice in their encounters with the police positively impact their views of police legitimacy, satisfaction with police, and confidence in the police (Donner et al., 2015). These conclusions are mirrored in an earlier review and meta-analysis conducted by Mazerolle, Bennett, and colleagues (2013). Specifically, this review found that in addition to enhancing individuals' perceptions of police, police interventions incorporating procedural justice positively impact citizen intentions to comply or cooperate with the police in the future (Mazerolle, Bennett, et al., 2013; see also Mazerolle et al., 2014).

Notably, these positive effects of procedural justice are supported across different contexts of police–citizen interactions and when using different types of samples, methodologies, and statistical analyses. For example, through survey research, these relationships have been found in tests of drivers stopped at random drunk driving checkpoints (Mazerolle, Bennett, Antrobus, & Eggins, 2012; Mazerolle, Antrobus, Bennett, & Tyler, 2013), in traffic stops by police (Engel, 2005; Lowrey et al., 2016), in police interactions with victims of crime (Elliott, Thomas, & Ogloff, 2012; Hickman & Simpson, 2003), and in general surveys of community members (Gau, Corsaro, Stewart, & Brunson, 2012; Sunshine & Tyler, 2003; Tyler & Fagan, 2008; Tyler & Jackson, 2013). Collectively, this body of evidence suggests procedural justice is closely associated with greater satisfaction with police encounters, improved perceptions of police, including higher assessments of police legitimacy, and increased cooperation and compliance. As such, it appears that police agencies stand to gain substantial benefits when they treat the citizens they encounter with fairness, objectivity, and equity (Donner et al., 2015).

Procedural Justice to Black Americans

The evidence base on the impact of procedural justice has motivated police reformers, such as those involved in the President's Task Force on 21st Century Policing, to point to the procedural justice model of policing as an important step in improving confidence, enhancing trust, and forging positive relationships with disenfranchised individuals in disadvantaged communities—that is, those communities characterized by poverty, various social and physical disorders, violence, and high crime (Mazerolle et al., 2014; Wilson, 1987). This push for procedural justice in policing is based on the belief that the effects of procedural justice are generalizable. Indeed, in his early work, Tyler (1990) presents procedural justice as a theory that applies equally across subgroups of people. Supporting this proposition, studies have found that individuals from both majority and minority groups are concerned with how the police treat people and, in turn, consider quality of treatment in their evaluations of legal authorities (Sunshine & Tyler, 2003; Tyler, 2001, 2005; Tyler & Huo, 2002). Scholars go on to suggest that the cognitive process related to perceptions of procedural justice and subsequent outcomes is the same across racial/ethnic groups (Tyler & Huo, 2002). Therefore, if majority and minority group members perceive procedural justice within a police encounter similarly, the effects of the procedural justice model should be the same. But what is the likelihood that a White American and Black American will perceive fairness and justice within an encounter similarly? Research exploring more general, or global, public attitudes toward police suggests that substantial racial variation in perceptions exists (see below). We argue that this variation has important implications for the application and effectiveness of the procedural justice model of policing in minority communities.

Black Americans' Perceptions of Police

Since the 1960s, studies have observed consistent racial disparities in Americans' attitudes toward police (National Research Council, 2004; for an exception, see Frank, Brandl, Cullen, & Stichman, 1996). Black Americans are consistently found to report lower levels of confidence and trust in and/or satisfaction with police (Peck, 2015). Additionally, research finds Black Americans are more likely to perceive the police as racially biased (Stewart, Baumer, Brunson, & Simons, 2009; Weitzer, 2000; Weitzer & Tuch, 1999, 2002, 2005), less courteous (Brunson & Weitzer, 2009; Gau & Brunson, 2010), and to perceive police use of force as more of a problem (Weitzer, 2002). A national survey conducted by the CATO Institute reiterates these findings (Ekins, 2016). Specifically, this study found that only 40% of Black respondents reported favorable views of the police, compared to 68% of White respondents. Additionally, only 31% of Black respondents (versus 64% of White respondents) suggested that police treat everyone equally. Furthermore, Black respondents were much more likely to suggest police are too quick to use lethal force (73% compared to 35% of White respondents) and that police tactics are generally too harsh (56% of Black respondents compared to 26% of White respondents) (Ekins, 2016).

It is possible these findings are even more dramatic among Black Americans living in truly disadvantaged neighborhoods. For example, in a recent survey of residents in high-poverty, high-crime neighborhoods conducted by the Urban Institute, the majority of respondents (two-thirds of which identified themselves as Black) did not believe that the police act in procedurally just ways, suggesting that police rarely make fair and impartial decisions in the cases they deal with.[3] Additionally, respondents indicated limited perceptions of police legitimacy, proposing that the police do not behave according to the law, often arrest individuals without a good reason, and usually act in ways inconsistent with respondents' ideas about what is right and wrong (La Vigne, Fontaine, & Dwidevi, 2017).

Implications for Race and Procedural Justice

Research indicates that citizens' evaluations of their encounters with police are strongly affected by pre-existing global attitudes, such as those outlined above (Brandl, Frank, Worden, & Bynum, 1994; Rosenbaum, Schuck, Costello, Hawkins, & Ring, 2005). Stated differently, citizens' prior attitudes and broader orientations toward the police impact their perceptions of their interactions with police officers. Therefore, individuals with contrasting global attitudes are likely to perceive similar police encounters differently—that is, individuals that hold generally unfavorable views of police are likely to evaluate their contacts unfavorably, while those with more favorable general views will also view their encounters more favorably. Notably, these global attitudes are typically found to be stable, meaning individual police–citizen encounters are unlikely to substantially shift a citizen's broader view of police (Brandl et al., 1994).

Furthermore, the effects of global attitudes on subjective experiences may be greater for Black citizens than White. For example, in a survey examining racial variation in perceptions of police–citizen interactions, Hurwitz and Peffley (2005) found that Black Americans' global attitudes toward the police had a significant impact on their interpretation of police encounter scenarios. Specifically, Black respondents who viewed the criminal justice system as unfair reported greater suspicion of police encounters, particularly when the encounter involved a Black citizen. In contrast, the global attitudes of White respondents were found to have smaller effects. Additionally, White respondents typically reported perceiving the criminal justice system as fair, ignoring differences in police encounters with Black versus White citizens (Hurwitz & Peffley, 2005). From these findings, Hurwitz and Peffley (2005) observed that fairness "often takes on a radically different meaning for the races" (p. 765).

The significant influence of global attitudes suggests that while concern regarding procedural fairness in police encounters and the cognitive process related to the procedural justice model may be similar across racial/ethnic groups (see, e.g., Sunshine & Tyler, 2003; Tyler & Huo, 2002), an individual's interpretation of police encounters (procedurally just or not) may differ according to their race. Specifically, Black Americans—who have consistently reported less favorable global attitudes toward the police—may be less likely to perceive and interpret their specific interactions with police officers as fair and just, effectively limiting the impact of the procedural justice model. Unfortunately, however, current research sheds little light on the effects of Black citizens' preexisting attitudes on perceptions of procedural justice and subsequent outcomes. Instead, the procedural justice model provides a prescriptive model for police where the role of the citizen in police encounters—including the opinions, emotions, and/or preconceptions they import into those encounters—is largely ignored.[4] Indeed, the current procedural justice model presents citizens as empty vessels that will react similarly if police behave similarly in those encounters.

Therefore, while procedural justice is touted as a reform to aid in improving police relations with minority communities, as a model, it makes little reference to how minority citizens within these communities might perceive their encounters with police. This failure to explore global attitudes of Black Americans—including the origins of those attitudes and their influence on encounters with police—produces an incomplete model with potentially limited effects for police relations with minority communities. It must be recognized that procedural justice occurs in context. If we are going to hypothesize how strategies might affect Black communities, the theoretical base of those strategies must consider the unique perspectives and experiences of Black citizens in American society.

A Black Criminology Model of Procedural Justice

A Black Criminology model of procedural justice would emphasize the role of race in perceptions of fairness and equity in police encounters. Discarding the idea that procedural justice functions as a general model for policing, this Black Criminology approach suggests that Black Americans' perceptions of police are related to their incomparable past and contemporary experiences. As such, this model facilitates (1) exploration of the unique factors that influence Black Americans' global attitudes toward police, (2) examination of the impact of these attitudes on perceptions of procedural justice in police encounters and subsequent outcomes depicted in the procedural justice model of policing (i.e., encounter satisfaction, perceptions of police legitimacy, cooperation and compliance), and (3) discussion concerning the implications of procedural justice for police relations with minority communities. Figure 12.2 presents the Black Criminology model of procedural justice. This model identifies three important contributors to Black Americans' formulation of global attitudes toward police: general discrimination, experience with police, and legal socialization.

Figure 12.2
Black Criminology Model of Procedural Justice

Contributors to Black Americans' Global Attitudes

First, the global attitudes of Black citizens in the United States are likely a product of the *general discrimination* inherent in the history of Black America. Slavery, Jim Crow laws, segregation, the War on Drugs, and mass incarceration—these legal and social constraints on Black lives across American history have systematically designated a second-class status to Black Americans (Alexander, 2012; Butler, 2017; Hayes, 2017). Importantly, police agencies in the United States have historically been used as the enforcers of both explicitly racist and implicitly discriminatory laws and norms (National Academies of Sciences, 2018). This enforcement role has consistently placed police officers and minority citizens at odds, producing a "multi-generational—almost inherited—mistrust between communities of color and their law enforcement agencies" (Jackman, 2016). Given this history, Black Americans are more likely to view police through a racial lens, demonstrating greater vigilance to signs of discrimination. Indeed, incidents of police bias, brutality, and other misconduct may be so familiar to certain individuals that they create "chronically accessible scripts" that guide both their general attitudes of police and their interpretations of individual police encounters (Hurwitz & Peffley, 2005, p. 767).

Second, the global attitudes of Black Americans are likely influenced by their high rates of direct and vicarious *experience with police* (Browning, Cullen, Cao, & Stevenson, 1994; Feagin, 1991; Rosenbaum, Schuck, Costello, Hawkins, & Ring, 2005). As discussed previously, Black Americans are often subject to more frequent police–initiated contacts (Smith et al., 2017). Research suggests the nature of these specific encounters has some influence on an individual's broader perceptions of police, though the influence of positive and negative encounters is asymmetrical in nature (Frank, Smith, & Novak, 2005; Hurst & Frank, 2000; Weitzer & Tuch, 2002). Skogan (2006), for example, observed that the impact of having a negative experience on attitudes toward police is 4–14 times greater than that of having a positive experience. This finding has substantial implications for the global attitudes of Black Americans. Indeed, the law of large numbers would suggest, given their high rate of contact with police, Black Americans are more likely to experience a negative encounter with an officer.

Negative perceptions can also be amplified through vicarious experience. Specifically, the concentration of proactive policing initiatives in inner-city, minority communities increases the likelihood of Black citizens knowing someone (i.e., friends, family) who has had a negative contact with the police (Brunson, 2007; Weitzer, 2000). For example, in their interviews with middle-class Black Americans, Feagin and Sikes (1994) observed that "a black victim frequently shares [their] account with family and friends, often to lighten the burden, and this sharing created a domino effect of anguish and anger rippling across an extended group" (p. 16). The effects of these experiences are increased by perceptions that these policing strategies target minority neighborhoods because they are predominantly Black and disadvantaged (see, e.g., Gau & Brunson, 2010). Furthermore, the rate of vicarious experience has expanded with the proliferation of news and social media. These sources have increased citizens' exposure to high-profile incidents of police misconduct and use of lethal force against Black citizens (Desmond, Papachristos, & Kirk, 2016), fueling broader perceptions of police in America.

Finally, the *legal socialization* of Black citizens in America is likely to affect their global attitudes of police. Legal socialization refers to the development of an individual's ties to law and legal actors (Fagan & Tyler, 2005). This socialization process is identified to begin in childhood and adolescence—"a time when young people's initial impressions of the justice system are translated into conscious and subconscious expectations about how police will treat them and how they should respond" (Henning, 2017, p. 63). Parents and other guardians are observed to play a large role in childhood legal socialization (see, e.g., Cavanagh & Cauffman, 2015; Wolfe, McLean, & Pratt, 2016). For many Black American families, the legal socialization process involves the transmission of norms regarding how to best handle interactions with police (Henning, 2017). Indeed, literature examining the Black experience with the American criminal justice system often note "the talk" parents and guardians must inevitably have with their children. Specifically, parents and other guardians instill in Black children the wisdom of their personal experiences with police, outlining rules ranging from what to wear to how to act—all designed to reduce their chances of coming to the attention of police or, *when* (not if) they are stopped, increase the likelihood that they will walk away from the encounter (see, e.g., Burley, n.d.; Gandbhir & Foster, 2015). The content of "the talk" socializes Black youths to be suspicious, even fearful, of legal authorities. In turn, these orientations are carried into adulthood, creating lasting effects on adults' attitudes toward police (Fagan & Tyler, 2005; Searing, Wright, & Rabinowitz, 1976).

Implications for Procedural Justice Research and Reform

This Black Criminology approach to the procedural justice model of policing frames our understanding of the impact of fair and impartial policing on police–community relations by race. This model recognizes the influence of the unique lived racialized experiences of Black Americans (i.e., general discrimination, experience with police, legal socialization) in the formulation of their global attitudes toward police and the subsequent effects of those attitudes on encounter-specific perceptions of procedural justice. While we do not deny overlap in public perceptions of police, this model suggests that Black Americans are more likely to view police through a racial lens. As such, they do not enter police–citizen encounters with the same mindset as White Americans.

More generally, this Black Criminology model highlights the need for rigorous examinations of procedural justice and race. This chapter has emphasized the influence of race on perceptions of procedural justice at the encounter level. However, it should be noted that the Black Criminology framework for procedural justice might be expanded in another direction. For example, it is possible that Black Americans have a racialized interpretation or understanding of procedural justice itself. Stated differently, it is possible that Black Americans have different conceptions from their White counterparts of what constitutes "fairness," and those definitions may influence both their global and specific attitudes toward police. Understanding this variation will require asking Black Americans what they want and expect from authorities in the criminal justice system. Indeed, Tyler (1990) recognized that issues of procedural justice must be explored from the public's perspective. What does procedural justice mean to Black Citizens in the United States? How do they view the core components of participation, neutrality, respect, and trustworthiness? Would they identify other elements that constitute fair and impartial policing? A Black Criminology framework for the general model of procedural justice would facilitate the exploration of questions like these—providing greater insight into the origins and nature of individuals' understanding of "fairness" in policing and the impact of that understanding on police–citizen interactions.

Overall, recognizing the potential for differences in citizens' interpretation of procedural justice and police events raises important questions regarding the efficacy of procedural justice in minority communities. Specifically, the persistent and pervasive nature of unfavorable attitudes among Black Americans toward police suggests that police incorporation of procedural justice in their encounters with these citizens is not sufficient on its own to improve police–community relations. Instead, police efforts must be made to address the components of global attitudes at both the encounter and community levels. "Black Americans" attitudes toward police are not uniformly negative. The challenge, however, is for police to tap into the positive perceptions and enhance experiences in the community. While the general model of procedural justice provides one avenue for these efforts, continued development and exploration of a Black Criminology model can facilitate the advancement of strategies that address Black Americans' historical and contemporary experiences with police that are key to improving police–community relations.

Conclusion

For years, scholars have debated whether there is an inevitable tradeoff between police efficiency and effectiveness in preventing and controlling crime and the fairness and equity of police services (Engel & Eck, 2015; Packer, 1968). In a recent example, the proactive policing movement demonstrates the power of the police to manage problems of crime and disorder but also reveals the substantial collateral consequences of some of these efforts—particularly for communities of color. Indeed, the subsequent crisis in police relations with minority communities caused many policing scholars, practitioners, and policymakers to explore how police can be both effective and fair in their practices. Procedural justice appears to provide the answer. The procedural justice model of policing emphasizes the importance of the quality and fairness of citizens' interactions with police. This model of policing is certainly the ideal. Police agencies should undoubtedly encourage equity in policing by training their officers to incorporate procedurally just behavior and decision making in their interactions with citizens.

However, the procedural justice model of policing should not be treated as a general model—suggesting all citizens and communities will react to these procedurally just encounters similarly. To do so risks overstating the impact of experiences in police–citizen encounters on general perceptions of police and increases the likelihood that the procedural justice model of policing will remain a symbolic reform (National Academies of Sciences, 2018; see Johnson et al., 2017; Maguire, Lowrey, & Johnson, 2017). Stated simply, "[a]dult attitudes are not simple functions of the treatment they receive from the police" (Worden & McLean, 2017, p. 51). Instead, to effect real change in police relations with disadvantaged minority communities, community context and global attitudes must be taken into consideration.

A Black Criminology approach to the procedural justice model of policing would do just that—providing a race-specific approach to the procedural justice model of policing to enhance our understanding of the impact of procedural justice on police–race relations. Specifically, a Black Criminology model of procedural justice would incorporate the unique experiences of Black Americans into the procedural justice model of policing, connecting research on the origins and impact of global attitudes to the procedural justice model. In particular, this model emphasizes the importance of enhancing individuals' experiences with the police both in encounter-specific scenarios and in broader community contexts to bridge the historically based divide between police agencies and communities of color. In sum, the application and evaluation of this model can help inform both procedural justice and community-based efforts—clarifying best practices for enhancing perceptions of fair and impartial policing, particularly in those communities that are policed the most.

Notes

1. Readers should note *The President's Task Force on 21st Century Policing Final Report* is now unavailable on federal websites.
2. For more discussion on measurement, see Gau, 2011; Jonathon-Zamir, Mastrofski, & Moyal, 2015; and Maguire & Johnson, 2010.
3. Using a purposive sampling methodology, the Urban Institute conducted in-person surveys across six cities: Birmingham, Alabama; Fort Worth, Texas; Gary, Indiana; Minneapolis, Minnesota; Pittsburgh, Pennsylvania, and Stockton, California. The sampling process resulted in 1278 survey respondents—66.3% of the respondents identified as Black, 11.9% identified as White, and 10.6% identified as Latino or Hispanic.
4. It should be noted that Murphy and Tyler (2008) provide some examination of the role of emotions in procedural justice. However, their study frames emotion as a mediator in the procedural justice model—viewed as a response to perceptions of procedural justice that can impact subsequent compliance behavior.

References

Alexander, M. (2012). *The new Jim Crow: Mass incarceration in the age of color-blindness*. New York, NY: The New Press.

Alpert, G. P., Dunham, R., & Smith, M. R. (2007). Investigating racial profiling by the Miami-Dade Police Department: A multi-method approach. *Criminology & Public Policy*, *6*, 25–55.

Bayley, D. H. (1990). *Police for the future*. New York, NY: Oxford University Press.

Brandl, S. G., Frank, J., Worden, R. E., & Bynum, T. S. (1994). Global and specific attitudes toward the police: Disentangling the relationship. *Justice Quarterly, 11*, 119–134.

Browning, S. L., Cullen, F. T., Cao, L. Kopache, R., & Stevenson, T. J. (1994). Race and getting hassled by the police: A research note. *Police Studies, 17*, 1–11.

Brunson, R. K. (2007). "Police don't like black people": African-American young men's accumulated police experiences. *Criminology & Public Policy, 6*, 71–102.

Brunson, R., & Weitzer, R. (2009). Police relations with black and white youths in different urban neighborhoods. *Urban Affairs Review, 44*, 858–885.

Burley, U., III. (n.d.). A letter to my unborn [black] son. *The Salt Collective*. Retrieved from http://thesaltcollective.org/letter-unbornblack-son/

Butler, P. (2017). *Chokehold: Policing black men; A renegade prosecutor's radical thoughts on how to disrupt the system*. New York, NY: The New Press.

Cavanagh, C., & Cauffman, E. (2015). Viewing law and order: Mothers' and sons' justice system legitimacy attitudes and juvenile recidivism. *Psychology, Public Policy, & Law, 21*, 432–441.

Desmond, M., Papachristos, A. V., & Kirk, D. S. (2016). Police violence and citizen crime reporting in the black community. *American Sociological Review, 81*, 857–876.

Donner, C. M., Maskaly, J., Fridell, L. A., & Jennings, W. G. (2015). Policing and procedural justice: A state-of-the-art-review. *Policing: An International Journal of Strategies and Management, 38*(1), 153–172.

Eck, J. E., & Maguire, E. R. (2000). Have changes in policing reduced violent crime? An assessment of the evidence. In A. Blumstein & J. Wallman (Eds.), *The crime drop in America*. New York, NY: Cambridge University Press.

Eck, J. E., & Rosenbaum, D. (1994). The new police order: Effectiveness, equity, and efficiency in community policing. In D. Rosenbaum (Ed.), *Community policing: Testing the promises*. Newbury Park, CA: Sage.

Ekins, E. (2016). *Policing in America: Understanding public attitudes toward police. Results from a national survey*. Washington, DC: CATO Institute.

Elliott, I., Thomas, S. D. M., & Ogloff, J. R. P. (2012). Procedural justice in contacts with the police: The perspectives of victims of crime. *Police Practice and Research, 13*, 437–449.

Engel, R. S. (2005). Citizens' perceptions of distributive and procedural justice during traffic stops with police. *Journal of Research in Crime and Delinquency, 42*, 445–481.

Engel, R. S., & Eck, J. E. (2015). Effectiveness vs. equity in policing: Is a tradeoff inevitable? *Ideas in American Policing, 18*, 1–12.

Engel, R. S., & Johnson, R. (2006). Toward a better understanding of racial and ethnic disparities in search and seizure rates. *Journal of Criminal Justice, 34*, 605–617.

Engel, R. S., Smith, M. R., & Cullen, F. T. (2012). Race, place, and drug enforcement. *Criminology & Public Policy, 11*, 603–635.

Epp, C. R., Maynard-Moody, S., & Haider-Markel, D. (2014). *Pulled over: How police stops define race and citizenship*. Chicago, IL: University of Chicago Press.

Fagan, J., Geller, A., Davies, G., & West, V. (2010). Street stops and broken windows revisited: The demography and logic of proactive policing in a safe and changing city. In S. K. Rice & M. D. White (Eds.), *Race, ethnicity, and policing:*

New and essential readings (pp. 309–348). New York, NY: New York University Press.

Fagan, J., & Tyler, T. R. (2005). Legal socialization of children and adolescents. *Social Justice Research, 18*, 217–241.

Fagan, J., Zimring, F. E., & Kim, J. (1998). Declining homicide in New York City: A tale of two trends. *The Journal of Criminal Law & Criminology, 88*, 1277–1324.

Feagin, J. R. (1991). The continuing significance of race: Antiblack discrimination in public places. *American Sociological Review, 56*, 101–116.

Feagin, J. R., & Sikes, M. P. (1994). *Living with racism: The Black middle class experience*. Boston, MA: Beacon.

Floyd v. City of New York, 959 F. Supp. 2d 540 (2013).

Folger, R., & Greenberg, J. (1985). Procedural justice: A interpretative analysis of personnel systems. In K. Rowland & G. Ferris (Eds.), *Research in personnel and human resources management* (Vol. 3). Greenwich, CT: JAI Press.

Forman Jr., J. (2017). *Locking up our own: Crime and punishment in black America*. New York, NY: Farrar, Strauss, and Giroux.

Frank, J., Brandl, S, G., Cullen, F. T., & Stichman, A. (1996). Reassessing the impact of race on citizens' attitudes toward police: A research note. *Justice Quarterly, 13*, 321–334.

Frank, J., Smith, B. W., & Novak, K. J. (2005). Citizen attitudes toward the police: Exploring the basis of citizen attitudes. *Police Quarterly, 8*, 206–228.

Gandbhir, G., & Foster, B. (2015). A conversation with my black son: Op-docs. *The New York Times*. Retrieved from www.nytimes.com/2015/03/17/opinion/a-conversation-with-my-black-son.html

Garza, A. (2014). A herstory of the #BlackLivesMatter movement. *The Feminist Wire*. Retrieved January 27, 2016, from www.thefeministwire.com/2014/10/blacklivesmatter-2/.

Gau, J. M. (2011). The convergent and discriminant validity of procedural justice and police legitimacy: An empirical test of core theoretical propositions. *Journal of Criminal Justice, 39*(6), 489–498.

Gau, J. M., & Brunson, R. K. (2010). Procedural justice and order maintenance policing: A study of inner-city young men's perceptions of police legitimacy. *Justice Quarterly, 27*, 255–279.

Gau, J. M., Corsaro, N., Stewart, E. A., & Brunson, R. K. (2012). Examining macro-level impacts on procedural justice and police legitimacy. *Journal of Criminal Justice, 40*, 333–343.

Gelman, A., Fagan, J., & Kiss, A. (2007). An analysis of the New York City police department's "stop-and-frisk" policy in the context of claims of racial bias. *Journal of the American Statistical Association, 102*, 813–823.

Gottfredson, M. R., & Hirschi, T. (1990). *A general theory of crime*. Palo Alto, CA: Stanford University Press.

Greenberg, J., & Tyler, T. R. (1987). Why procedural justice in organizations? *Social Justice Research, 1*, 127–142.

Greenwood, P., Chaiken, J., & Petersilia, J. (1977). *The criminal investigation process*. Lexington, MA: Heath.

Hagan, J., Shedd, C., & Payne, M. R. (2005). Race, ethnicity, and youth perceptions of criminal injustice. *American Sociological Review, 70*, 381–407.

Hayes, C. (2017). *A colony in a nation*. New York, NY: W. W. Norton.

Henning, K. (2017). Boys to men: The role of policing in the socialization of black boys. In A. J. Davis (Ed.), *Policing the Black man*. New York, NY: Pantheon Books.

Hickman, L. J., & Simpson, S. S. (2003). Fair treatment or preferred outcome? The impact of police behavior on victim reports of domestic violence incidents. *Law & Society Review, 37*, 607–634.

Hurst, Y. G., & Frank, J. (2000). How kids view cops: The nature of juvenile attitudes toward the police. *Journal of Criminal Justice, 28*, 189–202.

Hurwitz, J., & Peffley, M. (2005). Explaining the great racial divide: Perceptions of fairness in the U.S. criminal justice system. *The Journal of Politics, 67*, 762–783.

Jackman, T. (2016). U.S. police chiefs group apologizes for "historical mistreatment" of minorities. *The Washington Post*. Retrieved from www.washingtonpost. com/news/true-crime/wp/2016/10/17/head-of-u-s-police-chiefs-apologizes-for-historic-mistreatment-of-minorities/?utm_term=.812eb2e73cba

Johnson, D., Wilson, D. V., Maguire, E. R., & Lowrey-Kinberg, B. V. (2017). Race and perceptions of police: Experimental results on the impact of procedural (in) justice. *Justice Quarterly, 34*, 1184–1212.

Jonathan-Zamir, T., Mastrofski, S. D., & Moyal, S. (2015). Measuring procedural justice in police-citizen encounters. *Justice Quarterly, 32*(5), 845–871.

Kelling, G. L., Pate, T., Dieckman, D., & Brown, C. E. (1974). *The Kansas City preventive patrol experiment: A summary report*. Washington, DC: Police Foundation.

Kochel, T. R., Wilson, D. B., & Mastrofski, S. D. (2011). Effect of suspect race on officers' arrest decisions. *Criminology, 49*, 473–512.

La Vigne, N., Fontaine, J., & Dwidevi, A. (2017). *How do people in high-crime, low income communities view the police?* Washington, DC: Urban Institute, Justice Policy Center.

Lind, E. A., & Tyler, T. R. (1988). *The social psychology of procedural justice*. New York, NY: Plenum Press.

Lowrey, B. V., Maguire, E. R., and Bennett, R. R. (2016). Testing the effects of procedural justice and overaccommodation in traffic stops. *Criminal Justice and Behavior, 43*, 1430–1449.

MacQueen, S., & Bradford, B. (2015). Enhancing public trust and police legitimacy during road traffic encounters: Results from a randomised controlled trial in Scotland. *Journal of Experimental Criminology, 11*, 419–443.

Maguire, E. R., & Johnson, D. (2010). Measuring public perceptions of the police. *Policing: An International Journal of Police Strategies & Management, 33*(4), 703–730.

Maguire, E. R., Lowrey, B. V., & Johnson, D. (2017). Evaluating the relative impact of positive and negative encounters with police: A randomized experiment. *Journal of Experimental Criminology, 13*, 367–391.

Mazerolle, L., Bennett, S., Antrobus, E., & Eggins, E. (2012). Procedural justice, routine encounters and citizen perceptions of police: Main findings from the Queensland Community Engagement Trial (QCET). *Journal of Experimental Criminology, 8*, 343–367.

Mazerolle, L., Antrobus, E., Bennett, S., & Tyler, T. R. (2013). Shaping citizen perceptions of police legitimacy: A randomized field trial of procedural justice. *Criminology, 51*, 33–64.

Mazerolle, L., Sargeant, E., Cherney, A., Bennett, S., Murphy, K., Antrobus, E., & Martin, P. (2014). *Procedural justice and legitimacy in policing*. New York, NY: Springer.

Mazerolle, L., Bennett, S., Davis, J., Sargeant, E., and Manning, M. (2013). Proce-dural justice and police legitimacy: A systematic review of research evidence. *Journal of Experimental Criminology*, *9*, 245–274.

Meares, T., & Tyler, T. (2017). Policing: A model for the twenty-first century. In A. J. Davis (Ed.), *Policing the black man*. New York, NY: Pantheon Books.

Murphy, K., & Tyler, T. (2008). Procedural justice and compliance behaviour: The mediating role of emotions. *European Journal of Social Psychology*, *38*(4), 652–688.

National Advisory Commission on Civil Disorders. (1968). *Report of the national advisory commission on civil disorders*. Washington, DC: U.S. Government Printing Office.

National Academies of Sciences, Engineering, and Medicine. (2018). *Proactive polic-ing: Effects on crime and communities*. Washington, DC: National Academies Press.

National Research Council. (2004). *Fairness and effectiveness in policing* (W. Skogan & K. Frydll, Eds.). Washington, DC: National Academies Press.

Nix, J., Campbell, B. A., Byers, E. H., & Alpert, G. P. (2017). A bird's eye view of civilians killed by police in 2015. *Criminology & Public Policy*, *16*, 309–340.

Packer, H. (1968). *The limits of criminal sanction*. Stanford, CA: Stanford Univer-sity Press.

Paoline, E. A., Gau, J. M., & Terrill, W. (2016). Race and the police use of force encounter in the United States. *The British Journal of Criminology*, *58*, 54–74.

Peck, J. H. (2015). Minority perceptions of the police: A state-of-the-art review. *Polic-ing: An International Journal of Police Strategies & Management*, *33*, 173–203.

President's Commission on Law Enforcement and Administration of Justice. (1967). *The challenge of crime in a free society*. Washington, DC: U.S. Government Printing Office.

Reisig, M. D., Bratton, J., & Gertz, M. G. (2007). The construct validity and refine-ment of process-based policing measures. *Criminal Justice and Behavior*, *34*, 1005–1028.

Rosenbaum, D. P. (2006). The limits of hot spots policing. In D. Weisburd & A. A. Braga (Eds.), *Police innovation: Contrasting perspectives* (pp. 245–263). New York, NY: Cambridge University Press.

Rosenbaum, D. P., Schuck, A. M., Costello, S. K., Hawkins, D. F., & Ring, M. K. (2005). Attitudes toward the police: The effects of direct and vicarious experi-ence. *Police Quarterly*, *8*, 343–365.

Sahin, N. M. (2014). Legitimacy, procedural justice and police-citizen encounters: A randomized controlled trial of the impact of procedural justice on citizen per-ceptions of police during traffic stops in Turkey (Unpublished doctoral disserta-tion). Newark, DE: Rutgers University.

Schulhofer, S. J., Tyler, T. R., & Huq, A. Z. (2011). American policing at a cross-roads: Unsustainable policies and the procedural justice alternative. *Journal of Criminal Law & Criminology*, *101*, 335–374.

Searing, D., Wright, G., & Rabinowitz, G. (1976). The primacy principle: Attitude change and political socialization. *British Journal of Political Science*, *6*, 83–113.

Sherman, L. W. (2018). Reducing fatal police shootings as system crashes: Research, theory, and practice. *Annual Review of Criminology*, *1*, 421–449.

Skogan, W. G. (2006). Asymmetry in the impact of encounters with police. *Polic-ing & Society*, *16*, 99–126.

Smith, M. R., Rojek, J. J., Petrocelli, M., & Withrow, B. (2017). Measuring dis-parities in police activities: A state of the art review. *Policing: An International Journal of Police Strategies & Management*, *40*, 166–183.

Sparrow, M. (2016). *Handcuffed: What holds policing back and the keys to reform.* Washington, DC: Brookings Institution.

Spelman, W., & Brown, D. K. (1981). *Calling the police: A replication of the citizen reporting component of the Kansas City response time analysis.* Washington, DC: Police Executive Research Forum.

Stewart, E. A., Baumer, E. P., Brunson, R. K., & Simons, R. L. (2009). Neighborhood racial context and perception of police-based racial discrimination among Black youth. *Criminology, 47*, 847–887.

Sunshine, J., & Tyler, T. R. (2003). The role of procedural justice and legitimacy in shaping public support for policing. *Law & Society Review, 37*, 513–548.

Taylor, R. B. (2006). Incivilities reduction policing, zero tolerance, and the retreat from coproduction: Weak foundations and strong pressures. In D. Weisburd & A. A. Braga (Eds.), *Police innovation: Contrasting perspectives* (pp. 98–114). New York, NY: Cambridge University Press.

Thibaut, J., & Walker, L. (1975). *Procedural justice: A psychological analysis.* Hillsdale, NJ: Erlbaum.

Tyler, T. R. (1987). Procedural justice research. *Social Justice Research, 1*, 41–65.

Tyler, T. R. (1988). What is procedural justice? Criteria used by citizens to assess the fairness of legal procedures. *Law & Society Review, 22*, 103–135.

Tyler, T. R. (1990). *Why people obey the law.* Princeton, NJ: Princeton University Press.

Tyler, T. R. (2001). Trust and law abidingness: A proactive model of social regulation. *Boston University Law Review, 81*, 361–405.

Tyler, T. R. (2003). Procedural justice, legitimacy, and the effective rule of law. In M. H. Tonry (Ed.), *Crime and justice: A review of research* (Vol. 30). Chicago, IL: University of Chicago Press.

Tyler, T. R. (2004). Enhancing police legitimacy. *The Annals of the American Academy of Political and Social Science, 593*, 84–99.

Tyler, T. R. (2005). Policing in black and white: Group differences in trust and confidence in the police. *Police Quarterly, 8*, 322–341.

Tyler, T. R., & Caine, A. (1981). The influence of outcomes and procedures on satisfaction with formal leaders. *Journal of Personality and Social Psychology, 41*, 642–655.

Tyler, T. R., & Fagan, J. (2008). Legitimacy and cooperation: Why do people help police fight crime in their communities? *Ohio State Journal of Criminal Law, 6*, 231–275.

Tyler, T. R., & Folger, R. (1980). Distributional and procedural aspects of satisfaction with citizen-police encounters. *Basic and Applied Social Psychology, 1*, 281–292.

Tyler, T. R., Goff, P. A., & MacCoun, R. J. (2015). The impact of psychological science on policing in the United States: Procedural justice, legitimacy, and effective law enforcement. *Psychological Science in the Public Interest, 16*, 75–109.

Tyler, T. R., & Huo, Y. J. (2002). *Trust in the law: Encouraging public cooperation with the police and courts.* New York, NY: Russel Sage Foundation.

Tyler, T. R., & Jackson, J. (2013). *Future challenges in the study of legitimacy and criminal justice.* Public Law Working Paper No. 264. Yale Law School.

Tyler, T. R., Jackson, J., & Mentovich, A. (2015). The consequences of being an object of suspicion: Potential pitfalls of proactive police contact. *Journal of Empirical Legal Studies, 12*, 602–636.

Walker, L., & Lind, E. A. (1984). Psychological studies of procedural models. In G. M. Stephenson & J. H. Davis (Eds.), *Progress in applied social psychology* (Vol. 2). New York, NY: Wiley.

Weisburd, D., & Braga, A. A. (2006). *Police innovation: Contrasting perspectives*. New York, NY: Cambridge University Press.

Weisburd, D., & Eck, J. E. (2004). What can police do to reduce, crime, disorder, and fear? *The Annals of the American Academy of Political and Social Science, 593*, 42–65.

Weitzer, R. (2000). Racialized policing: Resident's perceptions in three neighborhoods. *Law & Society Review, 34*, 129–155.

Weitzer, R. (2015). American policing under fire: Misconduct and reform. *Social Science and Modern Society, 52*, 475–480.

Weitzer, R., & Tuch, S. A. (1999). Race, class, and perceptions of discrimination by the police. *Crime and Delinquency, 45*(4), 494–507.

Weitzer, R., & Tuch, S. A. (2002). Perceptions of racial profiling: Race, class, and personal experience. *Criminology, 40*, 435–456.

Weitzer, R., & Tuch, S. A. (2004). Race and perceptions of police misconduct. *Social Problems, 51*, 305–325.

Weitzer, R., & Tuch, S. A. (2005). Racially biased policing: Determinants of citizen perceptions. *Social Forces, 83*, 1009–1030.

Weitzer, R., & Tuch, S. A. (2006). *Race and policing in America*. Cambridge, UK: Cambridge University Press.

Wilson, W. J. (1987). *The truly disadvantaged: The inner city, the underclass, and public policy*. Chicago, IL: University of Chicago Press.

Wolfe, S. E., McLean, K., & Pratt, T. C. (2016). I learned it by watching you: Legal socialization and the intergenerational transmission of legitimacy attitudes. *British Journal of Criminology, 57*, 1123–1143.

Worden, R. E., & McLean, S. J. (2017). *Mirage of police reform: Procedural justice and police legitimacy*. Oakland, CA: University of California Press.

Worden, R. W., & McLean, S. J. (2014). *Assessing police performance in citizen encounters: Police legitimacy and management accountability*. Report to the National Institute of Justice. Albany, NY: John F. Finn Institute for Public Safety, Inc.

Zimring, F. E. (2007). *The great American crime decline*. New York, NY: Oxford University Press.

Zimring, F. E. (2017). *When police kill*. Cambridge, MA: Harvard University Press.

13

The Paradox of a Black Incarceration Boom in an Era of Declining Black Crime: Causes and Consequences[1]

Ojmarrh Mitchell

In this chapter, I explain how criminal justice policy changes led to dramatic increases in Black imprisonment despite falling Black crime rates. I argue that policy changes designed to reduce discretionary sentencing and racial disparities in sentencing were later usurped by punitive policy initiatives aimed at reducing crime. Most notably, the "war on drugs" and the "tough-on-crime" movement dramatically increased the likelihood of imprisonment and the length of prison terms for many offense types, often by using structured sentencing mechanisms (e.g., long mandatory minimum prison sentences for drug offenses). Further, structured sentencing mechanisms aimed at reducing judicial discretion were undermined by prosecutors, whose discretion was left untouched by structured sentencing. Prosecutors used their discretion in more punitive ways, which is an important but often unacknowledged cause of rising imprisonment rates.

I also argue that each of the major policy initiatives causing mass imprisonment has failed to reach its stated goals, but these harsh policies have had major collateral consequences on the lives of those caught in the criminal justice system. These collateral consequences in varied ways reduce employment opportunities, income, and family formation, but not parenthood, which results in millions of children growing up without one of their parents in their life, typically a father, and, once labeled a felon, parents experience greater difficulty in providing for their children. Perhaps most important, the collateral consequences of conviction lead to political disenfranchisement, leaving those affected by America's punitive shift in crime and punishment without the ability to directly change these policies by voting against them and their proponents. All of these collateral consequences are most concentrated among Blacks, and many of them have larger negative effects on Black Americans. In the end, the shifting landscape of punishment in America has resulted in a large, expensive prison system and a large population of Blacks who have been marginalized socially, economically, and politically.

This chapter is organized in six sections. In the first section, I begin by discussing trends in Black crime and imprisonment. These trends reveal a seemingly contradictory pattern of falling Black crime for all crime types historically associated with imprisonment but growing Black imprisonment rates. I then examine the criminal justice factors causing the growth of prison populations in the second section. This examination finds that the explosion in Black imprisonment is primarily due to increases in the likelihood of imprisonment given an arrest, especially for drug crimes, and increases in the length of prison terms, particularly for violent crimes. Little of the growth is explained by changes in offending or the likelihood of arrest, with the exception of drug arrests, which boomed in the 1980s and remain elevated to this day. In the third section, I discuss the policy changes that produced increases in the likelihood of imprisonment and length of imprisonment. I attribute prison growth to three factors: efforts to structure sentencing, the war on drugs of the mid-1980s, and the subsequent tough-on-crime movement. Structured sentencing intended to make sentencing more predictable and race neutral by reducing judicial and parole board discretion but had the unintended consequence of empowering prosecutors. The drug war and the tough-on-crime movement made sanctions more punitive in an effort to reduce drug-related crime and crime generally. In section four, I review the evidence assessing the effectiveness of these policy changes in achieving their intended goals. I contend that the noted policy changes increased sentencing predictability and punitiveness; however, these changes largely failed to reduce racial disparities in sentencing or reduce crime. I discuss the unintended, collateral consequences of America's punitive policy shifts with a particular emphasis on the concentration of collateral consequences among Blacks in the fifth section. The sixth and final section is perhaps the most controversial. In this section, I argue that the policy changes causing the explosion in the prison population in all likelihood were motivated by racial politics, and the continued existence of these policies is *proof positive* of racial bias.

Trends in African American Imprisonment

Between 1980 and 2014, Black crime rates as measured by arrests have dropped markedly for all Uniform Crime Reporting (UCR) Index crimes (see Table 13.1). Violent crimes involving Black offenders were down approximately 40% overall in 2014 compared to 1980 (Snyder, Cooper, & Mulako-Wangota, 2017). Black arrests for murder declined 65%, rape fell 75%, robbery dropped 62%, and aggravated assault sank by 24%. Likewise, Black property offending dropped by 51% overall in this time period, led by declines in burglary (-70%), motor vehicle theft (-69%), and larceny (-41%). These declines in Black crime are even larger if measured from their respective peaks instead of the 1980 rate. Black rates of burglary (1982), rape (1986), robbery (1989), larceny (1989), and motor vehicle theft (1989) all peaked in the 1980s, and murder (1991) and aggravated assault (1995) reached their apex in the 1990s. Thus, Black crime has been on a downward trajectory for most UCR Index crimes for more than 25 years. And these reduced crime rates are found among the types of crimes historically most likely to lead to imprisonment.

Notably, this finding of reduced Black offending is not confined to UCR arrest data. The same finding of reduced Black offending is evident

Table 13.1 Black UCR Crime Rates per 100,000: 1980–2014

Offense Type	1980 Rate	Peak Rate (Year)	2014 Rate	% Change Peak to 2014	% Change 1980 to 2014
Murder	35	42 (1991)	12	−71	−65
Rape	55	60 (1984)	14	−78	−75
Robbery	314	352 (1989)	120	−66	−62
Aggravated assault	366	638 (1995)	280	−56	−24
Burglary	545	585 (1982)	163	−72	−70
Motor vehicle theft	152	314 (1989)	47	−85	−69
Larceny	1,338	1,738 (1989)	786	−55	−41

Source: Snyder, Cooper, and Mulako-Wangota, 2017

in self-reports of offending (see, e.g., Western, 2006). Likewise, victim reports of crimes involving Black perpetrators has fallen for both Black-on-Black violence and Black-on-White violence (Morgan, 2017). Undeniably, Black crime has fallen precipitously in the past 25 years or so.

Black imprisonment rates, in stark contrast to Black rates of crime, have risen dramatically in the same period of time (see Figure 13.1). In 1980, for every 100,000 Blacks in the United States, 550 were under the jurisdiction of a state or federal prison (serving a sentencing of any length) (U.S. Department of Justice, 2015). This rate grew continuously from 1980 to 1999—reaching a peak of 1,770 per 100,000. Since that time, Black imprisonment rates have fallen modestly and sit at approximately 1,420 per 100,000 in 2014. Taken together, Black imprisonment rates in 2014 are approximately 150% greater than those of 1980, despite Black Index crime rates falling by more than 50%.

Another notable feature of the boom in Black imprisonment is the remarkable rise in imprisonment for drug offenses despite falling Black drug use (see Figure 13.2). In 1983, which is the first year these data are available, less than 6% of Blacks admitted to prison were committed on

Figure 13.1
Black Crime vs. Imprisonment Rates, 1980–2014

Sources: National Prisoner Statistics, 1978–2015; Snyder, Cooper, and Mulako-Wangota, 2017

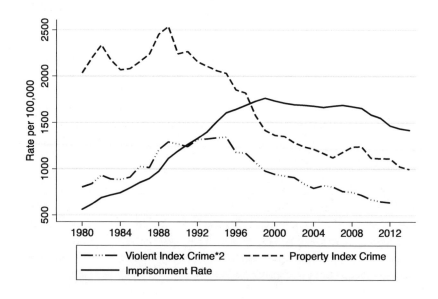

Figure 13.2
Black Drug Use vs. Drug Prison Admissions

Sources: National Corrections Reporting Program, 1983–2014 & National
Survey on Drug Use and Health

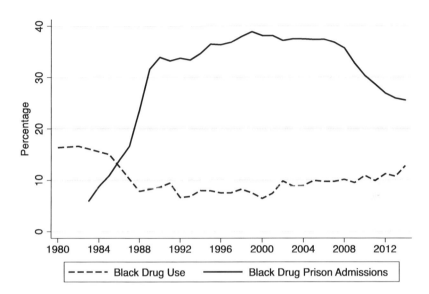

a drug offense as their most serious offense. This percentage grew on a nearly annual basis until 1999, when the percentage peaked at 39%. Thereafter, the percentage of Black prison admissions for drug crimes fell slowly at first and then more rapidly beginning in 2009. In the year 2014, 27% of Black admissions to prison were for a drug offense—350% greater than the percentage in 1983. Yet once again, Black crime does not explain this increase, as Black drug use fell, as measured by past-month drug use from the National Survey on Drug Use and Health. In the 1980s, when Black drug admissions were surging, drug use was falling substantially. And Black drug use remained at relatively low levels in the 1990s, when Black drug admissions reached their highest rates.

The rate of White imprisonment has also risen markedly. The White rate of imprisonment in 1980 was approximately 85 per 100,000, peaked in 2011 at 270 before falling to approximately 240 in 2014—for an overall increase of 180% between 1980 and 2014 (United States Department of Justice, 2013). A 180% increase in the White rate of imprisonment in an era of falling crime rates is remarkable. However, this percentage increase is a bit deceptive because of the initially low rate of White imprisonment (85 for Whites in comparison to 550 for Blacks in 1980). Moreover, even at its peak, the White rate of imprisonment was less than half the *lowest* rate of Black imprisonment in this period.

It comes as no surprise that this massive growth in the U.S. prison population has caused prison expenditures to soar. While prison cost data are not consistently collected, it is apparent that the cost per year to keep a prisoner behind bars has increased only modestly; for example, by my calculations, including adjustments for inflation (2015 dollars), the average yearly cost to keep an inmate in a state prison was approximately $31,000 in 1986 (based on Stephan, 2004) and $33,000 in 2015 (Mai & Subramanian, 2017). Yet state prison costs skyrocketed simply because of the explosion in state prisoners. For instance, the total cost of state prisons in 1986 was roughly $15.6 billion, and this figure ballooned to more than $43 billion in 2015, after adjusting for inflation. Simply put, prison expenditures ballooned in direct response to the swelling prison population.

Decomposing Prison Growth by Criminal Justice Factors

Changes in prison populations are a function of four major criminal justice factors: (1) rates of offending, particularly for offenses that are commonly punished by imprisonment; (2) the likelihood of arrest, given an offense; (3) the likelihood of imprisonment, given an arrest; and (4) the length of prison stays, given commitment to prison. Any one of these factors could in theory cause the imprisonment rate to rise, holding the other factors constant. Several recent studies estimate the amount of prison growth attributable to each of these factors (Beck & Blumstein, 2017; Blumstein & Beck, 1999; Pfaff, 2017; Raphael & Stoll, 2013; Western, 2006). These studies produce comparable findings when they examine the same time periods, but the influence of these four factors varies over time. As a result, studies examining different time periods reach different conclusions about the relative influence of these four factors. Here I briefly summarize the key findings of this body of research.

All of these decomposition studies referenced above find that changes in offending and the likelihood of arrest for an offense account for little of the growing prison population. For most of the period of interest, crime was falling so offending played no role in America's imprisonment binge. And contrary to the popular belief pushed by television shows and movies glamorizing advances in police technology (e.g., forensics, profiling), police effectiveness in clearing crime by arrest has not improved appreciably. For example, Raphael and Stoll (2013) estimate that police clearance rates for murder, rape, and larceny fell somewhat in the period of interest, and the clearance rates for other Index crimes were essentially unchanged. Thus, increases in crime and clearance rates generally do explain the explosion in imprisonment.

The exception to this general finding is the massive increase in drug arrests since 1980. During the 1980s, drug arrests spiked, going from about 580,000 to 1,360,000 between 1980 and 1989 (135% increase), even though drug use was dropping precipitously (see Figure 13.3). Drug use in modern America peaked around 1979 and fell throughout the 1980s. For instance, in 1979, a national survey of Americans aged 12 and over found that 14% had used an illicit drug in the past month (National Institute on Drug Abuse, 2015). These rates fell continuously in subsequent years, with 7.7% reporting past-month use in 1988, and bottomed out in 1994 at 6%. Thereafter, drug use rebounded but past month drug use only exceeded 10% once (2014) (National Survey on Drug Use and Health, various years). Other drug use surveys

Figure 13.3
Drug Use vs. Drug Arrest Rates, 1980–2014

Sources: National Survey on Drug Use and Health; Snyder, Cooper, and Mulako-Wangota, 2017

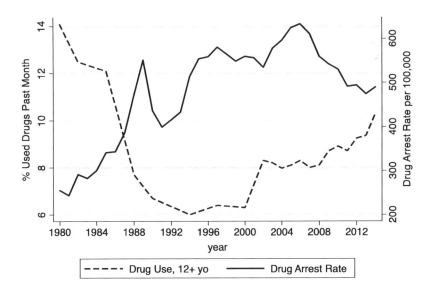

such as the annual Monitoring Future survey reveal similar trends (Johnston, O'Malley, Miech, Bachman, & Schulenberg, 2016; Johnston, O'Malley, & Bachman, 2002). Therefore, the surge in drug arrests was not due to an increase in drug use; instead, it was due to increased emphasis on drug enforcement. This increase in drug arrests accounted for nearly 5% per year of the prison population growth in the period 1980 to 1996 (Blumstein & Beck, 1999). This contribution may seem small, but it was larger than any other individual contribution, except for the increase in number of prison commitments per drug arrests.

The two major factors driving the explosion in imprisonment were increases in the likelihood of being sentenced to prison, given an arrest, and increases in the length of prison terms (see Table 13.2, which is derived from Beck & Blumstein, 2012). In the 1980s, the period with the steepest rise in imprisonment, the likelihood of being committed to a prison given an arrest increased markedly, and this change accounts for 79% of prison growth in the 1980s. Length of prison terms also increased in the 1980s, but lengthening sentencing explain only 14% of the 1980s' growth in imprisonment. In the 1990s, the relative influence of these factors reversed, with time served contributing to 73% of prison population expansions and commitments accounting for 27%. Since 2000, a period with very little growth in prison populations, all of the limited growth was accounted for by increased prison commitments given an arrest.

In the full period of interest, approximately half of the prison population growth was explained by increases in time served and increases in the likelihood of prison commitment. Increases in commitment and length of imprisonment were evident for each Index crime category; however, increased commitments were especially large for drug

Table 13.2

Decomposing Mass Imprisonment

Factor	1980–89	1990–99	2000–09
% Change in Prison Population	107%	55%	1%
Increased Offending	0%	0%	0%
Increased Arrests, per Offense	7%	0%	0%
Increased Prison Commitments, per Arrest	79%	27%	100%
Increased Time Served, per Commitment	14%	73%	0%

Source: Beck & Blumstein, 2012

offenses, and prison terms became much longer for violent offenses. For example, Raphael and Stoll (2013) estimate that prison commitment per arrest doubled for Index crimes between 1984 and 2004, and drug commitments per arrest tripled in the same period. The same authors calculate that time served for violent offenses (murder, rape, robbery, and aggravated assault) went up by roughly 50%, and burglary rose by 20%. Yet contrary to popular belief, time served for drug offenses did not increase significantly; the average time served for drug offenders increased from 1.4 years to 1.75 years between 1983 and 2009 and never exceeded 1.92 years (Beck & Blumstein, 2012). Thus, the imprisonment boom is explained by increased prison commitments for all major crime types but especially steep increases in prison commitments for drug offenses and increased sentence lengths with particularly large increases in time served for violent offenses.

Which Policies Caused Punitiveness to Increase?

The decomposition research finds that prison growth is primarily attributable to changes in the likelihood of commitment, length of prison terms, and increases in drug arrests. These changes in punitiveness are directly related to policy changes adopted in this period. Broadly defined, there were three kinds of policy changes that led to increased punitiveness: (1) structured sentencing, (2) the war on drugs, and (3) the tough-on-crime movement. These policy changes in various ways increased the punitiveness of the criminal justice system and made prosecutors more influential but did nothing to constrain their discretionary power.

The earliest of these policy changes was the structured sentencing movement, which began in earnest in the late 1970s and accelerated in the early 1980s. The structured sentencing movement sought to reduce discretion in sentencing, increase the predictability of sentences imposed, and reduce demographic disparities in sentencing—especially racial disparities. To achieve these goals, jurisdictions fundamentally reshaped American sentencing. Prior to this movement, sentencing in America relied almost exclusively on indeterminate sentencing for many decades. Indeterminate sentencing systems typically provided judges with a maximum permissible sentence (e.g., 10 years) and rarely a minimum sentence. Judges were free to choose a sentence range (e.g., 2 to 4 years) within this wide range of permissible sentences. Once sentenced, parole boards had the power to discretionarily release prisoners once they had been sufficiently rehabilitated, after a portion (typically a third) of the maximum sentence had been served. So a sentence pronounced in court as "2 to 4 years" might in practice lead to a prison term of 1.2 years or less with good time. Opponents claimed that indeterminate sentencing provided judges and parole boards with too much discretion, this discretion was used in a manner that disadvantaged some demographic groups, especially racial minorities, and the whole system was "dishonest" because pronounced sentences did not match time actually served in prison (Tonry, 1996).

The structured sentencing movement had two prongs. The first prong eliminated the discretion of parole boards by abolishing discretionary parole release or by structuring this discretion using parole guidelines. By 2000, 33 states had abolished discretionary parole release or restricted parole release to certain offense types (Western, 2006), and roughly half of the remaining states use parole guidelines (Ruhland, Rhine, Robey, & Mitchell, 2016). The second prong of the structured sentencing movement was the creation and implementation of sentencing guidelines and determinate sentencing systems to constrain judicial discretion. Only 2 states had had sentencing guidelines in 1980; by 2000, this number had grown to 17 states (Western, 2006), and several other states used some form of determinate sentencing. Currently, only 12 states retain the indeterminate sentencing model that was nearly ubiquitous throughout the United States prior to 1980 (Ruhland et al., 2016). To be clear, these structured sentencing mechanisms initially restrained the use of prison (Marvell & Moody, 1996); however, later policy movements described below usurped structured sentencing by using its mechanisms to increase sentencing severity and made prison sentences more common.

The war on drugs, the second major cause of prison growth, was launched to curtail drug use and drug-related crime, both of which were problematic in the mid-1980s. This war called for a massive increase in drug arrests, greater use of incarceration for drug offenders, and longer terms for drug offenders (Office of National Drug Control Policy, 1989). Long mandatory prison sentences became the hallmark of the war on drugs. Most notoriously, the Anti-Drug Abuse Act of 1988 required a mandatory 5-year prison sentence for those convicted of *simple possession* of 5 grams or more of crack cocaine. Yet federal law required the possession of 500 grams of powder cocaine to trigger the same 5-year mandatory sentence. This disparity became to be known as the 100-to-1 crack-to-powder cocaine ratio. The adoption of mandatory minimum prison sentences for drug crimes was a stunning reversal of federal law, which had removed all federal mandatory minimums for drug offenses in 1970 (see Murakawa, 2014).

The federal push for a drug war was transferred to the states by the political atmosphere created by the federal call to arms and by policies that provided federal funds to states. These funds were used to create drug task forces, which increased drug arrests, and to increase prison capacity to make room for more convicted drug offenders. Further, states followed the federal government's lead and enacted mandatory minimums for a plethora of drug offenses as a means to increase the certainty and severity of prison sentences for drug offenders. By 1994, 36 states had adopted at least one mandatory minimum for a drug crime (Bureau of Justice Assistance, 1996).

The war on drugs was a harbinger of a broader "tough-on-crime" movement that began in the late 1980s and reached full fruition in the 1990s. Tough-on-crime policies sought to deter crime by making sanctions more certain, severe, and onerous. In this era, correctional boot camps that required vigorous exercise, rigorous adherence to rules, and confrontational discipline for rule infractions flourished; only two states operated boot camps in 1983, but by 1995, at least 30 states, numerous counties, and even the federal system operated boot camps (Mitchell, 2013). States went on a frenzy and enacted mandatory minimums and sentence enhancements for a variety of offenses, especially violent offenses and offenses committed while in the possession of a firearm. The signature policies of tough-on-crime reformers were "three strikes" and truth-in-sentencing laws, which were adopted in 24 and 40 states, respectively, by 2000 (Western, 2006). Three-strikes laws mandate long prison sentences including life in prison for those convicted of a third felony offense; usually but not always the third felony had to involve a violent offense. And truth in sentencing laws require prisoners convicted of a violent offense to serve at least 85% of the sentence imposed by the judge before release, but a few states applied this 85% rule to all prison sentences.

Again, federal tough-on-crime policies were transferred to the states via federal grants. Most notably, the Violent Crime Control and Law Enforcement Act of 1994 enacted a smorgasbord of tough-on-crime measures and provided billions of federal dollars to states in an effort to crack down on violent crime. Penalties were stiffened for violent and drug crimes committed by gang members, drive-by shootings, sex offenders, "criminal aliens" (i.e., undocumented immigrants convicted of a crime), and repeat offenders, including a federal three-strikes provision (U.S. Department of Justice, 1994). The act made federal funds available to state and local jurisdictions to add 100,000 new police officers, hire more prosecutors ($150 millions), and a whopping $9.7 billion to build and operate new prisons and boot camps (U.S. Department of Justice, 1994).

Notably, the war on drugs and the tough-on-crime movements hijacked and undermined structured sentencing initiatives. Both the drug war and tough-on-crime policies led to the enactment of mandatory penalties such as mandatory minimums and three-strikes laws. Yet unlike the earlier structured sentencing movement that used mandatory minimums primarily to promote uniformity in sentencing, these later mandatory minimums were adopted to make sentencing more punitive. Moreover, these mandatory minimums essentially overrode the sentencing guidelines for targeted offenses. Stated differently, offenses that normally would have been sentenced using sentencing guidelines were instead sentenced based on other structured sentencing mechanisms, such as mandatory minimums or three-strikes laws, which universally required longer sentences than the sentence recommended under the applicable guidelines. Last, sentencing guidelines themselves were utilized by tough-on-crime politicians seeking to enhance punitiveness. Such motivations were easily accomplished by simply revising the whole guideline structure to shift sentences upwards, and that's exactly what happened in many states such as Florida (Griset, 2002) and North Carolina (Truitt, Rhodes, Kling, & McMullen, 2000), among several others.

Hidden beneath the surface of these policy changes is the fact that they granted greater discretionary powers to prosecutors in several ways. Most fundamentally, prosecutors have been empowered by the implementation of sentencing structures that closely tie sentences to the conviction offense and prior record. Where such sentencing structures exist, prosecutors can simply obtain the sentence they desire by selectively charging the offender with a crime mandating the desired sentence. And because prosecutors have the discretionary power to pursue or not to pursue charges triggering these mandatory minimums, just the presence of draconian mandatory minimums gives prosecutors more leverage to compel offenders to plead guilty to the desired charge(s) (Pfaff, 2017). Succinctly stated, there can be no doubt that "prosecutors are the most powerful officials in the criminal justice system, bar none" (Davis, 2017, p. 178).

The evidence suggests that prosecutors used their increased influence and unbridled discretion in more punitive fashions. Pfaff (2017) finds that prosecutors were twice as likely to file felony charges against an arrestee since 1990 in comparison to earlier times. Pfaff also finds that the number of prosecutors nearly doubled between 1970 and 2000, with most of this increase occurring after 1990. Pfaff finds even if prosecutors had not become more aggressive, the dramatic increase in the number of prosecutors would have led to more criminal cases being filed, and ultimately more felony convictions, despite falling crime rates.

Harder to measure, but perhaps every bit as important as the policy changes enacted during this period, is philosophical change in the criminal justice system. Rehabilitation and the possibility of reformation were replaced by a widespread emphasis on harsh sanctions to achieve deterrence. This philosophical change is important because it provided both an action plan (more arrests, prosecutions, and prison sentences) and a rationale for these actions (i.e., harsh sanctions will reduce crime). This rationale not only motivated prosecutors to seek felony charges more frequently but also encouraged police to stringently enforce minor laws (via "zero tolerance" and "broken windows" policing) and proactively hunt for drugs and weapons using tactics such as stop-and-frisk and drug courier profiles.

Taken together, these policy changes perfectly explain the findings of the prison growth decomposition research. Drug arrests and imprisonment rose in response to the war on drugs, even though drug use was declining before the drug war was mobilized. Prison commitments per arrest increased due to prosecutors using their increased influence and nearly limitless discretionary powers in more punitive ways, a marked increase in prosecutors available to oversee felony cases, and sentencing structures calling for increased imprisonment. Prison terms increased for all crime, but especially for violent crimes, because tough-on-crime laws required violent criminals to serve no less than 85% of their sentence.

Did Policy Changes Achieve Their Goals?

Globally, the policies driving the growth in Black prisoners were designed to achieve two stated goals. First, the discretion of judges and parole boards were reduced to make sentencing more consistent, and thereby reduce racial disparities in sentencing outcomes as well as prison populations. Second, sanctioning was enhanced to reduce crime generally with a special emphasis on drug and violent crimes. Given the tremendous financial and human costs associated with America's experiment with mass incarceration, it becomes important to assess the extent to which these goals were achieved. I do not assess any unstated policy goals. For example, several scholars have argued that the policy shifts noted previously were designed to control undesirable populations (see, e.g., Alexander, 2010; Russell, 2001; Wacquant, 2001) assessing such goals is outside the current scope.

Clearly, the war on drugs and the tough-on-crime movements accomplished their intermediate goal of increasing the punitiveness of criminal justice sanctioning. Drug arrests skyrocketed and the probability of imprisonment given a drug arrest soared. Similarly, violent crimes which already had large probabilities of imprisonment pushed higher and prison terms that were already generally long became longer. As demonstrated above, the increase in the likelihood of imprisonment and time served were not isolated to drug and violent offenses—these trends were evident for all Index crime categories.

The existing evidence indicates that these enhanced sanctions had only a marginal effect on crime—most of the crime drop after 1990 would have occurred without enhanced sanctions. While a few influential studies estimate that mass imprisonment caused large drops in violent (~33%) and property (~25%) crime (Levitt, 1996; Spelman, 2000), most studies indicate that only roughly 10% of the crime drop is due to large-scale imprisonment (Becsi, 1999; Western, 2006). Regardless of which of these estimates one finds most convincing, the bulk of the crime drop would have happened in the absence of mass incarceration. Likewise, the research focusing on the effect of harsh drug sanctions finds that these policies have had a limited general deterrent effect (see, e.g., MacCoun & Reuter, 2001) and little to no specific deterrent effect (see, e.g., Mitchell, Cochran, Mears, & Bales, 2017). And the drug war was supposed to reduce drug use by increasing drug prices, but drug prices have fallen (Abt Associates Inc., 2001). This evidence clearly establishes that the goal of crime reduction via the deterrent effects of enhanced sanctions is only weakly supported by the existing research.

The available evidence assessing the effects of structured sentencing initiatives finds that these effects have reduced the discretion of judges and parole boards, yet overall discretion may not have been reduced, because these efforts to structure sentencing extended the broad, unreviewable discretion of prosecutors. Early studies clearly demonstrate that sentencing was made more predictable and consistent after the implementation of sentencing guidelines, particularly presumptive guidelines (Tonry, 1996). Likewise, parole discretionary release was tamed by parole guidelines (Gottfredson, 1979). These gains in the predictability of time to be served gives the illusion of rationality and overall predictably. Behind this veil, however, prosecutorial discretion runs rampant and has been made more influential by sentencing structures. Given these developments, it is ambiguous whether sanctioning in the American criminal justice system is really more rational and predictable than in earlier eras.

Structured sentencing was motivated in part by a desire to reduce racial disparities in sanctioning and overall racial disproportionality in the criminal justice system. Yet both early and contemporary studies looking at racial disparities in sentencing typically find African Americans receive harsher sentences than Whites, even after taking into account legally relevant factors such as current offense seriousness and criminal history. For example, a meta-analysis of the race and sentencing research found that on average, Blacks had 28% greater odds of receiving a harsh sentence (e.g., imprisonment) than Whites in state courts (Mitchell, 2005). The same research found that the overall magnitude of racial disparities has remained highly similar in research conducted since the 1970s. For instance, after taking legally relevant factors into account, the odds of Blacks receiving a more punitive sentence than Whites were 24%, 29%, and 24% in studies conducted in the 1970s, 1980s, and after 1990, respectively. And very recent research examining racial disparities in the federal system continues to find that Blacks received sentences 20% longer than those of Whites (Schmitt, Reedt, & Blackwell, 2017). Altogether, there is evidence to suggest that structured sentencing caused racial disparities in sentencing to decrease, but there is still ample evidence that racial disparities persist.

Another more global means of assessing the racial fairness of the criminal justice system is to focus on explained racial disproportionality. Explained racial disproportionality refers to the amount of overall racial disproportionality that is accounted for by race differences in arrest for a particular crime type. For example, if 50% of imprisoned murderers are Black and race plays no race in imprisonment decisions, then 50% of those arrested for murder should also be Black. But if Blacks are discriminated against by the criminal justice system, then the percentage of Blacks imprisoned for murder should exceed the percentage of Blacks arrested for murder.

Table 13.3

Percentage of Black Prison Disproportionality Explained by Arrests

Offense Type	1979	2011
Murder	103%	104%
Rape	74%	85%
Robbery	84%	72%
Aggravated Assault	95%	61%
Burglary	67%	61%
Larceny	54%	79%
Drug Offenses	51%	52%
Overall	80%	70%

Source: 1979 estimates from Blumstein (1982), 2011 estimates from Beck and Blumstein (2017)

Table 13.3 compares the explained racial disproportionality in 1979 and 2011 using the results of Blumstein (1982) and Beck and Blumstein (2017), respectively. In both studies, explained disproportionality is highest for the most serious violent offenses (murder, rape, robbery) and lowest for drug offenses. Most telling is the comparison between total explained disproportionality from these studies. Total explained disproportionality dropped from 80% in 1979 to 70% in 2011. This finding indicates that the criminal justice system *writ large* appears to be no more racially fair today than a generation ago, despite many efforts to reduce overall and racial disparities via discretion reduction.

The bottom line is that all three of the primary policy shifts causing the prison boom did not achieve their stated goals. Structured sentencing did not reduce overall discretion in sentencing; instead, discretion was ceded to prosecutors. And while structured sentencing has curtailed overall sentencing disparity, racial disparities and racial disproportionality persist at levels comparable to those before sentencing structures were put in place. The war on drugs ratcheted up sanction severity for drug offenses but has had limited effects on drug use and drug-related crime. Similarly, tough-on-crime policies elevated the punitiveness of America's criminal justice system to new heights, yet their crime control effects have been modest.

Collateral Consequences

Thus far, I have emphasized that the shift toward punitiveness led to a massive expansion of the prison population, but this focus obscures another crucial effect of this shift; namely, these policies also have led to an unprecedented number of former prisoners and Americans with a felony conviction. There are currently 7.3 million Americans who have been in prison, representing over 3.1% of adult Americans (Shannon et al., 2017). These numbers are shocking, particularly in a nation touted as the world's greatest democracy and "the land of the free." Even more shocking is the fact that the wars on crime and drugs have resulted in 8.1% of adult Americans (19 million) having a felony conviction on their record (Shannon et al., 2017). Among Blacks, these figures are more than thrice as high, with 9.6% having been imprisoned and 23.4% with a felony conviction. The concentration of prisoners, former prisoners, and felons among Blacks is incontrovertible evidence of the criminal justice system's disparate effects on Blacks.

Felony conviction and incarceration come with a host of collateral consequences that in varied and numerous ways diminish the life chances of felons by excluding them from prosocial institutions and opportunities (see, e.g., Travis, 2002). Socially, men who have been previously incarcerated are just as likely as other men to be fathers; however, formerly incarcerated men have higher likelihoods of divorce, and among Black men (but not White men), a history of incarceration reduces the likelihood of getting married (Western, 2006). These effects result in a large number of children, particularly Black children, with fathers who have been or are currently incarcerated. Western (2006) estimates that 9.3% of Black children have a father who has been incarcerated in comparison to 1.3% of White children. These statistics are notable because children without their father in their lives are at greater risk for criminal behavior (see, e.g., Derzon, 2010). And conversely, fathers not residing with their children are at greater risk of involvement in crime and arrest (Mitchell, Landers, & Morales, 2017).

A felony conviction has a substantial negative effect on employment outcomes. Felons have harder times getting hired (Decker, Ortiz, Spohn, & Hedberg, 2015; Pager, 2003; Pager, Western, & Sugie, 2009). For instance, Pager (2003) found in a field study that applicants with a history of incarceration and Black applicants were less likely to receive a call back from prospective employers. The effect of prior incarceration varied by race, with the largest negative effects evident among Blacks. In fact, Pager found that Black applicants without a history of incarceration were less likely to receive a call back than White applicants with a history of incarceration. Incarceration also reduces the number of weeks worked, wages, and annual income of men (Western, 2006). Once again, the negative effects of incarceration on wages and yearly earnings were most pronounced among Blacks (Western, 2006).

Convicted felons lose their ability to lawfully vote until they are either no longer incarcerated or no longer under correctional supervision in most states (Manza & Uggen, 2006). A few states (Florida, Kentucky, and Virginia) permanently rescind the voting rights of felons unless they petition for and are granted restoration of their voting rights. Because of these policies, more than 5 million Americans, 2.5% of voting-eligible Americans with a felony conviction on their records, were barred from voting in the 2000 election, which George W. Bush won by a historically thin margin (Manza & Uggen, 2006). By 2010, this figure had grown to nearly 6 million Americans (Uggen, Shannon, & Manza, 2012). It comes as no surprise that Blacks are most affected by this collateral consequence, with 7.7% of Blacks in comparison to 1.8% of Whites of voting age disenfranchised by state rules barring felons from voting. There is tremendous variation in the Black felon disenfranchisement rate, with two states (Maine and Vermont) barring no felons from voting and three states barring more than 20% of Blacks from voting, including the key swing state of Florida (Uggen et al., 2012). Last, these authors note that Black rates of felon disenfranchisement are up markedly in comparison to 1980, before the latest drug war and tough-on-crime movement.

Clearly, Blacks are most affected by the collateral consequences of conviction. The concentration of felony convictions and imprisonment among Blacks guarantees that Blacks are disproportionately affected by the collateral consequences of conviction. On top of this disproportionality, in several domains, collateral consequences have more negative effects on Blacks than Whites. As noted above, the collateral consequences on marriage and employment outcomes vary by race, with the largest negative effects on Blacks. In all, these collateral consequences and the stigma of criminal conviction have further marginalized Black Americans and exacerbated racial inequality in America.

Was the Prison Boom Racially Motivated?

Many scholars have argued that the punitive policies implemented in the 1980s and 1990s giving rise to the explosion in the prison population, former prisoners, and felons were motivated by racial politics (see, e.g., Alexander, 2010; Edsall & Edsall, 1992; Murakawa, 2014; Tonry, 1995; Weaver, 2007). The details of these arguments vary, but in a nutshell this argument contends: Beginning in the 1960s, conservative politicians, such as Barry Goldwater, used crime control as a racially coded message to disaffected White voters. The purpose of this coded message was to pry Whites tired of Black demands for full civil rights from the Democratic party. This racially coded theme of resistance to Black civil rights cloaked behind crime control was honed by Nixon and later used by Ronald Reagan and George H.W. Bush to win the presidency. These ostensibly colorblind calls for crime control were used as a racially coded dog whistle to achieve political advantage—not to reduce crime. And in all likelihood, these politicians knew or should have known that their punitive policies would not meaningfully drive down crime. Yet they also knew that these initiatives would win with voters, and the lives of those affected by these policies would be the disadvantaged minorities referenced in the dog whistle. Punitive crime control policies were such an effective political tool that eventually even liberals, such as Bill Clinton, adopted it to nullify conservatives' political advantage on crime.

While I find such arguments to be compelling, I imagine that political conservatives would counter by noting the rising crime of the 1960s, 1970s, and postcrack 1980s to undermine these arguments. In other words, according to the conservative perspective, crime control was not a racially coded means to fight Black civil rights—crime control was a real, pressing problem in need of punitive countermeasures. As someone who came of age during the crack era and lived two blocks from the projects, I can attest that the three-headed monster of crack cocaine, gangs selling crack, and the proliferation of guns was in fact a crime crisis. So I have some sympathy for the conservative counterargument. In the end, how one views the argument that racial politics motivated America's punitive shift toward crime control serves as a sort of Rorschach test, leaving liberals seeing one vivid picture, conservatives seeing another very different image, and neither side being able to see the other side's perspective.

Rather than cosign the liberal account of the racial motivations of America's punitive shift in crime, I'll make a simpler and, arguably, more persuasive case that the politics surrounding crime control are in fact racially biased. My argument relies on one fact: The policies and practices causing the prison boom are largely still in place. The fact that these policies persist, despite overwhelming evidence of their ineffectiveness, high cost, and racially disparate effects, unmistakably demonstrates racial bias. I consider this set of findings to be indisputable evidence of racial bias, because it is inconceivable that these policies would remain largely unchanged if Whites bore the burden of these policies. In fact, history provides numerous examples of punitive shifts in criminal justice policies when a crime problem is associated with racial minorities but no such shifts when Whites are associated with a similar crime problem. As one example, Musto (1999) documents that in the 1970s marijuana laws were eased, and in some states, marijuana was decriminalized in response to the large and growing number of Whites arrested at the time for marijuana law violations. Likewise, Murakawa (2014) shows that drug laws requiring mandatory minimum prison terms have been consistently adopted in periods with rising and large percentages of non-White drug arrests, and these laws are repealed in periods with rising and large percentages of White drug arrests. As another example, compare the nation's response to the current opioid epidemic, which overwhelmingly has affected Whites, to that of the crack cocaine crisis of the 1980s, which largely affected racial minorities. In contrast to the punitive policies put in place in response to crack cocaine, thus far there has not been a national call for increased punitiveness aimed at users. Instead, the most frequently discussed policy options involve treating users and preventing overdose deaths by making naloxone more readily available. These are but a few historical examples of punitiveness shifting with race, yet there are many others.

Discussion and Conclusion

Black imprisonment rates exploded in the 1980s and 1990s and remain high when viewed in historical context. The current Black imprisonment rate is more than 150% higher than that of 1980. Further, decades of unusually high levels of Black imprisonment have led to an unprecedented proportion of Black Americans having been previously imprisoned or convicted of a felony. The labels of felon and ex-prisoner have enormous collateral consequences. These labels undermine Black progress toward economic and social equality, as well as strip the vote from a large portion of Blacks.

In this chapter, I have demonstrated that the primary causes of the rise in Black imprisonment and felony conviction were punitive changes to criminal justice policies and practices—not increases in Black crime. Law enforcement became more stringent, particularly against drug law violations. Prosecutors became more likely to file felony charges. Judges became more likely to imprison convicted offenders, and sentence lengths increased, especially for violent offenders, who were required by new truth-in-sentencing provisions to serve at least 85% of their sentences. This punitive shift was fueled by the war on drugs and tough-on-crime movement of the 1980s and 1990s, which called for cracking down on crime in order to reduce crime. These punitive crime control movements were aided and abetted by sentencing structures designed to increase fairness and predictability in sentencing, but these structures were easily transformed to achieve increased punitiveness.

I have also demonstrated that the empirical research assessing the effectiveness of structured sentencing and enhanced punishments finds that they are only modestly successful in achieving their goals. While sentencing is more predictable, there are persistent racial disparities in sentencing outcomes. And there is little research that finds punitive sanctions effectively deters those sanctioned or would-be offenders. Instead, enhanced punishments have little effect in reducing the recidivism of those sanctioned and limited general deterrent effects.

The punitive shift in crime policy reeks of racial politics of the most repugnant sort. Conservative, and later liberal, politicians arguably used the seemingly race-neutral issue of crime as a dog whistle to subvert Black efforts to gain equality and to appeal to White voters. These politicians were successful in both regards. White voters supported proponents of the tough-on-crime stance, and Black progress was slowed, if not halted, by the disparate effects of these sometimes draconian policies.

The racial politics of American crime and punishment are still potent. Politicians are reluctant to reverse even the most patently racially biased crime laws. As an example, consider that the aforementioned Anti-Drug Abuse Act of 1988, which established the notorious 100-to-1 crack/powder cocaine sentencing disparity, was finally changed in 2010 by Congressional *voice votes*. Voice votes do not record how individual legislators voted or even the tally of votes—just which side of an issue apparently had more support. Voice votes are commonly used when an issue is expected to pass unanimously or when legislators want to avoid documenting the voting record on a piece of legislation. Given that previous efforts to change this law were unsuccessful, I suspect that a voice vote was used for the latter purpose, as policy makers see anything that can be seen as "soft on crime" as politically dangerous.

Yet the American public clearly favors abandoning punitivism, especially for drug offenses. According to a recent poll, 91% of Americans say that the criminal justice system has problems that need fixing, 71% believe that there are too many people in prison, the same percent believe that incarceration is often counterproductive, and 72% stated that they would vote for a candidate supporting the repeal of mandatory minimums (Benenson Strategy Group, 2017). The public is calling for criminal justice reform, but politicians are too squeamish to heed these calls. In fact, the vast majority of recent changes in drug laws, such as the legalization of medical and recreational marijuana as well as laws mandating treatment instead of incarceration for drug offenders, have come from voter initiatives—not elected politicians.

Despite the negative empirical research, clear evidence of racially disparate effects, and public sentiment running counter to these policies, they have been allowed to persist. It is inconceivable that these policies would remain in place if the racial roles were reversed to disadvantage Whites in the same manner that they disadvantage Blacks. This is the clearest evidence of persistent racial bias in criminal justice policy making. Given the public support to reverse course, the fact that legislators sit idly by while Blacks suffer under the failed policies of the war on drugs and tough-on-crime movement is immoral and indefensible.

Note

1. I would like to acknowledge and thank Katheryn Russell-Brown, who provided helpful and insightful comments on an earlier version of this work.

References

Abt Associates Inc. (2001). *The price of illicit drugs: 1981 Through the second quarter of 2000*. Washington, DC: U.S. Office of National Drug Control Policy.

Alexander, M. (2010). *The new Jim Crow: Mass incarceration in the age of colorblindness*. New York, NY: The New Press.

Beck, A. J., & Blumstein, A. (2012). *Trends in incarceration rates: 1980–2010*. Paper prepared for the National Research Council Committee on the Causes and Consequences of High Rates of Incarceration, Washington, DC.

Beck, A. J., & Blumstein, A. (2017). Racial disproportionality in U.S. state prisons: Accounting for the effects of racial and ethnic differences in criminal involvement, arrests, sentencing, and time served. *Journal of Quantitative Criminology*. Advance online publication. doi:10.1007/s10940-017-9357-6

Becsi, Z. (1999). Economics and crime in the states. *Economic Review-Federal Reserve Bank of Atlanta, 84*(1), 38.

Benenson Strategy Group. (2017). *ACLU national survey: Fielded October 5–October 11, 2017 among 1,003 Americans nationwide*. New York, NY: American Civil Liberties Union.

Blumstein, A. (1982). On the racial disproportionality of United States' prison populations. *Journal of Criminal Law & Criminology, 73*, 1259–1281.

Blumstein, A., & Beck, A. J. (1999). Population growth in US prisons, 1980–1996. In M. Tonry & J. Petersilia (Eds.), *Prisons* (pp. 17–61). Chicago, IL: University of Chicago Press.

Bureau of Justice Assistance. (1996). *National assessment of structured sentencing*. Washington, DC: U.S. Government Printing Office.

Davis, A. J. (2017). The prosecution of Black men. In A. J. Davis (Ed.), *Policing the Black man: Arrest, prosecution, and imprisonment* (pp. 178–208). New York, NY: Pantheon Books.

Decker, S. H., Ortiz, N., Spohn, C., & Hedberg, E. (2015). Criminal stigma, race, and ethnicity: The consequences of imprisonment for employment. *Journal of Criminal Justice, 43*(2), 108–121. doi:https://doi.org/10.1016/j.jcrimjus.2015.02.002

Derzon, J. H. (2010). The correspondence of family features with problem, aggressive, criminal, and violent behavior: A meta-analysis. *Journal of experimental Criminology, 6*(3), 263–292. doi:10.1007/s11292-010-9098-0

Edsall, T. B., & Edsall, M. D. (1992). *Chain reaction: The impact of race, rights, and taxes on American politics*. New York, NY: W. W. Norton.

Gottfredson, M. R. (1979). Parole Guidelines and the Reduction of Sentencing Disparity: A Preliminary Study. *Journal of Research in Crime and Delinquency, 16*(2), 196–231. doi:10.1177/002242787901600203

Griset, P. L. (2002). New sentencing laws follow old patterns:: A Florida case study. *Journal of Criminal Justice, 30*(4), 287–301. doi:https://doi.org/10.1016/S0047-2352(02)00130-7

Johnston, L. D., O'Malley, P. M., & Bachman, J. G. (2002). *Monitoring the future national survey results on drug use, 1975–2001* (*Secondary school study*, Vol. 1). Bethesda, MD: National Institute on Drug Abuse.

Johnston, L. D., O'Malley, P. M., Miech, R. A., Bachman, J. G., & Schulenberg, J. E. (2016). *Monitoring the future national survey results on drug use, 1975–2015: Overview, key findings on adolescent drug use*. Ann Arbor, MI: Institute for Social Research, University of Michigan.

Levitt, S. D. (1996). The effect of prison population size on crime rates: Evidence from prison overcrowding litigation. *The Quarterly Journal of Economics*, 319–351.

MacCoun, R., & Reuter, P. (2001). *Drug war heresies: Learning from other vices, times, and places*. New York, NY: Cambridge University Press.

Mai, C., & Subramanian, R. (2017). *The price of prisons: Estimating state spending trends, 2010–2015*. New York, NY: Vera Institute of Justice.

Manza, J., & Uggen, C. (2006). *Locked out: Felon disenfranchisement and American democracy*. New York, NY: Oxford.

Marvell, T. B., & Moody, C. E. (1996). Determinate sentencing and abolishing parole: The long-term impacts on prisons and crime. *Criminology, 34*(1), 107–128.

Mitchell, O. (2005). A meta-analysis of race and sentencing research: Explaining the inconsistencies. *Journal of Quantitative Criminology, 21*(4), 439–466.

Mitchell, O. (2013). The history of boot camps. In G. Bruinsma & D. Weisburd (Eds.), *Encyclopedia of criminology and criminal justice* (pp. 2099–2106). New York, NY: Springer.

Mitchell, O., Cochran, J. C., Mears, D. P., & Bales, W. D. (2017). The effectiveness of prison for reducing drug offender recidivism: A regression discontinuity analysis. *Journal of experimental Criminology, 13*(1), 1–27.

Mitchell, O., Landers, M., & Morales, M. (2017). The contingent effects of fatherhood on offending. *American Journal of Criminal Justice*. Advance online publication. doi:https://doi.org/10.1007/s12103-017-9418-2

Morgan, R. E. (2017). *Race and Hispanic origin of victims and offenders, 2012–2015*. Washington, DC: Bureau of Justice Statistics.

Murakawa, N. (2014). *The first civil right: How liberals built prison America*. New York, NY: Oxford University Press.

Musto, D. F. (1999). *The American disease: Origins of narcotic control* (3rd ed.). New York: Oxford.

National Institute on Drug Abuse. (2015). *National household survey on drug abuse, 1979*. Retrieved from http://doi.org/10.3886/ICPSR06843.v5

Office of National Drug Control Policy. (1989). *National drug control strategy.* Washington, DC: Office of National Drug Control Policy.

Pager, D. (2003). The mark of a criminal record. *American Journal of Sociology, 108*(5), 937–975.

Pager, D., Western, B., & Sugie, N. (2009). Sequencing disadvantage: Barriers to employment facing young Black and White men with criminal records. *The Annals of the American Academy of Political and Social Science, 623*(1), 195–213. doi:10.1177/0002716208330793

Pfaff, J. F. (2017). *Locked in: The true causes of mass incarceration—and how to achieve real reform.* New York, NY: Basic Books.

Raphael, S., & Stoll, M. A. (2013). *Why are so many Americans in prison?* New York, NY: Russell Sage Foundation.

Ruhland, E. L., Rhine, E. E., Robey, J. P., & Mitchell, K. L. (2016). *The continuing leverage of releasing authorities: Findings from a national survey.* Minneapolis, MN: Robina Institute of Criminal Law and Criminal Justice, Regents of the University of Minnesota.

Russell, K. (2001). Toward developing a theoretical paradigm and typology for petit apartheid. In D. Milovanovic & K. K. Russell (Eds.), *Petit apartheid in criminal justice* (pp. 3–14). Durham, NC: Carolina Academic Press.

Schmitt, G. R., Reedt, L., & Blackwell, K. (2017). *Demographic differences in sentencing: An update to the 2012 Booker report.* Washington, DC: United States Sentencing Commission.

Shannon, S. K. S., Uggen, C., Schnittker, J., Thompson, M., Wakefield, S., & Massoglia, M. (2017). The growth, scope, and spatial distribution of people with felony records in the United States, 1948–2010. *Demography, 54*(5), 1795–1818. doi:10.1007/s13524-017-0611-1

Snyder, H. N., Cooper, A. D., & Mulako-Wangota, J. (2017). *Arrest in the United States, 1980–2014: Arrest data analysis tool.* Retrieved August 11, 2012, from Bureau of Justice Statistics www.bjs.gov/

Spelman, W. (2000). The limited importance of prison expansion. In A. Blumstein & J. Wallman (Eds.), *The crime drop in America* (pp. 97–129). New York, NY: Cambridge University Press.

Stephan, J. J. (2004). *State prison expenditures, 2001.* Washington, DC: Bureau of Justice Statistics.

Tonry, M. (1995). *Malign neglect: Race, crime, and punishment in America.* New York, NY: Oxford University Press.

Tonry, M. (1996). *Sentencing matters.* New York, NY: Oxford University Press.

Travis, J. (2002). Invisible punishment: An instrument of social exclusion. In M. Mauer & M. Chesney-Lind (Eds.), *Invisible punishment: The collateral consequences of mass imprisonment* (pp. 15–36). New York, NY: The New Press.

Truitt, L. T., Rhodes, W. M., Kling, R. N., & McMullen, Q. E. (2000). *Multi-site evaluation of sentencing guidelines: Florida and North Carolina.* Cambridge, MA: Abt Associates.

U.S. Department of Justice. (1994). *Violent Crime Control and Law Enforcement Act of 1994: Fact sheet.* Washington, DC: U.S. Department of Justice.

U.S. Department of Justice, Office of Justice Programs, & Bureau of Justice Statistics. (2015). *National prisoner statistics, 1978–2014*. Retrieved from http://doi.org/10.3886/ICPSR34540.v1

Uggen, C., Shannon, S., & Manza, J. (2012). *State-level estimates of felon disenfranchisement in the United State, 2010*. Washington, DC: Sentencing Project.

United States Department of Justice. (2013). *National prisoner statistics, 1978–2011*. Retrieved from http://doi.org/10.3886/ICPSR34540.v1

Wacquant, L. (2001). Deadly symbiosis: When ghetto and prison meet and mesh. *Punishment & Society, 3*(1), 95–133. doi:10.1177/14624740122228276

Weaver, V. M. (2007). Frontlash: Race and the development of punitive crime policy. *Studies in American Political Development, 21*(2), 230–265.

Western, B. (2006). *Punishment and inequality in America*. New York, NY: Russell Sage Foundation.

14

Race and Rehabilitation

Paula Smith and Christina Campbell

An evaluation of correctional rehabilitation in the United States requires an examination of the role race plays in policy and practice. Given ethnic minority individuals remain overrepresented at all stages of the judicial process, it is essential to consider effective strategies that address individual and structural factors that perpetuate racial disparities. Even when individualized rehabilitative efforts are used, research on race suggests that there remain structural constraints (e.g., inequality) that minimize and undermine successful treatment outcomes and experiences. If a central goal of corrections is to restore all offenders through a broad range of programs and services aimed at reducing offending, researchers would benefit from using a critical lens to consider factors that improve racial responsivity in correctional treatment.

Our central thesis is that the correctional rehabilitation literature has either downplayed or completely ignored racial differences in the effectiveness of offender treatment programs. This omission is evident in theories of criminal behavior, empirical evaluations of correctional treatment programs, and the tools that practitioners use to deliver services to offenders (e.g., risk assessment and classification systems, structured treatment manuals). Given that chronic racial and ethnic disparities in incarceration rates have been well-documented for decades in the United States, the neglect of research on Black individuals' involvement in correctional rehabilitation programs is even more striking (National Research Council, 2014; Unnever & Gabbidon, 2011). Moreover, there is a great need to better understand and document models of effective practice and rehabilitation across diverse groups. This question of "does race matter" must be explored in ways that does not pathologize ethnic minorities but instead raises awareness of social injustices, while understanding how race and cultural values may serve as a resource to promote the reduction of recidivism and effective rehabilitation. Unfortunately, the historical developments within corrections (e.g., the use of risk assessment) seem to suggest that race, especially from a strength-based lens, may have been an afterthought in both implementation and evaluation. This is not surprising given that the origins of well-known and commonly used risk assessments, such as the Level of Service Inventory and the Youth Level of Service/Case Management Inventory, are in Canada. Further, Canada has not been faced with the same degree of racial and class disproportionality and disparity as documented in the United States. As a result, one has to wonder if there might have been a greater attention to race and a sense of urgency to address disparities if the ratios were reversed.

It is our position that meaningful reforms cannot be accomplished without an acknowledgment of racial and ethnic disparities. Further, there is a need to focus attention on reducing disproportionate representation of Black individuals in the criminal justice system with consideration of how cultural and ethnic differences might serve as an asset in promoting responsivity in rehabilitation. While this type of reform requires the involvement of stakeholders from all components of the criminal justice system, correctional rehabilitation plays a vital role given their responsibility to allocate resources and provide services. This viewpoint is consistent with the call for a Black Criminology (Unnever & Owusu-Bempah, this volume) to understand how the experience of systematic racial oppression has shaped the experiences of Black individuals involved in the criminal justice system.

Correctional rehabilitation has been dominated by a White, middle-class perspective (although it might not be readily acknowledged by many criminal justice professionals). To illustrate, most treatment approaches have been developed and evaluated by White, middle-class men (Katz, 1985), and current formulations of "core correctional practices" (or key competencies related to service delivery with offender populations) do not contain any items directly related to cultural competence. Given that White perspectives have played a critical role in defining and developing what are considered best practices for all racial groups, it is important to consider potential conflicts of interest and the role that power might play in the establishment of correctional policies and practices. The potential harm of cultural incompetence is not a new concern. For example, some authors have questioned the role of child savers and the motivation behind the child savers movement in the development of the juvenile justice system (e.g., Caldwell, 1961; Fox, 1996, Platt, 1969). This longstanding debate concerning if those in power were more motivated by maintaining social control or rehabilitation and benevolence continues (e.g., Alexander, 2010). Clarity around this debate may also provide clarity around why certain racial groups are more successful than other racial groups when involved in rehabilitative efforts.

Race appears to be an obvious oversight when one considers the fact that more than half of the incarcerated population is Black (Nellis, 2016).[1] Regardless if the oversight is intentional or unintentional, race has huge implications in the development and evaluation of rehabilitation and correctional practitioners. For instance, research is limited in how corrections practitioners might project their own biases, values, and attitudes onto their clients and how this affects recidivism. In fact, some scholars have argued that the presence of White culture and Eurocentric ideals are so pervasive in correctional treatment that it can be difficult— even for skilled White facilitators—to recognize how their own cultural influences might negatively affect their interactions and interventions with Black offenders (see Essandoh, 1996; Spiropoulis, Salisbury, & Van Voorhis, 2014; Sue & Sue, 1990). From this perspective, correctional treatment in the United States is considered to be primarily a White American enterprise that advances the values and priorities associated with White culture and those individuals who profit from this industry. As a result, a critical lens concerning correctional treatment is paramount.

Black Criminology underscores the importance of studying the experience of systematic racial subordination in order to understand Black individuals' involvement in the criminal justice system (Unnever, 2014; Unnever, Barnes, & Cullen, 2016; Unnever & Gabbidon, 2011). Implications for understanding how ethnic minorities involved in corrections are marginalized may encourage the field to rethink or refine various aspects of treatment, which include offender classification and assessment. At a practical level, it makes intuitive sense that Black individuals experience disproportionality and various disadvantages in correctional settings (and treatment programs by extension) given that they are also marginalized in society more generally. In turn, these experiences influence program participation, postrelease outcomes, and the attitudes and behaviors of correctional actors who are responsible for identifying programming and/or delivering services. For all of these reasons, it is critical for criminologists to take the study of racial differences in correctional treatment programs more seriously. More research is needed that examines how marginalization impacts the individuals involved in the correctional setting and more importantly how correctional actors respond to individuals who are from marginalized groups, with an eye toward promoting and improving human rights.

This chapter is presented in five sections. First, the underlying assumptions of a Black Criminology are discussed in relation to our current understanding of correctional rehabilitation as a paradigm. Second, racial disparities in American corrections are described in order to provide a clear rationale for a Black Criminology in the field of corrections. Third, the empirical literature on the effectiveness of correctional rehabilitation is summarized. This section also reviews the principles of effective intervention and considers how racial responsivity might be operationalized within this context. Fourth, meta-analytic reviews of the corrections treatment literature that have included analyses relevant to racial differences are discussed. Fifth, the recent guidelines set forth by the American Psychological Association (APA) to define best practices in multicultural counseling are presented. In this section, we also review relevant studies from the field of corrections and offer comments about the implications for treatment and the development of a Black Criminology.

It should be noted that this chapter ultimately raises many more questions than it can answer and provides some hypotheses concerning how criminal justice actors might think about race/ethnicity. Perhaps, the main contribution of this chapter (and others in this volume) is that it serves to initiate conversations about strategies to reduce pervasive racial and ethnic disparities and consideration of the benefits of viewing race/ethnicity from a strength-based lens.

Racial and Ethnic Disparities in Corrections

Now, there are an estimated 2.3 million people incarcerated in the United States, and a disproportionate number of those incarcerated are Black (Wagner & Sawyer, 2018). Statistics for state-level correctional facilities indicate that Black individuals are incarcerated at a rate of 1,408 per 100,000, whereas White individuals are incarcerated at a rate of 275 per 100,000 (Nellis, 2016). This means that Black individuals are five times more likely to be incarcerated as compared to their White counterparts (Nellis, 2016). Although Black individuals make up 12 to 14% of the general population in the United States, they represent upward of 40% of incarcerated individuals in the United States. In some cases, Black individuals sometimes represent the largest racial population in correctional settings. To illustrate, the Bureau of Justice Statistics reports that 35% of state prisoners are White, 38% are Black, and 21% are Hispanic. While these trends, which are observed at the adult level, are alarming, disproportionate representation of Black youth is even more pronounced in the juvenile justice system (Wagner & Sawyer, 2018). As a result, there have been many calls to address disproportionality across both the criminal and juvenile justice systems.

In addition to understanding racial disparities based on the proportion of individuals who are involved in corrections, researchers have illustrated disproportionality when examining severity of dispositions and sentences. For example, community supervision, which is intended to be a lesser punishment reserved for lower-risk offenders, is more likely to be given to individuals who are White. The racial composition of offenders under community supervision as compared to the racial composition of those sentenced to prisons and jails is reversed. This demonstrates that racial minorities are more likely to receive more severe treatment and services as compared to their White counterparts. Additionally, at the present time, approximately 840,000 individuals are on parole, and another 3.7 million are on probation (approximately 55% are White and 30% are Black; Wagner & Sawyer, 2018). These numbers may further suggest that there might be biased ways in which court practitioners think about risk for recidivism or amenability to certain types of treatment/dispositions.

Differential treatment as it relates to how court practitioners respond to minorities has a long history within the justice system. Recent reform to address disparities in sentencing for illegal substances like crack versus powder cocaine highlights the role of social policies in perpetuating oppression among marginalized groups. For 20 years, courts responded more punitively for possession of crack as compared to powder cocaine. Unfortunately, this differential response systematically led to longer and more severe sentences for socioeconomically disadvantaged people and ethnic minorities. Although some progress has been made, as a result of state and federal social policies, there are important collateral consequences faced by ethnic minorities who have prior and current involvement in the correctional system.

A comprehensive review of the contributing factors associated with racial and ethnic disparities is well beyond the scope of this chapter (see Alexander, 2010, for an in-depth discussion). Nevertheless, the disparities that exist in corrections reflect cumulative consequences of racial bias in the criminal justice system. These disparities also provide sufficient evidence that there is a need to identify how individual- and community-level factors jointly affect offenders (Nellis, 2016). It is also clear that all levels of the criminal justice system must be involved in reform efforts. For corrections scholars, the refusal to take seriously the call for Black Criminology is a form of professional negligence, because Black individuals now constitute the racial majority in correctional populations *and* appear to derive less benefit from offender treatment programs in comparison with their White counterparts (see Spiropoulis et al., 2014). As a result, stakeholders must ask pertinent questions that promote human rights, social justice, and effective treatment.

Understanding Differential Treatment Effects

At the most fundamental level, there are two main theoretical frameworks proposed that explain Black individuals' involvement in the criminal justice system. The *racial invariance thesis* contends that Black individuals and White individuals offend for the same reasons (e.g., antisocial attitudes and values, affiliations with procriminal peers, self-control deficits, substance misuse, and educational and employment deficits). For example, the psychology of criminal conduct (described in a later section of this chapter) provides the theoretical framework for well-established "principles of effective intervention" in the field of corrections (Bonta & Andrews, 2017). From this perspective, race is described as an example of a *specific responsivity factor* (i.e., key offender characteristic that should be matched to the style and mode of service delivery). This perspective does not support the notion that Black individuals have a different set of risk factors from White individuals; instead, proponents recommend that correctional programs consider how to adjust cognitive-behavioral interventions in order to enhance program participation and treatment outcomes for Black individuals (Bonta & Andrews, 2017).

In contrast, a Black Criminology contends that the unique experiences of Black individuals in a racialized society should provide the starting point for understanding Black involvement in the criminal justice system (Unnever, 2014; Unnever & Gabbidon, 2011). The causes of crime (or at least some of them) might be different for Black individuals because of their unique experiences with racial socialization and racial subordination. Furthermore, these differences should then be translated into correctional interventions in order to enhance treatment outcomes for Blacks.

We embrace the idea that correctional rehabilitation should be undertaken as part of a coherent framework that integrates theory, research, and practice (as in the psychology of criminal conduct and the principles of effective intervention). At the same time, our main concern with the racial invariance thesis is that the influence of race tends to be neglected or treated as an afterthought. In contrast, the main value of Black Criminology is that it challenges academics and practitioners to develop a more complete understanding of how, when, and why race matters (Unnever, 2014; Unnever & Gabbidon, 2011). However, it is important to emphasize that Black Criminology does *not* assume that the correctional treatment literature is incorrect or that Black individuals and White individuals necessarily have different criminogenic needs. The main point here is that the study of Black involvement in the criminal justice system should be prioritized and undertaken with the same scientific rigor that has been applied to correctional treatment programs in general.

The idea that we should investigate meaningful variation in criminological theories is not a new one in the field of corrections; feminist criminologists who persuasively argued that our understanding of the causes of crime is enhanced when we can explain gender differences (Miller & Mullins, 2006) have championed this approach. Furthermore, this literature has led to the development of "gender-informed" assessments, better understanding of responsivity, and effective interventions that acknowledge the background and pathways to offending that are unique for female offenders (Gobeil, Blanchette, & Stewart, 2016). It is our hope that the call for a Black Criminology will provide the impetus for many of the same advancements.

"What Works" and the Principles of Effective Correctional Intervention

Correctional rehabilitation has been the dominant philosophy throughout most of the history of the criminal justice system in the United States (Rothman, 1980).[2] Most criminologists contend that rehabilitation should be embraced as a correctional policy for several reasons. First, unlike other correctional policies, it establishes a social and political imperative for the criminal justice system to provide services and assistance to offenders (Cullen & Gilbert, 1982); correctional rehabilitation injects a healthy dose of humanity into the criminal justice system. Second, previous studies have documented public support for both rehabilitation (Applegate, Cullen, & Fisher, 1997; Cullen, Fisher, & Applegate, 2000; Cullen & Gilbert, 1982) and early intervention programs (Cullen et al., 1998). Correctional rehabilitation aligns with the public desire to help offenders. Third, research on correctional treatment programs refutes the contention that punishment-oriented approaches reduce crime (Cullen & Gilbert, 1982; Gendreau, Goggin, Cullen, & Andrews, 2000).

While correctional rehabilitation has been shown to be effective in reducing recidivism, it has also been well documented that reductions in recidivism vary considerably across programs (Andrews, Zinger, et al., 1990; Andrews, Bonta, & Hoge, 1990; Bonta & Andrews, 2017; Gendreau, 1996); there are clear patterns in the theories, therapeutic models, and techniques that have been found to be the most effective with offender populations. Currently, there are more than 100 meta-analyses (or quantitative syntheses) of the correctional treatment literature and the main findings have been replicated with remarkable consistency (McGuire, 2013). A comprehensive review of these studies is beyond the scope of this chapter; see Gendreau, Goggin, French, and Smith (2006) and Smith (2013) for more detailed discussions of this topic.

The psychology of criminal conduct has been described as a *paradigm* in the field of corrections (Smith, 2013). The term *paradigm* is used in this context to denote the integration of theory, empirical evidence, and practitioner tools into an organized framework. The paradigm of correctional rehabilitation has three central and interrelated components: (1) the criminological component (theoretical framework); (2) the correctional component (empirical evidence); and (3) the technological component (tools for practitioners).

First, the *criminological component* refers to the theoretical framework that underlies the intervention. This component is based on the proximate causes of crime. For example, corrections might be able to change proximate factors (e.g., antisocial values, criminal peer associations), but it is not able to affect the more distal causal factors (e.g., concentrated disadvantage within neighborhoods that might sustain criminal cultures and networks). The key point is that the identification of criminogenic needs (or treatment targets) that are related to recidivism is critical to the success of the model.

Second, the *correctional component* involves empirical evaluations of the strategies that are most effective and linked to criminological theory. This includes knowing *what to target* (what risk factors, or criminogenic needs, to target—the need principle), *whom to target* (which offenders to target—the risk principle), and *how to target* (which treatment modalities to use—the responsivity principle). More broadly, the intervention employed should conform to a specified, empirically validated set of principles of effective intervention. This is also commonly referred to as "what works" in reducing offender recidivism, or the risk, need, and responsivity (or RNR) framework in corrections (Andrews, Bonta & Hoge, 1990; Bonta & Andrews, 2017; Gendreau, 1996).

Third, the *technological component* refers to the instruments (or tools) needed to ensure that the treatment is delivered as designed and intended (i.e., program fidelity). Examples include offender classification and assessment systems (to measure risk and need factors), structured treatment manuals (to ensure that cognitive-behavioral strategies are incorporated into sessions), and program fidelity instruments. In short, it is not sufficient to know *what to do*; it also is essential to know *how to do it*.

Finally, for any correctional intervention to be consistently effective across settings, it must be paradigmatic. In other words, it must have a solid theoretical framework, empirical evidence to demonstrate effectiveness, and tools and technologies for practitioners to ensure that services are delivered with fidelity. However, more than one paradigm is possible. In fact, correctional treatment might well be invigorated by competing approaches (as in the case of gendered theories of crime; see Miller & Mullins, 2006). A more complete understanding of the causes of crime for diverse populations has the potential to enrich (rather than threaten) our current approach to correctional rehabilitation.

The Principles of Effective Intervention

The "what works" literature provides evidence that correctional interventions should conform to a specified, empirically validated set of evidence-based practices. More specifically, the most effective programs use *cognitive-behavioral interventions* (the general responsivity principle) to target the *criminogenic needs* (the need principle) of *higher-risk offenders* (the risk principle). Furthermore, matching the style and mode of service delivery to key offender characteristics enhances treatment effects (*specific responsivity principle*). Moreover, correctional treatment programs that fail to adhere to these principles have been associated with *increases* in recidivism rates (Bonta & Andrews, 2017).

The principles of effective intervention have also been found to be applicable to treatment programs for many different special populations in corrections, including sex offenders (Hanson, Bourgon, Helmus, & Hodgson, 2009), violent offenders (Dowden & Andrews, 2000), female offenders (Dowden & Andrews, 1999), juvenile offenders (Lipsey, 1992, Lipsey & Wilson, 1998), and institutional populations (Bonta & Andrews, 2017; Baro, 1999; French & Gendreau, 2006). The psychology of criminal conduct is based on well-established theories of *human behavior*, and therefore it is not surprising that it has been found to be relevant for different correctional populations in a variety of correctional contexts.

Responsivity

The *responsivity principle*—also referred to as *matching* or *differential treatment* in earlier work (Palmer, 1975; Warren, 1969)—is based on the idea that correctional rehabilitation should not be undertaken as a "one size fits all" approach. In other words, cognitive-behavioral interventions should be carefully tailored to meet the individual needs of clients (Spiegler, 2016).

The responsivity principle is further subdivided into *general responsivity* and *specific responsivity*. General responsivity has been well established in the empirical literature, whereas specific responsivity is far less developed (Smith, Gendreau, & Swartz, 2009). General responsivity refers to the empirical finding that cognitive-behavioral treatment programs delivered by skilled facilitators produce the greatest reductions in recidivism (Andrews & Kiessling, 1980; Andrews, Bonta & Hoge, 1990). In a recent summary of the meta-analytic findings in the corrections literature, Smith et al. (2009) found that 73% (or 16 out of 22) of effect size estimates for cognitive-behavioral interventions reflected reductions in recidivism of more than 15%. Similarly, Bonta and Andrews (2017) updated their comprehensive review of the correctional treatment literature and determined that cognitive-behavioral programs outperformed nonbehavioral treatment programs by 19%. One important distinction should be made here. While cognitive-behavioral treatment programs have been found to be the most effective with the majority of offenders, it does not mean that this is the *only* approach that works for *all* offenders. There is risk associated with the assumption that we have definitively identified the *only* effective treatment modality for offenders.

The *specific responsivity principle* underscores the need to match the style and mode of treatment to key offender characteristics (Bonta & Andrews, 2017). For example, an offender with a lower IQ might benefit from an intervention that is more behavioral (and less cognitive) in nature. Similarly, it is important to consider the match between staff and offender characteristics (Bonta & Andrews, 2017). For example, an offender with higher levels of anxiety might not connect well with a practitioner who engages in very direct communication. Finally, the specific responsivity principle also encourages correctional programs to match facilitators to programs by considering their skills and personal qualities (Gendreau, 1996).

Racial Responsivity

A variety of offender characteristics have been cited as specific responsivity factors that should be incorporated into the style and mode of service delivery, including gender, age, race, personality, mental health, cognitive development, motivation, and counselor characteristics (Andrews, Zinger, et al., 1990; Bonta & Andrews, 2017). Specific responsivity is far less developed than the other principles of effective intervention (Smith et al., 2009), and race is arguably the least understood of these factors.

Although previous meta-analyses (e.g., Gendreau, Little, & Goggin, 1996) have found race to be correlated with recidivism, it is not clear how this effect size might reflect disparities caused by racism and/or implicit bias at other stages of the criminal justice system. Historically, literature reviews and meta-analyses have rarely examined racial differences in treatment outcomes. Only a small handful of studies have considered how Black individuals and White individuals respond differently to correctional interventions (Unnever, et al., 2016). And on the relatively rare occasion that an analysis of racial differences was reported, it was typically not central to the main purpose of the article.

There are several possible reasons to explain why race has been neglected in the correctional treatment literature. First, the specific responsivity is the least developed in the empirical literature (Smith et al., 2009). Second, some researchers argue that program effectiveness does not significantly differ by race (Wilson, Lipsey, & Soydan, 2003).[3] Third, race is a static predictor (cannot be changed), and therefore it does not provide any immediate information relevant to the identification treatment targets. Other dynamic (or changeable) factors have been found to be stronger predictors of recidivism *and* can be targeted for change (e.g., antisocial associates, antisocial thinking, substance misuse). This preoccupation with dynamic factors might have led many corrections scholars to ignore the influence of race in program evaluations. However, it is important to consider while race is a static factor, the ways in which race may lead to differential treatment are dynamic. Fourth, while the cognitive-behavioral model underscores the importance of an individualized approach to treatment (Spiegler, 2016), it does not necessarily readily lend itself to suspect that differences in treatment effects are rooted in race (Hays, 1995). To illustrate, cognitive-behavioral programs target factors that do not seem likely to be *caused* by race. Fifth, the concept of racial differences has been a controversial issue and one that many academics and criminal justice practitioners might prefer to avoid.

Regardless of the specific reasons, most research reviews have downplayed or simply ignored the differential treatment effects for Black offenders. The few available studies have produced mixed results; while some meta-analyses have not generated clear empirical support for racial responsivity (e.g., Lipsey, 1992; Wilson et al., 2003), other summaries of the literature have offered some limited insight into the role of race in correctional treatment (Garrett, 1985; Lipsey, 1995; Nangle, Erdley, Carpenter, & Newman, 2002). Of these, only one review of the correctional treatment literature was specifically designed to test for racial differences in treatment outcomes. Wilson et al. (2003) reviewed more than 300 studies and examined 11 behavioral outcomes. Although there were no significant treatment differences between groups, minorities performed worse than White individuals on most behavioral outcomes (7 out of 10). The authors cautioned that the failure to find significant treatment differences should not be interpreted to mean that the effectiveness of treatment could not be further enhanced for minorities by attending to racial responsivity (Wilson et al., 2003).

Three additional meta-analyses offer more limited insight into racial differences in correctional treatment. Lipsey (1992) evaluated the effectiveness of correctional treatment programs for juvenile delinquents and found that 64% of these studies ($n = 443$) demonstrated a reduction in recidivism. The tests of heterogeneity did not reveal any significant findings for juvenile characteristics (e.g., ethnicity, age, prior offenses) over research design (e.g., sample size, attrition, type of outcome measure) and/or treatment characteristics (e.g., treatment modality, dosage, researcher involvement). In a subsequent meta-analysis, Lipsey (1995) determined that juvenile characteristics (i.e., ethnicity, age, and prior arrest history) exerted a modest influence on effect size, although it was not as strong as treatment characteristics. Finally, Garrett (1985) conducted a meta-analysis of residential treatment programs and reported that race interacted with individual-level characteristics, program characteristics, and type of treatment.

One additional study merits comment here. Nangle et al. (2002) completed a narrative review of treatment for childhood aggression. Two main conclusions relevant to racial responsivity were noted: (1) few studies considered race in treatment or behavioral outcomes; but (2) the available evidence suggested that Black individuals performed worse than White individuals in treatment. Further, when race is considered, there is limited knowledge concerning in what ways race may serve as a strength and promotes successful outcomes.

Given that research examining the relationship of race and responsivity is limited and underdeveloped, more research in this area is needed. Much of the research available provides insight concerning what is not working for individuals from ethnic minority groups or how racially marginalized groups compare to White counterparts. While this approach provides insight concerning group differences, these comparisons do not focus on how ethnic groups and cultural values might promote treatment success. Moving forward, one strategy that can be used to understand the impact of race and treatment is through the use of an appreciative inquiry (AI) approach. AI focuses less on "fixing individuals" and treating problems, and more on how to elevate strengths in a group to promote success and determine which aspects of programming and treatment (if any) are most beneficial to the participant (Robinson, Priede, Farrall, Shapland, & McNeill, 2012). Criminologists might benefit from this approach to better understand the potential impact of specific responsivity because it requires researchers to ask questions concerning strengths, resources, and assets of a group and/or program in order to gain a better understanding of how to minimize barriers and maximize success.

Racial Differences in Outcome Measures

Recidivism. In comparison with White offenders, several studies have reported higher recidivism rates for Black offenders (Janetta, Breaux, Ho, & Porter, 2014; Steinmetz & Henderson, 2016). There are two hypotheses concerning differences in recidivism. The differential offending hypothesis suggests that racial differences are the result of differences in engagement in criminal activity, whereas the differential treatment (or differential selection) hypothesis suggests that the apparent differences in criminal activity (i.e., recidivism) are attributable to discriminatory decisions and practices. These practices might lead to increased surveillance, longer sentences, over estimating criminogenic risk, and over-programming. When examining racial differences in corrections, it is imperative for practitioners to consider how minority groups are treated differently within the criminal justice system, and how minorities have a long history of being subjected to social control (Alexandar, 2010). Without an understanding of explicit and implicit racial bias by correctional actors, there is limited consideration of the role that structures and society play in patterns of recidivism.

Treatment and Attrition.   Previous research supports the notion that Black individuals have an increased risk of attrition from counseling, and are more likely to report being mistrustful of mental health services (Sue & Sue, 1990). To illustrate, Sue and Sue (1990) found that Black individuals were more likely to terminate treatment after just one session (approximately 50% for Black individuals versus 30% for White individuals) and were more likely to report that treatment services did not help them to resolve life problems (Sue & Sue, 1990). Additionally, few studies have analyzed racial differences in perceptions of treatment and attrition from correctional treatment programs more specifically. One notable study involved an evaluation of the effectiveness of a cognitive-behavioral treatment program for domestic abusers (Taft, Murphy, Elliott, & Keaser, 2001). Results indicated that Black individuals were much less likely to attend sessions and complete treatment, even when other factors were controlled.

Implications for Correctional Treatment Programs

The multicultural counseling literature provides useful information about the factors associated with racial identity that should be considered in correctional treatment programs (American Psychological Association, 2017; Arrendondo et al., 1996; Parrott, 1997; Sue, Arrendondo, & McDavis, 1992). In the United States, the American Psychological Association (APA) is widely considered one of the most important influential professional organizations involved in the promotion of ethical, evidence-based interventions. Recently, it adopted guidelines that provide clear recommendations for best practices in multicultural counseling (APA, 2017).

We have structured our discussion of the factors that might be relevant for Black offenders around these standards; the APA guidelines, 10 in total, are provided verbatim in what follows, coupled with our comments and/or descriptions of relevant studies where appropriate. It is important to reiterate, however, that the research on racial differences in treatment outcomes is not well developed in the field of corrections. Therefore, our comments should *not* be interpreted as firm conclusions but rather as ideas to stimulate continued discussion. Moreover, it is important to point out that the discussion of racial differences should also acknowledge that there is often meaningful variation within as well as between races and ethnicities.

1. *Psychologists seek to recognize and understand that identity and self-definition are fluid and complex and that the interaction between the two is dynamic. To this end, psychologists appreciate that intersectionality is shaped by the multiplicity of the individual's social contexts.*

At the most fundamental level, practitioners should be knowledgeable about clients' cultural influences (Parrott, 1997). Within the context of correctional treatment, this would mean that practitioners would be remiss if they did not take the time to educate themselves about values, practices, and belief systems of Black culture, and the impact of racial oppression plays in day-to-day experiences. The therapeutic relationship is widely recognized as a ". . . necessary but not sufficient condition of treatment" (Spiegler, 2016, p. 8). Furthermore, therapeutic techniques based on social learning (i.e., anticriminal modeling and structured skill building) have found that the most effective models are ones that are perceived to be similar to the observer (Spiegler, 2016). Racial differences between offenders and corrections practitioners might interfere with this interpersonal connection and thus diminish treatment outcomes (Sue & Sue, 1990). For similar reasons, the racial composition of participants' in-group treatment might also influence the extent to which the facilitator can establish an atmosphere that is conducive to learning and/or the disclosure of personal information. This guideline also should serve to remind us that it is critical to understand how individual Black offenders have been impacted by racial socialization and exposure to racial discrimination. Furthermore, correctional treatment programs should incorporate strategies to consider how racial identity is formed and how it might be shaped to incorporate more positive messages.

2. *Psychologists aspire to recognize and understand that as cultural beings, they hold attitudes and beliefs that can influence their perceptions of and interactions with others as well as their clinical and empirical conceptualizations. As such, psychologists strive to move beyond conceptualizations rooted in categorical assumptions, biases, and/or formulations based on limited knowledge about individuals and communities.*

The APA guidelines emphasize that counselors need to be aware of the potential influence of their own culture on service delivery since the cultural affiliation and worldview of their clients might be different (APA, 2017). Practitioners might unwittingly impose aspects of White culture on Black offenders in the process of correctional treatment. For example, White culture values individual autonomy and personal responsibility for life outcomes (see Katz, 1985). These values are likely reflected in the preoccupation of the correctional system with "holding offenders accountable" for their actions. In contrast, Black culture tends to promote a sense of collectivism, group-centeredness, and cooperation (Phinney, 1996; Sue et al., 1992). Furthermore, White culture tends to prioritize competition, action-oriented behavior, and long-term goals (Katz, 1985; Sue & Sue, 1990).

Structured treatment manuals in correctional treatment programs are replete with instructions (or steps) to address skill deficits as well as goal-setting exercises. Furthermore, White culture values the scientific method, cause-and-effect relationships, rationality, and objective thinking (Katz, 1985; Sue & Sue, 1990). These values are reflected in cognitive therapies (e.g., cognitive restructuring, cognitive coping skills training) that train offenders to recognize the connection between risky thinking, emotional reactions, and behavioral responses. Finally, the structure and content of treatment programs are also influenced by White culture in other ways. Holidays are based on Christian religious practices, music and art are often based on European traditions, and the examples provided are often not culturally diverse.

3. *Psychologists strive to recognize and understand the role of language and communication through engagement that is sensitive to the lived experience of the individual, couple, family, group, community, and/ or organizations with whom they interact. Psychologists also seek to understand how they bring their own language and communication to these interactions.*

Previous research has documented differences in patterns of communication and social interactions between Black individuals and White individuals (Sue et al., 1992). For example, Black and White individuals tend to differ on how they conceal their emotions, sex expression, tone, confrontation, and social interaction (Sue et al., 1992). It is important that even when differences exist, the differences should be interpreted as strengths and/or assets, not as risk factors. Further, there are sometimes differences across racial groups relative to spoken and unspoken language. For instance, research has found that when Black individuals do not use what is traditionally considered mainstream or standard English, this may negatively influence how White practitioners view them (Katz, 1985; Sue & Sue, 1990). Finally, an understanding of body language, direct eye contact, physical space, and how physical and emotional boundaries are defined is key to establishing healthy interactions between client and practitioner (Katz, 1985; Sue & Sue, 1990).

4. *Psychologists endeavor to be aware of the role of the social and physical environment in the lives of clients, students, research participants, and/or consultees.*

It is essential as practitioners engage with clients that they understand the daily role social and physical environments play in rehabilitation. The use of an ecological lens provides a framework for practitioner to consider the impact of various settings and groups play in recovery, rehabilitation, and program success. For instance, through asset mapping, one might learn that church, community groups, family events, the local charity, and/or a social group may maximize progress success and or minimize program barriers. It is not just important to consider what settings and or environments may cause potential harm but also to consider what community and social resources and relationships can be used that will optimize treatment success.

5. *Psychologists aspire to recognize and understand historical and contemporary experiences with power, privilege, and oppression. As such, they seek to address institutional barriers and related inequities, disproportionalities, and disparities of law enforcement, administration of criminal justice, educational, mental health, and other systems as they seek to promote justice, human rights, and access to quality and equitable mental and behavioral health services.*

Black individuals experience the correctional system differently than do other racial groups (Mann, 1990; Sampson & Lauritsen, 1997; Unnever, 2008). Black individuals are more likely to endorse less-favorable attitudes about the criminal justice system (DeLisi, 2001; Jones-Brown, 2000; Taylor, Turner, Esbensen, Thomas, & Winfree, 2001; Unnever, 2008). If Black individuals perceive the correctional system to be racist and/or experience racism within the system, it is reasonable to assume that these perceptions and experiences will interfere with their willingness to trust and engage in treatment programs. Relatedly, Black individuals hold perceptions and experiences of harsher treatment by the criminal justice system (Sampson & Lauritsen, 1997; Bales & Piquero, 2012). Black individuals also appear to perceive and experience the harm associated with criminal sentences differently. For example, several studies have found that Black individuals were more likely than White individuals to select shorter incarceration sentences rather than longer community sentences (Crouch, 1993; Spelman, 1995; Bales & Piquero, 2012). This means that Black offenders perceive prolonged engagement in the criminal justice system as more harmful regardless of severity of sentence.

Black individuals comprise a smaller proportion of mentally ill offenders in comparison with White individuals (Ditton, 1999). There are two major hypotheses that explains this trend. First, this could be attributable to the fact that Black individuals are less likely than White individuals to report mental illness and seek treatment and/or have the means or access to services to be properly diagnosed. For instance, Black inmates who are in need of mental health services were less likely than their White counterparts to have received them within correctional facilities (Ditton, 1999). Second, research suggests that White offenders' antisocial behaviors and criminality are more likely to be explained and/or conceptualized from a mental health lens, while Black offenders' antisocial behaviors and criminality are viewed from a lens of criminogenic risk and deviance. This double standard is harmful in thinking about holistic approaches to rehabilitation.

The mental and physical health of offenders should be considered in holistic approaches to correctional rehabilitation treatment (and these factors are considered important specific responsivity characteristics). It is well documented that there are substantial differences in the health status of Black individuals compared to their White counterparts. Further, there is an array of structural factors that perpetuate such disparities (e.g., access to health care, education, insurance, employment, etc.). Given that Black individuals are at risk for poorer health outcomes (e.g., drug use, sexual encounters, injuries, and violence), despite targeted health promotion (e.g., Yee et al., 1995), more consideration is needed concerning how to address health status in addition to rehabilitative needs.

6. *Psychologists seek to promote culturally adaptive interventions and advocacy within and across systems, including prevention, early intervention, and recovery.*

The identification of the factors that might influence pathways to crime for Black individuals (e.g., level of education, differences in racial socialization experiences, the strength of their connection to social support/affiliation with the Black Church, exposure to racial discrimination, formation of racial identity, access to services and resources) also provides crucial information that can enhance outcomes by translating it into more specific services and interventions (Unnever et al., 2016; Unnever & Gabbidon, 2011).

7. *Psychologists endeavor to examine the profession's assumptions and practices within an international context, whether domestically or internationally based, and consider how this globalization has an impact on the psychologist's self-definition, purpose, role, and function.*

At the most fundamental level, cross-national projects have the potential to enhance our understanding of the common versus culture-specific factors that influence behavior and identity development. Furthermore, individuals across the globe experience stresses and illnesses in many ways. By examining assumptions and practices within an international context, we can identify and investigate the holes in certain U.S.-originating theories and fill in the gaps with knowledge derived from other populations. Finally, psychologists are well advised to learn about applications in other cultural contexts in order to embrace a healthy dose of cultural humility, where professionals learn *from* cultures rather than learn *about* them.

8. *Psychologists seek awareness and understanding of how developmental stages and life transitions intersect with the larger bio sociocultural context, how identity evolves as a function of such intersections, and how these different socialization and maturation experiences influence worldview and identity.*

A biosociocultural context is important to consider when understanding the person–environment fit. This ecological notion suggests that in order to understand how individuals develop, it is essential to have some knowledge of predispositions and the sociological context, which shapes how individuals behave and respond to social environments. Further, in the context of corrections, it is important that practitioners acknowledge the developmental stage of an offender. Information concerning, age, maturation, and previous experiences might inform which services are most appropriate and help provide practitioners with clarity around program and treatment expectations.

9. *Psychologists strive to conduct culturally appropriate and informed research, teaching, supervision, consultation, assessment, interpretation, diagnosis, dissemination, and evaluation of efficacy as they address the first four levels of the Layered Ecological Model of the Multicultural Guidelines.*

The priorities for research outlined by Unnever and Owusu-Bempah (this volume) align with this guideline. Similarly, in the field of developmental psychology, attention to both microlevel and macrolevel variables are imperative to promote treatment success. Individuals are embedded within a series of contexts and environments. Social groups and physical space define these ecological contexts. Using an ecological framework requires practitioners to identify key factors (e.g., schools, family, neighborhood) and stakeholders that are central to defining social problems in a comprehensive way and identifying strategies and solutions that promote health and reduce recidivism.

10. *Psychologists actively strive to take a strength-based approach when working with individuals, families, groups, communities, and organizations that seeks to build resilience and decrease trauma within the sociocultural context.*

There is a tendency to discuss race as a risk factor for criminal justice involvement, but this overlooks the fact that the history of Black America is rooted in the resiliency of Black individuals (Agnew, 2015; Jones, 2010). This resiliency accounts for why the vast majority of Black individuals do *not* experience criminal justice involvement and reflects how race might be viewed as a protective factor. Undoubtedly, there is substantial individual variation in how Black individuals perceive, interpret, and respond to racial oppression (Unnever & Gabbidon, 2011). Therefore, a *strength-based approach* to correctional rehabilitation might, for example, help Black offenders create a racialized narrative that highlights the positive aspects of Black culture and reinforces the theme of *racial resiliency.*

Conclusions

The development of a Black Criminology has important implications for correctional rehabilitation as a paradigm. The psychology of criminal conduct has led to an impressive literature base on the predictors of criminal behavior, as well as the strategies most likely to reduce the risk for recidivism (Bonta & Andrews, 2017). One of the values at the base of the psychology of criminal conduct is the commitment to explaining individual variation in criminal behavior (Bonta & Andrews, 2017). From this perspective, the development of a Black Criminology has the potential to expand our knowledge of the causes of factors that predict involvement in criminal activity for Black individuals. In many ways, this model is similar to the one established by feminist criminologists in identifying gendered pathways to crime and then translating this research into gender-informed interventions (see Gobeil et al., 2016).

The chronic racial and ethnic disparities in the American criminal justice system have been documented for decades. These trends reflect the racial subordination that Black individuals continue to face in a racialized society. At the same time, the criminological literature has either downplayed or completely ignored the importance of understanding the etiology of crime for Black individuals. This represents a critical gap in the correctional rehabilitation paradigm that must be addressed.

Notes

1. It is perhaps interesting to note that the principles of effective intervention were first articulated by Canadian psychologists (Don Andrews, James Bonta, and Paul Gendreau). These scholars are also responsible for delineating the *core correctional practices* related to service delivery with offender populations. Despite the fact that they were all well versed in American corrections, it is fair to say that they were immersed in a sociopolitical context that was not characterized by the same level of racial oppression.
2. There was a relatively short period of time in the early 1970s when the criminal justice system abandoned correctional rehabilitation and embraced the notion that "nothing works" to reduce recidivism (Martinson, 1974). This shift was influenced by the sociopolitical climate of the 1970s and led to the rise of "get-tough" approaches in the United States (Cullen & Gilbert, 1982). The rehabilitative ideal was revivified by research demonstrating the effectiveness of offender treatment programs (see Gendreau, Goggin, French, & Smith, 2006).
3. A limitation of this study is that it combined all minorities into a single comparison group (i.e., results were not reported for Black individuals specifically).

References

Agnew, R. (2015). Race and youth crime: Why isn't the relationship stronger? *Race and Justice, 6,* 195–221.

Alexander, M. (2010). *The new Jim Crow: Mass incarceration in the age of colorblindness.* New York, NY: The New Press.

American Psychological Association. (2017). *Multicultural guidelines: An ecological approach to context, identity, and intersectionality.* Retrieved from www.apa.org/about/policy/multicultural-guidelines.pdf

Andrews, D. A., Bonta, J., & Hoge, R. D. (1990). Classification for effective rehabilitation: Rediscovering psychology. *Criminal Justice and Behavior, 17,* 19–52.

Andrews, D. A., & Kiessling, J. (1980). Program structure and effective correctional practices: A summary of CaVIC research. In R. Ross & P. Gendreau (Eds.), *Effective correctional treatment.* Toronto, Canada: Butterworth.

Andrews, D. A., Zinger, I., Hoge, R. D., Bonta, J., Gendreau, P., & Cullen, F. T. (1990). Does correctional treatment work? A clinically relevant and psychologically informed meta-analysis. *Criminology, 28,* 369–404.

Applegate, B. K., Cullen, F. T., & Fisher, B. S. (1997). Public support for correctional treatment: The continuing appeal of the rehabilitative ideal. *The Prison Journal, 77,* 237–258.

Arrendondo, P., Toporek, R., Brown, S. P., Jones, J., Locke, D. C., Sanchez, J., & Stadler, H. (1996). Operationalization of multicultural counseling competencies. *Journal of Multicultural Counseling and Development, 24,* 42–78.

Bales, W. D., & Piquero, A. R. (2012). Racial/ethnic differentials in sentencing to incarceration. *Justice Quarterly, 29,* 742–773.

Baro, A. (1999). Effects of a cognitive restructuring program on inmate institutional behavior. *Criminal Justice and Behavior, 28,* 490–521.

Baumgartner, F. R., Johnson, E., Wilson, C., & Whitehead, C. (2015). These lives matter, those ones don't: Comparing execution rates by the race and gender of the victim in the U.S. and in the top death penalty states. *Albany Law Review,*

79, 797–860.Bonta, J., & Andrews, D. A. (2017). *The psychology of criminal conduct* (6th ed.). New York, NY: Routledge.

Caldwell, R.G. (1961). The Juvenile court: Its development and some major problems. *Journal of Criminal Law & Criminology, 51*: 493–511.

Crouch, B. M. (1993). Is incarceration really worse? Analysis of offenders' preferences for prison over probation. *Justice Quarterly, 10*, 67–99.

Cullen, F. T., Fisher, B. S., & Applegate, B. K. (2000). Public opinion about punishment and corrections. *Crime and Justice, 27*, 1–79.

Cullen, F. T., & Gilbert, K. E. (1982). *Reaffirming rehabilitation*. Cincinnati, OH: Anderson Publishing.

Cullen, F. T., Wright, J. P., Brown, S., Moon, M. M., Blankenship, B., & Applegate, B. K. (1998). Public support for early intervention programs: Implications for a progressive policy agenda. *Crime and Delinquency, 44*, 187–204.

DeLisi, M. (2001). The affordable hypothesis: Punitive beliefs, violent beliefs, and race. *Journal of Criminal Justice, 29*, 101-106.

Ditton, P. M. (1999). *Mental health and treatment of inmates and probationers, NCJ 174463*. Washington, DC: Bureau of Justice Statistics, U.S. Department of Justice.

Dowden, C., & Andrews, D. A. (1999). What works for female offenders: A meta-analytic review. *Crime and Delinquency, 45*, 438–452.

Dowden, C., & Andrews, D. A. (2000). Effective correctional treatment and violent offending: A meta-analysis. *Canadian Journal of Criminology, 42*, 449–467.

Essandoh, P. K. (1996). Multicultural counseling as the "fourth force": A call to arms. *The Counseling Psychologist, 24*, 126–137.

Fox, S. (1996). The early history of the court. *The Future of Children, 6*: 29–39.

French, S. A., & Gendreau, P. (2006). Reducing prison misconducts: What works! *Criminal Justice and Behavior, 33*, 185–218.

Garrett, C. J. (1985). Effects of residential treatment of adjudicated delinquents: A meta- analysis. *Journal of Research in Crime and Delinquency, 22*, 287–308.

Gendreau, P. (1996). The principles of effective intervention with offenders. In A. T. Harland (Ed.), *Choosing correctional options that work: Defining the demand and evaluating the supply*. Thousand Oaks, CA: Sage.

Gendreau, P., Goggin, C., Cullen, F. T., & Andrews, D. A. (2000). The effects of community sanctions and incarceration on recidivism. *Forum, 12*(2) 10–13.

Gendreau, P., Goggin, C., French, S., & Smith, P. (2006). Practicing psychology in correctional settings. In A. K. Hess & I. B. Weiner (Eds.), *The handbook of forensic psychology* (3rd ed., pp. 722–750). Hoboken, NJ: Wiley.

Gendreau, P., Little, T., & Goggin, C. (1996). A meta-analysis of the predictors of adult offender recidivism: What works! *Criminology, 34*, 575–608.

Gobeil, R., Blanchette, K., & Stewart, L. (2016). A meta-analytic review of correctional interventions for women offenders: Gender-informed versus gender-neutral approaches. *Criminal Justice and Behavior, 43*, 301–322.

Hanson, R. K., Bourgon, G., Helmus, L., & Hodgson, S. (2009). The principles of effective intervention also apply to sex offenders: A meta-analysis. *Criminal Justice and Behavior, 36*, 865–891.

Hays, P. A. (1995). Multicultural applications of cognitive-behavior therapy. *Professional Psychology: Research and Practice, 26*, 309–315.

Janetta, J., Breaux, J., Ho, H., & Porter, J. (2014). Examining racial and ethnic disparities in probation revocation: Summary of findings and implications from a multi-site study. *The Urban Institute.* Retrieved from www.urban.org/sites/default/files/publication/ 22746/413174-Examining-Racial-and-Ethnic-Disparities-in-Probation-Revocation.pdf

Jones, N. (2010). *Between good and ghetto African American girls and inner-city violence.* New Brunswick, NJ: Rutgers University Press.

Jones-Brown, D. D. (2000). Debunking the myth of officer friendly: How African American males experience community policing. *Journal of Contemporary Criminal Justice, 16*, 209–229.

Katz, J. H. (1985). The sociopolitical nature of counseling. *The Counseling Psychologist, 13*, 615–624.

Lipsey, M. W. (1992). Juvenile delinquency treatment: A meta-analytic inquiry into the variability of effects. In T. D. Cook, H. Cooper, D. S. Cordray, H. Hartmann, L. V. Hedges, R. J. Light, T. A. Louis, & F. Mostseller (Eds.), *Meta-analysis for explanation: A casebook* (pp. 83–127). New York, NY: Russell Sage Foundation.

Lipsey, M. W. (1995). What do we learn from 400 research studies on the effectiveness of treatment with juvenile delinquents? In J. McGuire (Ed.), *What works: Reducing reoffending: Guidelines from research and practice* (pp. 63–78). Chichester, UK: Wiley.

Lipsey, M. W., & Wilson, D. B. (1998). Effective intervention for serious juvenile offenders: A synthesis of research. In R. Loeber & D. P. Farrington (Eds.), *Serious and violent juvenile offenders: Risk factors and successful interventions.* (pp. 313–345) Thousand Oaks, CA: Sage.

Mann, C. R. (1990). Random thoughts on the ongoing Wilbanks-Mann discourse. In B. D. MacLean & D. Milovanovic (Eds.), *Racism, empiricism and criminal justice.* Vancouver, Canada: The Collective Press.

Martinson, R. (1974). What works? Questions and answers about prison reform. *The Public Interest, 35*, 22–54.

McGuire, J. (2013). What works to reduce reoffending: 18 years on. In. L. A. Craig, L. Dixon, & T. A. Gannon (Eds.), *What works in offender rehabilitation: An evidence based approach to assessment and treatment* (pp. 20–49). Chichester, UK: Wiley.

Miller, J., & Mullins, C. W. (2006). The status of feminist theories in criminology. In F. T. Cullen, J. P. Wright, & K. R. Blevins (Eds.), *Taking stock: The status of criminological theory* (*Advances in criminological theory*, Vol. 15, pp. 217–249). New Brunswick, NJ: Transaction.

Nangle, D. W., Erdley, C. A., Carpenter, E. M., & Newman, J. E. (2002). Social skills training as a treatment for aggressive children and adolescents: A developmental-clinical integration. *Aggression and Violent Behavior, 7*, 169–199.

National Research Council. (2014). *The growth of incarceration in the United States: Exploring causes and consequences.* Washington, DC: National Academies Press.

Nellis, A. (2016). The color of justice: Racial and ethnic disparities in state prisons. *The Sentencing Project.* Retrieved from www.sentencingproject.org/wp-content/uploads/2016/06/The-Color-of-Justice-Racial-and-Ethnic-Disparity-in-State-Prisons.pdf

Palmer, T. (1975). Martinson revisited. *Journal of Research in Crime and Delinquency, 12* (July): 133–152.

Parrott, L. (1997). *Counseling and psychotherapy.* New York, NY: McGraw-Hill.

Phinney, J. S. (1996). When we talk about American ethnic groups, what do we mean? *American Psychologist, 51*, 918–927.

Robinson, G., Priede, C., Farrall, S., Shapland, J., & McNeill, F. (2012). Doing 'strengths-based' research: Appreciative inquiry in a probation setting. *Criminology & Criminal Justice, 13,* 3–20.

Rothman, D. J. (1980). *Conscience and convenience: The asylum and its alternatives in progressive America.* Boston, MA: Little, Brown.

Sabol, W. J., Adams, W. P., Parthasarathy, B., & Yuan, Y. (2000). *Offenders returning to federal prison, 1986–97, 182991.* Washington, DC: Bureau of Justice Statistics, U.S. Department of Justice.

Sampson, R. J., & Lauritsen, J. L. (1997). Racial and ethnic disparities in crime and criminal justice in the United States. In M. Tonry & J. Petersilia (Eds.), *Crime and justice: A review of research.* Vol. 21, pp. 311–314 Chicago, IL: University of Chicago Press.

Smith, P. (2013). The psychology of criminal conduct. In F. T. Cullen & P. Wilcox (Eds.), *The Oxford handbook of criminological theory* (pp. 69–88). New York, NY: Oxford University Press.

Smith, P., Gendreau, P., & Swartz, K. (2009). Validating the principles of effective intervention: A systematic review of the contributions of meta-analysis in the field of corrections *Victims and Offenders, 4,* 148–169.

Spelman, W. (1995). The severity of intermediate sanctions. *Journal of Research in Crime and Delinquency, 32,* 107–135.

Spiegler, M. D. (2016). *Contemporary behavior therapy* (6th ed.). Belmont, CA: Cengage Learning.

Spiropoulis, G. V., Salisbury, E. J., & Van Voorhis, P. (2014). Moderators of correctional treatment success: An exploratory study of racial differences. *International Journal of Offender Therapy and Comparative Criminology, 58,* 835–860.

Steinmetz, K. F., & Henderson, H. (2016). Inequality on probation: An examination of differential probation outcomes. *Journal of Ethnicity in Criminal Justice, 14,* 1–20.

Sue, D. W., Arrendondo, P., & McDavis, R. J. (1992). Multicultural counseling competencies and standards: A call to the profession. *Journal of Counseling and Development, 70,* 477–483.

Sue, D. W., & Sue, D. (1990). *Counseling the culturally different: Theory and practice* (3rd ed.). New York, NY: Wiley.

Taft, C. T., Murphy, C. M., Elliott, J. D., & Keaser, M. C. (2001). Race and demographic factors in treatment attendance for domestically abusive men. *Journal of Family Violence, 16,* 385–400.

Taylor, T. J., Turner, K. B., Esbensen, F. A., Thomas, L., & Winfree, J. (2001). Coppin' an attitude: Attitudinal differences among juveniles toward police. *Journal of Criminal Justice, 29,* 295–305.

Unnever, J. D. (2008). Two worlds far apart: Black-White differences in beliefs about why African-American men are disproportionately imprisoned. *Criminology, 46,* 511–538.

Unnever, J. D. (2014). A theory of African American offending: A test of core propositions. *Race and Justice, 4,* 98–123.

Unnever, J. D., Barnes, J. C., & Cullen, F. T. (2016). The racial invariance thesis revisited: Testing an African American theory of offending. *Journal of Contemporary Criminal Justice, 32,* 7–26.

Unnever, J. D., & Gabbidon, S. L. (2011). *A theory of African American offending: Race, racism, and crime.* New York, NY: Taylor & Francis.

Wagner, P., & Sawyer, W. (2018). Mass incarceration: The whole pie 2018. *Prison Policy Initiative*. Retrieved from www.prisonpolicy.org/reports/pie2018.html

Warren, M. Q. (1969). The case for differential treatment of delinquents. *Annals of the American Academy of Political and Social Sciences, 62* (January): 239–258.

Wilson, S. J., Lipsey, M. W., & Soydan, H. (2003). Are mainstream programs for juvenile delinquency less effective with minority youth than majority youth? A meta-analysis of outcomes research. *Research on Social Work Practice, 13*, 3–26.

Yee, B. W. K., Castro, F. G., Hammond, W. R., John, R., Wyatt, G. E., & Yung, B. R. (1995). Panel IV: Risk-taking and abusive behaviors among ethnic minorities. *Health Psychology, 14*, 622–631.

Index

Note: Page numbers in *italic* indicate a figure and page numbers in **bold** indicate a table on the corresponding page.

Printed in Great Britain
by Amazon